Studies in Development Economics and Policy

General Editor: **Anthony Shorrocks**

UNU WORLD INSTITUTE FOR DEVELOPMENT ECONOMICS RESEARCH (UNU-WIDER) was established by the United Nations University as its first research and training centre and started work in Helsinki, Finland, in 1985. The purpose of the Institute is to undertake applied research and policy analysis on structural changes affecting the developing and transitional economies; to provide a forum for the advocacy of policies leading to robust, equitable and environmentally sustainable growth; and to promote capacity strengthening and training in the field of economic and social policy-making. Its work is carried out by staff researchers and visiting scholars in Helsinki and through networks of collaborating scholars and institutions around the world.

UNU World Institute for Development Economics Research (UNU-WIDER)
Katajanokanlaituri 6B, FIN-00160 Helsinki, Finland

Titles include:

Tony Addison and Alan Roe (*editors*)
FISCAL POLICY FOR DEVELOPMENT
Poverty, Reconstruction and Growth

Tony Addison, Henrik Hansen and Finn Tarp (*editors*)
DEBT RELIEF FOR POOR COUNTRIES

George J. Borjas and Jeff Crisp (*editors*)
POVERTY, INTERNATIONAL MIGRATION AND ASYLUM

Ricardo Ffrench-Davis and Stephany Griffith-Jones (*editors*)
FROM CAPITAL SURGES TO DROUGHT
Seeking Stability for Emerging Economies

David Fielding (*editor*)
MACROECONOMIC POLICY IN THE FRANC ZONE

Basudeb Guha-Khasnobis (*editor*)
THE WTO, DEVELOPING COUNTRIES AND THE DOHA DEVELOPMENT AGENDA
Prospects and Challenges for Trade-led Growth

Basudeb Guha-Khasnobis and Ravi Kanbur (*editors*)
INFORMAL LABOUR MARKETS AND DEVELOPMENT

Aiguo Lu and Manuel F. Montes (*editors*)
POVERTY, INCOME DISTRIBUTION AND WELL-BEING IN ASIA DURING THE TRANSITION

Mark McGillivray (*editor*)
HUMAN WELL-BEING
Concept and Measurement

Mark McGillivray (*editor*)
INEQUALITY, POVERTY AND WELL-BEING

Robert J. McIntyre and Bruno Dallago (*editors*)
SMALL AND MEDIUM ENTERPRISES IN TRANSITIONAL ECONOMIES

Vladimir Mikhalev (*editor*)
INEQUALITY AND SOCIAL STRUCTURE DURING THE TRANSITION

E. Wayne Nafziger and Raimo Väyrynen (*editors*)
THE PREVENTION OF HUMANITARIAN EMERGENCIES

Machiko Nissanke and Erik Thorbecke (*editors*)
THE IMPACT OF GLOBALIZATION ON THE WORLD'S POOR
Transmission Mechanisms

Matthew Odedokun (*editor*)
EXTERNAL FINANCE FOR PRIVATE SECTOR DEVELOPMENT
Appraisals and Issues

Laixiang Sun (*editor*)
OWNERSHIP AND GOVERNANCE OF ENTERPRISES
Recent Innovative Developments

UNU-WIDER (*editors*)
WIDER PERSPECTIVES ON GLOBAL DEVELOPMENT

Studies in Development Economics and Policy
Series Standing Order ISBN 0–333–96424–1
(*outside North America only*)

You can receive future titles in this series as they are published by placing a standing order. Please contact your bookseller or, in case of difficulty, write to us at the address below with your name and address, the title of the series and the ISBN quoted above.

Customer Services Department, Macmillan Distribution Ltd, Houndmills, Basingstoke, Hampshire RG21 6XS, England

Human Well-being

Concept and Measurement

Edited by

Mark McGillivray

palgrave macmillan

in association with the United Nations University – World Institute for Development Economics Research

First published 2007 by
PALGRAVE MACMILLAN
Houndmills, Basingstoke, Hampshire RG21 6XS and
175 Fifth Avenue, New York, N.Y. 10010
Companies and representatives throughout the world

PALGRAVE MACMILLAN is the global academic imprint of the Palgrave Macmillan division of St. Martin's Press, LLC and of Palgrave Macmillan Ltd. Macmillan® is a registered trademark in the United States, United Kingdom and other countries. Palgrave is a registered trademark in the European Union and other countries.

ISBN-13: 978–0–230–00498–6
ISBN-10: 0–230–00498–9

This book is printed on paper suitable for recycling and made from fully managed and sustained forest sources.

A catalogue record for this book is available from the British Library.

Library of Congress Cataloging-in-Publication Data
Human well-being: concept and measurement/edited by Mark McGillivray.
p. cm. — (Studies in development economics and policy)
Includes bibliographical references and index.
Contents: Human well-being: issues, concepts, and measures/Mark McGillivray — Human well-being: concepts and conceptualizations/Des Gasper — Income-based measures of average well-being/Steve Dowrick — Social and political indicators of human well-being/Susan Harkness — Composite indices of human well-being/Mark McGillivray and Farhad Noorbakhsh — Indicators of inequality and poverty/S. Subramanian — Gender-related indicators of well-being/Stephan Klasen — Sustainability and well-being indicators/Eric Neumayer — Subjective measures of well-being/Ruut Veenhoven — Participatory approaches and the measurement of human well-being/Sarah White and Jethro Pettit.
ISBN 0–230–00498–9 (cloth)
1. Social indicators. 2. Well-being. I. McGillivray, Mark.
II. World Institute for Development Economics Research.
HN25.H86 2007
301.072′3—dc22 2006047642

10 9 8 7 6 5 4 3 2 1
16 15 14 13 12 11 10 09 08 07

Transferred to Digital Printing 2007

Contents

List of Figures

List of Tables

Foreword

Social science research on human well-being has progressed a great deal in recent years, altering in response to changing global conditions, new research priorities and improved data resources. Two decades ago, for example, a comparison of well-being across countries was typically based on per capita incomes converted into US dollars at market exchange rates. Nowadays, a similar exercise would almost certainly take account of variations in purchasing power parity between countries and would be likely to embrace non-income and non-economic dimensions of well-being, given the increased recognition of the multidimensional nature of well-being. It might also encompass the distribution of well-being among and within countries, the extent to which current levels of achievement can be sustained over time, or even be founded on subjective or self-assessed measures of well-being.

This book emanates from a UNU-WIDER project on 'Measuring Human Well-being' (Social Development Indicators). It aims to provide a comprehensive and rigorous review of the concept and measurement of human well-being, with the main focus on well-being achievement at the level of nations. The topics covered include influential conceptualizations of well-being (such as Amartya Sen's capabilities approach), the construction of composite indices (such as the Human Development Index), social and political dimensions of well-being, the application of participatory methods, taking account of sustainability and gender-related issues, and subjective measures of well-being, including happiness scores.

While accepting that many aspects of well-being cannot be measured, the book offers many useful suggestions for future research on the construction and application of well-being indices. These include paying greater attention to human security issues; efforts to synthesise alternative conceptualizations of well-being – for example, by combining subjective and objective measures; and assigning degrees of confidence in comparisons of inter-country well-being, especially in the context of the measures used to track progress towards the Millennium Development Goals.

This book provides a timely and welcome addition to the literature on well-being. It will appeal in particular to those who have ever wondered about the ultimate goal of human development, and whether the elusive concept of human well-being can ever be captured satisfactorily in a measure that can be used to monitor and assess progress.

Anthony Shorrocks
Director, UNU-WIDER

Acknowledgements

This volume originates from the UNU-WIDER research project entitled 'Measuring Human Well-being' (Social Development Indicators). The Board of UNU-WIDER provided valuable suggestions during the early stages of the project. Tony Shorrocks, director of UNU-WIDER, provided considerable encouragement, advice and support throughout the life of the project. Tony Addison, deputy-director of UNU-WIDER, provided very useful advice, especially at the early stages of the project. Valuable comments from anonymous referees on a previous draft of the volume were extremely useful in shaping the final product. The following people also provided very useful comments on one or more of the chapters appearing in this volume: Mina Baliamoune-Lutz, Matthew Clarke, James Foster, Ian Gough, Ajeet Mathur, Lars Osberg, Ram Pillarisetti, Mozaffar Qizilbash and Mariano Rojas.

The Measuring Human Well-being project was supported by many UNU-WIDER staff. Special thanks are due to Anne Ruohonen and Adam Swallow. Anne served as the project secretary, providing extremely efficient support and consistently good humour. The book could not have ever come to completion without Anne's inputs. Adam provided incisive and timely publications advice, handling often complex matters with sound judgement and skill. Thanks are also due to Barbara Fagerman, Lea Hallbäck, Maria Kauppinen, Ara Kazandjian, Bruck Tadesse and Ans Vehmaanperä.

Special thanks are also due to Amanda Hamilton at Palgrave Macmillan for providing such effective publication and dissemination of outputs from the UNU-WIDER Measuring Human Well-being project.

UNU-WIDER gratefully acknowledges the financial contributions to the research programme by the governments of Denmark (Royal Ministry of Foreign Affairs), Finland (Ministry for Foreign Affairs), Norway (Royal Ministry of Foreign Affairs), Sweden (Swedish International Development Cooperation Agency – SIDA) and the United Kingdom (Department for International Development – DFID).

Notes on the Contributors

Steve Dowrick is Professor of Economics at the Australian National University in Canberra, Australia. His research interests are sources of economic growth, global income inequality and international income comparisons.

Des Gasper studied economics at the universities of Cambridge and East Anglia, and now teaches at the Institute of Social Studies, The Hague. He works currently on theories of well-being and human development, and is Visiting Professor in the Department of Economics and International Development at the University of Bath, UK, affiliated to the ESRC Research Group on Well-being in Developing Countries.

Susan Harkness is a lecturer in economics at the University of Bristol, a research associate at the Centre for Market and Public Organisation at Bristol and a research associate at the Centre for Analysis of Social Policy at the University of Bath. She is an applied labour economist with research interests on the economics of the family, poverty and inequality, and female employment and earnings.

Stephan Klasen is Professor of Economics at the University of Göttingen, Germany. He holds a PhD from Harvard University and has held positions at the World Bank, the University of Cambridge, and the University of Munich. His research focuses, among other things, on causes, measurement and consequences of gender inequality in developing countries.

Mark McGillivray is Senior Research Fellow at the World Institute for Development Economics Research of the United Nations University in Helsinki, Finland and an Inaugural Fellow of the Human Development and Capabilities Association. His research interests include the allocation and impact of development aid, and human well-being achievement.

Eric Neumayer is a Reader in Environment and Development in the Department of Geography and Environment at the London School of Economics and Political Science (LSE). He is the holder of a Philip Leverhulme Prize in Geography and has broad research interests in sustainable development, environmental commitment and performance, economic and human development, conflict and violence, globalization and migration.

Farhad Noorbakhsh is Professor of Development Economics and Head of the Department of Economics at the University of Glasgow, UK. His research interests include welfare and human development, economic planning, project planning, macroeconomic adjustments and regional disparities.

Jethro Pettit is a member of the Participation Group at the Institute of Development Studies, University of Sussex, UK where he works on participatory methodologies, power and social change. He is interested in the design of learning for reflective practice, and how development practitioners can contribute to shifting power relations and realising human dignity.

S. Subramanian is a Professor at the Madras Institute of Development Studies in Chennai, India. He has research interests in the fields of social and economic measurement, development economics and collective choice theory.

Ruut Veenhoven is Professor of Social Conditions for Human Happiness at Erasmus University of Rotterdam in The Netherlands. He is also Director of the World Database of Happiness and editor of the *Journal of Happiness Studies*. His current research interest is subjective quality of life.

Sarah White is a lecturer in Sociology and International Development and Director of the Centre for Development Studies, University of Bath, UK. She is a member of the ESRC Research Group on Well-being in Developing Countries, based at the University of Bath, and of the Research Programme in Faiths and Development, based at the University of Birmingham. Her main interests lie in the constitution of social difference and the scope of the personal and cultural in development.

List of Abbreviations

AIDS	Acquired Immune Deficiency Syndrome
CEC	Commission of the European Communities
CESifo	Center for Economic Studies and the Institute for Economic Research (Munich)
CFCs	Chlorofluorocarbons
CQLI	Combined Quality of Life Indexes
DALY	Disability Adjusted Life Years
DIAL	Développement et Insertion Internationale (Paris)
EAW	Economic Aspects of Welfare (Zolotas)
EBI	environmental behaviour indicator
ECA	Economic Commission of Africa
EEI	environment endangerment index
ESRC WeD	Economic and Social Research Council, Well-being in Developing Countries
Eurostat	Statistical Office of the European Communities
FX	foreign exchange
GDI	Gender related Development Index
GDP	gross domestic product
GEI	Gender Equity Index
GEM	Gender Empowerment Measure
GER	gross enrolment rate
GGI	Gender Gap Index
GID	General Index of Development
GK	Geary–Khamis
GLC	Generalized Lorenz Curve
GNI	gross national income
GNP	gross national product
GPI	Genuine Progress Indicator
GS	Genuine Savings
HALY	Happiness Adjusted Life Years
HDI	Human Development Index
HDR	*Human Development Report*
HLE	Happy Life Expectancy
HPI	Human Poverty Index
HSI	Human Suffering Index

HIV	Human Immunodeficiency Virus
IAHDI	Inequality Adjusted Human Development Index
ICP	International Comparison Project
IDS	Institute of Development Studies, University of Sussex
IIED	International Institute for Environment and Development
ILO	International Labour Organization
ISEW	Index of Sustainable Economic Welfare
LIS	Luxembourg Income Study
LLI	Level of Living Index
LSMS	Living Standards Measurement Surveys
MEW	Measure of Economic Welfare (Nordhaus and Tobin)
MDGs	Millennium Development Goals
NESA	New Entity for Social Action
NGO	Non-governmental organization
NSR	non-self-report
OECD	Organisation for Economic Co-operation and Development
OED	Oxford English Dictionary
OLS	ordinary least squares
OWB	objective well-being
PGI	person generated index
PPAs	participatory poverty assessments
PPP	purchasing power parity
PQLI	Physical Quality of Life Index
PAR	participatory action research
PRA	participatory rural appraisal
PRSPs	poverty reduction strategy papers
QOL	quality of life
RRA	rapid rural appraisal
SDI	Socioeconomic Development Index
SIGE	Standardized Index of Gender Equality
SFB	Sonderforschungsbereich 303 (University of Bonn)
SHDI	Sustainable Human Development Index
SOL	standard of living
SPA	Social Policy Association (UK)
SR	self-report
SSA	sub-Saharan Africa
SWB	subjective well-being
SWF	social welfare function
TISA	Total Incomes System of Accounts (Eisner)
TS	transfer sensitivity
UNDP	United Nations Development Programme
UNHS	Ugandan National Household Survey
UNRISD	United Nations Research Institute for Social Development

WB	well-being
WBA	well-being achievement
WBF	well-being freedom
WDR	*World Development Report*
WEF	World Economic Forum
WHD	World Happiness Database
WHO	World Health Organization
WHOQOL	World Health Organization's quality of life assessment
WIDER	World Institute for Development Economics Research (Helsinki)

1
Human Well-being: Issues, Concepts and Measures

Mark McGillivray

Introduction

National governments, civil society organizations and international agencies have for many years assembled and reported data on achieved human well-being, be it for individuals, families, regions or countries. Human well-being achievement at the level of countries receives special attention. It is now commonplace for international agencies, such as the United Nations Development Programme (UNDP) and the World Bank, to publish annual reports that rank countries according to various well-being or well-being related indicators.

These eagerly awaited reports receive much attention, in particular from national governments wanting to see where their country ranks internationally, and especially relative to neighbouring countries or those with which they have links. It is not uncommon for a positive outcome, be it a move up the league tables or consistently high rankings, to be attributed to specific policy interventions. Poor outcomes are linked either to an absence of appropriate policies, or the presence of inappropriate ones – or both. While one can question whether such attribution is always valid, achieved well-being measures are seen as important tools, used in the design and evaluation of policies, both domestic and international.

Well-being indicators are also used to measure progress towards various benchmarks or goals set by the international community. These include the 'Education for All' and 'Health for All' goals set in 1978 and 1990, respectively. More recently and ambitiously, the international community agreed at the United Nations Millennium Summit in 2000 to adopt the now very well-known Millennium Development Goals (MDGs). Unanimously adopted by the UN member states, these goals involve the attainment of various well-being or related benchmarks or targets, defined in terms of corresponding indicators. The Education for All and Health for All goals involved achieving universal primary education and universal access to health care, worldwide, by 2000. The MDGs are more ambitious, both in the nature and number of targets. Fundamentally, they aim at reducing worldwide the proportion of people living in extreme income poverty and suffering from hunger to half the levels of 1990 by 2015. They also aim to achieve various targets in education and health by 2015 (UN Millennium Project Report 2005).

Countries that fall well short of agreed targets or benchmarks as such can expect, ceteris paribus, to receive more support from the international community, in the form of aid and other interventions aimed at increasing levels of achieved well-being. International donors are often urged to increase aid levels based on gaps between these benchmarks and actual well-being levels. The UN Millennium Project Report in 2005, for instance, called on the international donor community to double official aid levels so that the MDGs can be achieved. More generally, the agencies of international aid donors make much use of well-being indicators in the design, implementation and evaluation of aid and related policies.

Human well-being achievement has not only been the focus of the above-mentioned organizations; it has for many decades been extensively researched, attracting attention from numerous academic disciplines within the social sciences. This research has come a long way in recent years, responding to changing global conditions, new research priorities, more sophisticated conceptualizations and improved data resources. Yet many measurement and conceptual issues still require attention and some of the most widely used well-being measures should be interpreted with great care. There is, in particular, no one conceptualization or measure that is accepted above all others.

Human Well-being: Concept and Measurement aims to provide insights into how human well-being might be better conceptualized and measured. It does this by taking stock of – and reviewing – research directions, assessing efforts over recent decades to conceptualize and, in particular, measure human well being achievement. The main focus of this volume is national human well-being achievement, cross-country comparisons in particular. Given its overall survey orientation, the volume does not set out substantively to develop new measures or conceptualizations. It does, however, point to many new areas that subsequent research should address, with a view to developing better ways of understanding and measuring achieved well-being. The volume also provides some cautions on the use of existing measures. These pointers and cautions are original contributions to the research literature.

This first chapter provides a broad descriptive sketch of well-being research, focusing primarily on attempts to measure achieved well-being, but also on various well-being conceptualizations. This sketch is intended to: (i) describe and compare various well-being conceptualizations that have emerged in recent decades; (ii) provide a brief history of research on developing well-being measures; (iii) describe and compare characteristics of various well-known or widely-used well-being and related measures; (iv) discuss how the construction of various well-being measures relate (or should relate) to the intended application; and (v) provide a backdrop for the nine chapters that follow, each of which picks up and examines in much more detail a number of the concepts or measures introduced.

The coverage of the sketch, and the volume as a whole, therefore, is selective. But it is intended to focus on the main issues examined in the research literature in recent decades and, in particular, on those measures that have been most widely reported and used internationally by policy makers and other practitioners. The coverage also reflects the fundamental premise that well-being should be seen as a multidimensional concept, encompassing many diverse dimensions. It is no coincidence, therefore, that much of the research examined in this volume has been motivated by the recognition that income-based measures of well-being, which have for many decades been dominant in well-being assessments, do not adequately capture these dimensions and a number of related factors.

The remainder of this chapter is structured as follows. The next two sections provide the above-mentioned sketch of the literature, looking at conceptualization and measures. A brief outline of the contents of Chapters 2 to 10 then follows, before highlighting some of the recommendations for future research provided for herein. The final section offers some additional recommendations.

Well-being conceptualizations

Many different well-being conceptualizations have been provided but, as Gasper (2002), Travers and Richardson (1997) and others point out, the term 'well-being' is a concept or abstraction used to refer to whatever is assessed in an evaluation of a person's life situation or 'being'. In short, it is a description of the state of individuals' life situation. An array of different terms has appeared in the research literature to label this situation. Along with well-being, the most common ones include the quality of life, living standards and human development. Others include welfare, social welfare, well-living, utility, life satisfaction, prosperity, needs fulfilment, development, empowerment, capability expansion, poverty, human poverty and, more recently, happiness. Some have distinct meanings, but there is usually a high degree of overlap in underlying meanings. Individual studies tend to adopt a particular term, others use different terms interchangedly. Easterlin (2001), for example, goes so far as to equate explicitly happiness, subjective well-being, satisfaction, utility, well-being, and welfare. Similarly, McGillivray (2005) equates human well-being, quality of human life, human development and basic human needs fulfilment.

Early well-being conceptualizations were utilitarian, often reducing well-being to well-feeling (or pleasure) and further reducing it to the scalar of unitary pleasure or utility (Gasper 2004). It subsequently became more common, and arguably appropriate, to treat well-being as a multidimensional concept. Better known multi-dimensional conceptualizations include the capabilities approach (Sen 1982, 1985, 1993, among many other publications), the basic human values approach (Grisez *et al.* 1987), the intermediate needs approach (Doyal and Gough 1991, 1993), the universal psychological needs approach (Ramsay 1992), the axiological categories approach (Max-Neef 1993), the universal human values approach (Schwartz 1994), the domains of subjective well-being approach (Cummins 1996), the dimensions of well-being approach (Narayan *et al.* 2000), and the central human capabilities approach (Nussbaum 2000). Other contributions to the literature include Andrews and Withey (1976), Stewart (1985), Lasswell (1992), Allardt (1993), Rawls (1993), Galtung (1994) and Qizilbash (1996a, 1996b).[1]

Many well-being dimensions have been identified. The list is extremely diverse, covering such aspects as knowledge, friendship, self-expression, affiliation, bodily integrity, health, economic security, freedom, affection, wealth, and leisure (Alkire 2002). The fundamental nature of dimensions has received much attention. Finnis (1980) argues that dimensions are: (i) self evident, in that they are potentially recognizable by anyone; (ii) incommensurable, in the sense that all of the desirable qualities of one are not present in the other; (iii) and irreducible, as there is no one denominator to which they can be totally reduced; and (iv) non-hierarchical, since at any point in time any one dimension can seem to be the most important (Alkire 2002). Doyal and Gough (1991: 5) consider universal needs, which 'apply to everyone in the same way'. As in Alkire (2002), these needs are not seen as well-being itself, but preconditions of well-being. Doyal and Gough conclude that universal needs do exist, and that vectors of basic and intermediate needs and degrees of need satisfaction can be identified. They identify two universal basic needs: physical health and autonomy of agency, the latter defined as the capacity to initiate and act through the formulation of aims and beliefs (Doyal and Gough 1991).

The most influential well-being conceptualization, arguably, is the abovementioned capabilities approach of Amartya Sen. A person's capability, according to this approach, reflects the alternative combinations of 'functionings' a person can achieve, and from which they can choose a particular collection. Functionings, in turn, are the 'parts of the state of person – in particular the things that he or she manages to do or be in leading a life' (Sen 1993: 31). Well-being is assessed in terms of the capability to achieve valuable functionings. In contrast to much of the literature, Sen resists identifying a set of capabilities on the grounds it is a value judgement that needs to be made explicitly, in many cases through a process of public debate (Sen 1999).[2]

Well-being measures

Attempts to measure well-being achievement have largely followed developments in the conceptualization of well-being. These include attempts to measure this achievement at the level of nations, often using national averages of chosen variables. Early attempts to assess these achievements, dating back to the 1940s, relied on some measure of national income per capita. This is consistent with the utilitarian conceptualization of well-being. Higher income allows for higher consumption and this provides greater utility. Income was thus the metric that conveyed utility. These attempts were also consistent with the national economic strategies that sought to maximize growth of income per capita, with some correction for externalities and distribution (Alkire 2002). The most popular measures of national income per capita are Gross National Income (GNI) per capita or Gross Domestic Product (GDP) per capita. The former is also known as Gross National Product (GNP) per capita. Data for these measures are very widely reported and extensively used. The World Bank, for example, in its *World Development Reports*, for many years since 1977 ranked countries in terms of achieved GNPs or GNIs per capita measured in United States dollars using weighted average prices and exchange rates (World Bank 1977–2004). It has also reported comprehensive cross-country income per capita data since 1969 in its *World Bank Atlas* (World Bank 1969–2004).

Differences in domestic price levels between countries are obviously important in income-based assessments of well-being achievement between countries. For this reason, purchasing power parity (PPP) estimates of national income per capita are being used increasingly. GNIs and GDPs per capita are converted into international dollars using PPP conversion factors. One international dollar, at the PPP rate, has the same purchasing power over domestic GNI as the US dollar has over US GNI. PPP conversion factors are currently derived from price surveys in 118 countries (World Bank 2004). The *World Development Report 2004* reports PPP GNI per capita data for 170 countries while the *Human Development Report 2004* reports PPP GDP per capita data for 177 countries (World Bank 2004, UNDP 2004). For many countries, these data are obtained using estimated PPP conversion factors. The most recent conversion factors for OECD countries are based on surveys conducted in 2000, with the remainder either based on surveys conducted in 1993, 1996 or earlier years (World Bank 2004).

Limitations of income per capita as an indicator of human well-being are well-known and often repeated. If we accept that well-being is multidimensional, then it at best captures only one of its many dimensions. It might well be correlated with other measures, but even then one would realistically expect that it cannot fully capture the essence of the various well-being conceptualizations (McGillivray 2005). Sen (1985) points out that the use of income per capita reduced well-being to being well-off or, put differently, to having much. What was important to Sen is not the level of income per capita per se but how income is used or what it finances. Will expenditure on tobacco, gambling, narcotics, and alcohol necessarily increase well-being at all levels of expenditure? One would think not. A broadly similar criticism of income as a measure of well-being has been expressed by the UNDP in its early *Human Development Reports*. In the 1990 report it emphasized that 'income is a means, not an end', observing that an excessive pre-occupation among policy makers and others with GNP growth had obscured that perspective (UNDP 1990: 9–10). In making this point, the UNDP invoked the teachings of Aristotle, who warned that 'wealth is evidently not the good we are seeking, for it is merely useful and for the sake of something else' (UNDP 1990: 9). While wealth and income are different concepts, the same basic message applies to both.

Hicks and Streeten (1979: 568) observe that 'problems inherent in using GNP as a measure of social welfare have been recognized almost since the inception of national income accounting'. They point to a long history of endeavours to address this issue quantitatively, including adjustments to GNP and the development of non-monetary measures of social progress in the form of so-called social indicators. The former adjustments include PPP conversions, which date back to the work of Clark (1940). Nordhaus and Tobin (1972) adjusted GNP to obtain the Measure of Economic Welfare (MEW). The MEW was obtained by deducting from GNP an allowance for defence expenditure, pollution, congestion, and crime, and adding an estimate for the value of leisure and services of consumer durables (Hicks and Streeten 1979). There have also been attempts to adjust GNP per capita according to how it is distributed among population sub-groups. This is an explicit acknowledgement that per capita income, as many other indicators, is simply a national mean or average that says nothing about how the total cake of a country is divided. An early attempt to adjust GNP in this way is that of Ahluwalia and Chenery (1974), who proposed measures based on weighted shares of the growth rate of GNP by population sub-groups. The weights are interpreted as welfare weights, and can be defined either in terms of the share of total income or population of each group (divided into quintiles), or in terms of the priorities assigned to improving the welfare of each group. There have been many subsequent attempts to modify GNP and other per capita national income measures.[3] Yet, despite these attempts and the well-known weaknesses of such measures, and alternative non- or non-exclusively income-based measures, 'GNP per capita continues to be regarded as the "quintessential" well-being indicator' (Dasgupta 2001: 53).

Broadly similar measures to those of Ahluwalia and Chenery (1974) have resulted not from attempts to adjust GNP per capita or other national income measures, but from efforts to construct better income based measures per se. They are consistent to varying degrees with the utilitarian conceptualization. Some are explicit well-being or welfare measures; others are income poverty measures. The latter provide well-being information only on those people living in poverty, but not others. As such, they are only partial measures of well-being achievement if applied at the national level. A general class of the former treats well-being as an increasing function of mean income and a decreasing function of the measured level of inequality.[4] A well-known example of these measures is the Shorrocks (1983) Generalized Lorenz Curve (GLC), which takes the standard Lorenz curve and scales it by the mean income of the distribution. As such, the GLC defines social welfare in terms of both equity and efficiency, the latter defined by the level of mean income.

The best known and most widely used income poverty measure is the headcount, typically defined as the number or proportion of the national population whose income falls below the chosen poverty line. A headcount measure of extreme income poverty, used to track progress towards the MDG poverty target, is the number of people living on less than one US$ PPP per day. The headcount does not provide information on the extent to which the incomes of those living in poverty fall below the poverty line. Put differently, it does not indicate the extent of immiseration, merely its existence. The poverty (or income) gap measure attempts this, by adjusting the headcount on the basis of the gap between the poverty line and the average income of those living below the line, in the population group under consideration. As such, it is interpreted as both a measure of poverty and of the amount of money required to raise the incomes of the poor to the poverty line (Blackwood and Lynch 1994). More elaborate measures have been proposed by Sen (1976) and Foster *et al.* (1984), among others. The Sen Index combines the income gap, the headcount, and the distribution of income among those living below the poverty line (measured by the Gini coefficient). Foster *et al.* provide a class of parametric poverty measures that are sensitive to changes in the income gap, changes in inequality, and changes in the number of poor (Blackwood and Lynch 1994).

The use of non-monetary measures gathered momentum in the mid- to late 1970s when a number of prominent international agencies compiled various sets of what have been described, rather loosely, as social indicators. Often interpreted as measures of basic human needs fulfilment, these indicators sought to capture achievements in such areas as health, education, the environment, culture, and politics. Specific indicators therefore include life expectancy, child mortality, access to health services, access to water, access to sanitation, infant mortality, calorie intake, literacy, years of schooling, and school enrolment ratios. While some of these indicators reflect the progress countries are making towards attaining fundamental well-being or developmental goals, others act primarily as intermediate indicators of progress. There is also a wide range of variables that address political participation, civil liberties, and human and labour rights.

Data on social indicators are now widely published, often for large country samples. The UNDP, in its *Human Development Report 2004*, publishes data on life expectancy, adult literacy, and school enrolment ratios for 177 countries. There remain, however, concerns regarding the reliability and comparability of these indicators. Most of the widely used social indicators are based on information obtained from national censuses. It is well-known that many countries do not have the resources to conduct accurate censuses. No country conducts a yearly national census and some countries conduct them at irregular intervals. Data for the intervening years have to be estimated. Given these and a number of methodological problems, the data tend to be incomparable both between countries at a given point in time and within given countries over time. As a consequence, differences among countries in the values of social indicators are difficult to interpret. Yet, these problems do not provide grounds against the use of social indicators per se, but grounds for attempting to improve their reliability.

Income per capita or any single social indicator is only a partial measure of well-being if we treat well-being as a multidimensional concept. They alone capture a single well-being dimension, or part thereof. A number of composite measures aim to provide more comprehensive, multidimensional assessments of well-being.[5] One of the better known indexes is the Physical Quality of Life Index (PQLI), which was intended as a complement to GNP per capita in the measurement of human well-being at the national level. Proposed in 1979 by the Overseas Development Council, the PQLI combines infant mortality, life expectancy, and adult literacy into a single index. PQLI values for up to 150 countries were published (Morris 1979). While the PQLI has been criticized heavily, perhaps one of its most important contributions (and certainly one intended by its designers) was to combine variables measuring achieved well-being. That is, these variables measure the results or outcomes of efforts to improve human well-being, rather than combining measures of attempts to improve human well-being. As such, it avoided variables such as expenditure on education and, instead, focused on an aim of this expenditure; namely, higher literacy.

The PQLI received much attention in the years immediately following its inception. Yet interest in composite human well-being indicators tended to wane, and income per capita, especially GNP per capita, remained the most widely used and reported indicator. This changed with the UNDP *Human Development Report 1990*, which launched the Human Development Index (HDI) (UNDP 1990). The HDI, which has been revised a number of times since 1990, currently combines US$ PPP GDP per capita, life expectancy at birth, adult literacy, and the combined primary, secondary, and tertiary education enrolment ratio. The inclusion of US$ PPP GDP per capita has been controversial. The UNDP has made it clear that its inclusion in the HDI is intended to capture a material dimension to human development or well-being. US$ PPP GDP per capita is therefore transformed to reflect diminishing returns to the conversion of income or purchasing power into well-being, and hence to better capture this dimension. Various transformations have been employed since 1990, some rather drastic involving capping this variable at an international poverty line income. Currently, the logarithm of US$ PPP GDP per capita is employed (UNDP 2004). While the HDI has received often heavy criticism from researchers on numerous grounds, it is used extensively in research and policy work, and is quite possibly the best known well-being or human development index. HDI values are currently available for 173 countries, with some extending back to 1960 for a number of countries (UNDP 1994, 2004).[6]

In the *Human Development Report 1995* the UNDP first introduced the Gender Empowerment Measure (GEM) and the Gender related Development Index (GDI) (UNDP 1995). These composite indexes are an attempt to incorporate gender dimensions into well-being measurement. The GEM contains information on: (i) percentage of women parliamentarians; (ii) the number female legislators, senior officials and managers as a percentage of the total number of people holding such positions; (iii) the number of female professional and technical workers as a percentage of the total number of such workers; and (iv) female earned income relative to that of males. The GDI adjusts the HDI on the basis of gender disparity in each of its four indicators (UNDP 2004). Any such disparity in these indicators for a country results in its GDI value being lower than its HDI value. The UNDP was not the first to adjust or disaggregate well-being indicators on the basis of gender disparities, as there is a long history of doing so. Three of the four variables on which the HDI is based (life expectancy, adult literacy, and the combined education enrolment ratio), had been available in gender disaggregated form for a number of years. The contribution of the GDI was to combine these variables, along with a gender disaggregated GDP per capita. There are also a number of gender specific well-being indicators, such as the maternal mortality rate.[7]

As with gaps in incomes between population groups, few would deny that gender gaps are irrelevant to achieved well-being assessments. Yet, the gender disparity adjusted indicators are subject to the same criticisms as the variables on which they are based. For instance, the gender adjusted or disaggregated social indicators are obviously subject to the same methodological and measurement error problems as their non-adjusted or disaggregated counterparts, given that the former are obtained from the latter. This is not, of course, an argument against using gender specific or gender adjusted indicators, merely one for improving their accuracy and comparability. Gender specific or gender adjusted indicators tend to be very highly rank-correlated with their non-specific or adjusted counterparts, and with other well-being indicators, including income per capita (McGillivray and Pillarisetti 2006). This has led to questions regarding the empirical contribution of these indicators, although such a correlation is not an argument for not monitoring changes in them, or for simply assuming that changes in the gender related indicators will necessarily follow those in their non-gender related counterparts. Conceptual problems also arise. Should gender equality in all indicators be the underlying well-being goal? Relatedly, what constitutes equality?[8] There is also the issue of whether gender empowerment can be considered as well-being. Sen (1999) makes the distinction between female agency (a very similar concept to empowerment) and female well-being, arguing that strengthening the former is a separate goal alongside improving the latter. From this it might be inferred that increasing female empowerment will lead to increasing female well-being achievement, but leaves open the question of whether empowerment is well-being.

There are ongoing attempts to incorporate notions of sustainability into well-being assessment. Anand and Sen (2000b) provide a conceptual basis for this, viewing sustainability as a concern for inter-generational equity and treating its demand as a reflection of the universality of claims, applied to future generations vis-à-vis the current one. Anand and Sen argue that this univeralism is an ethical one, characterized as an elementary demand for impartiality, applied both within generations and between them. They assert that 'not working towards guaranteeing the basic capabilities to the future generations would be scandalous', but also that not 'bringing those elementary capabilities within the reach of the deprived in the present generation would also be outrageous' (Anand and Sen 2000b: 2030). These comments might be interpreted as a case for integrating sustainability measurement into achieved well-being measurement.

There is a long history of attempts to integrate well-being and sustainability measures. The MEW, mentioned above, attempted this, through including a measure of pollution (Nordhaus and Tobin 1972). Another early such attempt was the Economic Aspects of Welfare measure, which deducts the costs of air pollution damage and pollution and solid waste control costs (Zolotas 1981). A more recent attempt is the Genuine Progress Indicator (GPI) (Daly and Cobb 1989). The GPI deducts from selected expenditure components of GDP the depreciation of environmental assets and natural resources, reduction of stocks of natural resources – such as fossil fuels or other mineral deposits, and effects of wastes and pollution.[9] Attempts to adjust well-being indexes using sustainability measures have been criticized. Neumayer (2001), for instance, considers this issue in the context of 'greening' the HDI through the inclusion in the index of sustainability variables. Rather than such inclusion, Neumayer instead favours simply comparing a well-being achievement measure with a measure of sustainability, to assess whether this achievement is potentially sustainable.

Arguably the most thriving area of well-being research in recent years is that on subjective well-being or, as it is otherwise known, happiness.[10] Subjective well-being has been defined as people's multidimensional evaluation of their lives, including cognitive judgements of life satisfaction and affective evaluations of emotions and moods (Diener 1984, Argyle 1987, Diener and Larsen 1993, and Eid and Diener 2003). People are surveyed to obtain their self-assessments of well-being in a number of pre-determined domains or dimensions. The World Health Organization Quality of Life assessment (the WHOQOL), for instance, focuses on 100 variables representing different life domains. The quality of life is defined in the WHOQOL as 'an individual's perception of their position in life in the context of the culture and value systems in which they live, and in relation to their goals, expectations, standards, and concerns' (WHOQOL Group 1994, cited in Skevington *et al.* 2004: 299). Respondents are required to self-assess their lives according to such factors as pain and discomfort, sexual activity, self-esteem, mobility, work capacity, freedom, physical safety and security, work satisfaction, and financial resources (WHOQOL Group 1998).[11] Another approach is simply to ask respondents to self-assess, on a finite scale, their satisfaction or dissatisfaction with life. For instance, scores reported on the World Happiness Database (WHD) are based on responses to the question 'All things considered, how satisfied or dissatisfied are you with your life-as-a-whole now?' (Veenhoven 2004).

Easterlin (1974), in a landmark study, examined links between income and happiness. Easterlin found that while individuals with higher incomes were happier than those with lower incomes at a particular point in time, the happiness of a particular cohort did not increase with income over time. Happiness levels actually appeared to remain constant even in light of substantial increases in income. This result was confirmed in later work by Easterlin. Known as the 'Easterlin paradox', this finding has been extensively examined, with many studies drawing the same conclusion or reporting broadly consistent results. A number of theoretical explanations for stable happiness over time has been put forward. Easterlin postulated that absolute income levels matter up to the point at which basic needs are met, and beyond that relative incomes are more important. If an individual's income remains constant relative to the incomes of that person's reference group, their happiness may remain unchanged. Another explanation put forward by Easterlin is that an individual's aspirations might rise with increases in income, offsetting an increase in well-being (Easterlin 2001). Cummins (1998) has proposed a specific theory to explain relatively constant happiness over time. Labelled the theory of subjective well-being homeostasis, this theory proposes that, in a manner similar to the homeostatic maintenance of blood pressure or temperature, happiness is actively controlled and maintained by a set of psychological devices that function under the control of personality. This theory predicts that good or bad events will cause a short-term change in subjective well-being, but that these psychological devices will return life satisfaction or happiness to its previous level. This level is seen as a 'set point', around which well-being varies, and is thought to be within the satisfied range of a satisfaction–dissatisfaction continuum (Cummins *et al.* 2003).

A challenge in measuring subjective well-being concerns the sensitivity of survey responses to momentary or immediate mood swings. As Campbell *et al.* (1976), Eid and Diener (2003), among many others, have pointed out, the information provided by these surveys should instead relate to changes in the conditions in which people live. Diener (1984), Veenhoven (1993) and others have considered this question and as Easterlin (2001) points out, the general conclusion is that happiness scores are not perfect but do accurately reflect substantive feelings of well-being. International comparisons of happiness levels are also an issue. France, Japan, and Austria have happiness scores of 6.4, 6.3 and 6.1, respectively, out of a possible 10, according to the WHD (Veenhoven 2004). Yet, according to the WHD, Nigeria has a happiness score of 6.3, despite the fact that 70 per cent Nigerians live below the US$ PPP1 per day poverty line and 91 per cent live below the US$ PPP2 per day line (Veenhoven 2004, UNDP 2004). Such an apparent anomaly might provide a case not to use a happiness score to compare well-being across countries at a point in time, but instead to confine the use of these scores to monitor changes in well-being over time. This view is seemingly countered by Easterlin (2001), who argues such comparisons have credence, given a similarity of feelings about the sources of happiness across individuals, in diverse cultures and living in countries in different stages of socio-economic development.

A criticism of most indicators, including those discussed above, concerns the related issues of ownership and relevance. Attempts to increase a country's HDI score, for example, might be half-hearted if the relevant decision makers were not involved in the selection of the variables on which the index is based. Similarly, citizens of a particular country might not support a drive to lift their country's HDI value if they think the index is irrelevant to their own circumstances. In general, of course, there is a need to ensure that measures are directly relevant to the well-being circumstances and aspirations of the individuals whose well-being is under consideration. The underlying issue here is one of country-level ownership. Without ownership of the indicators, there is no guarantee that they will be used effectively for the design of policy interventions or will be relevant to the circumstances of the citizens to whom they apply. The UNDP has seemingly recognized these points, especially the second, through the preparation of *Human Development Reports* and country-specific HDIs (see, for example, UNDP 2003).

The same argument can, of course, be made regarding individual or household level indicators, and there have been many attempts to build poverty or well-being indicators using participatory methods. These methods can viewed as a process enacted either by the people whose living standards are being assessed, for those people (initiated by an agency, but based on participation or consultation), or with those people (Laderchi 2001). They have their origins in Participatory Rural Appraisal (PRA). Chambers (1994: 954) describes PRA as methods intended for 'local people to share, enhance and analyse their knowledge of life and conditions'. Participatory Poverty Assessments (PPAs), increasingly common in attempts to assess the life conditions of individuals or households in developing countries, have their origins in PRA. Examples of the indicators produced using participatory assessments include whether the individual lives in a cement block house, whether they own a bullock and whether they have to always rely on borrowed clothing (Hanmer *et al.* 1997). The *Voices of the Poor* study, emanating from the World Bank, is a well known study that employed PPA (Narayan *et al.* 2000)

Overview of the volume

Human Well-being: Concept and Measurement contains a further nine chapters. As mentioned previously, these chapters look in far more detail at a number of the concepts or measures discussed in the preceding section.

Chapter 2, by Des Gasper, looks at well-being concepts and conceptualizations. Its basic premise is that prior to measuring something, we need to think hard about what it is that we wish to measure.[12] More broadly, before acting, we should think hard about purposes. Various legitimate but different purposes underlie the available conceptualizations of well-being. Chapter 2 seeks to clarify this variety of purposes, and the corresponding differences of focus and conceptualization, in a number of approaches to well-being which are influential in or very relevant to development theory and policy. It looks inter alia at: Sen's capability approach, Nussbaum's theory of human functional capabilities, Finnis's theory of core motives, and Alkire's attempted synthesis of these; as well as Dasgupta's specification of well-being, and Max-Neef's matrix of human needs. The chapter will consider how far one can integrate the various approaches.

Chapter 3, by Steve Dowrick, looks at issues relating to income per capita, focusing on GDP per capita. It was mentioned above that international comparisons of well-being are commonly made in terms of GDP per capita. Such comparisons might appear in newspaper articles examining the latest country rankings, quality of life, or in development reports assessing national well-being achievement or in economics journals analyzing the relative performance of countries. Yet, these comparisons are open to criticism, further to those mentioned above, on the grounds that GDP is more properly regarded as a partial measure of aggregate output than as an indicator of either current or future well-being. International GDP comparisons make no allowance for environmental differences, for resource depletion, for leisure, for household production of goods and services, for black market activities or for external costs and benefits associated with production and consumption. They are also bedevilled by index number problems. Chapter 3 suggests ways of combining working hours and life expectancy with income comparisons, and shows that the fixed-price indexes of real income, such as those in the Penn World Tables, substantially understate the income gaps between the poorest and richest countries.

Chapter 4, by Susan Harkness, critically surveys the vast range of indicators used to assess social and political well-being at the level of countries. It considers what contribution these indicators can make towards our understanding of human well-being. While many social and political indicators exhibit wide variations across countries, the chapter argues that the interpretation of these differences is not always clear. The chapter examines sources of cross-country variations, highlighting differences in data availability and measurement issues. Finally, the chapter examines the links and correlations between these various indicators of development across countries and their interpretation as measures of development.

Chapter 5, by Mark McGillivray and Farhad Noorbakhsh, surveys the various composite well-being indexes that have been inter-country assessments over the last 40 or so years. It pays particular attention to the HDI. A number of issues are considered, including the choice of components, component weights, scale equivalence, non-linearity, correlations among components, and the policy relevance of such measures. Several of these issues are examined in the context of a critical review of the many criticisms of the HDI and the UNDP's responses to these criticisms (some involving changes to the design of the index). A basic premise of the chapter is that indexes used for international well-being comparisons should be relevant to the policies and individual priorities of countries. Possible directions for the future design and application of composite well-being indicators are identified, including adoption of country specific variables, participatory, country and time variant component weighting schemes, and the inclusion of a human security vector.

Chapter 6, by S. Subramanian, aims at a broad, mainstream account of the literature on inequality and poverty measurement in the space of income and, additionally, deals with measures of disparity and deprivation in the more expanded domain of capabilities and functionings. In addition to introductory and concluding parts, the chapter has four sections. The first of these sections, on measurement of income inequality, deals with preliminary concepts and definitions; a visual representation of inequality (the Lorenz curve); real-valued indexes of inequality; properties of inequality indexes; some specific inequality measures; and the relationship between Lorenz, welfare and inequality orderings. The second section, on poverty, deals with the identification and aggregation exercises; properties of poverty indexes; some specific poverty measures; the problem of plurality and unambiguous rankings; poverty measures and anti-poverty policy; and other issues in the measurement of poverty. The third section considers aspects of both congruence and conflict in the relationship amongst poverty, inequality and welfare. The final substantive section advances the rationale for a more comprehensive assessment of human well-being than is afforded by the income perspective, it briefly reviews measurement concerns relating to generalized indexes of deprivation and disparity, and it discusses the data and policy implications of the more expansive view of well-being adopted in the section.

Chapter 7, by Stephan Klasen, discusses the rationale, as well as the challenges, involved when constructing gender related indicators of well-being. It argues that such indicators are critically important but that their construction involves a number of conceptual and measurement problems. Among the conceptual issues the chapter examines is the space in which gender inequality in well-being is to be measured, whether the indicators should track well-being of males and females separately or adjust overall measures of well-being by the gender inequality in well-being, whether gender equality in every indicator is necessarily the goal, how to assess gender inequality that is apparently desired by males and females, and what role indicators of agency or empowerment should play in gender-related indicators of well-being. Among the most important measurement issues to be addressed are the role of the household in allocating resources, the question of stocks versus flows, as well as significant data gaps when it comes to gender inequalities. Where appropriate, remedies to the conceptual and measurement issues are proposed. The chapter also briefly reviews UNDP's gender related indexes to illustrate some of the challenges involved.

Chapter 8, by Eric Neumayer, provides a review and critical discussion of indicators that attempt to combine the measurement of sustainability with that of well-being. It starts with some commonly agreed definitions of sustainability, showing how most well-being indicators tell us little, if anything at all, about this issue. Sustainability is most commonly defined in economics as non-declining utility or well-being over time. Yet, due to its future orientation, most indicators of sustainability such as Genuine Savings (GS) have merely focused on the capacity to provide utility in the future, but have not included the measurement of current well-being. Indicators of well-being such as the HDI, on the other hand, have typically failed to account for sustainability in their measurement of current well-being. The chapter then critically reviews the Index of Sustainable Economic Welfare (ISEW) and the Genuine Progress Indicator (GPI), which are the most prominent examples of an indicator that attempts to fully integrate the measurement of welfare with that of sustainability into one single indicator. Such an integration, whilst seemingly attractive, is rendered difficult by the fact that what contributes to current well-being need not contribute at all, or in the same way, to sustainability and vice versa. He also reviews various proposals of extending a welfare indicator – namely, the HDI – with sustainability considerations without full integration of both concepts. All of these proposals suffer from a range of fundamental conceptual problems. As one possible alternative, he proposes a combination of the HDI and GS, which holds great promise for an assessment of well-being and its sustainability, particularly in developing countries.

Chapter 9, by Ruut Veenhoven, looks at measures of subjective well-being. It addresses three questions: What are 'subjective' measures?; What is 'well-being'?; Are subjective measures of well-being of use for policy making, in particular in developing nations? The first question is answered by making a distinction between two kinds of 'subjectivity': subjective substance and subjective assessment. On that basis, nine types of indicators are discerned, varying in degree of subjectivity. The second question is answered by discerning four kinds of well-being. Examples are presented of indicators for each of these well-being variants. It is argued that there is little sense in combining these variants in one sum score of overall well-being, since this is the equivalent of adding apples and oranges. The much-used HDI is questioned on these grounds. In answer to the third question, a case is made for subjective measures of well-being, in particular for using 'happy life years' as an indicator of final policy effectiveness.

Chapter 10, by Sarah White and Jethro Pettit, considers the use of participatory methods in international development research, and asks what contribution they can make to the definition and, in particular, measurement of well-being. It draws on general lessons arising from the project level, two large-scale policy research processes sponsored by the World Bank, and the experience of quality of life studies. It also considers emerging experiments with using participatory methods to generate quantitative data. The chapter closes by assessing the future trajectory of participatory approaches in well-being research, and reflects on some dilemmas regarding the use of participatory data on well-being in the policy making process.

Well-being concepts and measures: looking ahead

A number of conclusions emerge from the body of this volume. Each is clearly articulated in the chapters that follow, but it is useful at this early stage to briefly mention some of them, together with some additional comments.

With regard to well-being conceptualizations, it is evident that there are many well-being concepts and conceptualizations. The relevant literature is both diverse and rich. One wonders whether some degree of consolidation is possible; in particular, looking for commonality in the various well-being dimensions that have been proposed. Ideally, this might provide some sort of overall, definitive multidimensional well-being concept. A particular line of enquiry is how one might combine subjective and objective well-being measures or whether, indeed, this is at all appropriate. Conceptual work is required on how this might be done, but consideration could be given to augmenting composite indexes, containing objective measures, with a subjective measure or measures, such as a self-assessed happiness rating. One such augmentation might be to interact the two types of measures in some way, on the premise that achievement in objective well-being is conditional on happiness and *vice versa*.

A recurring theme throughout this volume concerns the availability and quality of national well-being data. International price level data, permitting comparisons of incomes across countries, need to be improved; in particular, data on social indicators. Not only do data on the commonly used social indicators (such as life expectancy, adult literacy, and infant mortality) need to be made more precise, but the country coverage of other such indicators needs to be expanded. This might perhaps allow for the inclusion of additional dimensions into indices such as the HDI without significantly compromising country coverage. Data on subjective well-being also need to be improved.

In addition to improving the precision of data, recent advances in statistics could be used to assign standard errors to social indicators and degrees of confidence in comparisons of inter-country well-being achievement. Confidence degrees could also be assigned in judging whether countries have achieved particular targets or benchmarks. This has obvious relevance to the MDGs. Can we be certain that a given country has achieved the MDGs? It could be the case that some countries might be judged to have achieved the MDGs, when in reality they have not. The opposite also applies. Assigning degrees of confidence to the MDG target variables would at least allow for more informed answers to the preceding question. More precise data would also, quite obviously, allow for more efficient monitoring of progress towards the MDGs. A case for assigning standard errors and degrees of confidence in inter-country comparisons can of course be made for most well-being indicators.

It is often said that we live in an increasingly insecure world. It is also said that individuals are becoming increasingly sensitive to their own personal security. Irrespective of whether these claims have empirical support, it is clear that individuals do place a high value on personal security and that this security would appear to be a universal human value. If we accept these points, then there is a strong, indeed compelling, case for including a human security vector in well-being indexes. An obvious candidate for this treatment is the HDI. Better data on human security are required. Just as importantly, consideration needs to be given to the conceptual issue of how one might augment an index like the HDI. Should a vector of human security variables simply be added to the index, with an appropriate weighting? Should this vector interact with one or more of the vectors already included? Or should it enter some other way? One might be able to argue that a given threshold level of security exists. Below that level, well-being increases only slightly with increases in the variables capturing the other well-being dimensions; above that level, well-being increases by a greater margin in response to increases in those variables. Other possibilities will, of course, exist and it is up to both the research and practitioner communities to consider all viable alternatives.

The topics covered in this volume provide a good illustration of the range of current research on national well-being achievements, in particular its measurement. It is hoped that the chapters that follow will stimulate further research along similar lines. Just as importantly, or perhaps more so, it is hoped that they better inform the agencies that compile and disseminate well-being achievement statistics and the policy makers and others who base decisions on them.

Notes

The author is grateful for the excellent and comprehensive comments on an earlier draft of this chapter provided by three anonymous referees. The usual disclaimer applies.

1 Alkire (2002) provides an excellent survey of research on well-being (human development) dimensions and discussion of related issues.
2 See Qizilbash (1996a) for an excellent survey of related material. Alkire (2002) provides a succinct, more detailed coverage of this issue.
3 Anand and Sen (2000a) provide an excellent discussion of conceptual and measurement issues in relation to the use of income per capita as a human development measure, including inter alia formulations which reflect diminishing marginal returns to the conversion of income into human development or well-being.
4 See Lambert (2001) for an incisive treatment of such indexes.
5 It is should noted that GNP is a composite measure, in the sense that it is obtained by aggregating values of all goods and services purchased in an economy over a given period of time. Similar comments can be made of GDP per capita and many other well-being measures. The term 'composite measure' in the context of this volume refers to an indicator that has been obtained by combining measures of achievement in different well-being dimensions.
6 The HDI has generated a large academic literature. Among the reviews of the index are: Kelley (1991), McGillivray and White (1993), Acharya and Wall (1994), Ivanova *et al.* (1998), Noorbakhsh (1998), Sagar and Najam (1998), and Morse (2003). Anand and Sen (1992) and UNDP (1993) provide a survey of a number of early reviews.
7 See Saith and Harriss-White (1999) for an analysis of the gender sensitivity of well-being indicators, Bardhan and Klasen (1999) for a review of the GDI and GEM, and Pillarisetti and McGillivray (1998) for a review of the GEM.
8 Interestingly, the GDI defines equality in life expectancy as males having an expectancy five years lower than that of females (UNDP 1995).
9 The GPI is also known and the Index of Sustainable Economic Welfare (ISEW). See Neumayer (1999) for a review.
10 This should not imply that research on subjective well-being is new. As Easterlin (2001) observes, the bibliographic survey of Veenhoven (1993) contains approximately 2,500 references, and the measurement and analysis of various notions of subjective well-being in the social sciences has a history dating back 50 years. It does, however, imply that in recent years the amount of research on happiness has increased very substantially.
11 WHOQOL (1998) reports quality of life assessments for 15 urban centres. Ignoring sampling errors, Beer Sheva and Melbourne have the highest assessments (14.8 and 14.7, respectively), while St Petersburg and Harare have the lowest (11.5 and 11.3, respectively). Other assessments include those for New Delhi, Paris and Tokyo, which were 13.3, 13.6 and 14.0, respectively.

12 This was the central premise of the lead paper in a broadly similar publication to this current volume, published in 1969 as a special issue of the *Journal of Development Studies*. That paper was entitled 'What are we Trying to Measure?', Seers (1972).

References

Acharya, A. and H. J. Wall (1994) 'An Evaluation of the United Nations' Human Development Index', *Journal of Economic and Social Development*, 20(1): 51–65.

Ahluwalia, M. and H. Chenery (1974) 'The Economic Framework', in H. Chenery, M. S. Ahluwalia, C. L. G. Bell, J. H. Duloy and R. Jolly (eds), *Redistribution with Growth* (New York: Oxford University Press).

Alkire, S. (2002) 'Dimensions of Human Development', *World Development*, 30(2): 181–205.

Allardt, E. (1993), 'Having, Loving, Being: An Alternative to the Swedish Model of Welfare Research', in M. Nussbaum and A. Sen (eds), *The Quality of Life* (Oxford: Clarendon Press for UNU-WIDER) 88–94.

Anand, S. and A. Sen (1992) 'Human Development Index: Methodology and Measurement', Background Paper for *Human Development Report 1993* (New York: UNDP).

Anand, S. and A. Sen (2000a) 'The Income Component of the Human Development Index', *Journal of Human Development*, 1(1): 83–106.

Anand, S. and A. Sen (2000b) 'Human Development and Economic Sustainability', *World Development*, 28(12): 2029–49.

Andrews, F. M. and S. B. Withey (1976) *Social Indicators of Well-being: Americans' Perceptions of Life Quality* (New York: Plenum Press).

Argyle, M. (1987) *The Psychology of Happiness* (London: Routledge).

Bardhan, K. and S. Klasen (1999) 'UNDP's Gender-Related Indices: A Critical Review', *World Development*, 27(6): 985–1010.

Blackwood, D. L. and R. G. Lynch (1994) 'The Measurement of Inequality and Poverty: A Policy Makers Guide to the Literature', *World Development*, 22(4): 567–78.

Campbell, A., P. E. Converse and W. L. Rodgers (1976) *The Quality of American Life: Perceptions, Evaluations and Satisfactions* (New York: Russell Sage Foundation).

Chambers, R. (1994) 'The Origins and Practice of Participatory Rural Appraisal', *World Development*, 22: 953-69.

Clark, C. (1940) *Conditions of Economic Progress* (London: Macmillan).

Cummins, R. A. (1996) 'Domains of Life Satisfaction: An Attempt to Order Chaos', *Social Indicators Research*, 38(3): 303–28.

Cummins, R. A. (1998) 'The Second Approximation to an International Standard of Life Satisfaction', *Social Indicators Research*, 43: 307–34.

Cummins, R. A., R. Eckersley, J. Pallant, J. van Vugt and R. Misajon (2003) 'Developing an Index of Subjective Well-being: The Australian Unity Well-being Index', *Social Indicators Research*, 64: 159–90.

Daly, H. and H. E. Cobb (1989) *For the Common Good* (Boston: Beacon Press).

Dasgupta, P. (2001) *Human Well-being and the Natural Environment* (Oxford: Oxford University Press).

Diener, E. (1984) 'Subjective Well-being', *Psychological Bulletin*, 95: 542–75.

Diener, E. and R. J. Larsen (1993) 'The Experience of Emotional Well-being', in M. Lewis and J. M. Haviland (eds), *Handbook of Emotions* (New York: Guilford).

Doyal, L. and I. Gough (1991) *A Theory of Human Need* (Basingstoke: Macmillan).

Doyal, L. and I. Gough (1993) 'Need Satisfaction as a Measure of Human Welfare', in W. Blass and J. Foster (eds), *Mixed Economies in Europe* (London: Edward Elgar).

Easterlin, R. A. (1974) 'Does Economic Growth Improve the Human Lot? Some Empirical Evidence', in P. A. David and M. W. Reder (eds), *Nations and Households in Economic Growth. Essays in Honour of Moses Abramovitz* (New York: Academic Press).

Easterlin, R. A. (2001) 'Income and Happiness: Towards a Unified Theory', *Economic Journal*, 111(473): 465–84.

Eid, M. and E. Diener (2003) 'Global Judgements of Subjective Well-being: Situational Variability and Long-term Stability', *Social Indicators Research*, 65: 245–77.

Finnis, J. (1980) *Natural Law and Natural Rights* (Oxford: Clarendon Press).

Foster, J., J. Greer and E. Thorbecke (1984) 'A Class of Decomposable Poverty Measures', *Econometrica*, 52: 761–6.

Galtung, J. (1994) *Human Rights in Another Key* (Cambridge: Polity Press).

Gasper, D. (2002) 'Is Sen's Capability Approach an Adequate Basis for Considering Human Development?', *Review of Political Economy*, 14(4): 435–61.

Gasper, D. (2004) 'Human Well-being: Concepts and Conceptualizations', WIDER Discussion Paper 2004/06 (Helsinki: UNU-WIDER).

Grisez, G., J. Boyle and J. Finnis (1987) 'Practical Principles, Moral Truth and Ultimate Ends', *American Journal of Jurisprudence*, 32: 99–151.

Hanmer, L., G. Pyatt and H. White (1997) *Poverty in Sub-Saharan Africa: What Can we Learn from the World Bank's Poverty Assessments* (The Hague: Institute of Social Studies Advisory Service).

Hicks, N. and P. Streeten (1979) 'Indicators of Development: The Search for a Basic Needs Yardstick', *World Development*, 7: 567–80.

Ivanova, I., F. J. Arcelus and G. Srinivasan (1998) 'An Assessment of the Measurement Properties of the Human Development Index', *Social Indicators Research*, 46: 157–79.

Kelley, A. C. (1991) 'The Human Development Index: "Handle with Care" ', *Population and Development Review*, 17(2): 315–24.

Laderchi, C. R. (2001) 'Participatory Methods in the Analysis of Poverty: A Critical Review', QEH Working Paper Series 62 (Oxford: Queen Elizabeth House).

Lambert, P. J. (2001) *The Distribution and Redistribution of Income* (Manchester and New York: Manchester University Press).

Lasswell, H. D. (1992) *Jurisprudence for a Free Society: Studies in Law, Science and Policy* (New Haven: New Haven Press).

Max-Neef, M. (1993) *Human Scale Development: Conception, Application, and Further Reflections* (London: Apex Press).

McGillivray, M. (2005) 'Measuring non-Economic Well-being Achievement', *Review of Income and Wealth*, 51(2): 337–64.

McGillivray, M. and R. Pillarisetti (2006) 'Adjusting Well-being Indicators for Gender Disparities. Empirically Insightful?', in M. McGillivray and M. Clarke (eds), *Understanding Human Well-being* (Tokyo: United Nations University Press for UNU-WIDER).

McGillivray, M. and H. White (1993) 'Measuring Development? The UNDP's Human Development Index', *Journal of International Development*, 5(2): 183–92.

Morris, M. D. (1979) *Measuring the Conditions of the World's Poor: The Physical Quality of Life Index* (New York: Pergamon).

Morse, S. (2003) 'For Better or for Worse, till the Human Development Index do us Part?', *Ecological Economics*, 45(2): 281–96.

Narayan, D., R. Chambers, M. K. Shah and P. Petesch (2000) *Voices of the Poor: Crying out for Change* (New York: Oxford University Press for the World Bank).

Neumayer, E. (1999) 'The ISEW: Not an Index of Sustainable Economic Welfare', *Social Indicators Research*, 48: 77–101.
Neumayer, E. (2001) 'The Human Development Index and Sustainability – A Constructive Proposal', *Ecological Economics*, 39(1): 101–14.
Noorbakhsh, F. (1998) 'A Modified Human Development Index', *World Development*, 26(3): 517–28.
Nordhaus, W. and J. Tobin (1972) 'Is Growth Obsolete?', *Economic Growth* (New York: NBER and Columbia University Press).
Nussbaum, M. C. (2000) *Women and Human Development: The Capabilities Approach* (Cambridge: Cambridge University Press).
Pillarisetti, J. R. and M. McGillivray (1998) 'Human Development and Gender Empowerment: Conceptual and Measurement Issues', *Development Policy Review*, 16(2): 197–203.
Qizilbash, M. (1996a) 'Capabilities, Well-being and Human Development: A Survey', *Journal of Development Studies*, 33(2): 143–62.
Qizilbash, M. (1996b) 'Ethical Development', *World Development*, 24(7): 1209–21.
Ramsay, M. (1992) *Human Needs and the Market* (Aldershot: Avebury).
Rawls, J. (1993) *Political Liberalism* (New York: Columbia University Press).
Sagar, A. and A. Najam (1998) 'The Human Development Index: A Critical Review', *Ecological Economics*, 25: 249–64.
Saith, R. and B. Harriss-White (1999) 'The Gender Sensitivity of Well-being Indicators', *Development and Change*, 30(3): 465–97.
Schwartz, S. H. (1994) 'Are there Universal Aspects in the Structure and Contents of Human Values?', *Journal of Social Issues*, 50(4): 19–45.
Seers, D. (1972) 'What are we Trying to Measure?', *Journal of Development Studies*, 8(3): 21–36.
Sen, A. K. (1976) 'Poverty: An Ordinal Approach to Measurement', *Econometrica*, 44: 219–13.
Sen, A. K. (1982) *Choice, Welfare and Measurement* (Oxford: Basil Blackwell).
Sen, A. K. (1985) *Commodities and Capabilities* (Cambridge: Cambridge University Press).
Sen, A. K. (1993) 'Capability and Well-being', in M. Nussbaum and A. Sen (eds), *The Quality of Life* (Oxford: Clarendon Press for UNU-WIDER).
Sen, A. K. (1999) *Development as Freedom* (New York: Knopf).
Shorrocks, A. F. (1983) 'Ranking Income Distributions', *Economica*, 50: 3–17.
Skevington, S. M, M. Lotfy and K. A. O'Connell (2004) 'The World Health Organization's WHOQOL-BREF Quality of Life Assessment: Psychometric Properties and Results of the International Field Trial. A Report from the WHOQOL Group', *Quality of Life Research*, 23(2): 299–310.
Stewart, F. (1985) *Basic Needs in Developing Countries* (Baltimore MD: Johns Hopkins University Press).
Travers, P. and S. Richardson (1997) 'Material Well-Being and Human Well-Being', in F. Ackerman, D. Kiron, N. R. Goodwin, J. M. Harris and K. Gallagher (eds), *Human Well-Being and Economic Goals* (Washington DC: Island Press).
United Nations Development Programme (UNDP) (1990–2004) *Human Development Report* (New York: Oxford University Press for UNDP).
United Nations Development Programme (UNDP) (2003) *Latvia Human Development Report 2002/2003* (Riga: UNDP).
UN Millennium Project Report (2005) *Investing in Development: A Practical Plan for Achieving the Millennium Development Goals* (New York: UNDP).

Veenhoven, R. (1993) *Happiness in Nations. Subjective Appreciation of Life in 56 Nations, 1946–1992* (Rotterdam: Erasmus University).
Veenhoven, R. (2004) *World Happiness Database*, www.eur.nl/fsw/research/happiness
WHOQOL Group (1994) 'Development of the WHOQOL: Rationale and Current Status', *International Journal of Mental Health*, 23: 24–56.
WHOQOL Group (1998) 'The World Health Organization Quality of Life Assessment (WHOQOL): Development and General Psychometric Properties', *Social Science and Medicine*, 46: 551–8.
World Bank (1969–2004) *World Bank Atlas* (Washington, DC: World Bank).
World Bank (1977–2004) *World Development Report* (New York: Oxford University Press for the World Bank).
Zolotas, X. (1981) *Economic Growth and Declining Social Welfare* (New York: New York University Press).

2
Human Well-being: Concepts and Conceptualizations

Des Gasper

Introduction

What should those who measure well-being try to measure? To address this question one must consider the nature of well-being, and the various purposes of the exercise of conceptualizing and measuring. This chapter concentrates on the nature of well-being, especially in the earlier sections; purposes will be addressed too, especially in the second part.

The chapter stresses the diversity both in well-being and the approaches to it. We will move towards a framework gradually, since, as Griffin (1986) argues, well-being concepts come as parts of complex conceptualizations which reflect pictures of personhood and of science. Insight grows through first surveying the terrain of well-being, and some of the range of concepts and conceptualizations, before risking blinkering one's vision in a framework. Then is presented an imperfect comparative and integrative framework, before we use the framework to examine some current re-conceptualizations of human well-being by Dasgupta, Sen, Nussbaum, Doyal and Gough, and Alkire, and compare their purposes.

The primary objective of the chapter is thus to identify different conceptualizations of well-being, and view them in relation to relevant evidence and an integrative framework. A necessary intermediate objective is to clear away presumptions linked to the enthroning of income per capita as the key indicator of well-being – necessary given that indicator's long predominance and continuing centrality in policy analysis and public discourse. Concepts derived for purposes of measurement of market transactions, and prediction of market behaviour, were taken over for purposes of wider evaluation of life situations and trajectories. The result was well-being measurement without an adequate theoretical frame, and the distortion of such measurement by the presence since the 1940s of national accounts and related data, even though economic measures of income have ignored large areas of well-being and are weak measures of well-being in the areas to which they attend.

The preoccupation with explanation of market behaviour and measurement came to obscure the different purposes of various types of normative judgement about human well-being. Increasing recognition of the distortions has had relatively little practical impact; in very many circles 'GNP per head continues to be regarded as the quintessential indicator of a country's living standard' (Dasgupta 2001: 53). One reason is the difficult requirement that alternative measurement should be guided by a unifying alternative vision while respecting the complexity and diversity of well-being. Hence the interest now in, for example, Sen's approach, which proposes such a vision.

The nature of well-being: terms, foci and blind-spots

Literature on 'well-being' is massive and diverse. A large part nowadays consists of books of advice on how to feel fine, through diet, exotic substances and aromas, music, posture techniques, exercise routines, giving more priority to one's family and other personal relationships, or religion. The 'in' term is well-being, not happiness. Perhaps the Aristotelian standpoint is widely shared: that well-being is not merely a sensation of happiness. Human beings have more faculties than just feeling happiness, pleasure or pain; notably they are creatures of reasoning and of meaning-making, of imagination, and of intra- and inter-societal links and identities.

A smaller part of contemporary publication on well-being comes from academic philosophy, as in the work of James Griffin or Wayne Sumner, which examines a limited set of concepts with reference to a rather limited range of evidence and methods. One encounters few real people or cases and usually little behavioural science there. Their theories of the good have a narrow basis; 'work' does not figure in the indexes to Griffin and Sumner's books. Such analysis does still probe and query assumptions behind the treatment of 'welfare', personal and social, in modern economics.

A third body of investigation, consciously on well-being, is the huge literature from other social sciences, especially psychology. These use a broader range of evidence and concepts. Whereas the 'ordinal revolution' in economics rejected cardinal measurement of utility and interpersonal utility comparisons, the other social science that matches it in scale – psychology – retained the study and measurement of subjective well-being (SWB). It shows that SWB is measurable, often relatively little related to consumption levels, and not simply imputable from choices – people do not try to maximize their own utility/SWB and/or are not very good at it (Kahneman 1994, Kiron 1997). Only exceptional cases in economics, such as Tibor Scitovsky's remarkable *The Joyless Economy* (1976), have delved into these sources, until very recently. SWB work has however long been available, and has grown greatly in the past generation, as in the so-called positive psychology movement (e.g. Seligman and Csikszentihalyi 2000). 'Positive' refers here to the study of success, as Abraham Maslow stressed from the

1930s: study of mentally healthy people and high achievers, not only the sick and disturbed. What outsiders may call SWB research includes, arguably, at least two different streams, the hedonic and the eudaimonic, the latter of which may sometimes call itself psychological well-being research rather than SWB research (Ryan and Deci 2001).[1] Also partly distinct are the great streams of research on quality of life (QOL) and social indicators, often from sociology, health sciences and related areas.[2]

Another philosophical style reflects less on generalized impersonal social science sources, and more, as in the Aristotelian or existentialist traditions, on insights from history, fiction, drama, biography and the narrative study of lives; for example, as in Theodore Zeldin's *An Intimate History of Humanity* (1994) or Andre Comte-Sponville's *A Short Treatise on The Great Virtues* (2002). Martha Nussbaum's *Upheavals of Thought* combines this tradition with intensive evidence from behavioural sciences.

A look across this variety of literatures generates many considerations, some of which we should mention here. We need to look at quantity as well as quality of life, at time budgets, and at the quality of death; and to acknowledge that 'well-being' refers to many different things.

The term 'well-being' is ambiguous: it has many usages, meanings and conceptions

The category 'well-being' (WB) seems to be used to refer to whatever is assessed in an evaluation of a person's situation, or, more fittingly and narrowly, in any such evaluation that is focused on the person's 'being' (Gasper 2002). The term 'welfare' can mean how well people live, or what is done by others to help the needy; these are the two *OED* meanings. In the former usage, 'welfare' is typically treated interchangeably with WB; the *OED* defines it as 'well-being; happiness; health and prosperity'.[3]

The concept of well-being is thus best seen as an abstraction, which is used to refer to any or all of the many well-evaluated aspects of life (Travers and Richardson 1993). But it has often been reified as a single entity, especially in most utilitarianism and utilitarian influenced economics. Most utilitarianism reduced well-being to *well-feeling* (typically seen as pleasure), and further reduced well-feeling to a scalar (unitary pleasure, 'utility').[4] People were presented as simple creatures, with just one sort of appreciative system, and with that one system having just one currency – as if we could only see shades of one colour. In contrast, even the simpler, hedonic stream of SWB research distinguishes three major aspects of well-being, which vary partly independently of each other: experiences of happiness, experiences of unhappiness, and experiences of contentment. A further ambiguity lurked in utilitarianism: was utility the psychic pay-off or was it the usefulness or pleasure-producing quality of the goods? (Bonner 1995). Lionel Robbins *et al.* claimed Pareto's legacy but conflated his terms that distinguished these two: ophelimity versus utility (Cooter and Rappaport 1984). They thus obscured that even if pleasure is hard to measure, usefulness is not always so (e.g. we can measure mobility).

In practice, mainstream economics declared that each person's utility (as ophelimity, this unitary well-feeling; or as preference fulfilment) is well reflected by income. Sen (1985) noted that this reduced well-being to being well-off, financially or materially; in other words to 'well-having' or 'having much' (cf. Fromm 1978). To test this reduction, one must consider how income is used. Some forms of consumption, such as heavy alcohol intake and compulsive gambling, damage the consumers and those close to them. In countries with less margin for luxury expenditure, alcoholism has massive impact on families. Janakarajan and Seabright (1999: 341), for example, record the escalating alcohol abuse by men in an economically booming settlement in South India, and the 'noticeably less positive' responses from women than men about changes in their family's situation.

The Aristotelian tradition takes well-being instead as *well-living*. People are seen as complex – reasoning, social, and thus in part moral – actors, who live in groups, for finite lives with an unavoidable rise and fall. In contrast to the abstracted utilitarian notion of a person as a smart rat who pulls the levers to maximize the reading on his utility meter, well-being is seen as the fulfilment of a deep and various nature, not just one particular type of sensation (Segal 1991). The range of important goods includes things that are not merely instrumental to our flourishing, as routes to our psychic utility, but which rather are 'constitutive of our flourishing' (O'Neill 1993: 24). Culyer (1990: 11) argues that 'being reassured' leads to 'pleasure' – but does it? Is there a single mental currency, or is being reassured itself the pay-off? One could distinguish many aspects within well-living; perhaps well-thinking and well-doing, as emphasized in, for example, some religious and quasi-religious communities.

Well-living can become denigrated as an elitist notion. Distanced labels may aid calmer debate. As we saw, Ryan and Deci (2001) define the conception of well-being as happiness or pleasure the *hedonic* conception; versus the *eudaimonic* conception of well-being as well-considered fulfilment.

Well-living is perhaps a superior term to well-being (at least for eudaimonists)

'Well-being' is such an established term that we will use it too. However, 'well-living' has claims to be a better label for what most people conceive of as well-being. 'Well-living' is a more active term, and in economics the term 'well-being' still carries a utilitarian baggage. Thus even for Sen, coming out of the tradition of welfare economics, 'well-being' referred only to one's own gratification, and was distinct from the pursuit and fulfilment of one's ideals and commitments. To an Aristotelian this seems a strange usage. Max-Neef's model of human needs illustrates a richer conception, with dimensions of *having*, *doing*, and *interacting*, as well as *being*, in each of a series of life spheres (see e.g. Ekins and Max-Neef 1992, which links this perspective to well-being measurement).

Being is a prerequisite for, and central component of, well-being

Lethal epidemics amongst the poor can raise average per capita income and other per capita indicators. Clearly, well-being measures should instead in some way reflect quantity of life as well as quality of life. The central importance of quantity is revealed in the notional choice between a life of 70 years with pre-Industrial Revolution living standards in all non-mortality related aspects and one of 35 (or maybe even 55) years with contemporary rich country living standards (at an income level purportedly 100 times higher). The poor country dweller would live as a family and community member, not in a prison, but with few material comforts. Possibly most people would choose the non-opulent life of 70 years (which happens to be a reality in a few remote corners of the world). This puts opulence sharply into perspective.

Time-patterns in being/living are of central importance for well-being

If we look empirically at quality of living, time-use too is central and little reflected in most well-being measures. Naila Kabeer's study of women textile-workers in Bangladesh found many with 18 hour work days: a factory job preceded and followed by housework, sometimes even as a second job (Kabeer 2000). 'Housework' for most women includes caring time, often including care for the handicapped, elderly and sick. While, remarkably, the self-assessed well-being of some people permanently handicapped by accidents can return to near their previous level, that of their unpaid carers is unlikely to. In low-income countries, unmanageable carer time-budgets can affect life-quantity of the cared for; in India few of the mentally retarded survive to adulthood (Harriss-White 1999: 138–9).

In apartheid South Africa, many black workers commuted three hours each way each day, in desperate conditions. In contrast to that, first, the time required for material reproduction by some hunter-gatherer peoples historically has been strikingly low; second, commuting time in the North has for some fortunate cases evolved into a new life sphere of seclusion and self-cultivation: the car driver cocooned in his luxury vehicle on the freeway, replete with snacks and music-system, free from interruptions and duties. And what is one to make of figures of TV watching times in the North: four hours daily on average in the USA, with the set often switched on for longer (*The Economist*, 12 April 2002; and 3.5 hours daily in the UK for the middle-aged), or of the new mass opium of communing with the muse of pornography from the Internet – reportedly the leading personal use of the most powerful new medium? The consensus academic reaction to Robert

Nozick's (1974) famous thought-experiment, the Experience Machine, was to assert that people will not choose to live cocooned in a world of electronic substitute experience, however high it raises their utility meter; yet perhaps many come to live so.

Concern for well-being and well-living must include central attention to people's work involvements, and domestic involvements, not only their consumption

Welfare economics has historically looked largely at consumption (Goodwin 1997) and measures derived from national income statistics have ignored the unhappiness from involuntary unemployment (Clark and Oswald 1994) and the satisfactions (and dissatisfactions) from employment. The pattern found in *Voices of the Poor* and many other studies is, however, that ordinary people's lists of priorities include both 'material' and 'non-material' aspects (Alkire 2002: 179–80). There is evidence for affluent countries that non-market sources – family, friends, health, recreation – are more important in general for happiness than are market sources, and that amongst the market sources, experiences during work hours or unemployment are more determinant of personal satisfaction than is the level of income or consumption (Oswald 1997, Lane 1998a, 1998b). We consider this more fully later.

External work is a major source of socializing, stimulation, challenge, and achievement (see e.g. Parker and Gerard 1990, Lane 1991); 'freed' from work, some lottery winners become miserable. Some of the low-income Bangladeshi women workers studied by Kabeer reported that they took their jobs for the non-monetary rewards: to avoid boredom and have company. The satisfactions from work are only slightly reflected in economic accounting. That applies the perspective of a capitalist to a nation, with work assumed to be a cost rather than a benefit.

Many aspects of well-being pass outside markets, and may be competitive with them

Travers and Richardson (1993) summarize many findings that there are only weak observed correlations between all of the following: (i) material well-being ('well-having'), (ii) happiness, (iii) health, and (iv) participation in society. Concerning the link between material well-being and happiness/SWB, while the rich in all countries have higher SWB, there is surprisingly little difference between the SWB levels recorded in many richer and poorer countries, and especially between many middle-income, rich and very rich countries.[5] Myers and Diener (1995) report almost no relation between income and happiness over time in the postwar USA, suggesting that richer people enjoy their relative superiority rather than their opulence, and/or that expectations grow with opportunities and that new unfulfilled ambitions emerge. Many other studies confirm this 'Easterlin paradox' (see e.g. the set in Easterlin 2002b).[6]

Some other factors retain a stronger relation to happiness. Lane (1991,1998a) documents that considerably more important than wealth for happiness in America are (i) marital satisfaction, (ii) self-esteem (and other psychological traits; Myers and Diener (1995) add: extraversion, optimism), (iii) self-management skills, (iv) financial stability, and (v) leisure. Myers and Diener add to such a list: (ia) other good personal relations, (iiia) feelings of progress towards goals that one accepts, and (vi) religious belief. (Camfield and Skevington 2003 give a similar recent multi-national survey.) Does a preoccupation with material opulence compete with these other factors, given the mind-set and time-use it may bring? Lane and others argue that the competition is serious. There is, at the very least, no reliable presumption that material opulence consistently promotes these other factors or is even across-the-board neutral towards them.

All this goes against the expectations of the material well-being school represented by Marshall and Pigou (Cooter and Rappaport 1984). They expected material WB to correlate well with, or at least not interfere with, other sources so that they could focus on it alone.

Well-living includes well-becoming and well-dying

Even a utilitarian rat, assiduously pulling its pleasure levers, exists in time. First, the person must be created, formed, emerge. Interestingly, developmental psychology suggests that 'well-becoming', personal growth, requires pain.[7] And eventually each person must decline, cease, un-be. In grindingly poor mid-twentieth century China, the Communists gained much respect for their commitment to ensuring decent burials. The 1990's *Voices of the Poor* study shows the strong importance attached to funerals in most milieux (Narayan *et al.* 2000a: 70). Funerals reflect death as a very special aspect of existence, both for those whose lives end and for their associates, not just 'an external limit on existence', suggests Hodge (1990: 52). They are less for the dead than, in fact, for the living. Inability to cope with death represents an inability to face life. The hospices movement is one relevant response. A well-living perspective considers the life cycles of real people, not only the imputed wish fulfilment of faceless moneyed consumers. It must look at Quality of Death as part of the QOL, including in particular the quality of decline, fade-out and departure (see e.g. Jennings *et al.* 2003). Ignoring the quality of death brutalizes both the ignored and the ignorers.[8]

Given the many relevant aspects of well-being, it seems better to use WB as an umbrella term rather than seek for a single key aspect or theme

Feeling and thinking, becoming and living and dying, and more, make up being. Well-being thus has diverse aspects. Rather than set up a precisely delimited, narrow, single notion of well-being, and then try to police its 'correct' usage, we would do better to see WB as an umbrella notion. The next section introduces the standard philosophy list of interpretations of well-being, only now that we have established this point.

A danger arises of disappearing, as a result, under an avalanche of indicators. Hodge argues that we must not isolate indicators from meanings and life-purposes in the situation concerned. We still need organizing frameworks. The next section goes on to the main dichotomy used to organize the field: between subjective and objective aspects or interpretations of well-being. Is this dichotomy itself objective?

Attempts to theorize and categorize

A standard philosophy categorization of conceptions of well-being, and additions

A categorization of conceptions of well-being by Derek Parfit (1984) has become widely used in philosophical ethics (see e.g. Griffin 1986, Crisp 2001). It contains both so-called subjective and objective conceptions. All make plausible claims.

Hedonism Well-being seen as pleasure. Hedonism fails as a full concept of well-being, due to both the diversity of our types of value and the nature of some of the factors that strongly influence pleasure. It is only one part of a family of conceptions of well-being as satisfaction or SWB. They all remain vulnerable to the significance of 'framing' and adaptive response, which we consider further later in this section. A severely retarded person might feel fine; likewise someone whose brain and nervous system have been damaged by drugs.

Desire theories Well-being seen as preference/desire fulfilment. One origin of this conception is in economists' operationalization of the previous conception, well-being as pleasure or satisfaction. From the days before systematic SWB research this has been done by the assumption that preference fulfilment always or nearly always brings satisfaction.[9] In the attempt, in turn, to operationalize this second conception without even measuring preference fulfilment either, the stream evolved into 'revealed preference theory', which imputes preference fulfilment from the fact of choice. That choices reveal preferences became taken as a tautology. So, well-being was reduced to choice. Ironically, the choice involved in this reduction was often done in a veiled way, such that many economists and their students and clients remained unclear about the methodological and value choices that were being made. In effect, it merged the preference fulfilment stream into a libertarian stream instead, which insists on people's right to make their own mistakes: to pursue their own goals, regardless of whether they are likely to fulfil them and of what that would bring. The libertarian stream is not highlighted in Parfit's list; arguably it is not even a conception of well-being. Next, theories of well-being as desire fulfilment or desire pursuit are vulnerable, like hedonism, to the existence of perverted desires and of addictions like alcoholism (see e.g. Scanlon 1993, Sagoff 1994). So, the more plausible versions are formulated in terms of fully informed desires – which would have to be fully informed from birth in order to rule out all addictions. These versions are also insufficient (as well as hard to convert into well-being measures): people with perverse desires to damage others may not be put off by full information on how to avoid damage to themselves or about the harm they can bring others, nor would be any people who are inclined to damage themselves. Why would one consider such people's desires objectionable? Probably because one held that there exists some set or list of justified criteria that is not identical to people's desires and excludes some types of desire pursuit and fulfilment.

Objective list theories The term 'objective' can be misleading, as we see later; Scanlon (1993) offered the better title of 'substantive good theories'. Each such theory has a listing of (the) elements that make a life well lived; as, for example, in theories in the eudaimonic tradition, such as Nussbaum's. In a way, pleasure and desire theories are objective list theories that have just one element on their list. Crisp (2001) notes that while objective list theories of the good are elitist in one sense – based on tested knowledge rather than on desires or pleasures alone – they need not entail a Big Brother state. They may be combined with theories of the right that establish areas for individual self-determination.[10]

How a 'substantive list' is derived varies greatly. The following ideal types exist, amongst which mixtures are possible: (a) Some lists are direct stipulations, drawn from intuition, religion, or tradition; (b) others are derived through formal analytical procedures, as we see later with Doyal and Gough's theory of need. That proffers objectively implied needs, derived from and conditional on some (not purely objective) more general specification of the good; and (c) some lists are derived through consultation and, perhaps, debate within a particular political community. Nussbaum's list has aspects of all these types: it derives from the use of formal criteria combined with ethical intuitions, and is to be elaborated and operationalized in each political context.

So, to accommodate current theories of well-being, Parfit's categorization should be extended. Let us underline and supplement some important additional variants that have already been mentioned.

1 Hedonism is just one member of a family of related but significantly distinct theories. In other members, there are many types of utility, pleasure, or satisfaction, not all of which can be reliably or meaningfully traded-off against each other.

2 The libertarian stance, wherein one's good means one's choice: this may be qualified by requirements of not harming others, but such requirements are not a part of the conception of one's own well-being.
3 Sen uses a conception of informed, rational preferences, applied to functionings and 'capabilities', the latter meaning access to particular valued functionings. This is in contrast to desire theories, which use the language of pure preference and apply it to alternative goods baskets. Capability is perhaps better seen as a criterion for personal advantage as opposed to well-being, we suggest later. The theory might be classified as an objective list theory, but of a peculiar type, since Sen insists, at least formally, on not specifying any of what would or should be the outcomes of informed and rational preference. To call it a desire theory is also unsatisfactory: it stresses public discussion and informed public decision for some priorities, rather than monetizable calculations based only on individuals' desires for themselves.

In contrast, Nussbaum specifies a series of functionings to which, she argues, all persons should have access. But, as does Sen, she does not seek to enforce use of the access (except for the schooling of children, control of infectious diseases, and such like).

Within objective list theories we should thus distinguish those that assess well-being only or mainly by access, from those that look primarily at achievement of valued functionings. The latter is the approach to well-being in much (Physical) QOL and social indicators research, with the valued functionings specified in some general public list rather than separately by every individual.

With Nussbaum and QOL research we return to the richness and realism of discussion of well-being we encountered earlier, from a wider range of literatures than the analytic philosophy tradition to which Parfit's list belongs. A considerable gulf has existed between most work in this tradition and substantive research on the content of well-being.[11]

Scanlon (1993) compares WB theories according to their relevance for different decision-makers: for oneself; for a policy maker acting in relation to others; and for moral argument. He proposes that desire theories are only relevant in the political context, where political leaders may conclude not to interfere with many pernicious and damaging desires. In contrast, he argues, for moral argumentation we are led inexorably to a substantive good conception. One might add that the informed desire conception seems more at home for the notional case of the individual choosing purely for him/herself, and that the capability criterion appears more relevant to public decision-making about persons' advantage.

Kagan (1994) contextualizes the conceptions in a different, complementary way. He underlines that they describe different things. For him, (personal) well-being refers to feelings in a person's body and mind – in other words, to well-feeling – and he adopts a common usage of 'quality of life' to refer instead to various availabilities and non-feeling functionings – in other words, (other aspects of) well-living. Many other authors employ a language of 'subjective versus objective' indicators of well-being.

The language of 'subjective versus objective' measures of WB is misused

Many authors use a single contrast between 'subjective and objective indicators of welfare'. This tends to oversimplify. It misleads when combined with two tendentious assumptions: that WB is unitary, and that the class of indicators derived without the judgement of the subject have an epistemological privilege. We should instead use two more cautious contrasts.

1 Measures of subjective WB (SWB) versus measures of objective WB (OWB); meaning, measures of feelings versus measures of non-feeling aspects such as longevity. We have here measures of different (families of) things, not different measures of a single thing.
2 Self-report versus non-self-report (subject-independent) measures of WB (Diener's terms; Camfield and Skevington 2003). Self-report can cover more than feelings of (dis)satisfaction; subjects can use other modes and criteria of judgement.

Some people propose (opposite to Kagan) that we reserve the term QOL for self-report judgements, perhaps on the grounds that quality of *life* is about the nature of perceived or felt experience. Yet, the QOL term has been so long and diversely used that it may be beyond reform through stipulation; and further, life involves also the unperceived, the unconscious, and the unfelt.

Figure 2.1, then, distinguishes four types of indicator.[12] Such a chart adds non-self-report measures of subjective well-being (the top right quadrant) to

	Self-report (SR) indicators	*Non-self-report (NSR; subject-independent) indicators*
Measures of subjective WB	'Self-report subjective' (e.g.: 'I am very satisfied with how far I can walk')	E.g. types of brain function and physiological indicator that express SWB
Measures of objective WB	'Self-report objective' (e.g.: 'I can walk 100 metres')	'Objective' – observing how far people really (can) walk, etc.

Figure 2.1 Refined terms for subjective/objective

the three categories which Camfield and Skevington (2003) use. I have used their titles in quote marks, while the examples are mine; in similar vein, one could label the top-right quadrant 'objective indicators of perceptions'.

We need at least one more distinction:

3 between measures that are applied to all times and places ('universalist'), and measures chosen per time and place ('relativist').

If we look at this closely we may find a continuum rather than a dichotomy, but the continuum is worth at least one distinction rather than none. One source of the popularity of income per capita measures for measuring human well-being, a task for which they were not devised and are fundamentally unsuited, has been their combination of two appeals, as universal and 'objective' measures which yet, in principle, in part reflect the subjective preferences of consumers. But they only refer to wishes that achieve expression in market terms. Things only enter GNP and similar calculations in proportion to how much people are willing *and able* to pay for them.

Shaffer (1996) makes a composite contrast, between economists' income/consumption approach and the alternative participatory approach to the study of poverty. In the income/consumption approach, well-being/poverty is determined by an external expert who, typically by use of a questionnaire survey, measures degrees of basic needs fulfilment/deprivation by reference to the proxies of income and/or consumption of goods and services. S/he usually takes no critical stance towards consumer preferences (for example, for heavy alcohol use), seeing his/her work and role as descriptive.

In the participatory approach, well-being/poverty is investigated by interactive internal and external discussion and participation in assessment, to look at multiple aspects of deprivation, employing multiple criteria and a mixture of qualitative and quantitative methods. There is a critical dialogue about current preferences, and the objective is to contribute both to understanding and empowerment of the people whose situation is studied. Robert Chambers and others have influentially collected and disseminated examples of local people's own criteria of well-being and ill-being (see e.g. UNDP 1997: 17).

Social exclusion theory gives a third perspective on well-being. It looks at the nature of a person's social relationships with others, and at illicit discrimination (e.g. on grounds of caste or gender) and unequal access to benefits that are supposed to be available to everyone. It uses a norm of citizenship and estimates its prerequisites. Different conceptions of citizenship lead to different interpretations of social exclusion (Gore 1996). Further, social exclusion can be assessed in a participatory or a subject-independent way.

Shaffer outlines how such approaches in poverty studies reflect different ways of looking at life, each of which will have strengths and weaknesses.

The participatory approach and social exclusion approach use more complex pictures of persons and of human lives than does the income/consumption approach. The approaches also use different philosophies of knowledge and different ethics. They will not, therefore, easily displace each other. Each has its own audience (cf. Dean 2003).

We must consider both SWB and OWB

The distinction between the issues of what is measured and how it is measured puts the contrast between SWB and OWB into perspective. First, 'objective *well*-being' is a normative concept: we measure what is proposed as having value. The question is how well argued and/or widely accepted those values are. For example, assessing lives in terms of longevity, morbidity, and the requirements for autonomy of agency gives a value laden but cogent, widely accepted, subject-independent, conception of well-being (cf. Doyal and Gough 1991). Second, measures of SWB can be valid and reliable: they can acceptably measure certain perceptions (Myers and Diener 1995, Camfield and Skeffington 2003).

On the other hand, this validity and reliability concerns the focus and quality of the measurement of SWB, not *necessarily* the stability or good judgement of the perception that is measured. First, psychology research shows that SWB is highly conditional upon 'framing effects'; for example, conditional upon with whom/when/where one compares one's present situation. For example, Frank (1997) notes how strongly in the USA the satisfaction from consumption depends on how the consumer's consumption level compares to his/her previous consumption level and to the consumption level of his/her reference group. Second, adaptive preference (sometimes called 'response shift') is widespread, notably where one's preferences and perceptions adjust to one's situation, however good or bad, to reinterpret it as normal and tolerable. Cummins *et al.* (2002) and others hold that this adjustment is not merely widespread but normal.[13] Such shifts would strengthen the case for subject-independent measures, as Sen, Nussbaum, Sunstein and others have argued – unless one equates well-being with preference-fulfilment regardless. Third, more generally, one can simply misassess one's situation (Kagan). So, measures of SWB cannot be identical to those for QOL. This is quite apart from the possibility, recognised in tragedy and also by Sen, that one may be committed to goals that do not give one SWB.

We must not ignore the information in measures of SWB. They tell us about something(s) different and important: people's feelings. If people did not feel, then we would be much less likely to feel for and with them and to be motivated to help the disadvantaged. And the messages that these measures have brought concerning such important variables are massively significant.

First, even if preferences are often adaptive, the gap that SWB data shows between the weak or often negligible impact of increases in measured real income and the substantial impacts of other promotor factors on SWB in richer countries is one of the major findings of modern social science (Easterlin 2002a).

Second, while such impact findings are less common (although so is the research, notes Easterlin) they sometimes also occur in poorer countries. They should lead us to review the measures for income and other 'objective' aspects of well-being, the values and assumptions hidden in the choice of indicators, and the uses made of income. For example, Janakarajan and Seabright compare the changes between 1985 and 1992 in two areas of Tamil Nadu (India) which had experienced contrasting recent economic fortunes. They find no strong and easily explainable correlations between the levels of various 'objective' welfare indicators and the perceptions of change. 'There is [also] a striking difference between the answers given to questions about respondents' own families and questions about the fortunes of the village as a whole. The latter are markedly more positive' (Easterlin 2002b: 339–40), about matters of which the respondents probably knew less. Some 'objective' measures of improved welfare in these villages, notably the shift to supposedly preferred, higher status, foods, may instead 'owe a good deal to social and life style pressures and are not necessarily perceived as bringing benefits to the household' (ibid.: 342).

Quite different discrepancies can occur, equally significant. N. S. Jodha found major divergences between the stagnant figures for real rural incomes in a set of North Indian villages, figures provided by India's relatively well respected economic statistics bureaucracy, and the declarations of improved well-being by the majority of villagers. In this case, the gains in SWB were strongly related by the villagers to changes in objective but non-monetized aspects of their lives: diversity of diet, ability to send children to school, increased access to cheap but life changing products such as transistor radios, and increased ability to survive without labouring for others, even if this meant a fall in monetary income. Such patterns of affect are widespread, not specific to a few villages or to India. Here, there was no discrepancy between SWB and non-income OWB, but a divergence between their trends and those in income.

Well-being is a vector

Utilities not utility, and life spheres not only the market

At least three types of fundamental plurality impinge here. One is well-known in economics: that there are diverse individuals, not only a societal aggregate. The other two have been neglected (despite e.g. Sen 1981): that there are various types of mental attitude, not a single 'utility', and various spheres of life with distinct forms of thought, not only the impersonal utilitarian market.

The language of 'weighing up' conflicting considerations (e.g. Crisp 2001) presumes commensurability and aggregation, rather than some other form of choice. But psychology confirms what introspection and the arts always suggested: we have diverse types of psychic 'currency', not only one.[14] Scitovsky (1976/1992), for example, considerably deepened the economics of welfare by distinguishing the 'currencies' of comfort and stimulation. Eudaimonic-WB research covers a range of emotional, cognitive and existential dimensions. We saw that even the simpler palette of hedonic-WB research distinguishes positive emotions, negative emotions, and life satisfaction, as basic dimensions of subjective well-being (e.g. Myers and Diener 1995: 174, 'Positive and negative emotions are only weakly correlated with one another').[15]

Different spheres of life can involve different types of thinking and feeling (see e.g. van Staveren 2001). As eludicated by authors such as Isaiah Berlin, Bernard Williams and Amartya Sen, these cannot be all subsumed by a single type of calculation (see e.g. Sen and Williams 1982, Gray 1993). Alkire surveys 39 lists, largely similar, of proposed fundamental, irreducible, aspects of well-being (2002: 59–85).

Since the mainstream of economics has derived from a priori and abstracted theorization about one type of life situation (the cool, calculating and assiduous choice-maker in markets), it often has not faced or accepted the vector nature of WB. No advance in indicators and indexes will find the one correct index that converts WB or poverty to a scalar. Scalar indexes have their uses, but not as all-purpose measures.

Mainstream economics has generally recognized the third type of plurality affecting well-being: plurality of persons. The response in Paretian welfare economics was perverse: to try to avoid interpersonal comparisons, rather than to be conscious about and analyze the value choices involved in the comparisons that are inevitable in public life. We might even say that interpersonal comparisons are feasible and legitimate *except* within the market-metric. Interpersonal comparisons of non-utility variables, such as holdings of Rawlsian primary goods, are perfectly feasible; and comparisons are now standard and well-validated for satisfaction measures too, as we have seen. But 'money-tarianism' – aggregation across persons in terms of monetary benefits and costs – too readily makes comparisons across persons. We cannot equate a Euro more for the rich person with a Euro less for a pauper and declare the redistribution societally neutral. Money-tarianism similarly ignores the worth of cataract operations and hospices for the poorest, since they cannot afford them.[16]

'Poverties not poverty'

Poverty means the lack of something(s) of special importance. As remarked by the Chilean economist and needs theorist, Manfred Max-Neef (1989), we must speak then of poverties not poverty, for different important things may be lacking. As in needs theory, what is lacking can be specified as the requisites for survival, or health, or dignity, or flourishing, and so on – or as those things themselves.[17] In other words, poverty (like development) is a vector not a scalar concept, though sometimes, for purposes of making decisions, we find aggregation useful.

Poverty concerns not only lack of income and wealth: 'I am illiterate. I am like a blind person' remarked an illiterate mother in Pakistan (cited by Narayan *et al.* 2000a: 53). Narayan *et al.* at first stipulate that 'While poverty is material in nature, it has psychological effects' (ibid.: 37): but others call these effects psychic poverties; having no voice, no dignity, being humiliated, feeling powerless, being unable to participate in one's community. These poverties also vary independently of material poverty. And the ability to participate and to have voice is not mere subjective perception. Any claim that poverty is *only* material in nature is swept away by the end of that chapter in *Voices of the Poor.* While the definitions by poor people vary, Narayan *et al.* find that 'What is striking, however, is the extent to which dependency, lack of power and lack of voice emerge as core elements of poor people's definitions of poverty' (ibid.: 64). These aspects are not only 'material in nature'. At least part of the World Bank thus acknowledged that 'Poverty Is Multidimensional' (ibid.: 32).

Baulch (1996) suggested that we use a series of poverty concepts, progressively more inclusive, rather than attempt to devise a single 'correct' concept:

1 private consumption;
2 #1 plus income from common property resources;
3 #2 plus income from social provision/consumption;
4 #3 plus assets;
5 #4 plus dignity;
6 #5 plus autonomy.

To organize these and similar ideas, we will look further at the notion of levels, and at the purposes and context of an analysis of well-being.

Bridging the means–ends divide: a comparative and integrative framework

Poverty can be conceptualized at different levels. Kabeer (1996) contrasts: (i) the 'means perspective', which focuses on the resources and requisites that people possess or obtain and can use to fulfil their (basic) needs or preferences; these means are often (inadequately) summarized by a measure of their income; and (ii) the 'ends perspective', which focuses on the actual degree of fulfilment of their needs or preferences. Economists typically adopt the means perspective, though they can also consider consumption, which moves us part way to an 'ends' perspective. Measures of income or personal consumption often neglect non-commoditized goods and services.

The traditional economics foci and presumptions can be summarized as a chain: (exogenous) preferences and resource endowments → income → choice/expenditure → preference fulfilment → satisfaction (utility). Much work, especially in psychology, has demonstrated the limits of these presumptions and, for example, of the model of expected-utility maximization. Consumer expenditure, to take a concrete example, is a weak proxy for the quantity and quality of consumption: are purchased goods actually used, how long do they last, how useful are they? Sen has built a framework for welfare economics that enlighteningly adds levels to the conventional set, notably the levels of functionings and capability. Each level can be the focus for defining and/or measuring poverty: so we can define 'income poverty', 'capability poverty', and so on. Sen's categories and the work of Doyal and Gough underlie the next two figures.

Table 2.1 presents an elaborated set of levels, grouped into three ranges (inputs, intermediate events, and outcomes), and some of the corresponding types of study of well-being and/or poverty. The figure includes rows for each of the interpretations of well-being that we saw earlier. Some readers might place value fulfilment in either the desire fulfilment or functionings row (the latter allocation would match an 'objective list' approach), but it may be worth highlighting separately.

National income measures concern only range I, the money-metric focus. They measure monetized activity. If treated as measures of net benefits, they at most measure opportunities, not achieved well-being in terms of actual consumption or functioning or satisfaction. Even as measures of value opportunities, they include much that should be excluded, exclude much that should be included, and weight inequitably whatever is included.[18]

The narrative structure in Table 2.1, resources through to felt satisfaction and value fulfilment, is still not ideal for a descriptive and explanatory micro-economics. Each of the categories contains ambiguities (see e.g. Gasper 2002); this is common, though, in social science. The focus on a chain-narrative brings a danger, too, of neglecting process values. Further, the structure of Table 2.1 should not make us assume that the level (or levels) having normative priority must be the final one. The set of levels still serves to permit useful organization and comparison of diverse literatures; and it highlights the intermediate range of categories (set II in Table 2.1) between economists' two traditional foci, the monetizable inputs to life and, secondarily, the presumed psychic outputs expressed in the mental money of utility. Economists have studied the inputs empirically and in general imputed the psychic outputs from those inputs.

Partha Dasgupta calls the difference in focus here between economists and other relevant sciences 'a cultural divide' (2001: 33). He initially represents the groups involved too narrowly, identifying only philosophers – who, he says, examine *constituents* of well-being – and economists and statisticians, who focus on its *determinants*. Absent, at first, from this colloquy on well-being are the rest of the social sciences and humanities. They provide richer

Table 2.1 Alternative levels of focus in studies of well-being

Putative narrative sequence (from bottom to top)	**Who has studied the category?**
III Fulfilment/satisfaction information	
HUMAN FULFILMENT – as value fulfilment	Studied by humanistic psychologists and philosophers
Utility – as SATISFACTION (this is not necessarily a unitary category; different aspects can be distinguished)	Traditionally not directly measured by economics (instead presumed unitary and imputed via long chains of assumptions). Studied empirically in psychology, especially in SWB research, and by others.
Utility – as DESIRE FULFILMENT	Imputed from choice, in much economics; i.e. (choice → desire fulfilment) is presumed. Studied directly by some others.
II Non-fulfilment non-money-metric information	
FUNCTIONINGS (other than satisfaction)	Little studied by economics traditionally (health economics is one exception). Studied by functional specialisms, social statistics, sociology, psychology: in work on social indicators and objective QOL.*
O-CAPABILITY (the range of lives that people could attain)	Hard to measure; often functionings are taken as the proxy. But see e.g. medical measures of (dis)ability.
S-CAPABILITIES (people's skill and capacities); and other characteristics of people (Culyer 1990)	Measured by functional specialisms, see e.g. various psychological and health indicators.
CHARACTERISTICS OF GOODS, which are acquired through consumption	Not much researched by economics traditionally, except in some basic needs work. Investigated by functional specialisms, such as in nutrition, health, education, transport, fashion, and in psychology.
CONSUMPTION proper – viz., actual *use* of purchases / acquisitions	Not much researched by economics, except in some basic needs work. Left to psychology, anthropology, medicine, cultural studies, etc.
I Information on inputs; money-metric focus	
PURCHASES and other acquisitions	More researched by marketing, psychology, anthropology, sociology; less intensively by economics.
Utility as CHOICE, which is assumed to reflect preference, and (as the base case) is weighted according to purchasing power.	These assumptions have been normal in economics; including 'revealed preference' (that choices reliably indicate preferences) as an *axiom*.
INCOME AND RESOURCES/POWER TO ACQUIRE GOODS/ COMMODITIES	Researched by economics; usually not also the power to acquire many other basic goods: political freedom, dignity, rewarding personal relations, satisfying meanings.

Note: * e.g. WHO's categories of social, emotional and physical well-being perspectives on both the constituents and the determinants, and find that the connection between well-being and the means studied in economics is weak and not infrequently perverse. As we will see, Dasgupta later reaches out somewhat across this second disciplinary divide, a greater one than that between economists and many Anglo-American philosophers. Oswald (1997) adds that a gap has existed too between psychologists working on SWB and sociologists *et al.* working on non-self-report measures of QOL.

Table 2.2 uses the sequence of levels presented in Table 2.1 for exposition and comparison of the conceptions of well-being in a selection of recent work, with emphasis on lower income countries. One point that arises concerns the insufficiency of the traditional economics chain, mentioned above; a second concerns the variety of alternative conceptions, which reflects partly different purposes and contexts.

A major finding is the repeated confirmation that the realm of means on which economics has focused is often only weakly connected to the world of ends, of satisfaction, valued functioning, and fulfilment. For both SWB and OWB the main determinants seem often not to be the monetary ones on which economists have concentrated. Robert Lane calls the incoherence of the economics narrative of welfare 'the economistic fallacy' (Lane 1991). This implies a need for alternative or additional base-narratives, with different variables to be highlighted in the bottom rows of Table 2.2.

While well-being is a plural category, some conceptualizations are perhaps better seen as part of a wider category of 'advantage'. Sen has stressed that people often pursue goals that do not further their own well-being, in the narrow sense of their own comfort and convenience but, instead, goals concerning other people or general ideals. (This is different from saying that they do things against their own benefit due to errors.) Some other authors say that the narrow sense is too narrow and that well-being covers such wider goals too. In any case, freedom to achieve well-being is different from achieved well-being. Freedom is one conception of personal advantage, but assessing freedom could be different from assessing well-being. Whether or not people prefer to be free to make their own mistakes, arguably clarity is aided if we do not define well-being as freedom.

Assessments of well-being can be for a variety of purposes. Some are descriptive, such as the measures of SWB; some are evaluative judgements of people's state-of-being, according to particular normative conceptions of WB. (SWB measures themselves reflect of course, we expect, the normative conceptions of the subject.) Some are better seen as prescriptive, concerning how people should be treated; for example, provided with opportunities even if it is expected that some people will make severe mistakes and blight their own well-being in the more usual sense. I have suggested that such concepts could in fact be seen instead as concepts of what is advantage, not well-being. Money-metric measures, then, concern opportunities (but only a narrow range of these: opportunities to purchase), not well-being in the achievement sense. So does Sen's criterion of range of valued options.

Table 2.2 Comparative overview of the focus and assumptions of selected writers on human development and well-being

	Coudouel *et al.*	**Baulch**	**Kabeer**	**Dasgupta**	**Sen**	**Nussbaum**	**Doyal and Gough**	**Diener**	**Ryan and Deci**
General nature of the author's perspective on well-being	*World Bank's Poverty Measurement manual (originally mis-titled Well-Being Measurement)*	*Six aspects of absence of poverty, including: (5) dignity and (6) autonomy*	*Contrasts the means focus in economics with the ends focus in other social science on well-being*	*In practice a combination of individual desire-fulfilment, health, education, political and civil liberties*	*Attention to all levels, but stresses functionings and especially capability and capability poverty*	*A substantive conception of key elements of a decent human life*	*A rigorous theory of need, which derives the needs implied by alternative specifications of required well-being/functioning*	*Prominent researcher on 'subjective well-being' (SWB), a multi-dimensional field in psychology*	*A more theorized approach to SWB: priority of fulfilment of humans' posited true/best nature*

SATISFACTIONS	(Perfunctory reference)	(5) dignity	'The ends perspective': considers powers, functionings, satisfactions	Individuals' desire-fulfilment (measured by WTP: Willingness to pay)	1. Own-well-being achievement (happiness and/or (self-oriented) preference fulfilment and/or other objective outcomes) 2. Agency achievement		SWB: 1. Positive affect (happiness) 2. Negative affect (unhappiness) 3. Life satisfaction	1. Happiness: hedonic well-being; 2. Fulfilment: eudaimonic well-being

Table 2.2 (Continued)

	Coudouel *et al.*	**Baulch**	**Kabeer**	**Dasgupta**	**Sen**	**Nussbaum**	**Doyal and Gough**	**Diener**	**Ryan and Deci**
FUNCTIONINGS (term ambiguously covers both activities and outcomes, even – for Sen – satisfactions)	(No reference)			Health		Implied priority function-ings	Criterion of required function-ings, e.g. avoidance of serious harm	Systematic investigation of functionings that conduce to satisfaction. Most key determinants are outside economic life (but can be affected by it): warm personal relations; clear goals, and progress towards them	Valued function-ings, including vitality, physical and mental health

CAPABILITIES/ POWERS: as ability to attain specific functionings	(No reference)	(6) autonomy		Civil and political liberties (assumed usable)	'Capability', in terms of: 1. own-well-being or 2. own goals.	Specified priority functional capabilities, especially practical reason and affiliation	Implied required capabilities: health, autonomy of agency	Key cases of valued functioning: 1. autonomy 2. competence 3. relatedness
CAPABILITIES/ SKILLS: persons' characteristics				Education		Highlighted		
Generalized satisfier CHAR-ACTERISTICS OF GOODS			Intermediate, shared focus: consump-tion fits in both means – and ends – perspectives	Not studied directly			Implied required universal satisfier character-istics: food and water; housing; health care, work, etc.	

Table 2.2 (Continued)

	Coudouel *et al.*	**Baulch**	**Kabeer**	**Dasgupta**	**Sen**	**Nussbaum**	**Doyal and Gough**	**Diener**	**Ryan and Deci**
CONSUMPTION	Poverty is seen as lack of income and consumption; with reference also to their inter-personal and inter-temporal distribution (vulnerability)	1. Private consumption 2. Use of common property resources 3. Societally provided consumption		Not studied directly			Implied required satisfier goods/commodities, in a specific society	*Consumption → satisfactions link:* *– significant in low income countries* *– insignificant in high income countries*	

PURCHASES/ ACQUISITIONS			'The means perspective': considers assets, income, purchases (but not work; Kabeer herself studies the worlds of work in depth)	Private consump-tion, measured by expenditure				
INCOME				Downgraded	Income-poverty, or its reverse, opulence		(Implied minimum required income)	
(EFFORT/ WORK) Located here in an economic means–ends chain as an input rather than also as a central functioning in living	Ignored. Treated in the economics tradition as a cost not a benefit	Conceivably implied under dignity and autonomy?		No attention to well-being in work. Shows how malnutri-tion affects work effect-iveness.	(Little attention?)	Fuller attention than Sen (via her categories of practical reason and affiliation)	Work is specified under the general require-ments for health and autonomy of agency	Work is highlighted by SWB researchers – it is found to be a major determinant of satisfactions; and so are several other aspects, in contrast frequently to the aspects focused on (wealth, income, acquisitions, consumption) by economics

Table 2.2 (Continued)

	Coudouel *et al.*	**Baulch**	**Kabeer**	**Dasgupta**	**Sen**	**Nussbaum**	**Doyal and Gough**	**Diener**	**Ryan and Deci**
ASSETS		4. Assets; which reduce vulnerability		Attention to natural resources					
(IMPLIED REQUIRED SOCIETAL CONDITIONS)				Attention to preconditions of civil and political liberties and to 'social capital'			Conditions concerning: production; reproduction; cultural transmission; political authority		

The next section will use this framework to understand the conceptualizations of well-being by a number of leading recent contributors on human development, including some of those presented in Table 2.2: Partha Dasgupta, Amartya Sen, Martha Nussbaum, and Len Doyal and Ian Gough.

Some current human development theorists

Dasgupta on technically superior substitutes for GNP

Partha Dasgupta proposes two measures as major advances over both GNP and the HDI. His measure for current well-being includes attention to liberties as well as to income, health and education. To measure the sustainable level of well-being, he proposes a comprehensive measure of wealth. He calculates (2001: ch. 9) that in many low income countries the rise in present well-being has been achieved by such degradation of natural assets that societal wealth, his measure of societal well-being over time, has fallen.

Dasgupta argues as a contractarian that the state's responsibility is not the management of happiness and the guarantee of achievement but, instead, the provision of opportunity, of preconditions for all to pursue their own purposes (1993: 53–5). As with other contract theories, this ignores the major cases of children and the mentally infirm. Given that WB is one of nearly everyone's purposes, we also still need to understand and measure it and what promotes or facilitates it, and his book *An Inquiry into Well-Being and Destitution* adopts this agenda. It originally views WB as 'flourishing' (ibid.: 34; and also uses the concept of 'a well-lived life', ibid.: 44), but deems the idea elusive, not well-captured by any of 'happiness', 'pleasure', 'satisfaction', or 'utility'. He proceeds though to a definition: 'A person's well-being is an aggregate of its constituents: utility (because it is the most reliable approximate of her rational desires), and an index of the worth to her of the freedoms she enjoys' (ibid.: 70). He omits any independent value to functionings. In practice, to Dasgupta well-being is largely a subjective category (being subject specified or concerning feelings). He proceeds, however, not to measure it directly (2001: 34ff.) as psychologists do, but instead in traditional economics fashion via long chains of assumptions.

His recent study, *Human Well-Being and the Natural Environment* (2001), now includes no preliminary Aristotelian flourish; the categories stay closer to his practice. For example, he explicitly makes no distinction between WB and QOL (Dasgupta 2001: xviii), unlike Sen. He adopts a flexible subjective concept of 'welfare', as the valuation by a person of her own situation. This potentially includes pleasure obtained from abuse of others. Thus, 'welfare' should be traded-off sometimes against respect for others' rights. Perhaps unfortunately, he uses 'welfare' and 'utility' interchangeably, but (ibid.: 15) 'well-being' remains a wider notion that includes other concerns ('non-welfare characteristics'), notably for human rights but also health, 'associational life, various kinds of freedoms to be and to do' (ibid.: 22). Thus, he recognizes that a drug-user's valuation of his own situation could diverge from his well-being (ibid.: 36), given 'non-welfare' concerns such as health, and also because the drug-user's valuation is flawed. Dasgupta has held to the peculiar notion of 'welfare' that is traditional in economics although, etymologically, welfare could arguably be a wider notion than well-being: 'fare' means to travel, travel through life, rather than only to be at a moment.

He adopts in both books the assumptions of sum-ranking across persons and of comparability of all objectives. The assumptions may reflect a view that choices can only be made after aggregation of costs and benefits (e.g. ibid.: 23), rather than sometimes by other procedures (e.g. lexicographic, or by voting). His version of current WB is, thus, a national measure that adds political and civil liberties to HDI-type concerns, as the *Human Development Report* 1991 tried; but, unlike the *HDR*s, he measures private consumption not GNP per capita and he synthesizes the concerns differently.

Dasgupta notes briefly but dismissively sociologists' work on measures of objective well-being (ibid.: 36), but treats more favourably and uses at least some of psychologists' work on measures of subjective well-being, consistent with his definition of individual 'welfare' in terms of self-valuation of situation. He uses, first, the finding that whereas at very low levels of material living subjective well-being is undoubtedly increased by material gains, in rich countries it is not. Commendably, he holds back from any further income based claims on levels of well-being in rich countries (ibid.: 38). Second, in both rich and poor countries, other things contribute to happiness. From the literature he emphasizes health, employment and civic participation. He feels this supports his inclusion of indices of consumption, health (viz., life expectancy), and civic and political liberties in his well-being measures, and concludes that in poor countries they are adequate proxies for happiness (ibid.: 38). The conclusion ignores many other determinants of happiness, such as employment (which he treats only as a badge of social status), and the distribution of consumption, and assumes that liberties are converted into participation. Yet, he himself later notes, for example, that longevity is an insufficient measure of health status: 'it isn't difficult to remain alive even when malnourished and weak' (ibid.: 79); and complains of the neglect of measures of nutrition in assessing the quality of growth (n. 42).

Dasgupta's index of current well-being significantly diverges in many important cases from GNP per capita, notably in the most unequal cases (ibid.: 62). So, too, does the HDI, but he attacks this; first, for being ad hoc and, second, for not showing the decline in long-term prospects due to 'mining' of natural capital, as shown by his own index of well-being over time. The HDI does not of course claim to be a measure of wealth or of well-being over time, and we need measures of present well-being precisely in order to then see the trade-offs over time. The role of the HDI should instead be seen as tactical and political – to be accessible for an audience of politicians, administrators and the wider public, in order to indicate the inadequacy of income per capita – and it has succeeded in that. To fulfil the role, it had to be easily understandable and universally calculable, hence its simple and 'ad hoc' nature. The economists and others who constructed the HDI were aware of its limitations. The wider UNDP human development approach explicitly highlights other relevant dimensions of present well-being, including distribution, employment, civic and political liberties, and their use, including security, and more. Concluding that there is no adequate single synthesis, the *Human Development Reports* amongst others mainly use a disaggregated approach.

Having delegitimated GDP as a well-being measure, various paths lie open. One is to construct better composite indicators, the path trodden by Dasgupta. What their additional value-added is, for whom and what, needs to be considered. Would they be used to allocate, say, international aid? One doubts it. Another path is to accept that no composite indicator is very good, and to consider how to handle plurality and incommensurabilities intelligently, with an eye to the variety of contexts and purposes. There is not as much depth in Dasgupta's discussion of the notion of WB as in his disturbing examination of our exploitation of and impacts on the natural environment, and in his case for appropriate measures of wealth as measures of sustainable WB. Those merits of his discussion no doubt survive his limited conceptualization of WB. Let us proceed to others who investigate the concept of WB further.

Sen: a conceptual backdrop to analyze personal advantage and quality of life

The ethical visions of various great economists such as Mill, Marshall and Pigou had limited long-term impact in economics since they often remained as non-integrated, non-formalized supplements to their economic theories (Ackerman 1997). In contrast, Amartya Sen has got major ethical messages relatively far into the discipline. He has built an alternative economic approach that is influential in theory, applied research, and policy.

Analytically, Sen has critiqued the conflation in modern welfare economics of numerous categories (self-interest = preference = choice = satisfaction = WB) which has been exacerbated by giving several of them the name 'utility'. He has pluralized our conceptual armoury for discussion of 'human advantage', as we noted earlier and will elaborate. He recognizes, for example, how satisfaction can come both from one's own situation and from others' situations. At the same time, he stresses that interpretations of ambiguous ideas 'must try to capture that ambiguity rather than hide or eliminate it' (1993: 34).

Normatively, he has argued convincingly that many types of information are relevant to the assessment of WB and QOL, and has warned against focus on hedonic well-being alone. As we saw earlier, he argues for a focus on some specific functionings and, especially, capabilities, more than on satisfaction; and, in effect, he adopts an analogue to the 'informed desire' or, better, 'reasoned desire' conception in this different space for evaluation; namely, a priority to those capabilities (and functionings) that we 'have reason to value'. While he shares the eudaimonic conception's concern for valued functionings, he stresses in a policy context the capability to attain these functionings above the actual attainment; and he eschews a general statement of what are priority functionings, leaving the prioritization to legitimate decision procedures in each situation.

My purpose here is to elucidate rather than assess Sen's conceptualization of well-being. (For more on assessment, see e.g. Giri 2000, Gasper 2002, Gasper and van Staveren 2003.) Let us look at his usage of the term 'well-being', and at whether capability is better seen as an interpretation of a person's 'advantage'.

Is Sen's capability approach really a theory of WB?

Sen's capability approach does not centre on the content of living – specific functionings – nor make functionings the primary evaluative criterion. It gives priority in evaluation to capability (e.g., 'quality of life to be assessed in terms of the capability to achieve valuable functionings', 1993: 31), though it retains a secondary evaluative role for functionings (e.g., ibid.: 32 'sees the evaluative space in terms of functionings and capabilities to function'). Capability, then, seems best read as a freedom centred concern relevant in policy prescription, an appropriate concept of advantage rather than of achieved well-being or quality of life. Indeed, Sen writes of 'The capability approach to a person's advantage' (though also, a few lines earlier, of 'a particular approach to well-being and advantage', ibid.: 30).[19]

Is Sen's usage of the term 'well-being' still too utilitarian?

Sen formalizes various choices in assessing a person's advantage. Two are: reference to opportunities or to achievements; and assessment in terms of a person's own costs and benefits, or in terms of the person's values, which could ignore aspects of their own welfare and include concerns about other matters. Assessment in terms of a person's own costs and benefits itself includes two cases: first, where we refer to satisfactions, which can be affected by other person's situations (via sympathy or Schadenfreude); and second, where we refer only to those aspects of a person's well-being determined by 'the nature of his own life, rather than from "other-regarding" objectives or impersonal concerns' (ibid.: 37). Sen describes the second as the person's 'standard of living' (a label that only makes sense coming out of the economics tradition). He thus generates five categories for describing and assessing a person's situation, shown in Figure 2.2. And he then adds a sixth, quality of life.

	In terms of an agent's personal/own well-being	*In terms of the agent's objectives*
Actual achievement	(Own) well-being achievement (WBA) 'Standard of living' (SOL) = WBA minus 'sympathy'	Agency achievement (AA)
Potential for attainment	(Own) Well-being freedom (WBF)	Agency freedom (AF)

Figure 2.2 Sen's categories for ranking a person's situation

In understanding an ambiguous idea, Sen tries to reveal the ambiguity. Are all the five categories faces of well-being; or only the 'well-being' column; or only the shaded cell whereas other cells represent other aspects of a person's 'advantage'; or even WBA only, since that is about being, not just potential, and about the individual's being, not other people's, but inclusive of what she feels about others? He seems to conclude that all are relevant aspects, with their relevance depending upon the context; but his choice of terms seems to prioritize the well-being column. His sixth term, 'quality of life', could fit the agency column or represent an evaluative summing-up of AA and WBA, or of the whole table.

Sen reserved the label 'well-being' for the categories in the first column. Within that column, we could interpret well-being in terms of pleasure, or of reasoned desire, or of externally specified valued functionings (e.g. life-span, etc., as in QOL research); but, in all cases, for self-referential concerns only (including, except in SOL, the pleasures from the benefit of others whom one cares for, and from the sufferings of one's enemies). Sen himself does not present an externally specified list but, in practice, uses an implicit partial list in his examples and his policy-oriented work. He continually refers to certain good functionings (such as longevity, health, and self-respect) in order to criticize assessments of well-being instead in the spaces of income, commodities, or felt utility. But he also gives space for well-being in terms of pleasure/satisfaction (hence the issue about whether or not to include pleasures caused by others' situations). Arguably his linguistic privileging of the first column is consistent with still seeing well-being (in his terms) as preference fulfilment, but that conception fits more readily his agency column, since many preferences are about other people and other types of concern, and the 'utility' imputed from choices would reflect this.

Some people advocate 'agency achievement' as the best single candidate for the title 'well-being': the fulfilment of one's goals, whatever their subject. This matches a less self-enclosed conception of personhood, and a less utilitarian conception of satisfaction. For Sen, WB is self-referential; agency is anything-referential. This is one standard usage, matching the idea of WB as 'prudential value': 'the notion of how well a person's life is going for that person'(Crisp 2001: section 1). It encounters criticism from various authors (e.g. Gore 1997, Giri 2000, Nussbaum 2000). First, it rests on assumptions about sharp bounds of the self. Second, Sen uses the category of 'commitment' to cover the pursuit of objectives that bring the agent no utility, in contrast to the pleasures of 'sympathy'. 'Commitment' thus falls outside 'well-being', perhaps reflecting a utilitarian assumption that there is only one currency of feeling ('utility'). Third, the debatable contrast between being and agency may lead to a further separation in Sen's vocabulary, between being and living (WB versus QOL).

Sen's main focus has however been on the last row in Figure 2.2: on the lives that people could attain, with reference to those functionings that people 'have reason to value'. He concentrates on well-reasoned desires (for him, 'reason' implies reasoning, not mere whim or habit) and on the capabilities space, not directly the functionings space (except for proxy purposes, or with secondary status), let alone the commodities space. He emphasises the contrast between rows in Figure 2.2, and chose to describe his approach as 'the capability approach'.

To some people the contrast between columns seems more important. It starts to add a theory of personhood. Over time, Sen has come to stress the language of 'freedom' above that of capability, perhaps partly because it links to this contrast between columns too. People freely commit themselves to things other than their own narrowly-defined well-being. What he calls the process aspect of freedom (e.g. 1999: 291) refers to people's sharing in choices, on the basis of their various values and objectives. The opportunity aspect of freedom concerns the extent of people's capability set.

It may be wise to adopt different labels, and to break from the welfare economics and utilitarian tradition in vocabulary as well as in concepts. Table 2.3 thus points to the need for an alternative vocabulary in which the

Table 2.3 Towards a replacement vocabulary

	PERSON'S 'OBJECTIVE' STATE (excludes 'sympathy')	***PERSONAL GRATIFICATION (includes 'sympathy')***	***GOAL FULFILMENT (includes commitment)***
ACHIEVEMENT	Objective well-being	Gratification achievement/subjective well-being	Goal achievement
POTENTIAL/ FREEDOM	OWB potential	SWB potential	Potential for goal achievement

term well-being no longer has singular reference but functions, at most, as the ambiguous umbrella for a complex field.

The roles of lists: Nussbaum, Doyal and Gough, Alkire

Nussbaum: a richer exploration of human well-being, for backing human rights

Martha Nussbaum provides an objective list conception of well-being plus, in a policy context, a liberal focus on the capabilities to achieve the functionings highlighted in the list. In the Aristotelian tradition, pride of place is given to practical reason and to affiliation with others. Nussbaum's list in various versions has attracted great attention. Rather than repeat the details of the list or the discussion around it (see e.g. Nussbaum 2000, Alkire 2002, Gasper 2003), let us situate her work.[20]

Although her list contrives to keep, in general, a Mosaic length of ten (with sub-parts), it is not ad hoc. It is derived, first, through Aristotelian procedures. Her criteria for the 'well' in well-being arise as criteria for what is human, and, more extensively, for what are capabilities essential to live at a minimum decent level: 'with dignity'. These hypotheses are then cross-checked with a variety of sources and interlocutors, including those from diverse cultures and literatures on well-being. The list yet lacks the degree of theorized order found in, for example, Doyal and Gough's model with its rigorous distinctions between levels, which influenced Table 2.2. Why does it still deservedly draw attention?

First, it consciously builds a basis for core rights, as parts of a legal constitution, to give a set of entrenched priorities without which we would leave too much open to domination by the powerful. It is best seen as conveying a method of thinking for developing such a priority set. A key audience consists of legislators, lawyers and judges, and those who seek to influence them. Second, it buttresses Sen's move to increase the range of types of information used in evaluation, for it provides a substantive language to express people's multi-faceted concerns (Nussbaum 2000: 138–9). Third, using such language helps to open up observers' perceptions of the content of others' lives and their own, and contributes to building sympathy and commitment (Gasper 2003).

Doyal and Gough's synthesis for discussing policy priorities

Existentialist work on well-being attacks perspectives such as the Aristotelian that derive an extensive picture of well-being from a relatively full picture of human nature. It uses a different and less extensive picture, asserting that self-determination is 'the defining characteristic of what it is to be human' (Hodge 1990: 43). The meaning of well-being is for people themselves to determine. Thus, existentialists dispute objective list approaches, as in QOL research. For them, after self-determination all other aspects are not given as good or bad by human nature but depend on mental attitude.

However, we should not equate choice with self-determination; addiction must be distinguished from autonomy. And the criteria of autonomy and self-determination have limited application also to the very young, the very old and the mentally infirm.

The work of Doyal and Gough is important; first, for seeking to draw out an objective list of implications of a commitment to autonomy and, second, for integrating many of the elements found in Sen, Nussbaum, QOL research (notably on physical and mental health), the existentialists and others. By a layered conception of well-being's aspects and determinants, similar to that above, and by systematically studying the links between levels, Doyal and Gough bridge the 'cultural divide' described by Dasgupta and Kabeer, and integrate the discussion of means and ends, establishing agendas for measurement and institutionalization at the various levels (Gasper 1996).

Doyal and Gough ask what are the prerequisites for avoiding serious harm and for functioning as an effective member of one's society. These are their criteria for basic needs. By focusing on the requirements of functioning as a society member, they are close to a social exclusion perspective. They argue that autonomy of agency, plus physical and mental health, are the minimum prerequisites. More striking than the specific inclusions in this list of posited basic needs – Nussbaum, existentialists and desire-fulfilment theories also prioritize goal formation and pursuit, though they make them directly central to human being – is the exclusion of other things from this level of priority, as a result of constructing their needs list by using explicit criteria, not ad hoc. The same principles of systematic derivation are applied down the hierarchy of levels that we saw earlier, rather than declaring needs/priorities by intuition. Given the layered structure of the model, moving from general ideals down through levels of increasingly specific means, it generates not a single list but lists at each level.

This is an ethical theory not a psychological theory, although it uses psychological evidence. It is a theory about needs as posited high priorities for policy; not a theory about motives, nor about every normative concern. Still, psychological evidence on what people care about is certainly relevant, and Camfield and Skevington (2003) report that the focus on autonomy matches the findings of decades of psychological research.

Bowlby's Attachment Theory holds that relatedness is a key condition for building autonomy: a person will operate more effectively when he feels he has a 'secure base' of other persons on whom he can rely for support if and when needed (Downes 1990). This finding emerged also in eudaimonic WB research. Thus, Ryan and Deci (2001) highlight relatedness, besides autonomy and competence, as a key determinant of felt well-being; and Nussbaum highlights affiliation as the second key capability. Doyal and Gough's theory could readily absorb an additional posited basic need such as affiliation/relatedness/conviviality, and draw out its implications. The theory offers space for partly different specifications of derived need according to what are the specified desirable functionings.

Alkire's synthesis for project management

Focused at a different operational level – not the national (and even global) constitution-making of Nussbaum or the policy-design level of Doyal and Gough, but rather at a local or project planning level – Alkire argues that a list of core aspects of well-being serves as a tool to give structure to, rather than replace, processes of discussion in particular situations (2002: 38). A list is an aid, to avoid forgetting matters that are often found important. For fuller ideas on how to structure such processes, Alkire uses the work of an Australian philosopher, John Finnis. Finnis seeks to identify basic reasons for action: reasons for which no other reason has to be given in order to be intelligible. He and collaborators have generated their own such list, in various versions. Interestingly, providing happiness is absent, perhaps considered as too undifferentiated, our reasons are not reducible to one. To judge such intelligible motives and their fulfilment to be good or bad is declared to involve a further step. However, also absent from the list are, for example, competitive spirit, aggression, and malice; so the list may be already more moralized than it claims.[21]

The list of motives is used as the set of dimensions to be covered in local discussions about evaluating past or prospective changes, as the hypothesized dimensions of human well-being. Alkire shows how, without necessarily measuring well-being directly, a deeply considered and enriched conception of well-being (again, with an emphasis on capability) can guide local planning and resource allocation. What she finds she needs in order to operationalize Sen are the methods of Nussbaum and Finnis (Alkire 2002: 224–6): a 'thick' (multi-dimensional), 'vague' (stated generally and requiring local interpretation) conception of the good, applied through a process of practical reasoning. This leads us to a successor of the basic human needs approach (ibid.: 168 and 173) and to multi-criteria analyses, including some in aggregating mode and some non-aggregating, with each of these now given a more complex philosophical basis.

Conclusion: what should we try to measure?

The conceptions, explanation and measurement of use values have needed to avoid domination by categories derived from the examination of exchange values. Unfortunately, much work on *well*-being has been based on insufficient evidence and theory about *be*-ing. The role of theory is to make sense of evidence; concepts should reflect plentiful experience rather than screen it out. Hence, this chapter on concepts started with some of the evidence and has tried throughout to relate conceptualization to evidence.

The following ideas were drawn from the evidence. There are many major aspects of 'objective' well-being (such as health, family life, employment, recreation, quality of death), and these are also major determinants of subjective well-being. These aspects are far from invariably strongly positively correlated with access to commodities via income, so that income cannot act as proxy for the others. Indeed, the aspects can sometimes be negatively correlated with income and each other, so that to use income, or any other variable, as proxy for all the others can be seriously misleading. One possible explanation for the Easterlin paradox, besides concerns with status and relative position, and the emergence of new aspirations, is this: even if higher income would, other things being equal, raise SWB, the generation of the income might often have substantial negative side effects on major determinants of SWB such as family life; the 'other things' do not remain equal, under many arrangements. We need disaggregated pictures that highlight various aspects of life. In looking at information on persons, we must study good outlier cases too, as the 'positive psychology' movement does, and not rest content with the measures of central tendency and crude macro correlations.

Of course, we sometimes have good reason to aggregate; not because this reveals a shared essence such as 'utility', but because we need to make choices, and this is one way. The HDI, too, had a good reason to aggregate, for its rationale was to provide a contrast to the ruling aggregate – GNP – to suggest how that misleads us on welfare, not to claim that it was itself a great indicator of overall welfare. Aggregation is unlikely to ever give a great overall indicator here; any appropriate weights might be far from fixed, for example.

The other theme that emerged was that numerous, different concepts and measures are required to match the various contexts and purposes. For example, in distributing international aid between countries, one would probably not adjust (or supplement) national income figures for the quality of family life; whereas for assessing QOL and explaining social dynamics one might do so. Dasgupta (2001: 31–2) points out that different organizational contexts generate differences in purpose: responsibilities need to be divided, and the different institutions then need to pursue different objectives and, hence, to measure different things.

Amongst the authors we discussed, Dasgupta appeared focused on providing a more robust alternative to GNP as an aggregate measure of WB, not just to delegitimate it as the HDI had done. Such an aggregate measure that makes normative claims remains in demand for some purposes. Sen's purposes have been different: to delegitimate GNP as a WB measure, as a prelude to opening us up to the use of diverse types of information that should feed into various types of decisionmaking. Alkire's work on project planning and evaluation exemplifies this. Max-Neef, too, is oriented to project action and the workshop format, not to technocratic measurement.

Nussbaum is less oriented to measurement of WB, more to the design and use of legal constitutions. Operationalization of concepts includes institutionalization, not only measurement. Not everything important needs to be measured; thus, informed desire theory carries many policy implications, even if we could not come up with an informed desire measure of WB. We must address well-being not only by measurement but also, and sometimes instead, by, for example, rich qualitative description. The traditional methods of economics will be insufficient to capture and communicate all of importance that is involved. We need, in addition, cases of particular, real people in their complexity, in their social and historical contexts (Gasper 2000). Testimony, 'voices of the poor', life histories, and the languages of feelings are indispensable complements to social science abstraction.

Notes

This is a revised version of a paper presented at the workshop on Measuring Well-being, at UNU-WIDER, Helsinki, in May 2003, and at seminars in Trivandrum, Pavia, Barcelona and Bath. My thanks to workshop participants and to Achin Chakraborty, David Clark, Mark McGillivray, Irene van Staveren and three anonymous referees for their comments, and especially to Mozaffar Qizilbash for detailed helpful advice. The usual disclaimer applies.

1 'Current research on well-being has been derived from two general perspectives: the *hedonic approach*, which focuses on happiness and defines well-being in terms of pleasure attainment and pain avoidance, and the *eudaimonic approach*, which focuses on meaning and self-realization and defines well-being in terms of the degree to which a person is fully functioning' (Ryan and Deci 2001: 141; emphases added).
2 We will see 'quality of life' referred to as concerning (1) self-report indicators, (2) non-self-report indicators, or (3) both; and as identical to well-being (van Praag and Frijters, Dasgupta) or explicitly distinguished from it (Sen). Standardization of terms appears to be lacking.
3 In the well-being literature, we encounter various usages of 'welfare' besides (1) the same as well-being, including narrower meanings such as (2) the valuation by a person of their own situation (Dasgupta 2001), and (3) 'the evaluation assigned by the individual to income or, more generally, to the contribution to his well-being from those goods and services that he can buy with money' (van Praag and Frijters 1999: 427).
4 Easterlin (2001: 206) equates six concepts in one sentence: 'I use the terms happiness, subjective well-being, satisfaction, utility, well-being, and welfare interchangeably'.
5 In recent studies, many former Communist countries are major outliers, with exceptionally low SWB, while many Latin American countries are in the top SWB echelon.
6 Debate on these issues can fail to distinguish questions of statistical significance and socio-economic significance (cf. McCloskey and Ziliak 1996). Income could be closely statistically correlated with well-being measures when we compare different large populations (e.g. different periods in one country), yet the slope of the relationship could be tiny or negligible.
7 I am indebted to Ajeet Mathur for this observation and for the term 'well-becoming'.

8 Models for health policy analysis based on economics focus on the Quality Adjusted Life Years (QALY) returns from health expenditures; they look only to the future of the care-receiver, not also to the carers and survivors, or the meanings and obligations shared between the actors. The work of hospices might fail a QALYs evaluation. Similarly, '"distributive models" of health care justice cannot supply a rationale for expanded access to hospice care. These models fail because they are based on ...[a] picture of the moral agent, who resembles few of us as we lie dying' (Nelson 2003: S18). Rather than 'fail', one can say that their picture of living is too narrow – it ignores dying, and an inevitable stage for many old people of reduced autonomy.

9 Conflation was eased by a linguistic trick: fulfilment of preferences was often described as 'satisfaction of desires', which could too easily be identified with 'satisfaction'.

10 Further, more complex pictures of WB such as Nussbaum's can probably incorporate rights and liberties, because they go beyond the crude picture of personhood that underpins a theory of the good that has no reference to those aspects.

11 Richard Brandt was one notable exception; he enriched his theory of the good by considerable attention to evidence from psychology (Brandt 1979).

12 Veenhoven (Chapter 9 in this volume) gives a more refined, 3 × 3, classification, which distinguishes also an intermediate option in each of the dimensions.

13 David Clark queries this from his work in South Africa (e.g. Clark 2003). Elster (1983) examines adaptive preferences in detail.

14 The plurality of types of psychic 'currency' must not be confused with the plurality of ways of 'earning' even if there were only a single 'currency'.

15 Economists' typical assumption of full comparability, and hence of only one type of 'utility', derives from other conventional assumptions: of agents' unbounded powers of reason and/or of agents' responsibility for their own processes of comparison and decision, whatsoever those are.

16 More precisely, particular assumptions are required to support 'money-tarianism'; for example, a value principle that members of a political community are obliged to accept, whatever the personal losses, for the collective benefit, without guarantee that their turn to benefit will come; or an optimistic predictive hypothesis that everyone's turn to benefit will come. Admittedly, even the HDI or PQLI, as aggregative measures, can rise when conditions of the worst-off decline yet conditions of the best-off sufficiently further improve. However, this outweighing is enormously less likely when the currency of comparison is life expectancy, morbidity, or so on, than when it is monetary.

17 Baulch (1996: 38) tries to distinguish poverty, deprivation, and ill-being. For him, poverty means lack of the requisites for well-being – a person may have the requisites, and so not be poor, but misuse them and so have low well-being. He takes deprivation to mean feelings of dissatisfaction.

18 In the first of these categories, many things that typically reflect lack or loss of well-being are treated as benefits, such as most commuter travel and 'defensive expenditures' which merely counteract costs caused by economic growth, such as environmental pollution or increased stress and conflict. These expenditures grow far faster than overall GDP in rich countries (Ekins and Max-Neef 1992: 254). Net economic performance can be conventionally recorded as improving while net societal performance declines (see e.g. Daly and Cobb 1994).

19 Sen's Nobel lecture (2002: 82–5) speaks alternately of (inter-personal comparisons of) personal well-being, personal welfare, and individual advantage, though

without equating them; p. 94 differentiates between well-being and overall advantage. Alkire (2002) also moves to and fro between these names.

20 One should refer to her work published from 1999 onwards, which significantly revises and refines her theory, and no longer to the widely read predecessor papers.

21 In contrast, Jeremy Bentham's *Table of the Springs of Action* included such factors (Collard 2003).

References

Ackerman, F. (1997) 'Overview Essay on Utility and Welfare: Modern Economic Alternatives', in F. Ackerman, D. Kiron, N. R. Goodwin, J. M. Harris and K. Gallagher (eds), *Human Well-Being and Economic Goals* (Washington, DC: Island Press) 81–92.

Ackerman, F., D. Kiron, N. R. Goodwin, J. M. Harris and K. Gallagher (eds) (1997) *Human Well-Being and Economic Goals* (Washington, DC: Island Press).

Alkire, S. (2002) *Valuing Freedoms – Sen's Capability Approach and Poverty Reduction* (Oxford: Oxford University Press).

Baldwin, S., C. Godfrey and C. Propper (eds) (1990) *Quality of Life – Perspectives and Policies* (London: Routledge).

Baulch, B. (1996) 'Neglected Trade-Offs in Poverty Measurement', *IDS Bulletin*, 27(1): 36–42.

Bonner, J. (1995) 'Jeremy Bentham', Summary in F. Ackerman, D. Kiron, N. R. Goodwin, J. M. Harris and K. Gallagher (eds) (1997), *Human Well-Being and Economic Goals* (Washington, DC: Island Press) 61–4.

Bowlby, J. (1991) *Attachment and Loss: Attachment*, Penguin Psychology series (London: Penguin Books).

Brandt, R. (1979) *A Theory of the Good and the Right* (Oxford: Clarendon Press).

Camfield, L. and S. Skevington (2003) 'Quality of Life and Well-being', WeD Working Paper (Bath: WeD, University of Bath).

Clark, A. and A. Oswald (1994) 'Unhappiness and Employment', *Economic Journal*, 104(424): 648–59.

Clark, D. (2003) 'Concepts and Perceptions of Human Well-Being: Some Evidence from South Africa', *Oxford Development Studies*, 31(2): 173–96.

Collard, D. (2003) 'Research on Well-Being: Some Advice from Jeremy Bentham', Working Paper 02, ESRC Research Group on Wellbeing in Developing Countries, University of Bath.

Comte-Sponville, A. (2002) *A Short Treatise on the Great Virtues* (London: Heinemann).

Cooter, R. and P. Rappoport (1984) 'Were the Ordinalists Wrong about Welfare Economics?', *Journal of Economic Literature*, XXII: 507–30.

Coudouel, A., J. Hentschel and Q. Wodon (2001) 'Poverty Measurement and Analysis', (ch. 1 of PRSP Sourcebook) http://www.worldbank.org/poverty/strategies/chapters/data/data.htm#

Crisp, R. (2001) 'Well Being', *Stanford Encyclopedia of Philosophy* (Stanford, CA: Stanford University).

Culyer, A. J. (1990) 'Commodities, Characteristics of Commodities, Characteristics of People, Utilities, and the Quality of Life', in S. Baldwin, C. Godfrey and C. Propper (eds), *Quality of Life – Perspectives and Policies* (London: Routledge) 9–27.

Cummins, R., E. Gullone and A. Lau (2002) 'A Model of Subjective Well-being Homeostasis: The Role of Personality', in *The Universality of Subjective Wellbeing Indicators* (Netherlands: Kluwer) 7–46

Daly, H. and J. B. Cobb (1994) *For the Common Good*, 2nd edn (Boston, MA: Beacon).

Dasgupta, P. (1993) *An Inquiry into Well-Being and Destitution* (Oxford: Clarendon Press).

Dasgupta, P. (2001) *Human Well-Being and the Natural Environment* (Oxford: Oxford University Press).

Dean, H. (2003) 'Discursive Repertoires and the Negotiation of Well-being', Working Paper 04, ESRC Research Group on Wellbeing in Developing Countries, University of Bath.

Diener, E. and R. Biswas-Diener (2000) 'New Directions in Subjective Well-Being Research', Mimeo (ediener@s.psych.uiuc.edu).

Downes, C. (1990) 'Security and Autonomy', in S. Baldwin, C. Godfrey and C. Propper (eds), *Quality of Life – Perspectives and Policies* (London: Routledge) 149–64.

Doyal, L. and I. Gough (1991) *A Theory of Human Need* (London: Macmillan).

Easterlin, R. A. (2001) 'Income and Happiness: Towards a Unified Theory', *Economic Journal*, 111 (July): 465–84.

Easterlin, R. A. (2002a) 'Introduction', in R. A. Easterlin (ed.), *Happiness in Economics* (Cheltenham: Edward Elgar).

Easterlin, R. A. (ed.) (2002b) *Happiness in Economics* (Cheltenham: Edward Elgar).

Ekins, P. and M. Max-Neef (eds) (1992) *Real Life Economics* (London: Routledge).

Elster, J. (1983) *Sour Grapes* (Cambridge: Cambridge University Press).

Frank, R. H. (1997) 'The Frame of Reference as a Public Good', *Economic Journal*, 107 (November): 1832–47.

Fromm, E. (1978) *To Have Or To Be?* (London: Jonathan Cape).

Gasper, D. (1996) 'Needs and Basic Needs – A Clarification of Foundational Concepts for Development Ethics and Policy', in G. Köhler, C. Gore, U.-P. Reich and T. Ziesmer (eds), *Questioning Development* (Marburg: Metropolis) 71–101 (also Working Paper 210, ISS: The Hague).

Gasper, D. (2000) 'Anecdotes, Situations and Histories: Varieties and Uses of Cases in Thinking about Ethics and Development Practice', *Development and Change*, 31(5): 1055–83.

Gasper, D. (2002) 'Is Sen's Capability Approach an Adequate Basis for Considering Human Development?', *Review of Political Economy*, 14(4): 435–61.

Gasper, D. (2003) 'Nussbaum's Capabilities Approach in Perspective – Purposes, Methods and Sources for an Ethics of Human Development', Working Paper 379 (ISS: The Hague).

Gasper, D. and I. van Staveren (2003) 'Development as Freedom – and as What Else?' *Feminist Economics*, 9(2–3): 137–61.

Giri, A. (2000) 'Rethinking Human Well-Being: A Dialogue with Amartya Sen', *Journal of International Development*, 12(7): 1003–18.

Goodwin, N. (1997) 'Interdisciplinary Perspectives on Well-Being: Overview Essay', in F. Ackerman, D. Kiron, N. R. Goodwin, J. M. Harris and K. Gallagher (eds), *Human Well-Being and Economic Goals* (Washington, DC: Island Press) 1–14.

Gore, C. (1996) 'Social Exclusion and the Design of Anti-Poverty Strategy in Developing Countries', Mimeo (Geneva: International Institute of Labour Studies).

Gore, C. (1997) 'Irreducibly Social Goods and the Informational Basis of Amartya Sen's Capability Approach', *Journal of International Development*, 9(2): 235–50.

Gray, J. (1993) *Beyond the New Right* (London: Routledge).

Griffin, J. (1986) *Well-Being* (Oxford: Clarendon Press).

Griffin, J. (1996) *Value Judgement* (Oxford: Oxford University Press).

Harriss-White, B. (1999) 'On to a Loser: Disability in India', in B. Harriss-White and S. Subramanian (eds), *Illfare in India* (New Dehli: Sage) 135–59.

Harriss-White, B. and S. Subramanian (eds) (1999) *Illfare in India* (New Delhi: Sage).

Hodge, J. (1990) 'The Quality of Life – A Contrast Between Utilitarian and Existentialist Approaches', in S. Baldwin, C. Godfrey and C. Propper, (eds), *Quality of Life – Perspectives and Policies* (London: Routledge) 42–54.

Janakarajan, S. and P. Seabright (1999) 'Subjective and Objective Indicators of Welfare Change Over Time', in B. Harriss-White and S. Subramaniam (eds) *Illfare in India* (New Delhi: Sage) 329–49.

Jennings, B., T. Ryndes, C. D'Onofrio and M. A. Bailey (2003) *Access to Hospice Care* (Garrison, NY: Hastings Center).

Jodha, N. S. (1989) 'Social Science Research on Rural Change: Some Gaps', in P. Bardhan (ed.), *Conversations between Economists and Anthropologists* (Delhi: Oxford University Press).

Kabeer, N. (1996) 'Agency, Well-Being and Inequality: Reflections on the Gender Dimensions of Poverty', *IDS Bulletin*, 27(1): 11–22.

Kabeer, N. (2000) *The Power to Choose – Bangladeshi Women Textile Workers in London and Dhaka* (London: Verso).

Kagan, S. (1994) 'Me and My Life', Summary in F. Ackerman, D. Kiron, N. R. Goodwin, J. M. Harris and K. Gallagher (eds) (1997), *Human Well-Being and Economic Goals* (Washington, DC: Island Press) 194–6.

Kahneman, D. (1994) 'New Challenges to the Rationality Assumption', Summary in F. Ackerman, D. Kiron, N. R. Goodwin, J. M. Harris and K. Gallagher (eds) (1997), *Human Well-Being and Economic Goals* (Washington, DC: Island Press) 177–180.

Kiron, D. (1997) 'Economics and the Good: Individuals – An Overview Essay', in F. Ackerman, D. Kiron, N. R. Goodwin, J. M. Harris and K. Gallagher (eds). Human Well-Being and Economic Goals (Washington, DC: Island Press) 165–73.

Lane, R. E. (1991) *The Market Experience* (New York: Cambridge University Press).

Lane, R. E. (1998a) 'The Joyless Market Economy', in A. Ben-Ner and L. Putterman (eds), *Economics, Values and Organization* (Cambridge: Cambridge University Press) 461–88.

Lane, R. E. (1998b) 'The Road Not Taken: Friendship, Consumerism and Happiness', in D. A. Crocker and T. Linden (eds), *Ethics of Consumption – The Good Life, Justice and Global Stewardship* (Lanham, MD: Rowman & Littlefield) 218–48.

Max-Neef, M. (1992) 'Development and Human Needs', in P. Ekins and M. Max-Neef (eds) *Real Life Economics* (Cheltenham: Edward Elgar) 197–214.

McCloskey, D. and S. Ziliak (1996) 'The Standard Error of Regression', *Journal of Economic Literature*, 34: 97–114.

Myers, D. G. and E. Diener (1995) 'Who Is Happy?', Summary in F. Ackerman, D. Kiron, N. R. Goodwin, J. M. Harris and K. Gallaghes (eds) (1997), *Human Well-Being and Economic Goals* (Washington, DC: Island Press) 174–7.

Narayan, D., R. Patel, K. Schafft, A. Rademacher and S. Koch-Schulte (2000a) *Voices of the Poor – Can Anyone Hear Us?* (New York: Oxford University Press).

Narayan, D., R. Chambers, M. Shah and P. Petesch (2000b) *Voices of the Poor – Crying Out for Change* (New York: Oxford University Press).

Nelson, H. L. (2003) 'Pictures of Persons and the Good of Hospices', in B. Jennings, T. Ryndes, C. D'Onofrio and M. A. Bailey (eds) *Access to Hospice Care* (Garrison, NY: Hastings Center) S18–19.

Nozick, R. (1974) *Anarchy, State and Utopia* (New York: Basic Books).

Nussbaum, M. (2000) *Women and Human Development* (Cambridge: Cambridge University Press).

Nussbaum, M. and A. Sen (eds) (1993) *The Quality of Life* (Oxford: Clarendon Press for UNU-WIDER).

O'Neill, J. (1993) *Ecology, Policy and Politics – Human Well-being and the Natural World* (London: Routledge).

Oswald, A. (1997) 'Happiness and Economic Performance', *Economic Journal*, 107 (November): 1815–31.

Parfit, D. (1984) *Reasons and Persons* (Oxford: Clarendon Press).

Parker, S. and K. Gerard (1990) 'Caring at Home for Children with Mental Handicaps', in S. Baldwin, C. Godfrey and C. Propper (eds), *Quality of Life – Perspectives and Policies* (London: Routledge) 131–48.

Ryan, R. M. and E. L. Deci (2001) 'On Happiness and Human Potentials: A Review of Research on Hedonic and Eudaimonic Well-Being', *Annual Review of Psychology*, 52: 141–66.

Sagoff, M. (1994) 'Should Preferences Count?', Summary in F. Ackerman, D. Kiron, N. R. Goodwin, J. M. Harris and K. Gallagher (eds) (1997), *Human Well-Being and Economic Goals* (Washington, DC: Island Press) 188–91.

Scanlon, T. (1993) 'Value, Desire and Quality of Life', in M. Nussbaum and A. Sen (eds), *The Quality of Life* (Oxford: Clarendon Press for UNU-WIDER) 184–200.

Scitovsky, T. (1976) (2nd edn 1992) *The Joyless Economy* (New York: Oxford University Press).

Segal, J. M. (1991) 'Alternative Conceptions of the Economic Realm', Summary in F. Ackerman, D. Kiron, N. R. Goodwin, J. M. Harris and K. Gallagher (eds) (1997), *Human Well-Being and Economic Goals* (Washington, DC: Island Press) 15–18.

Seligman, M. and M. Csikszentihalyi (2000) 'Positive Psychology: An Introduction', *American Psychologist*, 55: 5–14.

Sen, A. (1981) 'Plural Utility', *Proceedings of the Aristotelian Society*, 81: 193–215.

Sen, A. (1985) *Commodities and Capabilities* (Cambridge: Cambridge University Press).

Sen, A. (1993) 'Capability and Well-Being', in M. Nussbaum and A. Sen (eds), *The Quality of Life* (Oxford: Clarendon Press for UNU-WIDER) 30–53.

Sen, A. (1999) *Development as Freedom* (New York: Oxford University Press).

Sen, A. (2002) *Rationality and Freedom* (Cambridge, MA: Harvard University Press).

Sen, A. and B. Williams (eds) (1982) *Utilitarianism and Beyond* (Cambridge: Cambridge University Press).

Shaffer, P. (1996) 'Beneath the Poverty Debate: Some Issues', *IDS Bulletin*, 27(1): 23–35.

Staveren, I. van (2001) *The Values of Economics* (London: Routledge).

Sumner, L. W. (1996) *Welfare, Happiness and Ethics* (Oxford: Oxford University Press).

Sunstein, C. (1995) 'Gender, Caste and Law', in M. Nussbaum and J. Glover (eds) (1995), *Women, Culture, and Development* (Oxford: Clarendon Press for UNU-WIDER) 332–59.

Travers, P. and S. Richardson (1993) 'Material Well-Being and Human Well-Being', summary in F. Ackerman, D. Kiron, N. R. Goodwin, J. M. Harris and K. Gallagher (eds) (1997), *Human Well-Being and Economic Goals* (Washington, DC: Island Press) 26–9.

UNDP (1997) *Human Development Report* (Oxford and New York: Oxford University Press for UNDP).

van Praag, B. and P. Frijters (1999) 'The Measurement of Welfare and Well-Being: The Leyden Approach', reprinted in R. A. Easterlin (2002b) *Happiness in Economics* (Cheltenham: Edward Elgar) 113–33.

Zeldin, T. (1994) *An Intimate History of Humanity* (London: Sinclair-Stevenson).

3
Income-based Measures of Average Well-being

Steve Dowrick

Limitations of national income accounting data

International comparisons of living standards or development are most commonly made in terms of gross domestic product per person – whether in newspaper articles examining the latest country rankings or in economics journals analyzing the relative performance of countries. Such comparisons are open to criticism on the grounds that GDP is more properly regarded as a partial measure of aggregate output than as an indicator of either current or future well-being. International GDP comparisons make no allowance for environmental differences, for resource depletion, for leisure, for household production of goods and services, for black market activities or for external costs and benefits associated with production and consumption.

For example, World Bank measures adjusted for differences in the purchasing power of currencies show GDP per capita in Australia as close to that in Finland. Some part of the difference is due to higher expenditures by Finns on domestic fuel and power (2.6 per cent of GDP) in comparison with Australians whose warmer climate requires lower expenditure for domestic comfort (1.4 per cent of GDP). Also problematic for welfare interpretations of national income is the observation that if polluting industries cause illnesses requiring expensive medical treatment, both the output of the polluting industry and the expenditure on medical services will be counted as positive contributions to GDP. Thus, aggregate output and income, as measured in the national accounts, may be relatively high whilst actual well-being is low.

Comparisons of GDP per capita take no account of differences in hours of work or hours of leisure. Nor do they take account of the value of production for own use. Peasant farming activities are particularly problematic for national accountants, since much of the production may be directly consumed by the farming household and will therefore escape the measurement of market transactions. Furthermore, a large amount of household activity in both rural and urban societies is concerned with the unmeasured production of goods and services such as child-care, education, food preparation, cleaning, and so on for own-household consumption.

The failure of measured GDP to capture well-being accurately is not surprising given that the definitions and measurement practices of national accounts have been designed with a quite different purpose in mind; namely, to provide the accounting framework for the operation of monetary and fiscal policies. Dowrick and Quiggin (1998) argues that the System of National Accounts was designed with Keynesian short-run demand management in mind, hence its focus on the gross investment flows and government and market output which constitute the domestic side of the circular flow of funds in the familiar Macroeconomics I diagram. From the point of view of a central bank assessing the supply of money in relation to unemployment and inflation, GDP is a useful measure of the level of market activity without any inherent welfare implications.

These problems have long been recognized by economists. Eisner (1988) provides a survey of the problems and of various attempts to overcome them through amended and extended systems of national accounts. More recently, addressing the problem of valuing non-marketed productive activities, Folbre (2002) estimates that the average non-cash cost of bringing up a child in the United States in 2000 was around US$20,000 – valuing the supervisory time plus foregone wages of the parents. Folbre and Nelson (2000) discuss the welfare implications of transferring activities from families to the market.

Considerable research effort is required to calculate properly the adjustments required to convert national accounts data into a measure that has a clear relationship with well-being. Such research is a luxury good that can be afforded only by the richer countries. So, it may be useful to examine ad hoc adjustments to national accounts data that allow us to make more meaningful cross-country comparisons with readily available data. In the next section I look at two potential adjustments – one for hours of work and one for life expectancy. Then I go on to look at biases in the methods commonly used for calculating international income comparisons.

Income measures and alternative indicators of well-being

National governments devote considerable resources to the measurement of GDP in line with the internationally agreed standards of the System of National Accounts. Furthermore, an international programme has been in progress for over thirty years to enable cross-country comparisons of real income and expenditure. At five-year intervals, under the auspices of the International Comparison Project (ICP), detailed price surveys have been conducted in varying groups of countries. The results are published as tables of prices and real quantities for around 150 categories of goods and services that are purchased in each surveyed economy. A wealth of information has been generated on the price and quantity structures of the participating countries, enabling international comparisons of real GDP and its components at purchasing power parity. This information has been extrapolated across non-survey countries and across time to form the Penn World Table – see Summers and Heston (1991) – and in different forms has been analyzed and published by international organizations such as Eurostat, the OECD, and the World Bank.

Given the ready availability of economic statistics based on the national accounting definitions of GDP and income,[1] researchers are naturally tempted to use such data for international comparison of both economic performance and welfare. Even if GDP is not designed for the latter purpose, it is not unreasonable to enquire whether it might be a useful short-cut proxy for a measure of well-being, or whether it can be converted into a useful measure with readily available data.

Adjusting for hours of work

Recorded hours of employment in the total population vary according to rates of participation in the labour force and according to average hours of work. These rates are influenced by national differences in income levels, by differences in the age structure of the population and by legal or cultural factors that influence participation, including gender roles and gender discrimination. Other things being equal, we expect a country with high participation rates and high hours of work to record a higher level of output, but this will not necessarily reflect higher well-being if the additional market income is offset by the sacrifice of leisure and home production.

The data on recorded hours of work typically suffer from the same drawbacks as the data on GDP, failing to record time spent on productive activities that fall outside the market sector, such as household production and black market activities. But it is precisely the common nature of these drawbacks that make GDP per hour worked a better indicator of well-being than the ratio of GDP to population. This will be the case if the average value of non-market production is the same as the average value of recorded labour market activity.

Table 3.1 lists in descending order the average weekly hours of work per head of population for 24 OECD countries in 1990. The variation in recorded hours is remarkably large given that the OECD is a relatively homogeneous group of countries in terms of income levels. The average person in Japan is recorded as working almost double the hours of the average person in Spain. Table 3.1 also records indexes of GDP per person and of GDP per hour worked, with each index normalized to have an average value of 100.

GDP per person is 50 per cent higher in Japan than in Spain. But this does not mean that the average Japanese is that much better off than the average Spaniard, who has considerably more time available for both leisure and for home production. Indeed, anecdotal evidence suggests that many Japanese people consider that they are substantially overworked and fail to enjoy the

Table 3.1 Recorded hours of work and GDP in the OECD, 1990

	Hours per person	GDP per person OECD = 100	GDP per hour OECD = 100		Hours per person	GDP per person OECD = 100	GDP per hour OECD = 100
Japan	23.8	103.2	73.0	USA	16.6	125.4	127.0
Iceland	23.6	96.6	68.7	Austria	16.1	96.5	101.0
Switzerland	22.2	122.2	92.3	Australia	16.0	93.5	98.2
UK	20.4	92.8	76.6	Finland	16.0	96.4	101.3
Luxembourg	20.0	112.7	94.8	France	15.4	101.6	110.7
Sweden	19.8	99.6	84.6	Canada	15.2	112.1	124.3
Germany	18.1	106.5	99.1	Greece	15.1	42.9	47.8
Portugal	17.8	51.1	48.1	Italy	14.8	93.2	105.6
Norway	17.5	93.8	90.3	Turkey	14.0	27.1	32.6
Netherlands	17.3	91.8	89.1	Ireland	13.3	62.1	78.6
New Zealand	16.9	79.3	78.7	Belgium	12.9	95.6	124.7
Denmark	16.6	98.1	99.0	Spain	12.2	68.6	94.6

Source: OECD National Accounts and OECD Labour Force Statistics. Indexes calculated by author.

living standards of other high income countries, a judgement backed by the study of Castles (1992) who analyzes time use data and other indicators to compare living standards between Tokyo and Sydney. These judgements are backed by the index of GDP per hour, which shows that labour productivity is nearly one third higher in Spain than in Japan.

The Japan–Spain example is extreme, but other inter-country income comparisons also vary considerably depending on whether income is measured per person or per recorded working hour. These comparisons are illustrated in Figure 3.1, which is a scatter plot of GDP per hour versus GDP per person. Countries lying above the 45 degree line are those with below average hours of work.

We can see that although Canada and Belgium are well below the US in terms of GDP per capita, they are almost equal in labour productivity. A number of other countries appear to be substantially better off when we take account of hours of work, particularly Ireland and Spain, whilst those which appear substantially worse off include Iceland, Japan, the UK, Luxembourg, Sweden and Switzerland.

Output per hour, as a measure of labour productivity, may not be closely correlated with average well-being if there are large differences across countries in dependency rates. Equally, GDP per hour may be a poor measure of relative welfare if low hours of work do not reflect a voluntary choice of leisure/home-production but are imposed by high unemployment or by social norms that restrict participation by groups such as women. So, whilst

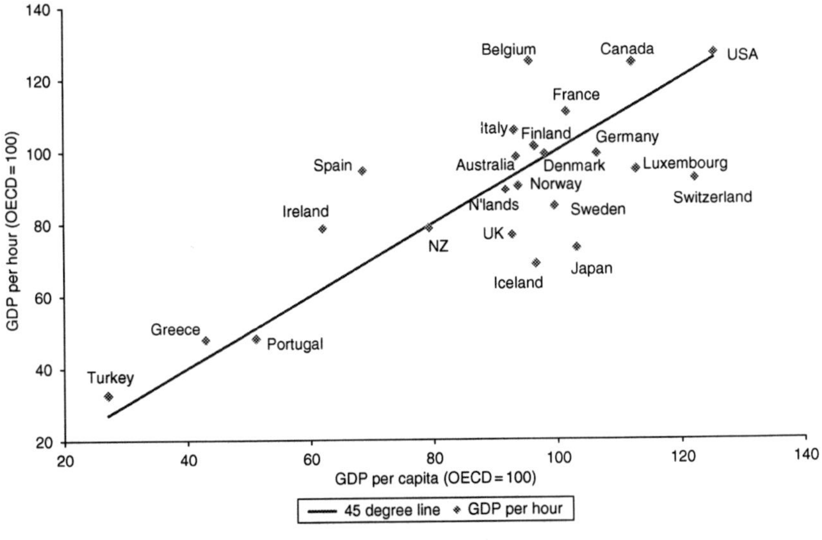

Figure 3.1 Scatter plot of GDP per hour versus GDP per person

we may not want to replace GDP per capita with GDP per hour as our preferred income measure, it may be instructive to compare the two measures as in Figure 3.1. Such comparisons are, however, more difficult to compute with accuracy for non-OECD countries, for which the hours of work data compiled by the ILO are often incomplete.

Adjusting for life expectancy

An approach that has been particularly popular in the development literature is to report multiple indicators of social development including GDP or GNP per capita, life expectancy, educational attainment, literacy rates, and so on. The best-known composite index is the Human Development Index (HDI), combining measures of income, life expectancy and literacy. Discussed in detail in Chapter 5 of this volume, it is regularly updated in the UNDP's annual *Human Development Report* (UNDP 1990–2003)

These approaches are intuitively appealing as a solution to the limitations of purely income-based measures, though the composite indicator approach inevitably raises serious questions concerning the rather arbitrary choices of scaling and weighting methods. These issues are addressed in depth in Chapter 5, and in the broader literature on composite well-being indices (see for example UNDP 1990–2003). For the purposes of this chapter, however, it is of interest to examine how closely the much criticized income measures are correlated with commonly used alternative indicators. If the correlation is high, then income based measures may serve as a reasonably good proxy for a variety of measures of development.

Life expectancy is probably one of the most important and widely used indicators of development. Figure 3.2 is a scatter plot displaying the relationship between GDP per capita and the life expectancy of a newborn across the 171 countries for which World Bank data was available, averaged over the years 1994 to 1998. We can observe immediately that a child's expectancy of life varies hugely according to their country of birth and that poorer countries tend to have much lower life expectancy.

The relationship between income and life expectancy is strongly positive but clearly non-linear. Figure 3.1 displays the OLS regression line and parameter estimates for the semi-log model:

$$LX_i = \beta \ln(GDP_i) + constant + \varepsilon_i \tag{3.1}$$

where LX represents life expectancy and GDP is real GDP per capita. This very simple model suggests that variations in income 'explain' over two thirds of the cross-country variation in life expectancy. If we interpret the relationship as causal, the estimated value for the slope coefficient, $\beta = 8.2$, implies that a 12 per cent increase in real income would increase life expectancy by one year.

Interestingly, this relationship is very close to that estimated on 1980 data by Dowrick *et al.* (2003) who find a β coefficient of 9.5 for the 60 countries

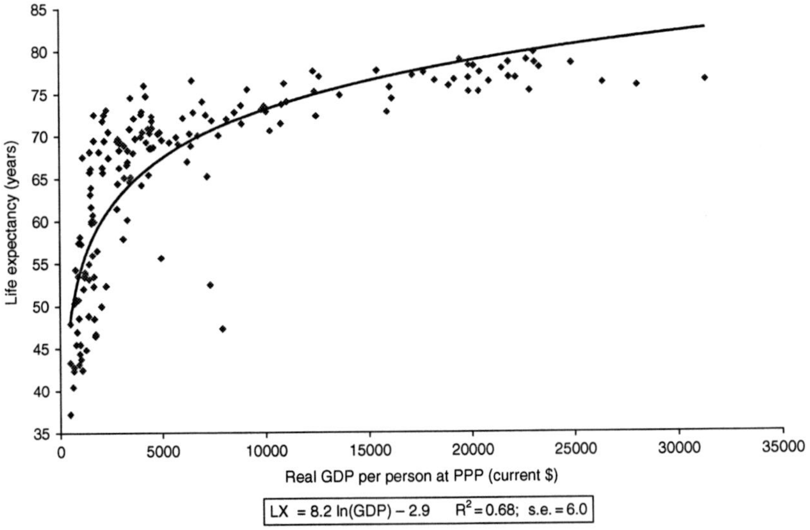

Figure 3.2 Real GDP per person and life expectancy across 171 countries, 1994–98

surveyed in that year by the ICP. Although the currency units in which GDP is measured differ between the two periods, the logarithmic formulation implies that this affects only the constant term, not the slope coefficient.

Of course, these correlations do not establish the direction of causation. But causation is not at issue here. Inasmuch as life expectancy is a crucial element in the measurement of well-being, GDP seems to act as a reasonable proxy and it is worthwhile examining the statistical relationship more closely.

Inspection of Figure 3.2 shows that the regression systematically over-predicts life expectancy for the very poorest and the very richest countries whilst it under-predicts for countries with average incomes between US$2,000 and US$10,000. Formal diagnostic tests also suggest that this simple semi-logarithmic relationship could be improved: the residuals exhibit heteroscedasticity, the functional form fails the Reset(2) test and, when the data are ordered by real GDP, the sequential application of the Chow test for parameter stability reveals significant structural breaks at low and middle income levels.

Accordingly, the model is re-estimated as:

$$LX_i = \beta_1 \ln(GDP_i) + \beta_2[DUM_i \ln(GDP_i)] + \beta_3 DUM_i + constant + \varepsilon_i \qquad (3.2)$$

where *DUM* is a dummy variable with a value of unity for countries with income levels below US$6,000 per year and a value of 0 for richer countries. Descriptive statistics are given in Table 3.2 and the regression results are summarized in Table 3.3.

Table 3.2 Life expectancy and GDP, descriptive statistics for 171 countries

		Mean	Standard deviation	Minimum	Maximum
Life expectancy 1994–98	*years*	65.6	10.7	37.2	79.8
GDP per capita 1994–98	*current PPP US$*	6,932.00	7,261	486.00	31,350.00
Log(GDP)		8.30	1.07	6.18	10.35

Note: Current PPP dollars are normalized to have the same value as the US$ in the USA. Variables are averaged.
Source: Global Development Finance and World Development Indicators. Accessed through http://www.worldbank.org/research/growth/GDNdata.htm

Table 3.3 Regression analysis of life expectancy on real GDP per capita

	Coefficient	s.e.	t-ratio
Log (GDP per capita)	6.78	1.31	5.17
Log (GDP) × dummy	5.81	1.50	3.86
Constant	9.56	12.9	0.74
Dummy	−44.8	4.16	−3.16

observations 171 countries
R^2 0.74
s.e. of estimate 5.5 years
Heteroscedasticity test (e^2 on predicted value): $\chi^2(1) = 5.85$

Estimation: OLS using heteroscedasticity-consistent covariance matrix.
Package: Shazam (White 1987).
Data: See Table 3.1. Dummy variable = 1 if GDP < US$6,000.
Note: With observations ranked in order of real GDP, a preliminary regression was run without the dummy variable and a Chow Test for parameter stability was applied with sequential breaks. Parameter stability was rejected between the sub-sample of 109 countries with GDP below US$6,000 and the sub-sample of 62 countries with GDP above US$6,000: $F_{2,167} = 22.5$.

Allowing for a structural break in the relationship reduces the standard error of estimated life expectancy from 6.0 to 5.5 years, but the diagnostic statistics show that heteroscedasticity is still present. Re-estimation of the relationship on the separate sub-samples reveals a higher standard error for the poorer countries (6.1 years) compared with the richer countries (4.4 years). But the slope coefficients for the independently estimated samples are almost identical to those implied by the pooled regression reported in Table 3.2.

The coefficient β_2 has a point estimate of 5.8 and is significant at the 1 per cent level. The implication is that the coefficient on GDP is nearly twice as high for the poorer countries in the sample, at 12.6, as it is for the richer countries, at 6.8. The causal interpretation of these estimates is that life expectancy will increase by one year when GDP increases by 15 per cent in a rich country or by just eight years in a poor country.

To the extent that real income is a good predictor of life expectancy, the combination of the two variables into a composite indicator seems to be a redundant exercise. But a standard error of over five years in predicting life expectancy is far from trivial, and inspection of Figure 3.2 indicates that, for a substantial number of countries, the prediction error is even greater. Indeed, the gap between income and life expectancy may indicate some of the most interesting, important features of the relationship between economic and human development. Figures 3.3 and 3.4 display the data and the regression lines separately for the poor and rich sub-samples of the 1994–98 data set.

I have labelled some of the outlying countries on both figures. Amongst the poor countries, the most prominent under-performers (in terms of lower than predicted life expectancy, given the level of income) are in sub-Saharan Africa. The over-performers include some Caribbean countries and some former Soviet Union countries. Amongst the rich economies, the under-performers include the three richest countries: Luxembourg, the USA and Singapore, whilst noticeable amongst the over-performers are Costa Rica, Greece, Sweden and Japan.

The size of the variations in life expectancy amongst countries at low and middle income levels suggests that per capita income is not always a satisfactory indicator of well-being. Looking at the figure above, it is hard

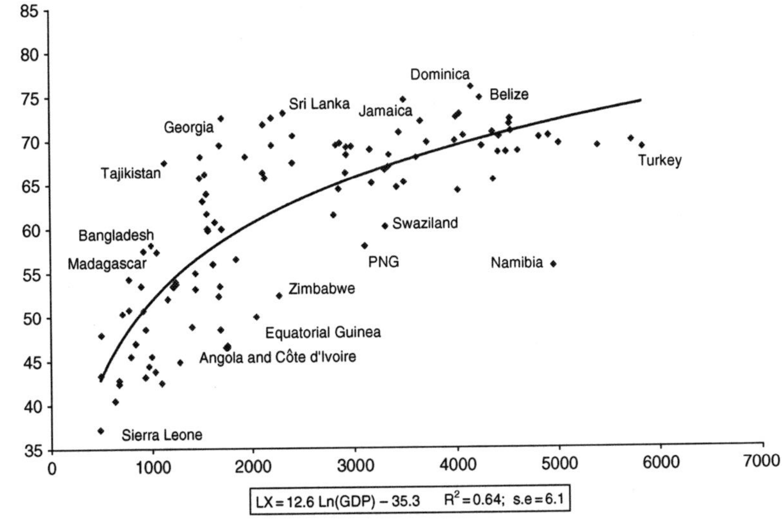

Figure 3.3 Life expectancy and GDP: countries with income under $6000

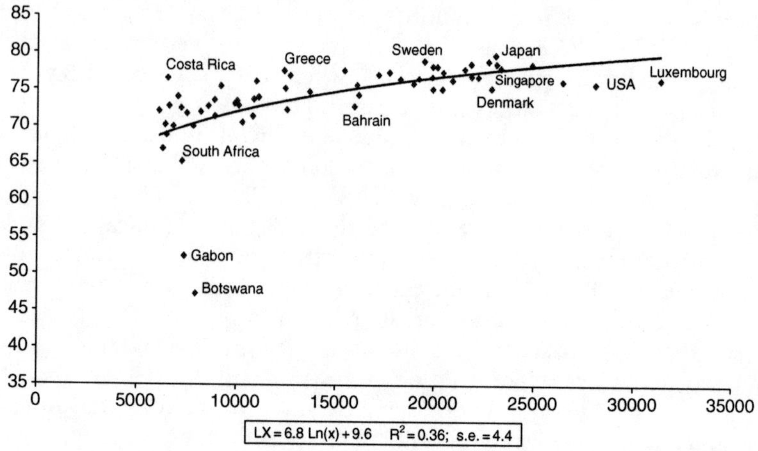

Figure 3.4 Life expectancy and GDP: countries with income over $6000

to believe that the average person in Botswana would regard themselves as better off than the average South African because their average income is 10 per cent higher, given that their average life expectancy is 18 years less.

The deviation of actual from predicted life expectancy can also highlight important questions for investigation. For instance, we might ask why Georgia and Sri Lanka have a so much higher life expectancy than other countries of comparable income. Does this reflect a better physical and social infrastructure? Does it reflect a more equitable distribution of income?

Index number bias in international income comparisons

In the preceding section I have discussed some of the problems arising from the national accounting conventions as to which activities are included in GDP and which activities are excluded. Here, I take the composition of the GDP bundle as a given and turn to the theory and practice of comparing expenditures that are expressed in different national currencies for consumers who face very different price structures.

A recent series of papers in the *Journal of Economic Perspectives* has addressed various index number problems in the measurement of the US Consumer Price index – see Abraham (2003), Hausman (2003) and Schultze (2003). These three papers are all addressing the problem of measuring a cost-of-living index, which is dual to an index of real incomes. Because the cost-of-living problem is examined in the context of inter-temporal rather than international comparisons, the authors give more emphasis to problems such as quality adjustment and the introduction of new goods.

Hausman (2003) argues that the bias arising from the incorrect treatment of new goods is a first order problem in contrast to the bias arising out of a failure to account for consumer substitution, which appears as a second order term in his Taylor expansion of the true cost-of-living index. This argument may well be correct in the context of annual changes in the relative prices of goods where a change as high as 10 per cent, such as might be observed between the price of computers and the price of restaurant meals, is exceptional. In the context of international comparisons, however, it is not uncommon for the ICP data to reveal price ratios that differ by 500 per cent or more. In this case, we may expect consumer substitution to have first order effects. Moreover, because the ICP redefines for each survey the basket of goods and services for which prices are collected, the problem of new goods is less likely to be significant in the context of cross-country comparisons.

It is well known, due to the work of Balassa and Samuelson, that the conversion of international incomes at currency market exchange rates induces biased comparisons that tend to understate the relative incomes of poorer countries. It is less well known that the most widely used method of estimating purchasing power parities, the Geary–Khamis method that underpins the Penn World Table, induces the opposite bias – tending to overstate the relative income of poorer countries.

The use of foreign exchange rates (FX) to translate international incomes into a common currency introduces a 'traded sector bias'. Whilst exchange rates tend to equate purchasing power over traded goods and services, much of world production is for domestic consumption only. Wide variations across countries in the prices of non-traded goods and services are not reflected in the market for foreign exchange. So FX-converted incomes do not reflect the purchasing power of consumers in their own countries. Indeed, FX income comparisons tend to exaggerate international income differentials by ignoring the lower cost of living that is typically observed in poorer economies, due to cheaper labour intensive services in the non-traded sector of low productivity economies.

The most widely used data set on purchasing power parity comparisons of GDP is the Penn World Table, the latest versions of which have been compiled by Summers and Heston (1991). They use the ICP price surveys to calculate 'international prices' as the weighted average of the price vectors of all of the countries participating in the survey. The Geary–Khamis (GK) index of real GDP is calculated by valuing each country's per capita GDP bundle at these 'international prices'. The GK purchasing power parities are not calculated directly, rather they are derived from the GK quantity index as the rates of currency exchange which, when applied to nominal GDP, yield the same relative quantities. The GK index is extended across non-ICP countries and over time to produce the full Penn World Table.

The GK approach typically results in substantial revisions to FX valuations of the income of poor countries relative to the rich. For example, the ratio of per capita GDP between the USA and Mali, the richest and poorest countries in the 1980 ICP sample, is 58:1 using market exchange rates (see UN and CEC 1987: part I, table 1). The ICP data reveal, however, that non-traded goods and services are much cheaper, relative to traded goods, in Mali than they are in the USA. The GK measure of the US/Mali real income ratio is almost half that of the FX measure, a ratio of 31:1.

The GK method is, however, just as problematic as the exchange rate approach. PWT analysts have themselves acknowledged that the GK index may impart a bias in the opposite direction.

> The issue arises out of a familiar problem in price and quantity index number construction... Valuation at other than own prices tends to inflate the aggregate value of the bundle of goods because no allowance is made for the substitutions in quantities toward the goods that are relatively cheap... The practical importance of this issue... may loom large in comparisons between countries that have widely divergent price and quantity structures. (Kravis *et al.* 1982: 7)

The economic approach to international income comparisons

In order to better understand these sources of bias in international comparisons, we turn to a model of a two good world where the representative agents of two economies, A and B, consume both tradable manufactures and non-tradable services, labelled m and s respectively.[2] The consumption bundle in country A is the quantity vector $\boldsymbol{A}$, where $\boldsymbol{A} \equiv (Q_m^A, Q_s^A)$, and the consumption bundle in $\boldsymbol{B}$ is the similarly defined quantity vector $\boldsymbol{B}$. We normalize the prices of manufactured goods in each country, measured in local currency, to unity. The price vector in country A is then defined as $\boldsymbol{a}$, where $\boldsymbol{a} \equiv (1, P_s^A)$, and $\boldsymbol{b}$ is the price vector in country B.

By assumption, the technology of each country is such that labour productivity is higher in the manufacturing sector of country A, whilst labour productivity in the labour intensive service sector is the same across countries. Competition in the tradable sector equalizes the exchange rate converted prices of manufactures and the productivity adjusted wage. Both real wages and the price of services are relatively cheap in the low productivity, low wage economy, B: $P_s^B < P_s^A$.

This situation is illustrated in Figure 3.5 where the solid lines through the consumption bundles $\boldsymbol{A}$ and $\boldsymbol{B}$ represent the budget lines for each representative consumer. With consumption of services measured on the vertical axis, B's budget line is steeper, reflecting the relative cheapness of domestic services. With manufactures as the numeraire good, the local currency values of national expenditure per capita are $\boldsymbol{A}'\boldsymbol{a}$ and $\boldsymbol{B}'\boldsymbol{b}$, represented by the intercept of each country's budget line with the horizontal axis. With no international capital flows and no depreciation, national expenditure, national income and GDP are all the same.

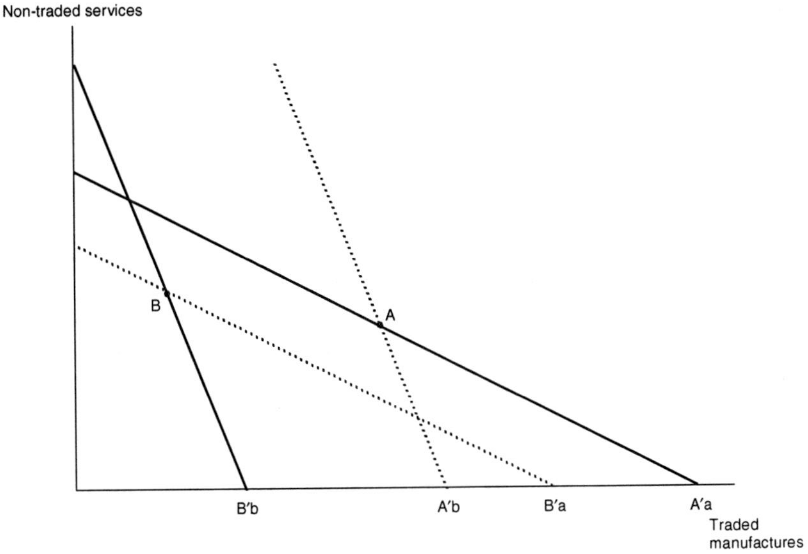

Figure 3.5 Revealed preference, Paasche and Laspeyre indexes

Assuming common preferences, full information and rational choice we can use standard economic principles to rank the welfare of *A* and *B*. By construction, the consumption bundle in the low productivity country ***B*** lies inside *A*'s budget set whilst ***A*** lies outside *B*'s budget set. *A* could have chosen the bundle ***B***, but instead chose ***A***. In this situation, the principle of revealed preference tells us that the bundle ***A*** is revealed preferred to ***B***, implying that consumer *A* is better off than consumer *B*. It is in this sense that we can say that country *A* is richer than country *B* or that country *A* has higher GDP per capita than country *B*.

The revealed preference argument can be expressed formally as:

$$L_{AB} \equiv \frac{A'\boldsymbol{b}}{B'\boldsymbol{b}} > 1 \text{ and } P_{AB} \equiv \frac{A'\boldsymbol{a}}{B'\boldsymbol{a}} > 1 \Rightarrow \boldsymbol{A} \text{ is revealed strictly preferred to } \boldsymbol{B} \quad (3.3)$$

where the first inequality is the condition that ***A*** lies outside *B*'s budget set whilst the second inequality is the condition that ***B*** lies inside *A*'s budget set. In (3.3) we have also noted that the first ratio, valuing *A*'s bundle at *B*'s prices, is the Laspeyres index, L_{AB}, whilst the second ratio is the Paasche index, P_{AB}. So the revealed preference condition is equivalent to the condition that both the Laspeyres and Paasche indexes exceed unity.

Revealed preference principles enable us to derive a partial ordering. It is an ordering, rather than a cardinal comparison, because whilst it may enable us to say that *A* is better off than *B* (or vice versa), it does not enable us to say that A is 10 per cent or 20 per cent better off. The ordering is partial because there may be situations where each consumption bundle lies outside the other's budget set (if $L_{AB} > 1$ and $P_{AB} < 1$) in which case we cannot tell which bundle is preferred. There may also be situations where $L_{AB} < 1$ and $P_{AB} < 1$; that is, each bundle lies inside the other's budget set, in which case we have to reject the joint hypotheses of common tastes and rational choice.

If we want to make a cardinal comparison, a natural starting point is to consider the Laspeyre and Paasche ratios, alternately comparing the values of the bundles at B's prices or at A's prices. Here, we start to confront some of the problems of index number theory. The L and P ratios will usually be different and there is no obvious reason to choose one over the other. In terms of Figure 3.5, B's budget line intersects the horizontal axis at $\boldsymbol{B'b}$ and the dotted line parallel to B's budget line through point A intersects the horizontal axis at $\boldsymbol{A'b}$. The Laspeyre index is the ratio of the distances of these two points from the origin. A similar construction with a line through point B parallel to A's budget line gives the Paasche index.

The diagram has been constructed to illustrate substitution bias: if A chooses to consume relatively more of the goods that are cheaper in country A than in country B, then valuing A's bundle at B's prices will tend to exaggerate A's relative welfare and vice versa. Given that substitution bias tends to make the L ratio too large and the P ratio too small, we might suppose that an unbiased measure would lie between the two ratios. We shall show later that this is indeed the case if the common utility function is homothetic. But at this point it is useful to explain how the foreign exchange and the Geary–Khamis income comparisons are calculated and their biases in relation to the Laspeyre and Paasche ratios.

With manufactures as the numeraire, nominal GDP per capita in each country is given by the intercept of the budget line with the horizontal axis in Figure 3.5. Abstracting from capital flows and from transport costs, we expect the law of one price to hold for traded goods; that is, the exchange rate converted price of manufactures is the same in both countries. In this case, the exchange rate converted ratio of GDP per capita is given by:

$$FX_{AB} = \frac{\boldsymbol{A'a}}{\boldsymbol{B'b}} \tag{3.4}$$

From Figure 3.5 we can see that this ratio exceeds both the Laspeyres and the Paasche ratios. This illustrates the Balassa–Samuelson result that foreign exchange comparisons tend to understate the relative income of the poorer country because the exchange rate is not influenced by the low price of non-tradables – see Balassa (1964) and Samuelson (1984).

The Geary–Khamis approach attempts to overcome the bias in exchange rate comparisons by valuing the GDP bundle in each country at a fixed price vector, g. This 'international price' vector is calculated as the GDP weighted average of price vectors of all the counties in the GK system. The Geary–Khamis quantity index is:

$$GK_{AB} = \frac{A'g}{B'g} \tag{3.5}$$

The weighting procedure biases the international price vector towards the price structures found in countries with the highest GDP; that is, countries with large populations and high per capita incomes. Since the ICP surveys do not include China, their sample is most heavily influenced by the price structures of the rich and populous countries such as the US, Germany, and Japan. This means that the international price vector, g, which underpins the Penn World Table, corresponds to the price structure of a high productivity economy with expensive non-traded services.

Valuing the GDP of poorer countries at rich country prices overstates their relative income levels. In Figure 3.6, valuation of GDP at the international price vector, g, is illustrated by the dashed lines through points A and $\boldsymbol{B}$. It is assumed that the international price vector corresponds to that of a country that is richer than both countries A and B. We see that in this case the GK ratio, $A'g/B'g$, is even smaller than the Paasche ratio, $A'a/B'a$. Since the latter ratio already overvalues the income level of the poorer country, we can see that the GK method compounds the problem of substitution bias.

Dowrick and Akmal (2003) show that this direction of bias is strongly evident in the GK measures, which substantially understate the true level of world income inequality.

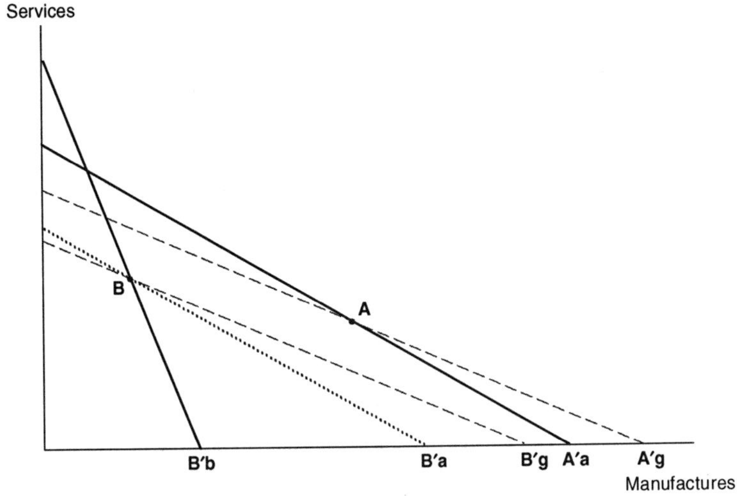

Figure 3.6 Substitution bias in the GK index

How can we construct an unbiased or 'true' income comparison? If substitution bias makes the Laspeyre index too high and the Paasche index too low, a natural candidate is the geometric mean of the two: $F_{AB} = \sqrt{L_{AB}P_{AB}}$, which is the Fisher Ideal index. A major drawback for international comparisons, however, is that the Fisher index is not transitive; that is, $F_{AC} \neq F_{AB}F_{BC}$. So, whilst the Fisher index is a natural choice for an unbiased bilateral comparison, it does not provide a consistent multilateral index.

The economic approach to the index number problem is based on the notion that there may be a common utility function generating the different observations. If we can estimate the common utility function, $u(.)$, then the welfare ratio is simply $u(\boldsymbol{A})/u(\boldsymbol{B})$. This procedure does not, however, yield a cardinal index because any particular utility function that fits the data can be subject to a monotonic increasing transformation to yield another function that fits the data equally well, preserving the utility ordering but yielding a different utility ratio.

The non-cardinality of utility functions can be overcome by using the Allen quantity index, $I(\boldsymbol{p})$, which is defined as the ratio of the expenditure functions:

$$I_{AB}(\boldsymbol{p}) \equiv \frac{e[u(\boldsymbol{A}),\boldsymbol{p}]}{e[u(\boldsymbol{B}),\boldsymbol{p}]} \tag{3.6}$$

where the expenditure function $e[u(\boldsymbol{Q}),\boldsymbol{p}]$ is the minimum expenditure required to attain the utility level $u(\boldsymbol{Q})$ at some reference prices $\boldsymbol{p}$.

Two special cases of the Allen index are worth noting. If country A's prices are chosen as the reference price vector, we have the Allen–Paasche index:

$$I_{AB}(\boldsymbol{a}) \equiv \frac{e[u(\boldsymbol{A}),\boldsymbol{a}]}{e[u(\boldsymbol{B}),\boldsymbol{a}]} \geq \frac{\boldsymbol{A'a}}{\boldsymbol{B'a}} \equiv P_{AB} \tag{3.7}$$

The Allen–Paasche index has a tight lower bound, the Paasche index. The derivation of this result is straightforward. Given utility maximization, the minimum expenditure required to achieve A's utility at A's prices is exactly $\boldsymbol{A'a}$, the value of A's chosen consumption bundle. On the other hand, whilst B's utility could be achieved at A's prices simply by spending $\boldsymbol{B'a}$ to purchase the bundle $\boldsymbol{B}$, there may be some other bundle which is cheaper but generates the same utility level.

Similar reasoning gives the result that the Laspeyre index is the upper bound to the Allen–Laspeyre index evaluated at country B's prices:

$$I_{AB}(\boldsymbol{b}) \equiv \frac{e[u(\boldsymbol{A}),\boldsymbol{b}]}{e[u(\boldsymbol{B}),\boldsymbol{b}]} \leq \frac{\boldsymbol{A'b}}{\boldsymbol{B'b}} \equiv L_{AB} \tag{3.8}$$

The Allen index is both transitive and cardinal. It is, however, not unique. It depends crucially on the choice of the reference price vector and in the context of cross-country comparisons there is no obvious price vector to choose. The only circumstance under which the Allen index is independent of the choice of reference price vector is where the common utility function is homothetic, $h(.)$. In this case, the inequalities in equations (3.7) and (3.8) can be combined to yield the result that the Paasche and Laspeyre indexes are the exact upper and lower bounds for the Allen-homothetic index, I^H:

$$P_{AB} \leq I^H_{AB} \equiv \frac{e[h(\boldsymbol{A}), \boldsymbol{p}]}{e[h(\boldsymbol{B}), \boldsymbol{p}]} \leq L_{AB} \qquad (3.9)$$

A special case that satisfies this inequality is the Fisher index which, by construction, must lie between the P and L indexes (and homotheticity ensures that $P < L$). We noted earlier that the Fisher index does not yield a consistent multilateral index because it is not transitive. Afriat (1973) presents a solution to the problem of defining a true multilateral index that can be viewed as a generalization of the Fisher approach. The attractiveness of the Fisher index is that it is a compromise between the Paasche and Laspeyre indices. But it is the specificity of the Fisher compromise – choosing the geometric mid-point – that makes transitivity impossible. The solution proposed by Afriat (1973) comes from asking a more general question: is there any set of real income numbers for our n country problem such that the income ratio for each pair of countries lies somewhere between the corresponding Paasche and Laspeyre ratios? Afriat's requirement that the ratios lie *between* rather than *at the mid-point* of the Paasche and Laspeyre ratios makes it feasible that there may exist such a set of numbers – a 'true index' in Afriat's terminology.

The Afriat index is not just a convenient set of numbers. It is a true welfare measure. Afriat (1981) has a remarkable theorem showing that the existence of such a true index, for a given set of observations on prices and quantities, is equivalent to the existence of a common homothetic preference relationship (or utility function) that rationalizes the data.[3] That is to say, if there exists a set of Afriat index numbers, then there must also exist some common homothetic utility function such that any country's observed consumption bundle maximizes the utility of a representative consumer facing the prices and budget constraint of that country.

If a true multilateral index does exist it will not be unique, but we can establish upper and lower bounds to each of the bilateral ratios. These will be tighter than the Paasche–Laspeyre bounds. We can also establish bounds to the deviation of any observation from the sample average income. Using these true bounds as our benchmark, we can evaluate the degree of bias in both the FX and the GK income measures.

Applying the economic approach to international income data

Criticism of the economic approach to international income comparisons comes from several angles. There are those who point out that individual preferences can only be aggregated to predict aggregate behaviour if they satisfy quasi-homotheticity, and that there is no evidence to suggest that individual preferences do satisfy that condition. Then there are those who argue that preferences are heterogeneous even within a nation, so the assumption of common preferences across countries is preposterously counter-factual.

My response to these criticisms runs as follows. Yes indeed, individuals do have different preferences which probably do not satisfy the conditions for aggregation. If, however, we find that aggregate patterns of expenditure do satisfy tests for common preferences, then we can use the economic approach to value the aggregate bundles. This allows us to assess the relative welfare of a notional representative consumer facing the relative prices and budget set of each country.

When John Quiggin and I first tested the hypothesis of common tastes on international average data, applying revealed preference tests to the 1980 ICP data for sixty countries, we found that the hypothesis of common preferences was not rejected (see Dowrick and Quiggin 1994). All of the variation in the composition of national expenditures could have been due solely to differences in relative prices and incomes. Subsequent research reported in Dowrick and Quiggin (1997) and Dowrick and Bruton (2000) showed that the much stronger hypothesis of common homothetic preferences could be sustained for a substantial majority, though not all, of the countries in the ICP surveys for 1980, 1990 and 1993. These findings, some of which are reproduced later, allow us to quantify the biases in both FX and GK indexes.

Hill (2000) has also addressed the problem of measuring substitution bias, adopting two utility based approaches to establishing bounds on income comparisons. He estimates the parameters of the linear expenditure system, which is derived from the Stone–Geary utility function, to derive utility numbers for each country. He notes the sensitivity of the income ratios to the choice of the reference price vector, illustrated by his finding that the USA/Turkey ratio could be as high as 7 or as low as 3.5, bounds that encompass the GK ratio of 3.7. His other approach is to assume homothetic preferences, implying that income comparisons based on expenditure function ratios are invariant to the reference price vector. This enables him to tighten the bounds on the US/Turkey ratio to the interval (5.4, 4.0), establishing that the GK measure does indeed overvalue the relative income of the poorer country. This latter approach is similar to that used by Dowrick and Quiggin (1997), but whereas Hill examines only bilateral comparisons, Dowrick and Quiggin develop results on the multilateral properties of true Afriat index numbers.

In order to highlight the magnitudes of bias involved, it is worth presenting results with respect to an extreme problem: what is the ratio of real GDP per capita in the richest country, the USA, relative to that in Mali, one of the very poorest? As discussed above, exchange rate comparisons give

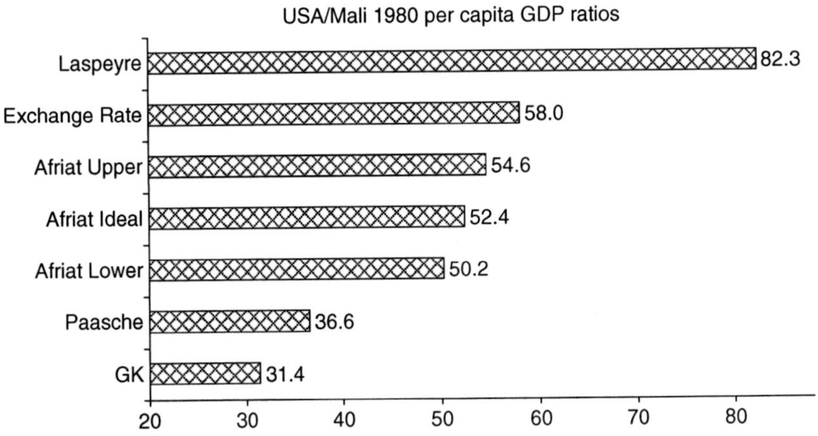

Figure 3.7 Quantifying the bias in FX and GK indexes

a measure of 58, whilst the GK method applied to the ICP data set for 1980 GDP in sixty countries, reduces the ratio to 31.

These ratios for USA/Mali GDP per capita are displayed in Figure 3.7, along with alternative index numbers. The Paasche and Laspeyre indexes give the income ratios that are obtained by evaluating the GDP bundles at US prices or Mali prices respectively. Given the very different price structures in the two countries, it is not surprising to see that the Laspeyre ratio of 82 is very much higher than the Paasche ratio of 36. The true multilateral index bounds, labelled the Afriat Upper and Afriat Lower, are necessarily tighter. We see that the bounds are tightened very considerably by the assumption of common homothetic preferences, giving a range between 50.2 and 54.6.

A conservative approach to the evaluation of bias is to measure it relative to the closest true bound. We see that the exchange rate measure lies above the true upper bound, overvaluing US income relative to Mali by more than 6 per cent. We can also see that the GK measure has undervalued USA–Mali relative incomes by nearly 40 per cent.

Our preferred choice of true multilateral index numbers is the geometric average of the upper and lower bounds relative to the sample mean. This measure, the Afriat Ideal index, gives a USA–Mali income ratio of 52.4.

Comparison of the FX and GK indexes with the Afriat Ideal index for 57 countries is illustrated in Figure 3.8, where countries are ordered in decreasing true income from left to right. All of the indexes have been normalized to the geometric mean of the FX index, measured in 1980 US$. We can see that the FX index does indeed overstate the income of the richer countries relative to the mean.

Because of the scaling, it is difficult to distinguish the index values for the poorer countries. So the data are re-presented in Figure 3.9 as log ratios

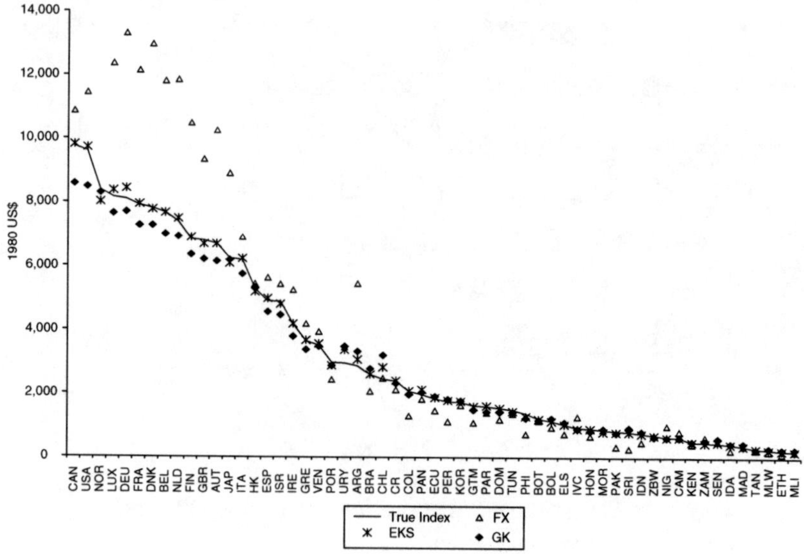

Figure 3.8 Indexes of GDP per capita

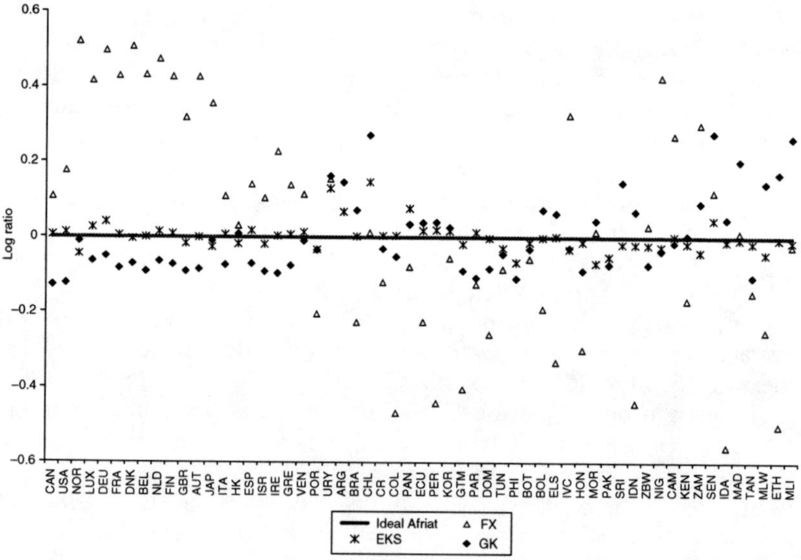

Figure 3.9 Deviations from Ideal Afriat index

Table 3.4 Standard deviation of log ratio to Afriat Ideal index

GK	FX	EKS
0.104	0.361	0.038

relative to the Afriat Ideal index. It is evident that the FX measure tends to understate the income levels of the poorer countries – sometimes by as much as 60 per cent – with an equal and opposite bias in relation to the rich countries. The bias in the GK index is smaller – rarely exceeding 30 per cent – and the direction of bias is opposite to that of the FX measure. The GK comparisons tend to overstate the incomes of poorer countries and understate the incomes of the richer countries.

Finally, I have displayed in both Figures 3.8 and 3.9 the EKS index, which is constructed for each country as the unweighted geometric average of the bilateral Fisher indexes with respect to each of the other countries. This index turns out to be very close to the Ideal Afriat index as measured by a standard deviation of the log ratio to the Afriat Ideal index. The same statistic for the GK and FX indexes are much higher, as reported in Table 3.4. It is also evident from Figure 3.9 that there is no systematic tendency for the EKS index to overvalue or undervalue incomes by level of development.

The EKS is of particular interest because it has become the preferred index number method of the OECD in calculating the purchasing power parity incomes of its member countries. Our analysis of the 1980 ICP data suggests that EKS is an unbiased and accurate approximation to the Afriat Ideal index. A disadvantage of the EKS index is that the EKS measures cannot be broken down into components such as private and government consumption and investment, as is done in the Penn World Table using the GK method. On the other hand, the EKS is clearly preferred when it comes to comparing income levels for the purpose of assessing relative well-being.

Concluding comments

International comparisons of GDP per capita are fraught with difficulties, if we want to use them as indicators of relative well-being. I have discussed the difficulties related to the limitations of national accounts data and the difficulties related to index number problems. Income comparisons can still be valuable, if we recognize their limitations. In particular I suggest the following guidelines for using and interpreting international income comparisons.

1 Where data availability allows it, comparisons should be carried out using the EKS index rather than the GK index or exchange rate conversions

in order to minimize index number bias. FX measures tend to overstate income differentials, whilst GK measures tend to understate them.

2 Measures of GDP per capita should be contrasted with measures of labour productivity to highlight differences that might reflect variation in levels of unrecorded productive activities. High labour productivity relative to GDP per capita may indicate that a country enjoys more leisure and/or home production – especially if recorded unemployment is low and if access to the labour market is unfettered.

3 Income measures can be used to predict life expectancy and other social indicators. Analysis of deviations from predictions can yield useful insights into important aspects of national well-being.

Notes

1 For the purposes of this chapter, I use the ICP definition of GDP per capita as my primary measure. The national accounting identity defines gross domestic income to be the same as gross output, so I use the terms income and output interchangeably. But note that this definition is different from that of net national income, which subtracts capital depreciation and adjusts for international income transfers.

2 This is a heuristic version of the modelling of Dowrick and Akmal (2003) where country *B* also produces an intermediate good that is exported. The arguments that follow are applicable in the case of many goods. The two good model is used to enable diagrammatic representation.

3 This equivalence is explained further by Varian (1983), who proposes a numerical algorithm to test for the existence of a true index given a set of observations on price and quantity vectors.

References

Abraham, K. G. (2003) 'Toward a Cost-of-Living Index: Progress and Prospects', *Journal of Economic Perspectives*, 17 (1): 45–58.

Afriat, S. N. (1973) 'On a System of Inequalities in Demand Analysis: An Extension of the Classical Method', *International Economic Review*, 14 (2): 460–72.

Afriat, S. N. (1981) 'On the Constructability of Consistent Price Indices between Several Periods Simultaneously', in A. Deaton (ed.), *Essays in the Theory and Measurement of Consumer Behaviour* (Cambridge: Cambridge University Press) 133–61.

Balassa, B. (1964) 'The Purchasing Power Parity Doctrine: A Reappraisal', *Journal of Political Economy*, 72 (6): 584–96.

Castles, I. (1992) 'Living Standards in Sydney and Japanese Cities: A Comparison', in K. Sheridan (ed.), *The Australian Economy in the Japanese Mirror* (Brisbane: University of Queensland Press).

Dowrick, S. and M. Akmal (2003) 'Explaining Contradictory Trends in Global Income Inequality: A Tale of Two Biases', Draft paper for World Institute for Development Economics Research on 'Inequality, Poverty and Human Well-being', May, http://ecocomm.anu.edu.au/economics/staff/dowrick/dowrick.html

Dowrick, S. and G. Bruton (2000) 'Quantifying Substitution Bias: True Comparisons across Countries', 4th Biennial Conference of the Pacific Rim Allied Economic Organizations, Sydney (13 January).

Dowrick, S., Y. Dunlop and J. Quiggin (2003) 'Social Indicators and Comparisons of Living Standards', *Journal of Development Economics*, 70 (2): 501–29.

Dowrick, S. and J. Quiggin (1994) 'International Comparisons of Living Standards and Tastes: A Revealed-Preference Analysis', *American Economic Review*, 84 (1): 332–41.

Dowrick, S. and J. Quiggin (1997) 'True Measures of GDP and Convergence', *American Economic Review*, 87 (1): 41–64.

Dowrick, S. and J. Quiggin (1998) 'Measures of Economic Activity and Welfare: The Uses and Abuses of GDP', in R. Eckersley (ed.), *Measuring Progress: Is Life Getting Better?* (Collingwood, VA: CSIRO) 93–107.

Eisner, R. (1988) 'Extended Accounts for National Income and Product', *Journal of Economic Literature*, 26 (4): 1611–84.

Folbre, N. (2002) 'Valuing Parental Time: New Estimates of Expenditures on Children in the United States', Meeting of the Allied Social Science Association, Draft paper (28/12/01): 1–23.

Folbre, N. and J. A. Nelson (2000) 'For Love or Money – or Both?', *Journal of Economic Perspectives*, 14 (4): 123–40.

Hausman, J. (2003) 'Sources of Bias and Solutions to Bias in the Consumer Price Index', *Journal of Economic Perspectives*, 17 (1): 23–44.

Hill, R. J. (2000) 'Measuring Substitution Bias in International Comparisons Based on Additive Purchasing Power Parity Methods', *European Economic Review*, 44 (1): 145–62.

Kravis, I. B., A. Heston and R. Summers (1982) *World Product and Income: International Comparisons of Real Gross Products* (Baltimore: Johns Hopkins University Press).

Samuelson, P. (1984) 'Second Thoughts on Analytical Income Comparisons', *Economic Journal*, 94 (June): 267–78.

Schultze, C. L. (2003) 'The Consumer Price Index: Conceptual Issues and Practical Suggestions', *Journal of Economic Perspectives*, 17 (1): 3–22.

Summers, R. and A. Heston (1991) 'The Penn World Table (Mark 5): An Expanded Set of International Comparisons, 1950–1988', *Quarterly Journal of Economics*, 106 (2): 327–68.

United Nations and Commission of the European Communities (UN and CEC) (1987) *World Comparisons of Purchasing Power and Real Product for 1980* (New York: UN).

United Nations Development Programme (UNDP) (1990–2003), *Human Development Reports* (New York: Oxford University Press).

Varian, H. R. (1983), 'Non-Parametric Tests of Consumer Behaviour', *Review of Economic Studies*, 50 (1): 99–110.

White, K. J. (1987) 'A General Computer Program for Econometric Methods – Shazam', *Econometrica*, 46 (1): 239–40.

4
Social and Political Indicators of Human Well-being

Susan Harkness

Introduction

Quality of life bears a complex relationship to a wide range of social and political indicators of development. Over recent years, the availability of data has increased appreciably in both the range and number of countries covered. In this chapter, I ask what contribution these indicators can make towards our understanding of human well-being. In so doing, the conceptualization of 'well-being' and development is discussed, and how these concepts may be applied to multidimensional approaches to welfare analysis. The issues surrounding the choice of indicator variables, data quality and availability are reviewed, before the interpretation of social indicators is discussed. I then look at issues surrounding aggregating and disaggregating social indicators, and review the literature on political indicators of well-being.

Conceptualizing human well-being and development

Since the 1990s, the United Nations Development Programme's *Human Development Reports* (hereafter UNDP and *HDR*) have argued that 'human development', and not economic growth, should be the objective of development policy. Indeed, it is now widely accepted that measures of income and poverty do not adequately measure human well-being. Instead income has increasingly become seen as a means towards achieving an end, rather than as an end in itself, and this has led to a substantial shift in emphasis in poverty analysis (see Dowrick, Chapter 3 this volume, for a further discussion of the limitations of using income as a measure of well-being). Instrumental to this shift have been the 'basic needs' approach, developed in the 1970s (Seers 1972, ILO 1976), and Sen's (1993a) 'capabilities' approach. The basic needs approach placed emphasis on the fact that the poor require access to certain basic goods and services, and that income may not be a necessary or sufficient condition for their provision. For Sen, on the other hand, development implied expanding the choices available to individuals, or their capabilities. As measurement of the capability space is problematic (as the set of choices available to individuals cannot be observed), Sen also distinguishes 'functionings' (or actual 'states of being and doings', such as being healthy) which can be measured. He suggests that the capabilities most essential for a good life are: adequate nourishment, leading a long and healthy life, literacy, and shelter. Other factors that influence the ability of individuals to participate in society – for example, gender or race – are also important determinants of capabilities.

The commonality of these approaches is their emphasis on the multi-dimensional nature of well-being. The UNDP's *HDR*s have attempted to quantify some of these non-monetary aspects of development. While these reports have been subject to considerable criticism by authors including Sen (1998) and Ravallion (1996b), they have helped focus attention on broader concepts of welfare. In particular, the development of composite indicators of development, such as the Human Development Index (HDI), has helped raise awareness of the multidimensional nature of poverty and have been instrumental in bringing non-income based measures of development to the fore of policy analysis. These increasingly multidimensional approaches to development have been mirrored in Europe, with concepts such as 'social exclusion' gaining increased credence since the 1990s. Atkinson (1998) identifies three key characteristics of social exclusion: relativity (i.e. exclusion occurs relative to some societal norm), agency (i.e. exclusion results from the actions of agents), and dynamics (i.e. future prospects are as relevant as current situation). While some have argued that this concept is of less relevance to developed countries (Saith 2001), its focus on identifying groups of the socially excluded and on the role of social circumstances in generating social exclusion is an area as yet little explored by development economists.

These developmental approaches all aim to improve human well-being, the ultimate goal of which is to maximize happiness or satisfaction. Yet each of these approaches to social development focuses on objective (or material) measures of living conditions and tend to ignore subjective measures of welfare (Anand and Ravallion 1993). More recent approaches to measuring well-being, particularly in developed countries, have taken improvements in happiness or satisfaction as the ultimate goal of economic development, and examined the correlations of economic and social factors with these measures. Easterlin's (1974) seminal paper showed that happiness varies little across countries, and that in the USA has increased little over time. This, he argues, suggests that subjective well-being does not increase with income but is, instead, dependent on individuals' relative economic position (Easterlin 1974, 2003). More recent studies link subjective measures of well-being to family status, health and social support, and employment (Berkman and Glass 2000, Blanchflower and Oswald 2000, Easterlin 2003). Sen (1993b, 1998) makes a similar point for developing countries. He notes that rates of morbidity (self-reported health status) are higher in the USA than those reported in the Indian state of Kerala, and concludes that high life expectancy and high morbidity move together and not in opposite directions. This, he suggests, is because well-being depends on 'positional objectivity'. A recent EU report on well-being by Berger-Schmitt and Noll (2000) concluded that subjective evaluations of well-being are 'dependent on the level of aspirations, and according to this approach do not represent appropriate criteria for guiding social policy which is considered as the primary function of welfare measurement' (see Veenhoven 2004 for a further discussion of these issues).

Application of multidimensional approaches to poverty

While multidimensional approaches to conceptualizing poverty have helped researchers understand the nature of poverty, attempts to make objective measurement of progress towards improving human development have been harder. The HDI, which is a weighted sum of three measures of deprivation (income, health and education), is perhaps the best known and most widely used aggregate indicator of well-being. While composite indexes provide a useful way of summarizing complex measures of development, they (and in particular the HDI) have been subject to considerable criticism (see, for example, Sen 1997 and Kanbur 2002). It has been argued that the index is conceptually weak (Srinivasan 1994), that interpretation of these indicators is unclear, that the aggregation of disparate measures of development does not lead to a meaningful index, and that the choice of components and weights attached to these components is value laden. How, for example, should a change in the index be interpreted if it rises because one indicator has gone up and another down? Are cross-country or time-series comparisons meaningful? Alternative approaches to poverty, and in particular analysis of chronic poverty in develope countries, and of 'social exclusion' in developed countries, have used multidimensional indicators of development to assess poverty using 'union' and 'intersection' approaches. 'Union' measures of poverty define an individual as poor where they fall below some critical threshold in *any* of the measured dimensions of poverty, while 'intersection' measures define poverty on the basis of a some combination of well-being scores (Atkinson *et al.* 2002). For Hulme *et al.* (2001), such an approach is particularly important; as it is the multidimensional nature of poverty typically experienced by the chronically poor that prevents their escape.

Numerous studies have examined specific indexes of well-being. Choice of individual indicator variables, measurement and interpretation are discussed in more detail in the following section. The basic needs literature suggests that well-being may be conceptualized within a production function framework describing this relationship between inputs and outputs (see Streeten 1981 and Fei *et al.* 1985). Following from this, Dasgupta (1990) suggests categorization of indicator variables into 'input' and 'output' measures of well-being. He suggests that the basic needs approach may be perceived as a production process, with the consumption of commodities, including nutrition, clean water and medicine, health facilities and education, being perceived as inputs, while outputs measure the 'achievement of vital interests of people', such as adult literacy rates, infant and child survival rates, and life expectancy. These output measures should, he argues, be conceived of as a different class of social indicator from those measuring inputs. Dasgupta, as Sen, also places importance on the 'environment of the production process which converts commodity inputs into outputs'. The extent to which people are able to play an active and critical role in the choice of leaders, are able to express opinions, to be protected from abuse and other environmental factors are, he argues, crucial in shaping individual well-being.

Sen's capability approach has been criticized on the grounds that it does little to enable comparative analysis. While Sen distinguishes between 'functionings' and 'capabilities', it is capabilities, rather than functionings that relate to concepts of well-being. Srinivasan (1994a) suggests that the importance of Sen's approach for applied analysis of well-being is limited, and reports Sudgen's critique of Sen:

> Given the rich array of functioning that Sen takes to be relevant, given the extent of disagreement among reasonable people about the nature of the good life, and given the unresolved problem of how to value sets, it is natural to ask how far Sen's framework is operational. Is it a realistic alternative to the methods on which economists typically rely – measurements of real income, and the kind of practical cost-benefit analysis which is grounded in Marshallian consumer theory? (Sugden 1993: 1,953, reported in Srinivasan 1994a: 239)

While Srinivasan suggests that income may be as good a measure of well-being as any alternative, Anand and Ravallion argue that this is in fact an empirical question:

> if only a weak link exists between 'income poverty' and 'capabilities', relative to other factors, then the human development approach would clearly imply less emphasis on private incomes, except insofar as growth facilitates the financing of public support. On the other hand, if private incomes are a powerful instrument for expanding capabilities, then a focus on income poverty may be justified from either perspective. An empirical question needs to be addressed fully before an assessment can be made of the policy implications of the human development approach. (1993: 137)

The empirical evidence does not, however, lead to a conclusive answer. Ravallion notes that although several studies have used household or individual data to look at the relationship between income and health or educational outcomes, the 'methodologies and data used have differed greatly among these studies'. The results from these studies have been inconclusive; some have found income to improve health and educational outcomes while others have found little or no effect. The results on public spending are similarly inconclusive (Anand and Ravallion 1993: 137) Nor is it clear that other indicators of well-being are well correlated; indeed, as Ravallion (1997) emphasizes, non-income measures of well-being, although showing 'considerable congruence' are 'not so congruent that any of them will do'. He therefore argues that there is a need to retain a focus on individual indicators of well-being. Other studies, such as those of Atkinson and Bourguignon (1982) and Laderchi *et al.* (2003), also suggest that a lack of overlap between multidimensional indicators of deprivation is common; and, in the context of examining social exclusion in Europe, Atkinson (2002b) concludes that there is no justification for placing primacy on one indicator over another.[1] A similar conclusion is drawn by Saith and Harriss-White (1998), who argue that the way in which the problem of human well-being is conceptualized is instrumental in shaping the choice of indicator because the 'considerable lack of overlap' between them means that targeting based on one indicator will mean serious mistargeting on others.

For developing countries, the Millennium Development Goals (MDGs) have been accepted as a gauge for measuring progress towards achieving human development. Many of these goals are compatible with Sen's 'functioning approach' to well-being, which suggests that the minimum requirements for individuals to function are that individuals should be healthy, educated, and nourished. The MDGs' targets and the indicator variables used to assess progress towards these goals are reported in Table 4.1. Of the eight goals, the first six in particular have substantial bearing on the debate on human well-being.[2] For each of the goals, targets have been set for achievement by 2015 based on a set of indicator variables.[3] While the goals have been ratified by the 189 member states of the United Nations, the choice of indicator variables remains the subject of debate. The Task Force on Education and Gender Equality, for example, has criticized the use of enrolment data rather than school completion rates as an indicator of educational attainment[4] because they believe this to be a more appropriate indicator of educational 'output'. Other indicators, such as literacy, have been criticized on the grounds of the poor quality of data availability. Issues concerning the choice of indicator variables, data availability, quality, and comparability are explored in greater detail in the following section.

Table 4.1 The Millennium Development Goals, targets and indicators

Goals	Targets	Indicators
1 Eradicate extreme poverty and hunger		
Poverty	Halve between 1990 and 2015 the proportion of people with income below $1 a day	Proportion of population below $1 per day (PPP values) Poverty gap ratio (incidence*depth) Share of poorest quintile in consumption
Hunger	Halve between 1990 and 2015 the proportion of people who suffer from hunger	Proportion of underweight children (under 5s) Proportion population with inadequate energy intake
2 Universal Primary Education		
	Ensure universal primary schooling for boys and girls by 2015	Net enrolment ratio in primary school Proportion pupils starting grade 1 reaching grade 5 Literacy rate of 15–24 year olds
3 Promote gender equality and empower women		
	Eliminate gender inequality in education	Ratio of girls to boys in primary, secondary and tertiary education Ratio of literate females to males 15–24 years Share of women in wage work in nonagricultural sector Proportion of seats held by women in national parliament
4 Reduce child mortality		
	Reduce the under-5s mortality rate by two thirds by 2015	Under-5s mortality rate Infant mortality rate Proportion of one year olds immunized against measles
5 Improve maternal health		
	Reduce by three-quarters maternal mortality ratio by 2015	Maternal mortality ratio Proportion of births attended by skilled health personnel
6 Combat HIV/AIDS, malaria and other diseases		
HIV/AIDS	Halt and reverse spread of HIV/AIDS	HIV prevalence among 15–24 year old pregnant women Condom use rate of contraceptive prevalence rate Number of children orphaned by HIV/AIDS
Malaria and other diseases	Reverse incidence of malaria and other major diseases	Prevalence and death rate of malaria Proportion of population using effective malaria prevention and treatment measures

Table 4.1 (Continued)

Goals	Targets	Indicators
		Prevalence and death rate from TB Proportion TB cases detected and cured under Directly Observed Treatment Short Course
7 Ensure environmental sustainability		
	Integrate principles of sustainable development into country policies and programmes and reverse the loss of environmental resources	Change in land area covered by forest Ratio of area protected to retain land area diversity Energy use per $1 GDP Carbon dioxide emissions and consumption of ozone depleting CFCs Proportion of population using solid fuels
	Halve by 2015 the proportion of people without sustainable access to safe drinking water	Share population with sustainable access to an improved water source
	Achieve by 2020 significant improvement in the lives of at least 100 million slum dwellers	Proportion of population with access to improved sanitation Proportion of population with access to secure tenure
8 Develop a global partnership for development		

Source: http://www.developmentgoals.org/About_the_goals.htm

Measuring well-being: data availability, data quality and the choice of indicator variables

Over the last decade there have been vast improvements in the quality of data available for developing countries on multidimensional indicators of well-being. In particular, the increased availability of large scale microeconomic datasets, such as the Living Standards Measurement Surveys (LSMS), which record indicators of social well-being, have considerably improved the potential for conducting high quality empirical research on developing countries. However, considerable data limitations remain particularly where researchers want to conduct comparative research either across countries or within countries over time. Ravallion (1996a), Bidani and Ravallion (1997) and Loup *et al.* (2000) all discuss in depth the data constraints that exist in applying multidimensional approaches to poverty analysis. Data problems arise both in terms of data availability and data quality. Table 4.2

Table 4.2 Data coverage for core development indicators (1990–95)

	Number of countries with data (out of 171)	Proportion of countries with data (out of 171)	Percentage of population represented
Economic well-being			
1 Incidence of extreme poverty: population below $1 per day	59	35	79
2 Poverty gap ratio: incidence times depth of income poverty	51	30	72
3 Inequality: poorest fifth's share of national consumption	74	43	85
4 Child malnutrition: prevalence of underweight under-5s	117	68	93
Social development			
Universal primary education			
5 Net enrolment in primary education	102	60	61
6 Completion of fourth grade primary education	101	59	79
7 Literacy rate of 15–24 year-olds	77	45	84
Gender equality			
8 Ratio of girls to boys in primary and secondary education.	126	74	87
9 Ratio of literate females to males (15–24 year-olds)	77	45	84
Infant and child mortality			
10 Infant mortality ratio	126	74	87
11 Under-5 mortality rate	77	45	84
Maternal mortality rate			
12 Maternal mortality ratio	162	95	100
13 Births attended by skilled health professionals	163	95	100
Reproductive health			
14 Contraceptive prevalence rate	159	93	99
15 HIV prevalence in 15–24 year-old pregnant women	124	73	98

Source: Hammond (1998).

summarizes the availability of key indicators of development from 1990–95, as reported by Loup *et al.* (2000). While this table reveals that considerable data gaps exist, these problems are even greater when it is considered that data is most frequently missing for the poorest counties. Data coverage for the world's poor is therefore considerably worse than suggested by this table.

Even more problematic for comparative research is the issue of data quality. As Srinivasan (1994a) has noted, for many countries data collected on key social indicators is old, measurement biases and errors abound, many indicators are estimated, and data is often incomparable both over time within countries and at a point in time across countries.[5] Even within official international organizations publications inaccuracies and inconsistencies in the data abound. As Loup *et al.* note, quoting from the 'Africa Poverty Status Report' (1999), prepared for the SPA Working Group on Social Policy:

> different numbers can be given for the same series. Maternal mortality, which for Ghana jumped from 400 to 1,000 from one issue of the *World Development Report* to the next, is often mentioned in this regard. Mauldin (1994) showed that, although they both used the same source, the WDR reported from 56 developing countries and the *HDR* for 55 of these, and a further 48. Counting differences of less than 50 points as the same, *HDR* gave higher values than the WDR for 26 countries, lower for 12 and about the same for 17. Some differences are substantial e.g.; Benin at 800 and 161, Mali at 850 and 2,325 and Malaysia at 120 and 26. The correlation coefficient between the two sets of figures is only 0.7, dropping to only 0.4 for high mortality countries. (Loup *et al.* 2000: 13)

In spite of these weaknesses the data recorded in official publications is commonly used to monitor developmental goals and to evaluate policies.[6] Several authors have argued that there is an urgent need to improve the data collection capabilities of countries, that weaknesses in reported data should be more clearly noted, and that where data is weak either conceptually because of wide differences in definitions or because data availability is poor and based on projections it should be omitted from the tables. Although the UN has recently made an attempt at standardizing concepts and methods of data collection, as Loup *et al.* note:

> There are currently no international methodological norms in the area of human development statistics (except possibly the DHS methodology for health and population surveys and the LSMS for surveys on living standards). In this regard the situation differs greatly from most other statistical fields, where such norms exist. One can mention, for instance, the UN methodology for national accounts, the GDDS and SDDS standards of the IMF for financial and economic statistics or the EUROTRACE method for external trade statistics, among others.
>
> In spite of this gap, there is at present to our knowledge no attempt to initiate work in this direction. This appears paradoxical given the high priority now given to human development statistics as well as the existing problems of data quality and comparability. (Loup *et al.* 2000: 50)

The last decade has also seen a rapid increase in the availability of microeconomic household datasets for developing countries. However, Ravallion (1996a) notes that common data problems for research and policy application are 'lack of survey integration (some surveys get health data, some get incomes, but fewer get both)' and 'too small a sample to capture low-frequency events (such as infant death)' (Bidani and Ravallion 1997). Moreover, in the past difficulties have arisen in making cross-country comparisons because data across developing countries has varied widely in terms of sampling and information collected, leading to varying conclusions about relationships between variables and limiting the generality of conclusions that can be drawn.

Even among high quality micro data sets problems of comparability remain. Strauss and Thomas (1996) compare actual and measured heights of children recorded in the United States' National Longitudinal Survey of Children and Mothers (NLSCM) and conclude that 'reported height of children is prone to systematic errors that render it of questionable value even in a high-quality socio-economic survey conducted in a well-educated society, like the NLSCM in the United States'. The problems of cost effective collection of socioeconomic data therefore remain large. Note, however, that the collection of income data is not in itself unproblematic. Fields (1994) has criticized the use of inappropriate and inconsistent data for analysis of income, inequality and poverty. He suggests that three criteria should exist for data admissibility; (i) data should come from actual household survey or census data, (ii) it should be national in coverage, and (iii) for comparisons over time the income concept (whether income or expenditure) and recipient unit (household, individual or per capita) must be constant. In the context of income distribution data, Fields suggests that of 70 countries with income distribution estimates, half fail to meet these minimum criteria. Moreover, estimates such as GDP/capita exclude the valuation of home production and do not account for differences in needs. Such limitations of income based measures of well-being are discussed further by Dowrick in Chapter 3 of this volume. The rest of this section details the problems attached to demographic, health, and education indicators of development and then goes on to review recent data developments.

Health and demographic data

Sen (1998) has argued that mortality data is a key indicator of human well-being because life has 'intrinsic value' (a longer life is desirable in own right), 'enabling significance' (as life necessary to function), and 'associative significance' (as life expectancy is linked with other aspects of welfare). Dowrick (Chapter 3, this volume) discusses the relationship between life expectancy, well-being and income in greater detail. However, as Chamie (1994) has noted, international data on life expectancy is particularly weak with the data required for estimating life expectancy at birth being available for only 30 out of 117 less developed countries. Moreover, mortality data is most likely to be missing in countries where mortality is highest, and for these countries where vital registration is absent (80 per cent of African and

Asian nations) mortality rates have to be estimated from other sources. While the information available on infant mortality rates is better, substantial gaps in the data exist, particularly for African countries where data is missing for around 30 per cent of countries. It is Chamie's conclusion that 'the repackaging of population data has greatly increased, and as a consequence, confusion regarding the original source and nature of the data has become widespread among users' (Chamie 1994: 145). While less concerned with data quality, Sen (1998) and Saith and Harriss-White (1998) have called for information of life expectancy to be disaggregated and for age specific life expectancies to be recorded.

Most recently, authors of the 'Task Force on Child Health and Maternal Health' have suggested that the maternal mortality ratio, one of the key indicators for achievement of the MDGs, is very hard to measure. They suggest that even in the USA maternal death rates are underreported by as much as 50 per cent, while in many LDCs a 'sisterhood method' of recording maternal death (which asks interviewees to recall deaths over the last 10–12 years) is even more unreliable (Freedman *et al.* 2003). In the 2002 *HDR*, maternal mortality rates were reported for only 27 out of 36 low human development countries. As an indicator variable for measuring progress towards achieving the MDGs, therefore, this indicator is weak. The number of births attended by skilled health professionals has therefore been included as a proxy for maternal deaths. However, this variable too is the subject of some criticism: Srinivasan (1994b) suggests that there are differences in defining health professionals, while Freedman *et al.* (2003) note that such indicators are subject to disintermediation because once countries know which statistic is to be used for measuring development progress, resources may be shifted towards achieving these goals (for example, if the number of health professionals attending births is monitored, resources may be diverted towards achieving this goal at the expense of other areas of the health system, even though these areas may also have a substantial impact on maternal mortality rates).

Other indicators of health and well-being include data on morbidity, nutritional intake and anthropometric measures of health status. Morbidity data, because of the subjective nature of the data, has been subject to considerable criticism with several authors suggesting that such data is useless of policy analysis.[7] The use of nutritional intake data, one of the key MDG indicator variables, has also been subject to considerable attack. Authors such as Ravallion (1994) have argued that the use of nutritional data as a measure of developmental outcomes is conceptually flawed because of its focus on consumption rather than outcomes. This, he argues, has led to problems with studies on the impact of income on nutrition finding conflicting results.[8] Moreover, Srinivasan (1994a) is critical of the data used to measure consumption, and in particular argues that collecting data on calorie intake over a short time period is inappropriate as it is long term nutritional intake that effects well-being. Conceptual flaws and shortcomings in measurement are therefore argued to limit the value of data on nutritional status as an indicator of development. Measures of outcomes are seen as conceptually superior to data on food intake and have led more recent studies, such as that of Micklewright and Ismail (2001), to focus on anthropometric measures of outcomes. While the interpretation of adult indicators well-being, such as Body Mass Indexes and height, are subject to criticism because genetic factors may have an impact on the data, indicator variables measuring children's health status are accepted as conceptually appropriate measures of well-being. However, the criticisms of Strauss and Thomas (1996) on errors in measurement on self-reported data on child height suggest that cost effective collection of anthropometric data remains.

Education data

Attainment of universal primary education is a key target of the MDGs. The three indicators selected to monitor progress towards attainment of this goal are: (i) net enrolment in primary school, (ii) proportion of pupils reaching grade 5, and (iii) literacy rate of 15–24 year olds. Most analysts concur that educational 'flow' variables are more informative measures of progress towards attaining human development than assessments of 'stocks'. The Task Force on Education and Gender Equality moreover concurs with the focus of the MDG on the completion of primary schooling (as defined by World Bank). The quality of data on literacy is generally thought to be poor. Grown *et al.* (2003) point out that there is no universal meaning of literacy,[9] that many countries are unable to provide even basic information on literacy. Behrman and Ronsenzweig (1994) note that much of the data on literacy is very old: that 1991 data on literacy is based on data from the 1970s for 60 out of 145 countries. While the accuracy of enrolment data may be better, differences in quality of schooling, dropout rates and so on may mean inconsistencies in measurement remain. Moreover, as enrolment data is a measure of inputs into the educational process, it is often regarded as a poorer indicator variable than school completion rates. However, the 2002 *HDR* records data on completion rates for just 11 out of 36 countries with low human development.

Developments in data collection, reporting and analysis

While the quality of development data has been subject to considerable criticism, there have been considerable efforts to improve the quality of data over recent decades. From the mid-1980s there has been a significant increase in the availability of comparable large scale microeconomic data sets for developing countries, in part thanks to the development of LSMS data sets. These data sets are household surveys which include detailed information on welfare, including data on consumption, income savings, employment, health, education, fertility, nutrition, housing and migration

(Grosh and Glewwe 1996). Currently, LSMS data is available for 40 countries, about half of which are for Eastern European countries. Kanbur (2002) notes that in spite of these data improvements, there are still many countries for which data does not exist or is dated. Moreover, sample sizes in the LSMS are variable, with sample sizes being as small as 780 households in the Chinese survey, and smaller than 2000 households in several of the other surveys.

There have also been changes in the availability and reporting of aggregate data. In particular, in the 2002 *HDR* 'the indicator tables have been streamlined to focus on indicators that are most reliable, meaningful and comparable across countries' (UNDP 2002: 141). The process has reduced the number of indicator tables, removing some tables altogether and consolidating others.

Meanwhile, data availability for other indicators has improved, with new surveys on literacy and crime meaning that comparable data should soon be available in future editions. Yet, the 2002 *HDR* notes that: 'despite these strides in measuring human development, many gaps and problems remain. Sufficient and reliable data are still lacking in many areas of human development. Gaps throughout the tables demonstrate the pressing need for improvements in both the quantity and quality of human development statistics' (UNDP 2002: 143). In particular, they note that in 2002 there were 29 countries excluded from the main indicator tables, reducing the total number of countries for which data is available by 12 over a period of just one year, so that data for only 162 countries was recorded.

Authors such as Srinivasan have painted a gloomy picture of the quality of data available on social indicators of development. Srinivasan argues that unreliable and biased data could seriously distort analyses and policy conclusions. Poor data quality is not exclusive to the analysis of developing countries, and other authors such as Atkinson (2002a) and Griliches (1986) have examined the importance of the quality of data to econometric research. Atkinson examines ways in which economists have chosen to deal with data deficiencies, and in particular examines the views that (i) 'the quality of the data does not matter', (ii) 'the data are not that bad' and (iii) 'we have learned to adjust for data deficiencies'. He concludes respectively that (i) the quality of data does matter and should be examined carefully to assess 'fitness for purpose' before it is used, (ii) while data is improving, there remains considerable room for improvement,[10] and (iii) that while economists are getting better at dealing with data deficiencies, more investment is needed in this area.[11] Atkinson (2002a: 25) concludes that:

> in my view we need a constructive approach to the very real problems of data deficiencies. We should not ignore them, nor should we paint a picture of total disaster. But to make further progress, issues of data quality should be higher in the priorities of the economics profession.

Ravallion (1996a) reaches a similar conclusion to Atkinson, arguing, 'closer scrutiny of sampling and survey methods is needed'. While, clearly, good data are highly desirable for informing policy, in reality data inadequacies are common. Ravallion continues, 'measurement errors can have profound implications for empirical poverty analysis'. Although methods of dealing with error, such as the construction of dominance tests to assess the robustness of poverty comparisons to certain structures of measurement errors, have improved, he notes that obtaining a robust ordering for poverty identification may be elusive. Cowell and Victoria-Feser (1998) have also proposed advances in methods for dealing with data problems, such as 'trimming' and data censoring or truncation. Ravallion (1996a) has also argued that the methods used to correct for measurement errors are rarely tested. He suggests that experiments to test the robustness of the data and the conclusions drawn should be implemented. While such improvements clearly improve the quality of research findings available to us, Ravallion concludes, 'substituting method for data is a long way from being perfect'. Srinivasan (1994a) and Atkinson (2002a) have also made similar points about the importance of checking the robustness of data by checking it against other sources.

Authors such as Atkinson (2002a) and Srinivasan (1994a) have called for greater transparency and discussion of the limitations of the data available. One further way in which the debate could be moved forward would be to pay greater attention to the *precision* of the indicators available. As Ravallion (1996a: 1339) notes, 'current practice in poverty analysis typically ignore the statistical imprecision of the measures used', yet for many of the indicators available, computations of standard errors would be a relatively straightforward process (particularly where data are obtained form household survey data). The inclusion of standard errors would allow analysts to be more confident in attaching rankings to countries for individual indicators, and would also guide policy makers by helping focus greater attention on variables whose values are relatively certain.

Interpreting social indicators

While studies abound on the relationship between individual indicators of human development, and income and economic growth, the relationship between other indicators of well-being are less well understood. The 1993 *HDR* reported very high correlations between HDI indicators, but goes on to argue that there is no automatic link between GNP and human development. Ravallion (1997) has argued that the *HDR*s pay too much attention to trying to explain outliers (such as Sri Lanka, which has high life expectancy and low income although, on average, life expectancy increases with income). Ravallion (1994) points out that those countries with high per capita income tend to do better on social indicators of development. His 1994 study therefore aims to 'inquire as to whether the fact that richer countries tend to have better social indicators implies that economic growth should be centre stage in discussions of how to promote human development'. However, if 'social expenditures and the reduction in income poverty are the main forces driving human development, rather than economic growth per se, then policy intervention can play a role in promoting human development independently of the promotion of aggregate influence' (1994: 144). He finds that the impact of economic growth on life expectancy and infant mortality depends on the way that the benefits from growth are distributed across people, in particular on the extent to which it leads to a reduction in poverty and its impact on raising public health expenditures. Similar findings are reported in Anand and Kanbur (1991) and Anand and Ravallion (1993). One caveat he notes, however, relates to causality: it may be that improved health and reduced income inequality has led to improved economic growth. Bruno *et al.* (1996) support this evidence, suggesting that the higher income inequality, the smaller the impact of economic growth on human development.

The impact of growth on other social indicators of development is also examined by other studies. Laderchi (1999) finds that in Peru factors other than money income affect individuals' outcomes, and she argues that this challenges the assumption of a correlation between income and other indicators of development. She calls for greater direct action to effect social development, including public spending for the weakest groups. Laderchi *et al.* (2003) suggest that microeconomic studies of Indian and Peruvian data show that the overlap between capabilities and monetary measures of poverty are limited, with large proportions of the population being capability poor but not monetarily poor, and vice versa.

Sen (1998) suggests that longer life expectancy is associated with improved adult literacy, female education, and lower fertility rates. This is illustrated by the following rank correlations for 'low income' and 'lower middle income' countries with life expectancy: total adult literacy, 0.88; female adult literacy, 0.82; lowness of birth rate, 0.88; lowness of fertility rate, 0.89; and 0.95 with the HDI. As mortality is influenced by the availability of health care, the nature of medical insurance, as well as the availability of social services including basic education, the 'orderliness of urban living' and 'access to modern medical knowledge in rural communities' he also suggests that analysis of mortality data can draw attention to these policy issues. Sen's analysis shows that while mortality rates are correlated with economic growth, economic growth is not the only cause of falling mortality. He illustrates these points with examples from the USA and UK. In the UK, he reports that age specific death rates fell rapidly over the decade of the Second World War in spite of a decline in total food supply per head. He argues that this was because of an increase in the public delivery of food, which led to a decline in the incidence of severe undernutrition.[12] On the other hand, in the USA age specific mortality rates among blacks have fallen behind those in many LDCs in terms of survival to old age, and Sen identifies lack of national medical coverage as part of the reason for this.

There is also a large literature suggesting that the relationship between health and income works in the opposite direction (see Ranis *et al.* 2000, for a review). Dasgupta (1997) provides a review of studies that relate nutritional intake and anthropometric measures of health status to wages and income. Some of these studies have suggested that the link between income and food expenditure is weak (Behrman and Deolalikar 1987, Subramanian and Deaton 1996), and hence dispute Dasgupta's thesis that nutrition is linked to wages (via 'efficiency wages'). However, Dasgupta (1997) argues that timing is central to this result and finds that malnutrition, especially in early childhood, scars and that this leads to lower adult wages.

Sen (1997) argues that capability expansion not only has a direct impact on well-being, but may also raise productivity (by expanding human capital), and encourage social development. The expansion of educational opportunities for girls in particular is correlated with reduced gender inequalities, declining fertility rates, and reductions in child mortality. Such associations are also noted by Levine *et al.* (2003) who note that child health and educational outcomes are related, while mothers' education is associated with improvements in child health and child nutrition.

Aggregation, disparities and dynamics

Aggregate and individual level data

Social indicators are typically used for one of two purposes, to *identify* those in need, or to provide an *aggregate* indicator of a country's development progress. The MDGs, for example, use aggregate indicators as means of measuring the progress of countries towards attaining human development. Construction of a single index of development may, in this context, be neither appropriate nor possible. Ravallion (1996a: 1340) argues that 'implementing a genuinely multi-dimensional approach will often make the welfare rankings of social states . . . more difficult, but that fact points to the non-robustness of low dimensional rankings, and it may also have important policy implication in its own right, given that there can be some degree of correspondence between policy instruments and welfare objectives'. He argues that the complexity of the relationships between variables, and their dynamics, however, offer a new line of attack on poverty and escape routes. Where researchers care about *identifying* needy groups, however, the ability to rank observations[13] according to need is important for targeting. Multiple indicator frameworks, which allow the assignment of ranks to families using multidimensional measures of poverty, have been suggested for targeting (see Abul Naga 1994).

Ravallion (1994) has drawn a distinction between the findings of research using nutritional data at an aggregate rather than individual level. Ravallion suggests that studies that have looked at the relationship between consumption and income have found conflicting results, in part because they are looking at the wrong indicator variable (inputs rather than outcomes).[14] Ravallion reports however that *aggregate* undernutrition (i.e. the number of individuals with nutritional intake below requirement) is very responsive to income gains.

> In Indonesia reasonable measures of aggregate undernutrition . . . have been found to respond quite strongly to income gains, even though intakes at the individual level show relatively small responses. (1994: 138)

The work of Micklewright and Ismail (2001) suggests a similar conclusion. They argue that average measures of child anthropometry may provide a useful guide for the allocation of government funds at a regional level. However, at an individual level they provide a poor guide for targeting as 'genetic source of variation in body size implies that this would result in substantial errors of both inclusion and exclusion (although the same is true of other imperfect measures of well-being)'.

Disparities

Aggregate indicators of social development may mask large disparities by gender, region, racial group, rural/urban areas or between the rich and poor. The 1993 *HDR* notes that making adjustments for gender has a large impact on the HDI ranking of countries. Similarly, adjusting for inequality can have a large impact (for Brazil they report that adjusting for inequality reduces the HDI by 14 per cent). However, as Ravallion (1997) notes, although most indicators can now be relatively easily adjusted for inequality, most are not.

Gender differences in social indicators have been extensively researched (see Sen 1997, Saith and Harriss-White 1998). Achieving a reduction in gender inequality is a priority of the MDGs, and this is reflected in the relatively good availability of disaggregated social indicators of development by gender. However, less attention is paid to other aspects of disparity, including racial and regional differences. One reason for this may be that disaggregation of data is difficult for different population sub-groups. This may arise because only aggregated data is available, or because the information required for disaggregation is only available in disparate data sets. Where data availability is poor, Bidani and Ravallion (1997) suggest decomposing socioeconomic indicators, using information on the distribution of the population across sub-groups, to arrive at estimates for different socioeconomic groups. However, he goes on to add that the accuracy of sub-group decompositions will depend on the extent to which other relevant variables (correlated with sub-groups shares) have been controlled for. Bidani and Ravallion suggest a model that disaggregates health indicators for the poor and non-poor. They find that life expectancy of the poor[15] is nine years lower than that for the non-poor, and that infant mortality is 50 per cent higher. Moreover, their results suggest important implications for policy, as they find that social spending has a differential effect on these two groups, with social spending having a smaller impact on the health of the non-poor who are better placed to substitute public for private spending.

Finally, while significant attention has been paid to gender differences in social indicators, less attention has been paid to the welfare of children. Children are rarely used as a unit of analysis, and while child health and education data are commonly recorded, these data are generally regarded as an inadequate measure of well-being (Ben-Arieh *et al.* 2001). Moreover, the tendency to regard child literacy rates as a 'flow' variable suggests that the fact that the data recorded for children is incidental. In assessing the well-being of children, it is also useful to ask whether the conceptualization of child well-being should differ from that of adults. In particular, the importance of childhood poverty and malnutrition to adult outcomes (or 'scarring') suggest that a separate analysis of the processes of poverty is warranted.

The current focus of social indicators in developing countries has been at the level of the individual (looking at nutritional intake, measures of health, education, employment and income), household (examining income, assets, fertility), and community (reporting data on crime, drugs, infrastructure and services, community and planning, governance). More recent indicators also include dimensions such as social cohesion, social exclusion, social capital and human development and sustainability.

Chronic poverty and income dynamics

A common criticism of static indicators of well-being is that they do little to distinguish between those who are transiently poor and chronically (or persistently) poor. Yet, distinguishing the chronically poor is critical for targeting assistance to the most needy. As Saith (2001) notes, time has been seen as an increasingly important dimension of poverty within Europe, with policy initiatives increasingly focusing on long-term unemployment and those facing recurring poverty. However, cross-sectional data can do little to help our understanding of chronic poverty, and dynamic approaches to the analysis requiring panel data are increasingly called for. For Hulme *et al.* (2001), such an approach is particularly important, as it is the multidimensional nature of poverty typically experienced by the chronically poor that prevents their escape. According to Hulme *et al.*, chronic poverty is most common among the young, the old, those facing discrimination (minorities), and those with health problems, and their work suggests that these matters should be the subjects of policy focus. Baulch and Masset (2002) find that monetary poverty is less persistent than malnutrition among children and school enrolment among children. Such findings may suggest that, in the absence of panel data, there may be some classes of non-monetary indicators of poverty that perform better at targeting the chronically poor than others.

The increasing availability of panel data in developing countries also presents opportunities for future analysis of poverty dynamics, and will allow improvements in the identification of periods of risk when individuals may be at particular risk of falling into poverty. In developed countries, life course events, such as births, deaths, divorce and changes in health, have been identified as particular times of risk. Improvements in the quality of data available may help identify further risk factors.

Political indicators of development

Political and civil rights have a fundamental impact on individuals' well-being. As Sen has argued, the ability of people to play an active and critical role in their choice of leaders, to express opinions, and to be protected from abuse and other environmental factors is critical in shaping welfare. Indeed, Sen (1999) has gone so far as to claim that the spread of democracy has been the greatest achievement of twentieth century. Recent *HDR*s have also taken increasing note of the impact of freedom and participation on well-being. In the 2002 report, they argue that democracies improve economic and social well-being by increasing accountability and political participation, and expanding the choices available to individuals. Where women have no access to the vote, for example, they argue that the choices available to them are restricted and their well-being reduced. Sen, who argues that a famine has never occurred in a democratic country with a free press and regular elections, has also noted the protective power of democracy.

The construction of political indicators of development is, however, fraught with difficulties. The 2002 *HDR* notes that the problem with attempting to construct such an indicator lies in the fact that there is no unambiguous, uncontroversial measure of political and civil rights. The 2002 *HDR* reports a range of subjective and objective measures of political rights. These include indexes on civil liberties, political rights, press freedom, voice and accountability, political stability and lack of violence, law and order, rule of law, government effectiveness, and corruption. The objective indicators included are the years of the last election timing, voter turn out, the year that women got the right to vote, the share of seats held by women in parliament, trade union membership, and the ratification of rights instruments. However, it also goes on to note that:

> Truly democratic governance requires widespread substantive participation – and accountability of people holding power. Objective measures fail to capture such concepts. Subjective measures should, in principle, capture more of what is meant by the concept of democracy. But being subjective, they are open to disagreement and perception biases. (UNDP 2002: 36)

The 1992 *HDR* had also introduced a freedom index, which was subsequently abandoned because the index was based on judgements and was not therefore quantitatively verifiable. It was also concluded that summarizing complex issues into single statistics did not help improve understanding of the sources of inter-country differences in indexes, or help explain their change. The disaggregated nature of the subjective data presented in the 2002 report appears to represent some improvement. It should be noted, however, that data on human rights abuses and other restrictions on freedoms are not reliably recorded. This, together with problems of measurement, leads the *HDR* to conclude that an exclusive focus on quantitative measure of political freedom should not be relied on.

Dasgupta (1990) notes that political rights (the right to participate in the governance of a country) and civil rights (press freedom and judicial independence) are rare in poor countries. He goes on to note that there is a 'temptation to suggest that very poor countries cannot afford the luxury of political and civil rights'. Dasgupta argues these rights are not however luxuries, but crucial in shaping the environment in which people live. He reports that political and civil liberties are positively and significantly correlated with per capita income and its growth, with improvements in infant survival rates and increases in life expectancy. In a later study, Dasgupta and Weale (1992) find similar correlations for the world's poorest countries. These studies however note the important caveat that correlation does not imply causality. Levine and Renelt (1992) test the robustness of the cross-country statistical relationship between long-run average growth, and find that the link between it and 'every other policy indicator' is fragile, with small changes in one explanatory variable overturning past results. They find that indexes of political stability are not robust in determining growth. The conclusions of the 2002 *HDR* are more muted, arguing that 'statistical studies find that neither authoritarianism nor democracy is a factor in determining either the rate of economic growth or how it is distributed' (UNDP 2002: 4), which they suggest challenges the assumption that there is a trade-off between economic and political rights.

Conclusion

The last decade has seen multidimensional indicators of welfare taking increasing precedence over monetary measures of welfare. This shift in focus has been accompanied by greatly improved efforts to collect and monitor socioeconomic data. However, substantial challenges for the future remain in terms of both conceptual development, and data collection and analysis. Kanbur (2002) has argued that while alternative measures of well-being are increasingly being analyzed, they are being examined separately, one-by-one, often within country-specific settings. This increasing micro-economic approach to data analysis leaves development economists with limited scope to draw generalized conclusions. Kanbur concludes that the primary conceptual challenge for the future will be to develop an overall framework for dealing with multidimensional indicators of poverty. Chapter 5 of this volume discusses recent developments in this area. However, it may also be argued that attempting to unite data into a single policy goal may be inappropriate. Instead, increasing micro management of targets within countries, and of specific rather than general targets, may be a more appropriate policy response.

Assessing the conceptual appropriateness and improving comparability of socioeconomic data are further key areas for future development. In particular, the purpose for which data are being collected needs to be made clear, and a distinction should be made between the data needs for aggregate reporting and those for identification of the poor. The data needs for these two purposes may be quite different. For aggregate data, the *HDR* 2000 notes 'neither governments nor the public can wait 20 years to find out whether policies have promoted human development and helped realize human rights'. In order to assess policy impact, therefore, socioeconomic indicators must be responsive to policy change and be up-to-date. Thus, focal indicator variables should be sensitive and quick to respond to policy change, allowing economic policies to be adjusted appropriately over time. As Sen's (1998) study has shown, this does not mean that indicators should be ruled out too quickly. He shows that although life expectancy may have been predicted to respond slowly to policy change (in the absence of famine or disaster), in Russia life expectancy declined dramatically from 1989 as the availability of medical and health facilities, and the social security system declined.

This chapter has also outlined some of the weaknesses in currently reported data. Authors including Atkinson (2002a) and Srinivasan (1994a) have called for greater transparency and discussion of the limitations of the data, and the most recent *HDR*s have responded to some of these criticisms by deleting from the reports some of the less reliable data. Improved international protocols for data collection, as argued for by Loup *et al.* would allow greater clarity in international comparisons. One further way in which the debate could be moved forward would be to pay greater attention to the *precision* of indicators. The reporting of standard errors would allow analysts to be more confident in attaching rankings to countries for individual indicators, and would also guide policy makers by helping focus greater attention on variables whose values are relatively certain. Data needs for targeting purposes may be quite different. In order to ensure data is appropriate for this purpose, ensuring adequate sample sizes and adopting an appropriate sampling framework will be crucial for the identification of the needy. This chapter has highlighted the inadequacies of currently existing data. Future research will rely on improvements in data quality.

Notes

This study has been prepared within the UNU-WIDER project on Social Development Indicators (Measuring Human Well-being) directed by Professor Mark McGillivray.

1. In the case of the EU, unemployment rates have typically been prioritized as indicators of deprivation.
2. The final goal of 'developing a global partnership for development' is viewed as a means of achieving the first seven goals, as many poor countries will require international assistance in achieving these (via ODA, debt relief, access to markets, etc.).
3. The set of indicators remains under consultation.
4. They argue that enrolment rates should be seen as an input into the schooling process, while completion rates are the outcome.
5. As examples, Srinivasan reports that Sen's (1998) study has used unreliable data on infant mortality, while Barro and Lee's (1993) influential growth study relied on unreliable schooling, investment and life expectancy data.
6. For example, data on infant mortality and life expectancy are commonly used as indicators of development in spite of the immense problems with data availability and quality.
7. Most studies show that self-reported health status tends to get worse as income rises.
8. He cites Behrman and Deolalikar's (1987) study of the impact of income on nutritional intake, which finds that calorie intake does not respond to increases in income even among the poor.
9. Three alternative indicators of literacy are generally accepted. Some of these are, however, relatively poor measures of actual literacy. UNESCO, for example, suggests 'a person is literate if s/he has completed five or more years of schooling'. However, some individuals with fewer years of schooling may be functionally literate, while some of those with five or more years of schooling may not have attained functional literacy.
10. In particular, he suggests that the availability of long-run data series would be a considerable improvement over examining single years or short time periods.
11. In particular, he notes that one commonly used method for correcting for differences in definitions, the inclusion of dummy variables, is not satisfactory on the field of economic inequality.
12. The emergence of the National Health Service also contributed to this change.
13. The unit of observation may range from individuals or families to regions.
14. These studies have found income to have little impact on nutritional intake. See Ravallion (1996a) for a review.
15. Defined as living on less than $2 per day.

References

Abul Naga, R. M. (1994) 'Identifying the Poor: A Multiple Indicator Approach', DARP Discussion Paper 9, STICERD, LSE.

Anand, S. and R. Kanbur (1991) 'Public Policy and Basic Needs Provision: Intervention and Achievement in Sri Lanka', in J. P. Dreze and A. Sen (eds), *The Political Economy of Hunger*, vol. 3 (Oxford: Oxford University Press for UNU-WIDER).

Anand, S. and M. Ravallion (1993) 'Human Development in Poor Countries: On the Role of Private Incomes and Public Services', *Journal of Economic Perspectives*, 7(1): 133–50.

Anand S. and A. Sen (2000) 'Human Development and Economic Sustainability', *World Development*, 28(12): 2029–49.

Atkinson, A. (1998) 'Social Exclusion, Poverty and Unemployment', in A. B. Atkinson and J. Hills (eds) 'Exclusion, Employment and Opportunity', CASE Paper 4, London School of Economics.

Atkinson, A. (2002a) 'Data Matter', Mimeo, Nuffield College, Oxford.

Atkinson, A. (2002b) 'Multidimensional Deprivation: Contrasting Social Welfare and Counting Approaches', Mimeo, Nuffield College, Oxford.

Atkinson, A. and F. Bourguignon (1982) 'The Comparison of Multi-Dimensional Distributions of Economic Status', *Review of Economic Studies*, 49: 183–201.

Atkinson, A., B. Cantillion, E. Marlier and B. Nolan (2002) *Social Indicators: The EU and Social Inclusion* (Oxford: Oxford University Press).

Barro, R. and Lee, J.-W. (1993) 'International Comparisons of Educational Attainment', *Journal of Monetary Economics*, 32(3): 363–94.

Baulch, B. and E. Masset (2002) 'Do Monetary and Non-Monetary Indicators Tell the Same Story about Chronic Poverty? A Study of Vietnam in the 1990s', Working Paper 17, Chronic Poverty Research Centre, Manchester.

Behrman, J. and A. Deolalikar (1987) 'Will Developing Countries Nutrition Improve with Income? A Case Study form Rural South India', *Journal of Political Economy*, 95: 492–507.

Behrman, J. and M. Ronsenzweig (1994) 'Cross Country Data on Education and the Labour Force', *Journal of Development Economics*, 44(1): 147–71.

Ben-Arieh, A., N. H. Kaufan, A. B. Andrews, R. M. George, B. J. Lee and J. L. Aber (2001) 'Measuring and Monitoring Children's Well-Being', *Social Indicators Research*, vol. 7, (Amsterdam: Kluwer).

Berger-Schmitt, R. and H.-H. Noll (2000) 'Conceptual Framework and Structure of a European System of Social Indicators', EU Reporting Working Paper 9.

Berkman, L. and T. Glass (2000) 'Social Integration, Social Networks, Social Support and Health', in L. Berkman and I. Kawachi (eds) *Social Epidemiology* (Oxford: Oxford University Press) 137–73.

Bidani, B. and M. Ravallion (1997) 'Decomposing Social Indicators Using Distributional Data', *Journal of Econometrics*, 77: 125–39.

Blanchflower, D. and A. Oswald (2000) 'Well-being Over Time in Britain and the USA', NBER Working Paper 7487 (Cambridge, MA: NBER).

Bruno, M., M. Ravallion and L. Squire (1996) 'Equity and Growth in Developing Countries: Old and New Perspectives on the Policy Issues', Policy Research Working Paper 1563 (Washington DC: World Bank).

Chamie, J. (1994) 'Population Databases in Development Analysis', *Journal for Development Economics*, 44(1): 131–46.

Cowell, F. A. and M. Victoria-Feser (1999) 'Statistical Inference for Welfare Under Complete and Incomplete Information', DARP Discussion Paper 47, STICERD, LSE.

Dasgupta, P. (1990) 'Well-being and the Extent of its Realization in Poor Countries', *Economic Journal*, 100 (Conference) 1–32.

Dasgupta, P. (1997) 'Nutritional Status, Capacity for Work and Poverty Traps', *Journal of Econometrics*, 77: 5–37.

Dasgupta, P. and M. Weale (1992) 'On Measuring the Quality of Life', *World Development*, 20(1): 119–31.

Easterlin, R. A. (1974) 'Does Economic Growth Improve the Human Lot', in P. A. David and M. W. Reder (eds) *Nations and Households in Economic Growth: Essays in Honor of Moses Abromavitz* (New York: Academic Press).

Easterlin, R. A. (2003) 'Building a Better Theory of Well-Being', Discussion Paper 742, March (Bonn: IZA).
Fei, J., G. Ranis and F. Stewart (1985) 'A Macro-Economic Framework for Basic Needs', in F. Stewart, *Planning to Meet Basic Needs* (London: Macmillan).
Fields, G. S. (1994) 'Poverty and Income Distribution: Data for Measuring Poverty and Inequality Changes in the Developing Countries', *Journal of Development Economics*, 44: 87–102.
Freedman, L., M. Wirth, R. Waldman, M. Chowdhury and A. Rosenfield (2003), 'Background Paper of the Task Force on Child Health and Maternal Health' (Washington DC: World Bank).
Griliches, Z. (1986) 'Economic Data Issues', in Z. Griliches and M. Intriligator (eds) *Handbook of Econometrics*, vol. 3 (Amsterdam: Elsevier) ch. 25, 1466–514.
Grosh, M. E. and P. Glewwe (1996) 'Household Survey Data from Developing Countries: Progress and Prospects', *American Economic Review* (Papers and Proceedings) 86(2): 15–19.
Grown, C., G. Gupta and Z. Khan (2003) 'Background Paper of the Task Force on Education and Gender Equality' (Washington DC: World Bank).
Hammond, B. (1998) 'Measuring Development Progress', INTERSTAT, October, reported in J. Loup, D. Naudet and DIAL (2000), 'The State of Human Development Data and Statistical Capacity Building in Developing Countries', Human Development Report Office Occasional Papers, New York.
Hulme, D., K. Moore and A. Shepherd (2001) 'Chronic Poverty: Meanings and Analytical Frameworks', Chronic Poverty Research Centre Working Paper 2, Institute of Development Policy and Management, University of Manchester.
ILO (1976) *Employment Growth and Basic Needs: A One World Problem*, (Geneva: ILO).
Kanbur, R. (2002) 'Conceptual Change in Poverty and Inequality: One Development Economist's Perspective', Introductory comments at the Cornell Conference on Conceptual Challenges in Poverty and Inequality, April 16–17, http://www.arts.cornell.edu/poverty/kanbur/CCPI.pdf
Laderchi, C. R. (1999) 'The Many Dimensions of Deprivation in Peru: Theoretical Debates and Empirical Evidence', Working Paper 29 (Oxford: Queen Elizabeth House).
Laderchi, C. R., R. Saith and F. Stewart (2003) 'Does it Matter that We Don't Agree on the Definition of Poverty? A Comparison of Four Approaches', *Oxford Development Studies*, 31(3): 243–74
Levine, R., N. Birdsall, A. Ibraahim and P. Dayal (2003) 'Background Paper of the Task Force on Education and Gender Equality' (Washington DC: World Bank).
Levine, R. and D. Renelt (1992), 'A Sensitivity Analysis of Cross-Country Growth Regressions', *American Economic Review*, 82(4): 942–63.
Loup, J., D. Naudet and Développement et Insertion Internationale (DIAL) (2000) 'The State of Human Development Data and Statistical Capacity Building in Developing Countries', Human Development Report Office Occasional Papers, New York.
Micklewright, J. (2002) *Social Exclusion and Children: A European View for the US Debate* (Florence: UNICEF).
Micklewright, J. and S. Ismail (2001) 'What can Child Anthropometry Reveal about Living Standards and Public Policy? An Illustration from Central China', *Review of Income and Wealth*, Series 47, 1, March.
Ranis, G., F. Stewart and A. Ramirez (2000) 'Economic Growth and Human Development', *World Development*, 28(2): 197–219.
Ravallion, M. (1994) 'Measuring Social Welfare with and without Poverty Lines,' *American Economic Review*, 84(2): 359–64.

Ravallion, M. (1996a) 'Issues in Measuring and Modelling Poverty', *Economic Journal*, 106(438): 1328–43.

Ravallion M. (1996b) 'How well can Method Substitute for Data? Five Experiments in Policy Analysis', *World Bank Research Observer*, 11(2): 199–221.

Ravallion, M. (1997) 'Good and Bad Growth: The Human Development Reports', *World Development*, 25(5): 631–8.

Saith, R. (2001) 'Social Exclusion: The Concept and Application to Developing Countries', Working Paper 72 (Oxford: Queen Elizabeth House).

Saith, R. and B. Harriss-White (1998) 'Gender Sensitivity of Well-Being Indicators', Working Paper 10 (Oxford: Queen Elizabeth House).

Seers, D. (1972) 'What are we trying to Measure', *Journal of Development Studies*, 8(3): 21–36.

Sen, A. (1993a), 'Capability and Well-being', in M. Nussbaum and A. K. Sen (eds) *The Quality of Life* (Oxford: Clarendon Press for UN-WIDER).

Sen, A. (1993b) 'Positional Objectivity', *Philosophy and Public Affairs*, 22.

Sen, A. (1997) 'Editorial: Human Capital and Human Capability', *World Development*, 25(12): 1959–61.

Sen, A. (1998) 'Mortality as an Indicator of Economic Success and Failure', *Economic Journal*, 108 (January): 1–25.

Sen, A. (1999) 'Democracy as a Universal Value', *Journal of Democracy*, 10(3).

Srinivasan, T. (1981) 'Malnutrition: Some Measurement and Policy Issues', *Journal of Development Economics*, 8: 3–19.

Srinivasan, T. (1994a) 'Destitution: A Discourse', *Journal of Economic Literature*, 32(4): 1842–55.

Srinivasan, T. (1994b) 'Data Base for Development Analysis: An Overview', *Journal of Development Economics*, 44: 3–27.

Srinivasan, T. (1994c) 'Human Development: A New Paradigm or Reinvention of the Wheel', *American Economic Review*, 84(2): 238–43.

Strauss, J. and D. Thomas (1996) 'Measurement and Mismeasurement of Social Indicators', *American Economic Review* (Papers and Proceedings), 86(2): 30–4.

Streeten, P. (1981) *First Things First: Meeting Basic Needs in Developing Countries* (Oxford: Oxford University Press).

Subramanian, S. and A. Deaton (1996) 'The Demand for Food and Calories', *Journal of Political Economy*, 104(1): 133–62.

Sugden, R. (1993) 'Welfare, Resources, and Capabilities: A Review of Inequality Reexamined by Amartya Sen', *Journal of Economic Literature*, 31(4): 1947–62.

UNDP (1993, 1997, 2001, 2002) *Human Development Report* (Oxford and New York: Oxford University Press for the United Nations Development Programme).

Veenhoven, R. (2004) 'Subjective Measures of Well-being', WIDER Discussion Paper 2004/07 (Helsinki: UNU-WIDER).

5
Composite Indexes of Human Well-being: Past, Present and Future

Mark McGillivray and Farhad Noorbakhsh

Introduction

Human well-being is often treated as a multidimensional concept, consisting of a number of distinct, separable dimensions. Theoretical research has identified an array of dimensions. Often specific to a particular conceptualization of well-being; these dimensions can be social, physical, psychological or material in nature (Alkire 2002).[1] Empirical research has proposed a number of composite indexes intended to measure multi-dimensional well-being, especially at the level of countries. At least twenty composite indices have received international attention in the last four decades (Booysen 2002). The best known, and that which has received the most attention, is the UNDP's Human Development Index (HDI) (UNDP 1990–2004). Others include the Physical Quality of Life Index (PQLI) (Morris 1979), the Combined Quality of Life Indices (CQLI) (Diener 1995), and the Human Suffering Index (HSI) (Camp and Speidel 1987, Hess 1989, Tilak 1992). Also included in these indexes are United Nations Research Institute for Social Development (UNRISD) Level of Living Index (LLI) (Drewnowski and Scott 1966), General Index of Development (GID) (McGranahan *et al.* 1972), and Socioeconomic Development Index (SDI) (UNRISD 1970). The designers of these indexes typically emphasize that there is more to well-being enhancement than material enrichment, and therefore often combine what might be loosely termed 'economic' and 'non-economic' well-being indicators. In some instances the indexes are intended to serve as alternative or competing indexes to traditional income-based measures, and therefore include non-economic variables only.

This chapter critically reviews composite well-being indexes. Its focus is on indexes of overall national well-being achievement, as opposed to more specific indexes of poverty, gender bias, sustainability or single well-being dimensions. Indexes such as the UNDP's Gender-related Development Index, Gender Empowerment Measure, Capability Poverty Measure, and Human

Poverty Index (UNDP 1990–2004), or the Combined Consumption Level Index (Bennett 1951), Real Index of Consumption (Beckerman and Bacon 1966), Index of Economic Well-being (Osberg and Sharpe 2002), and Human Freedom Index (Humana 1992) are not considered, therefore. A number of issues are examined, including the general structure of the index, the choice of components, universalism, component weights, scale equivalence, component transformations, the treatment of income, correlations among components and policy relevance. Most of these issues are examined in the context of a critical review of the many criticisms of the HDI and the UNDP's responses to these criticisms, some involving changes to the design of the index. Possible directions for the future design and application of composite well-being indicators are identified, including adoption of participatory country and time variant component weighting schemes. It should be stressed that there is a huge literature on the HDI that includes studies by McGillivray (1991), Murray (1991), McGillivray and White (1993, 1994), Acharya and Wall (1994), Gormely (1995), Lüchters and Menkhoff (1996, 2000), Hicks (1997), Ivanova *et al.* (1998), Noorbakhsh (1998a, 1998b, 2002), Sagar and Najam (1998), Neumayer (2001), Cahill (2002, 2005) and Morse (2003). The current chapter does not do justice to this literature as it does not look at the full ranges of issues raised in it or at the many useful revisions to the HDI it proposes. Nor does it do justice to a number of innovative, but less known, measures proposed in studies such as Maasoumi and Nickelsburg (1988), Slottje (1991), Majumdar and Subramanian (2001) and Zaim *et al.* (2001). The chapter is, instead, concerned with selected core issues.

Consisting of a further seven sections, this chapter begins with a critical overview of the structure of composite indexes and addresses some key issues in the selection of component variables. It pays special attention to the issue of universalism. Then we look at methods used to achieve scale equivalence in component variables, before examining transforming values to reflect perceived non-linear relationships, highlighting the case of the HDI income component. After looking at correlations between components and with other well-being measures and the weighting of components, we then discuss, mainly in the context of the HDI, the policy relevance of composite indexes used in international well-being assessments. The conclusion provides remarks on the future design and application of composite well-being indexes.

Structure and components

The general structure of most composite well-being indexes is:

$$W_i = \sum_{j=1}^{k} w_j C_{i,j} \qquad i = 1, \ldots, n \tag{5.1}$$

where w_j is a weight and $C_{i,j}$ is the jth component for country i. Each component is usually intended to measure achievement in some well-being dimension. Most indexes have common components capturing achievement in terms of health, education and incomes, although there is some variation among them. The PQLI, for example, contained years of life expectancy, the adult literacy rate and the infant mortality rate (Morris 1979). The HDI currently contains years of life expectancy, the adult literacy rate, the combined gross school enrolment ratio and the logarithm of purchasing power parity (PPP) GDP per capita (UNDP 2004).[2] Early versions of the index contained mean years of schooling instead of the third of these variables, and an adjusted PPP GDP per capita based on various thresholds (UNDP 1993). The HSI combined the following ten variables: GNP per capita, inflation rate, labour force growth, urban population growth, infant mortality, daily per capita calorie supply, access to clean drinking water, energy consumption per capita, adult literacy and an index of personal freedom (Camp and Speidel 1987, Tilak 1992). The UNRISD SDI contains 16 components, which include health and education status indicators but also newspaper circulation and a range of economic indicators such as electricity consumption, foreign trade per capita, economically active population with electricity, gas and water, agricultural production and GDP derived from manufacturing (UNRISD 1970).

The choice of component variables has promoted much discussion. Early indexes, including the GID and SDI, were criticized as measures of structural change or activity rather than measures of well-being achievement (Morris 1979, Thanawala 1990, Tilak 1992). The UNDP has, in many of its *Human Development Reports* sought to provide a solid conceptual basis for the HDI by linking the index to Amartya Sen's notion of capabilities (Sen 1985, 1990, 1993, among many other works). The *Human Development Report 1995*, for instance, noted that:

> The basis for selection of critical dimensions, and the indicators that make up the human development index, is identifying basic capabilities that must have to participate in and contribute to society. These include the ability to lead a long and healthy life, the ability to be knowledgeable and the ability to have access to the resources needed for a decent standard of living. (UNDP 1995: 18)

The three components of the HDI are intended to reflect these three (cap)abilities. The UNDP has also sought to provide a precise definition of human development, which is analogous to human well-being, linking it to the design of the HDI. The first *Human Development Report* noted:

> Human development is a process of enlarging people's choices. The most critical ones are to lead a long and healthy life, to be educated and to enjoy a decent standard of living. (UNDP 1990: 10)

The selection of component measures is subject to a number of criticisms. Irrespective of how elegantly and emphatically the justifications for components choices might be articulated, in the final analysis the selection is ad hoc. Hicks and Streeten (1979: 576) noted that, in the case of the PQLI, most serious scholars find it difficult to accept the results of a composite development index without stronger theoretical foundation. What is ultimately required, it would seem, is the known functional form of a well-being production function. This is acknowledged in *Human Development Report 1993*, which observed that, in an ideal world, the HDI's design would be guided by a meta production function for human development (UNDP 1993: 109). Unfortunately the precise form of this function is not known.

A related issue concerns the concept of universalism. As Anand and Sen (2000a) observe, universalism is the recognition of a shared claim of every person to the elementary or basic capabilities required to lead a worthwhile life.[3] This is in itself a defence of many composite indexes, including the HDI, as few would deny that health, education and purchasing power are universal elementary capabilities, and as such essential elements of a well-being vector. If so, then it is appropriate to measure well-being achievement among countries on the basis of these variables. But while universalism offers a justification for inclusion of certain variables in composite indexes, it also provides a telling criticism for the exclusion of others, as there are indeed many other elementary, universal capabilities or values that ought in principle be included in them. One such value is basic human security. While human security can be variously defined, not being the victim of physical violence or other intimidation would appear to be a universal value. Yet, it is one that has received little attention in discussions centred on the HDI and other composite indexes.

Another possible universal value is political freedoms or rights. Dasgupta (1990) criticized the HDI on these grounds, claiming that 'it is quite incomplete; as it is oblivious to what is commonplace to call human rights' (UNDP 1993: 105). On a similar vein, Hopkins (1991: 1471), in a critique of the HDI, observes that the index value would be high for someone living a long time with access to a library in a prison. Streeten (1995), however, argues against the inclusion of human rights variables on a number of grounds. These include the volatility of such variables which, if included in an index, could cause its values to drop from one year to the next, even though the other component variables might not have changed. Streeton also argues the subjectivity in the measurement of these variables. One may question the first of these grounds; if the value of a variable drops, and it is a valid measure of well-being, then it is entirely appropriate that the index value, ceteris paribus, drops. That is exactly what should happen. The UNDP also used the same argument to defend the choice of components in the first *Human Development Report*, published in 1990, and repeated this argument in the

1993 report. One suspects, however, that one important reason why human rights and many other variables are not included in composite indexes is their limited cross-country availability, and the related desire to report index values for as many countries as possible. Indeed, this would appear to have heavily guided the general choice of variables included in composite indexes.

While not challenging the universal nature of the HDI, Anand and Sen (1992) float the idea of different indicators for the capabilities that the index attempts to capture. Specifically, Anand and Sen consider different indicators for the low, medium, and high human development categories reported in the *Human Development Reports*. They propose, for example, combining child mortality and life expectancy as the long and healthy life component of the HDI for middle human development group countries. For high human development countries, they propose using a Gini-corrected mean national income instead of PPP GDP per capita (UNDP 1993). Similarly, the CQLI consists of two main components, which in turn contain sub-component variables: a basic quality of life index and an advanced quality of life index. Both contain seven variables, chosen to discriminate between developing and industrial countries in terms of the same general well-being domains (Diener 1995). Crucial here is the distinction between the choice of components and the choice of variables used to represent these components. We return to this crucial issue below when discussing the policy relevance of indexes.

Another common criticism of the choice of variables in composite indexes is that measures of the means by which well-being is achieved are combined with measures of well-being ends. In the cases of the PQLI and HDI, for example, life expectancy might be considered as an end but adult literacy and school enrolment only as means. Morris (1979), in defence of the PQLI, argued that indexes based on ends alone lack relevance on the grounds that policy interventions are designed on the basis of means (Booysen 2002). Veenhoven (1996) argues against the use of means variables, as ends variables are better suited to evaluate goals or outcomes of policy, and against the combination of means and ends variables as this lacks theoretical justification (Booysen 2002).

Ideology and politics can, not surprisingly, play an important role in the selection of variables and indexes have been criticized accordingly. For example, it has been asserted, possibly unfairly, that the choice of the components of the HDI was intended to elevate, in country rankings, those countries that perform better in terms of non-economic well-being indicators, thus providing greater justifications for activities, projects and programmes sponsored by the UNDP. A related assertion was that the HDI was an attempt by the UNDP to differentiate its activities and policy stances, especially vis-a-vis the World Bank.

Scale equivalence

Most component indexes combine variables that are measured in different scales. Consider the HDI. Two of its variables, as mentioned, are adult literacy and PPP GDP per capita. Adult literacy is a percentage and as such has a maximum value of 100. PPP GDP has no such upper limit, and current values range from 580 to 61,190 dollars (UNDP 2004). Scale equivalence is thus an issue. This equivalence is usually achieved by ensuring that the $C_{i,j}$ range from 0 to 1 or 0 to 100. A value of 0 was often assigned if $c_{i,j}$ (the actual value of $C_{i,j}$, prior to rescaling) is the lowest observed among n countries ($c_{i,j} = c_{i,j}^{\min}$). Either 1 or 100 is assigned if $c_{i,j}$ is the highest observed among these countries ($c_{i,j} = c_{i,j}^{\max}$). The formula used for this purpose (with the maximum being set at one) is:

$$C_{i,j} = \frac{c_{i,j} - c_{i,j}^{\min}}{c_{i,j}^{\max} - c_{i,j}^{\min}} \tag{5.2}$$

This formula assumes that $\partial c_{i,j}/\partial W_i$ is positive. Alternatively, in the event of $\partial c_{j,i}/\partial W_i$ being negative, a value of 0 is assigned if $c_{i,j} = c_{i,j}^{\min}$, or either 1 or 100 if $c_{i,j} = c_{i,j}^{\max}$, and 1 minus the value of (5.2) can instead be used.

This approach, employed by the PQLI and the 1990 HDI, attracted criticism on the grounds that a country could, over time, achieve improvements in each index component but experience a decline in the aggregate value of its index (McGillivray and White 1992). The underlying concern was that HDI values were not comparable over time. The reason for this is quite simple, as a closer look at (5.2) reveals. $C_{i,j}$ could increase, but if $c_{i,j}^{\min}$ increases by a sufficiently greater margin $C_{i,j}$ will decrease and, ceteris paribus, so too would W_i. The reverse can also happen, with $C_{i,j}$ increasing even though $c_{i,j}$ might have fallen.

UNDP responded to this criticism, in the *Human Development Report 1994*, by fixing the maximum and minimum values above and below the actual maxima and minima, respectively. These fixed values are described as 'goal posts'. The upper goal posts have been set at 'limits of what can be expected within the next 30 years' and the lower goal posts correspond to values 'observed historically, going back about 30 years' (UNDP 1994: 92). The lower goal posts for life expectancy, adult literacy, educational attainment and PPP GDP per capita are 25 years, 0 per cent, 0 per cent, and \$100, respectively. The corresponding upper goal posts are 85 years, 100 per cent, 100 per cent, and \$40,000, respectively (UNDP 1994–2004). These values have been used to obtain HDI values in every year since 1994, despite a number of countries having gross school enrolment ratios exceeding 100 per cent and Luxembourg's PPP GDP well-exceeding \$40,000. The UNDP's response to this is to simply cap the values of these variables at the upper goal posts.

Setting what are essentially arbitrary but reasonable values for the upper and lower values might on the surface appear to be justifiable. It certainly does not matter as far as individual components are concerned, to the extent that the ranking of countries for individual components will not change. Yet, it will matter for the ranking of countries according to the composite index if that index is constructed by either summing or averaging the rescaled variables, as is the case with the PQLI and HDI. This is due to the change in component means and variances that result from the rescaling. Consider the case of the HDI. Setting the lower value for life expectancy at 30 years would appear to be defensible, or at least no less defensible than the value of 25 years adopted by the UNDP. Yet, the former results in a larger mean, standard deviation and coefficient of variation for the corresponding rescaled value of life expectancy (see Table 5.1). Higher lower values for the education variables, compared to those used by the UNDP, results in a lower mean but higher standard deviation and coefficient of variation for the education attainment component on the HDI, and higher lower and upper values for PPP GDP per capita give the same results (see Table 5.1).[4] In each case, therefore, these equally defensible fixed values will result in different country HDI rankings.

The use of the fixed lower and upper values ensures that country HDI values will not fall over time even though the component variables, prior to rescaling, might increase. But would such a fall in this context be a bad thing? For the HDI, a more meaningful comparison might be achievement defined in terms of the benchmark set by the lowest and highest actual observed values of the component variables prior to rescaling. Indeed, if a country cannot match improvements achieved by the country or countries with the lowest values of each variable, then it might be especially appropriate that its HDI value falls over time. An HDI devised in this way would be seen as a

Table 5.1 Mean and standard deviation of rescaled variables

HDI component	Range	Mean	Standard deviation	Coefficient of variation
Life expectancy	25 to 85 years	0.674	0.193	0.286
Life expectancy	30 to 85 years	0.645	0.210	0.326
Educational attainment	Literacy: 0 to 100% Enrolment: 0 to 100%	0.756	0.196	0.259
Educational attainment	Literacy: 10 to 100% Enrolment: 15 to 100%	0.702	0.214	0.305
PPP GDP per capita	\$100 to \$40,000	0.646	0.189	0.292
PPP GDP per capita	\$400 to \$60,000	0.496	0.225	0.454

Note: Logarithmic values of PPP GDP per capita are used, as in the HDI.

relative well-being achievement measure used in the assessment looking at country's performance over time. Its values could even be reported alongside a HDI obtained using fixed upper and lower values which would in a sense be seen as absolute measure.

Non-linearity

Well-being is usually treated as a linear function of index components. The principal exception to this is income per capita, as it is generally accepted that there are diminishing returns to the conversion of income into well-being. In the first version of the HDI, income was treated as follows:

$$\begin{aligned} c_{i,3} &= \ln y_i \quad \text{for } 0 < y_i \le y^* \\ &= \ln y_i^* \quad \text{for } y_i > y^* \end{aligned} \tag{5.3}$$

where $c_{i,3}$ is the income component prior to rescaling, y_i is PPP GDP per capita, y^* is the average official poverty line income in nine industrial countries adjusted for purchasing power parities of \$4861 (UNDP 1990). It follows that the income component increases logarithmically with PPP GDP per capita up to the poverty, but is capped at this point. The UNDP expressed a change of view in the design of the second and many subsequent versions of the HDI, conceding that the capping of the income component was 'too drastic an adjustment' (UNDP 1991: 15). Accordingly, the 1991 to 1998 versions of the index the adjustment was as follows:

$$\begin{aligned} c_{i,3} &= y_i && \text{for } 0 < y_i \le y^* \\ &= y^* + 2\left[(y_i - y^*)^{1/2}\right] && \text{for } y^* < y_i \le 2y^* \\ &= y^* + 2\left[(y_i - y^*)^{1/2}\right] + 3\left[(y_i - 2y^*)^{1/3}\right] && \text{for } 2y^* < y_i \le 3y^* \\ &= y^* + 2\left[(y_i - y^*)^{1/2}\right] + 3\left[(y_i - 2y^*)^{1/3}\right] + 4\left[(y_i - 3y^*)^{1/4}\right] && \text{for } 3y^* < y_i \le 4y^* \end{aligned} \tag{5.4}$$

and so on (UNDP 1991). McGillivray and White (1992) demonstrated that the two preceding treatments of income were almost indistinguishable for incomes equal to or greater than y^*. For example, according to second equation in (5.4), an income per capita of \$9658, twice the 1991 poverty line of \$4829, is adjusted downwards to \$4968, a difference of only \$139 or 3 per cent as compared to the poverty line income of \$4829. The UNDP claimed otherwise, however, asserting that (5.4) significantly differentiated the adjusted incomes of countries for which $y_i > y^*$ (UNDP 1993: 100). McGillivray and White (1992) and Ravallion (1997), among others, argue that the discounting due to (5.4) is excessive, with the former recommending the use of the logarithm of income, for all incomes, instead of (5.4).

The UNDP further softened its line on the treatment on income in the *Human Development Report 1999*, acknowledging (5.4) also too heavily penalized countries with incomes above the poverty line. Following Anand and Sen (1999, 2000b), the UNDP wanted to put the treatment of income 'on a more solid analytical foundation' (UNDP 1999: 159). Anand and Sen refer to the well-known and frequently applied Atkinson formulation:

$$W(y_i) = \frac{1}{1-\varepsilon} y_i^{1-\varepsilon} \qquad (5.5)$$

where $W(y_i)$ is the utility or well-being derived from income and ε is the elasticity of the marginal utility of income with respect to income and measures the extent of diminishing returns. If $\varepsilon = 0$ there are no diminishing returns and $W(y_i)$ reduces to y_i. As ε approaches 1 $W(y_i)$ becomes the logarithm of y_i. In (5.4), ε increases with income. For example, for incomes less than y^*, between y^* and $2y^*$ and $2y^*$ and $3y^*$, $\varepsilon = 0$, 1/2 and 2/3, respectively.

In acknowledging that (5.4) too heavily discounted incomes above the poverty line, the UNDP simply elected to transform all incomes into their logarithmic values, hence electing for a value of ε that approaches 1. This transformation has been used in all *Human Development Reports* since 1999. While this would seem a better treatment than the transformations provided by (5.4), there remains profound ambiguity over precisely what the value of ε should be. In particular, 1 and 0 can be considered extremes, with the appropriate value being somewhere in between. Precisely what the value ought to be remains a matter of speculation.

If there is a case for discounting income due to diminishing returns, there might be also be a case for discounting other well-being index components on the same grounds. Noorbakhsh (1998a) considered this issue with respect to the educational attainment component of the HDI. A set of weights was devised to reflect constant rate of diminishing returns to the conversion of educational attainment to human development. These weights were applied to the individual sub-components of the educational attainment component as follows:

$$\sum_{k=1}^{K} c_{i,2,p,k} e^{x} \qquad p = 1, 2 \qquad (5.6)$$

where k denotes a fraction of the pth sub-component and the exponent e^x is a decreasing function of this component given that x decreases according to successive ranges of the sub-component.[5]

Correlations and weights

Most composite indexes are a response to the perceived inadequacies of income per capita as a measure of well-being; they are an attempt empirically to capture more fully the assumed vitality or complexity of the human well-being concept. This is not to say that income might not be an important determinant of well-being, but simply there is more to well-being than income alone. The HDI is such a response, being an attempt to shed more light on other aspects of human development than income per capita alone (Noorbakhsh 1998a). The UNDP made much of this point in early *Human Development Reports*. For instance, in the 1990 report it is noted that:

> Human development is a process of enlarging people's choices. In principle, these choices can be infinite and change over time. ...income is clearly one option that people would like to have, albeit an important one. But it is not the sum total of their lives. (UNDP 1990: 10, box 1.1)

Correspondingly, the UNDP went on to claim that the HDI 'ranks countries very differently from GNP per capita' and that 'the reason is that GNP per capita is only one of life's many dimensions' (UNDP 1990: 14).

A number of studies have looked at correlations between composite indexes, reporting zero- and rank-order correlation coefficients. Larson and Wilford (1979) looked at the correlation between the PQLI and GNP per capita for a sample of 150 countries, reporting zero- and rank-order coefficients of 0.496 and 0.766, respectively. On the basis of these coefficients, it was concluded that the PQLI was redundant, on the grounds that it 'does not provide any essential information for ranking countries other than that already provided by GNP per capita' (Larson and Wilford 1979: 583). McGillivray (1991) conducted a similar exercise for the 1990 version of the HDI, reporting for a sample of 119 countries with zero- and rank-order correlation coefficients between the HDI and the logarithm of GNP per capita of 0.859 and 0.889. McGillivray (1991: 1467) also concluded that the HDI for many country groups was empirically redundant, in that it largely provides us with little more information regarding inter-country well-being levels than the traditional indicator, GNP per capita, alone can provide.

A fundamental weakness with these studies is that it is not entirely clear what extent of statistical association deems a new indicator empirically redundant with respect to a pre-existing one. McGillivray and White (1992, 1993) and Cahill (2005) address this point. The former study specifies explicit thresholds to differentiate between redundancy and non-redundancy. Two thresholds are specified – correlation coefficients of 0.90 and 0.70 – and, hence, tests were performed to determine whether the coefficients between the HDI and income per capita are significantly less than these thresholds. The conclusion was that both the 1990 and 1991 HDIs were redundant according to both thresholds. Cahill repeated this exercise for the 2001 HDI, drawing the same conclusion. While these two studies are empirically superior to their predecessors, the thresholds they specify are, of course, arbitrary. Nor do they deny the non-empirical contribution of the HDI, as outlined above.

A related and arguably more important issue, if one retains the sorts of indicators used in indexes such as the HDI and PQLI, is the correlations between the individual components and also between individual components and the indices as a whole. Larson and Wilford (1979), McGillivray (1991) and McGillivray and White (1992, 1993) also consider this issue, showing that these correlations are very high, with zero- and rank-order coefficients often being above 0.90. The consequence of this is that basing either the PQLI or the HDI on any one of its component variables yields very similar insights into inter-country well-being to the indexes as a whole.

Table 5.2 contains correlation coefficients between the HDI appearing in UNDP (2002) and its components.[6] The coefficients between the HDI and its components (shown in column 2) are all high, and typical of those reported in the literature. Of course, one would expect some level of correlation between the HDI and its components by simple virtue of the components being just that, part of the index. McGillivray and White (1992) show, however, that for large samples of countries, even after removing one of the components from the index and correlating it with what remains, (that is, the restricted index) the coefficients remain very high.[7] The reason for this is the high correlations between each individual component, as Table 5.2 demonstrates.

Noorbakhsh (1998b) demonstrates, however, that while the correlation coefficients are high for the data for all countries, they can be much lower – sometimes statistically insignificant – for the sub-samples of countries. This is also demonstrated by Table 5.2, which reports coefficients for countries that are classified by the UNDP as either high, medium or low human development. The coefficients between the HDI and its components for these sub-samples, while remaining statistically significant, are much lower than those for the full sample of countries. The correlations between individual components are lower still, and often insignificant. The coefficient between the educational attainment and income components is negative. It follows that, for these sub-samples of countries, basing the index on any one component will yield very different information on well-being achievement among countries than the HDI as a whole. We return to this issue later in the chapter, when discussing policy relevance of composite indexes.

Observing correlation coefficients between composite indexes and other well-being indicators is an interesting and informative exercise. It is also reasonable to ask whether a new index might be redundant with respect to pre-existing indicators, despite ambiguity over the extent of correlation required to deem an indicator redundant. But this question needs to be considered in its proper context. If the purpose of the composite index under question is primarily statistical, to rank countries in terms of well-being achievement, then the high correlations reported in many studies, combined with some of the technical problems outlined above and in the relevant literature, do make differences in this achievement hard to interpret.

Table 5.2 Pearson correlation coefficients between HDI 2002 and its components

Sample	HDI	Life expectancy	Educational attainment	PPP GDP per capita
All Countries				
HDI	1.000			
Life expectancy	0.925**	1.000		
Educational attainment	0.916**	0.763**	1.000	
PPP GDP per capita	0.924**	0.794**	0.765**	1.000
High HDI countries				
HDI	1.000			
Life expectancy	0.819**	1.000		
Educational attainment	0.743**	0.395**	1.000	
PPP GDP per capita	0.869**	0.688**	0.388**	1.000
Medium HDI countries				
HDI	1.000			
Life expectancy	0.771**	1.000		
Educational attainment	0.692**	0.258*	1.000	
PPP GDP per capita	0.663**	0.264*	0.264*	1.000
Low HDI countries				
HDI	1.000			
Life expectancy	0.747**	1.000		
Educational attainment	0.611**	0.057	1.000	
PPP GDP per capita	0.567**	0.386*	−0.044	1.000

Notes: ** and * are significant at the 1 and 5 per cent levels, respectively. All component variables are scaled and GDP per capita is logged prior to scaling, as in the HDI.

As such, the conclusions drawn by Larson and Wilford (1979), McGillivray (1991) and others might have validity.[8] However, if the prime use of the index is policy or advocacy oriented with the purpose of highlighting the importance of social issues to human development, or shifting attention away from a possibly excessive focus on narrower well-being measure, then the statistical redundancy issue has much less relevance.

Component weighting is an especially difficult issue, and related in part to the high correlations between component variables. Ideally, as Hicks and Streeten (1979) among others point out, weights should be guided by theory. Anand and Sen (1992) note with respect to the HDI that a meta production function for human development would be specified, and the contribution of each variable to human development would be its weight (UNDP 1993). But the form of such a function is unknown, so weights must be assigned via another method. Most indexes simply take the sum or the average of the components, hence giving the appearance of equal weights. The three components of the HDI, for example, are assigned weights of one third each.[9] This, in principle, is almost certainly incorrect, as it implies that each component is equally important, in terms of well-being achievement, at all points of time and levels of achievement, and in all regions, countries, cultures, levels of development, and so on. The UNDP recognizes this but justifies the HDI weighting scheme on the basis of Occam's razor; that is, since it is probably impossible to achieve agreement on what the weights should be, the simplest response is the best, that being to assign an equal weight to each component.

The UNRISD LLI (Drewnowski and Scott 1966) and GID (McGranahan *et al.* 1972) attempt a more sophisticated weighting system. The LLI employed a system of sliding weights under which deviations from the normal were given more weight than variables close to the normal (Hicks and Streeten 1979) The GID gave greater weight to components that had the greatest inter-correlation with other components. These weighting systems have been criticized heavily, largely because of their arbitrary nature. Hicks and Streeten (1979), for example, criticized the GID weighting scheme, suggesting that the absence of a correlation with other components would be an equally valid reason for giving a component a high weight.

A number of studies address this issue by proposing the use of principal components analysis (Adelman and Morris 1967, Ram 1982, Desai 1993, Ogwang 1994, Srinivasan 1994, and Noorbakhsh 1998b, 2002, Lai 2000).[10] The weights are typically those assigned to the first principal component extracted from the data. While an accepted statistical method, it is purely data driven and the weights have no conceptual interpretation. As Hicks and Streeten (1979: 576) note, none of these attempts 'indicates that much effort was expended in developing a theoretically sound rationale for the weighting system.' One such rationale, consistent with economic theory, would be to apply a differential weighting system, in which the weights would be a decreasing function of the level of well-being achievement according to the particular component. This is broadly consistent with Veenhoven (1996), who suggested that some variables will be culturally less prominent in particular societies that have high achievement in them (Booysen 2002).

High correlations between components are relevant to weighting schemes. Even if we had sufficient information or an accepted procedure to assign differential weights, the exercise might be fruitless if these correlations are high. Table 5.3 reinforces this point. It reports correlation coefficients between the 2002 HDI and 12 versions of that index with different component weights. The weights of the first index version have been obtained by the principal components method. The weights are similar in value, reflecting the high correlations between components reported above in Table 5.2. The remaining 11 HDI versions have been obtained from various arbitrary combinations of weights. The weights vary from 0 to 0.8 and as such are very different to those used by the UNDP to calculate the HDI. Each combination sums to 1, as is the case with the UNDP HDI. Yet, the correlation coefficients are all close to 1.[11]

As mentioned above, the UNDP assigns weights of one third to each of the HDI components. Seemingly overlooked by the UNDP and others, there is, however, an implicit HDI weighting scheme that operates prior to the application of these explicit weights. It results from the rescaling procedure outlined above, where a gap between the upper and lower goal posts operates as an implicit reciprocal weight. The higher this gap relative to the mean value of the variable under consideration, the lower is the implicit weight (or higher the reciprocal weight) attached to the variable under consideration. In essence, this gap operates as a reciprocal weight. In the case of the HDI, income has the highest reciprocal weight and its influence on the index is

Table 5.3 Human Development Index with alternative weights

HDI Re-weight	**Correlation coefficient**	
	Pearson (zero-order)	**Spearman (rank-order)**
$HDI_i = 0.93LE_i + 0.91EA_i + 0.93Y_i$	0.935	0.941
$HDI_i = 0.4LE_i + 0.0EA_i + 0.6Y_i$	0.974	0.977
$HDI_i = 0.2LE_i + 0.8EA_i + 0.0Y_i$	0.954	0.935
$HDI_i = 0.6LE_i + 0.4EA_i + 0.0Y_i$	0.979	0.970
$HDI_i = 0.4LE_i + 0.6EA_i + 0.0Y_i$	0.977	0.961
$HDI_i = 0.8LE_i + 0.2EA_i + 0.0Y_i$	0.961	0.963
$HDI_i = 0.2LE_i + 0.6EA_i + 0.2Y_i$	0.985	0.979
$HDI_i = 0.2LE_i + 0.4EA_i + 0.4Y_i$	0.997	0.996
$HDI_i = 0.2LE_i + 0.2EA_i + 0.6Y_i$	0.987	0.986
$HDI_i = 0.0LE_i + 0.2EA_i + 0.8Y_i$	0.960	0.961
$HDI_i = 0.0LE_i + 0.8EA_i + 0.2Y_i$	0.953	0.946
$HDI_i = 0.2LE_i + 0.0EA_i + 0.8Y_i$	0.957	0.977

reduced as a consequence.[12] In contrast, the chosen upper and lower values for the educational attainment variables leaves the impact of these variables unchanged.[13] The general point to be made here is that component transformations – in the case of the HDI, its rescaling procedure – can introduce a form of implicit weighting. This not only applies to the HDI but potentially to any index that combines transformed variables.[14]

Policy relevance

One of the greatest impacts of composite indexes intended to assess national well-being achievement relates to the signals they send to policy makers. Both the PQLI and the HDI, for instance, were explicitly intended to send the message that there is more to well-being achievement than improvements in incomes alone. The HDI has been particularly successful in this regard, reminding policy makers in developing countries that achieving better levels of health, education and incomes is a particularly desirable outcome. Noorbakhsh (2002) observes, however, that the history of composite measures tells us that their impact is limited and not sustained over time if they are not geared to policy implementation at the national or sub-national levels. This observation is not new. Three decades earlier, Seers (1972: 32) observed that the 'most important use of development indicators is to provide the targets for planning', and Drewnowski (1972: 77) noted 'welfare indices are supposed to serve not only for assessing the results of development but also as targets for development plans'.

Consider the HDI. Policy makers in developing countries readily accept the basic message of the HDI. Given also that the literature has now identified vast, interrelated well-being domains and corresponding indicators, one is tempted to conclude that the UNDP's index might be seen in the same light as GNP per capita was more than a decade ago, when the HDI first appeared. That is, policy makers might simply attend to showing intertemporal improvement in the HDI in its present form at the cost of possibly more urgent priorities, in the same way that many sought simply to increase income growth in the decades preceding the 1990s. That the country specific *Human Development Reports* tend to emphasize the universal HDI, with a limited policy orientation, attests to this. Alternatively, attempts to increase HDI values might be half-hearted if they were not directly involved in the construction of the index, in the selection of components, the variables on which these components are based and the weights. The underlying issue here is one of country level ownership.

A core concern in making composite indexes more policy relevant would appear be to universalism. Consider again the HDI. The issue here is not so much the chosen components of the index as it would appear reasonable to identify a common set of measurable well-being components, applicable to all people in all societies. As Anand and Sen (2000a) noted 'not working toward bringing the elementary capabilities [that the components are intended to reflect] within the reach of the deprived would be outrageous'. The issue would instead appear to turn on the selection of a common set of variables that empirically capture each component. Are the four variables on which the HDI is based appropriate for measuring well-being in all countries, in terms of policy relevance, or at least for the 170 or more countries for which HDI values are reported?

The answer to the preceding question would appear to be a clear 'no', since universal indexes such as the HDI are currently more concerned with a measurement for ranking countries, and less concerned with the operational capability of the index in terms of policy making at a more practical level for different countries. A simple response would be simply to drop a universal index and adopt a set of country specific ones. But this would be at the cost of no longer being able to make inter-country well-being achievement comparisons. Such a cost is significant.

An index design that avoids this cost is to retain a universal set of components, but with variables on which these components are based varying across countries. It has already been pointed out that Anand and Sen (1992) proposed the use of different indicators for the low, medium and high human development categories, with, for example, the longevity component of the HDI being based on a combination of child mortality and life expectancy instead of life expectancy alone. Likewise, the Diener CQLI uses different variables for developing and industrial countries, as was also mentioned above. A more radical approach would be to allow policy makers in each country, or possibly even citizens, to select the variables for each component that are most appropriate to their own country. One could also do the same with component weights. Participatory techniques could be used to select variables and assign weights, which would need to be periodically re-assessed as conditions within countries change. The chosen variables should be better, more incisive and more relevant measures of each component in each country.[15] But because the same components are used across countries, a degree of inter-country comparability is maintained. The weights would presumably reflect contemporary priorities, with higher weights being attached to components that are more prominent and important. For example, in sub-Saharan Africa the longevity component would probably at present receive a very high weight given the enormity of the HIV/AIDS problem being faced on those countries. Country-specific variables and weights might also mean that the index provides more information, better capturing the assumed vitality of the well-being concept. Such a scheme might also address the redundancy of components and weights issue discussed above. Another approach might be to retain the universal structure of the index for inter-country comparisons at a particular point in time, but use country specific versions of the index for comparisons of performance over time.

Conclusion

This chapter surveyed the various composite well-being indexes that have been used over the last forty or so years, looking mainly at the Physical Quality of Life Index and the very well-known Human Development Index of the United Nations Development Programme. A number of issues are considered, including the choice of components, component weights, scale equivalence, component transformations, the treatment of income, correlations among components, and correlations with other well-being measures. Among the issues highlighted is the often very high correlation between the PQLI and the HDI and its components. It was argued that a main consequence of these correlations is that assigning differential component weights, which is appropriate on conceptual grounds, is largely a fruitless exercise. That is, such weighting produces index values that are generally indistinguishable from values of the equally weighted index.

Also highlighted was the issue of the policy relevance of composite indexes such as the HDI and PQLI. It was observed that the history of composite measures of development is such that their impact is limited if they are not geared to policy implementation at a practical level. It was argued that one way of addressing this issue is to retain a universal set of components, chosen on the basis of universal elementary capabilities, but with variables on which these components are based and their weights varying across countries. Thus, the variables and weights may well vary across countries and over time. Theory tells us that well-being components or dimensions will assume different priorities in different countries, depending on their levels of achieved well-being, different cultural priorities and so on. Empirical observation tells us that a standard set of variables, used across countries, will not appropriately measure the capabilities or other criteria indexes. Selection would either be based on the preferences of policy makers or citizens, gauged through participatory techniques. Essentially, this would involve surveys in which policy makers or citizens determine their own variable weights. This would be no small task, but if we can devote sufficient resources, for example, to obtaining information on purchasing power parities to adjust per capita incomes, then we could also devote resources to the gathering of such information on component weights and measures. Might the UNDP consider this for the HDI? Might it also consider adding a human security variable to the HDI, as it is a fundamental, universal well-being component? Time will tell, of course, but as Amartya Sen observed, 'the infant has now grown up and can take the rough with the smooth' (2000: 22).

Notes

This is a revised version of a paper presented at a workshop on Measuring Well-being at UNU-WIDER in Helsinki, May 2003. The authors are grateful to meeting participants, especially Des Gasper, Stephan Klasen and Mozaffar Qizilbash, for helpful comments. They are also grateful for the very helpful and comprehensive comments from three anonymous referees. The usual disclaimer applies.

1 For the purposes of this chapter, notions such as human well-being, quality of human life, human development, basic human needs fulfilment are treated as synonymous.
2 The second and third of these variables are actually formed into educational attainment index, which is the second HDI component. In essence, they are sub-components, therefore. This index can be written as follows:

$$C_{i,2} = \alpha_1 C_{i,2,1} + \alpha_2 C_{i,2,2}$$

where α_1 and α_2 are weights set at two thirds and one third respectively; $C_{i,2,1}$ is country i's adult literacy rate and $C_{i,2,2}$ is that county's gross combined primary, secondary and tertiary enrolment ratio. These variables are scaled with a range of 0 and 100. The scaling procedure is discussed later.
3 Strictly speaking, Anand and Sen refer to ethical universalism and not universalism per se.
4 Furthermore, averaging three variables that are spread around different means with different variances is also questionable. The gap between the lower and upper values also has significant implications for component weights, as outlined later.
5 For $c_{i,2,1}$ (adult literacy), for example, the following applies: $x = 0$ if $0 < c_{i,2,1} \leq 40$, $x = -0.1$ if $40 < c_{i,2,1} \leq 50$, $x = -0.2$ if $50 < c_{i,2,1} \leq 60$, and so on, through to $x = -0.6$ if $90 < c_{i,2,1} \leq 100$. For a country with a literacy rate of 50 per cent, for example, the discounted rate is calculated as $40 + 9.05 = 49.05$.
6 Spearman (rank-order) coefficients were also calculated, but were very similar in value to those shown in Table 5.2. Both Pearson and Spearman coefficients were calculated using HDI data for earlier years, with the results also being very similar to those in Table 5.2. Full results are available from the authors.
7 More precisely, McGillivray and White (1992) restrict the HDI by, for example, assigning a weight of 0 to the life expectancy component and correlate it against the restricted HDI. The resulting coefficient was found to be very similar in magnitude to that between the life expectancy component and the unrestricted HDI. This result held for each component.
8 It is worth noting that these studies do not argue that well-being achievement should be measured or assessed using income per capita alone, contrary to what has been attributed to them. McGillivray (1991: 1467), for instance, concludes that his research 'does not imply that social or human conditions are irrelevant to the assessment of development levels'.
9 As we note later, however, these weights are explicit as there is an implicit differential weighting scheme introduced into the HDI due to the way each component variable is normalized.
10 It is worth noting that the variant of principal component analysis used by a number of these studies relies on the high correlation among the components (Noorbakhsh 1998b, 2002).
11 See Cahill (2005) for a more detailed elaboration of this point.
12 It must be noted that the weight changes the magnitude of the index for all countries though not the country ranks.

13 Consider the variables within the educational attainment component. An adult literacy value 78 per cent, for example, according to the rescaling procedure outlined above becomes (78–0)/(100–0) = 0.78. A combined gross school enrolment of 56 per cent becomes 0.56 as the same range is used. As a result, the contribution of these variables to HDI values is purely determined by their levels and weights, and not the rescaling procedure.

14 The HDI rescaling procedure also reduces the variance of the life expectancy and income components, further reducing the impact of differential explicit weights and hence, in part, driving the results shown in Table 5.3.

15 Streeten (2000: 26) argues in the case of the HDI that 'work along the lines that improve the index or apply it to regions or groups within a country is most welcome'. For examples of the application of the index to policy making at a country level (Iran and India), see Noorbakhsh (2002, 2003).

References

Acharya, A. and H. J. Wall (1994) 'An Evaluation of the United Nations' Human Development Index', *Journal of Economic and Social Development*, 20(1): 51–65.

Adelman I. and Morris C. F. (1967) *Society, Politics and Economic Development: A Quantitative Approach* (Baltimore: Johns Hopkins University Press).

Alkire, S. (2002) 'Dimensions of Human Development', *World Development*, 30(2): 181–205.

Anand, S. and A. Sen (1992) 'Human Development Index: Methodology and Measurement', Background paper prepared for the *Human Development Report 1993* (New York: United Nations Development Programme).

Anand, S. and A. Sen (1999) 'The Income Component of the Human Development Index', Background paper prepared for the *Human Development Report 1999* (New York: United Nations Development Programme).

Anand, S. and A. Sen (2000a) 'Human Development and Economic Sustainability', *World Development*, 28(12): 2029–49.

Anand, S. and A. Sen (2000b) 'The Income Component of the Human Development Index', *Journal of Human Development*, 1(1): 83–106.

Beckerman, W. and R. Bacon (1966) 'International Comparisons of Income Levels: A Suggested New Measure', *Economic Journal*, 76: 519–36.

Bennett, M. K. (1951) 'International Disparities in Consumption Levels', *American Economic Review*, 41: 632–49.

Booysen, F. (2002) 'An Overview and Evaluation of Composite Indices of Development', *Social Indicators Research*, 59(2): 115–51.

Cahill, M. (2002) 'Diminishing Returns to GDP and the Human Development Index', *Applied Economics Letters*, 9(13): 885–7.

Cahill, M. (2005) 'Is the Human Development Index Redundant?', *Eastern Economic Journal*, 31(1): 1–6.

Camp, S. L. and J. J. Speidel (1987) *The International Human Suffering Index*, (Washington, DC: Population Crisis Committee).

Dasgupta, P. (1990) 'Well-being in Poor Countries', *Economic and Political Weekly*, 4 August: 1713–20.

Desai, M. (1993) 'Income and Alternative Measures of Well-Being', in D. G. Westendorff and D. Ghai (eds), *Monitoring Social Progress in the 1990s* (Aldershot: Avebury for UNRISD).

Diener, E. (1995) 'A Value-based Index for Measuring National Quality of Life', *Social Indicators Research*, 36: 107–27.

Drewnowski, J. (1972) 'Social Indicators and Welfare Measurement: Remarks on Methodology', *Journal of Development Studies*, 8(3): 77–90.

Drewnowski, J. and W. Scott (1966) *The Level of Living Index*, Report 4 (Geneva: United Nations Research Institute for Social Development).

Gormely, P. J. (1995) 'The Human Development Index in 1994: Impact of Income on Country Rank', *Journal of Economic and Social Measurement*, 21: 253–67.

Hess, P. (1989) 'The Military Burden, Economic Growth, and the Human Suffering Index: Evidence from the LDCs', *Cambridge Journal of Economics*, 13: 497–515.

Hicks, D. A. (1997) 'The Inequality Adjusted Human Development Index: A Constructive Proposal', *World Development*, 25(8): 1283–98.

Hicks, N. and P. Streeten (1979) 'Indicators of Development: The Search for a Basic Needs Yardstick', *World Development*, 7: 567–80.

Hopkins, M. (1991) 'Human Development Revisited: A New UNDP Report', *World Development*, 19(10): 1469–74.

Humana, C. (1992) *World Human Rights Guide*, 3rd edn (New York: Oxford University Press).

Ivanova, I., F. J. Arcelus and G. Srinivasan (1998) 'An Assessment of the Measurement Properties of the Human Development Index', *Social Indicators Research*, 46: 157–79.

Kelley, A. C. (1989) 'The "International Human Suffering Index": A Reconsideration of the Evidence', *Population and Development Review*, 15(4): 731–7.

Kelley, A. C. (1991) 'The Human Development Index: "Handle with Care" ', *Population and Development Review*, 17(2): 315–24.

Lai, D. (2000) 'Temporal Analysis of Human Development Indicators: Principal Component Approach', *Social Indicators Research*, 51(3): 331–66.

Larson, D. A. and W. T. Wilford (1979) 'The Physical Quality of Life Index: A Useful Social Indicator?', *World Development*, 7(7): 581–4.

Lüchters, G. and L. Menkhoff (1996) 'Human Development as a Statistical Artifact', *World Development*, 24(8): 1385–92.

Lüchters, G. and L. Menkhoff (2000) 'Chaotic Signs from HDI Measurement', *Applied Economics Letters*, 7(4): 267–70.

Maasoumi, E. and G. Nickelsburg (1988) 'Multivariate Measures of Well-being and an Analysis of Inequality in the Michigan Data', *Journal of Business and Economic Statistics*, 6(3): 327–34.

Majumdar, M. and S. Subramanian (2001) 'Capability Failure and Group Disparities: Some Evidence from India for the 1980s', *Journal of Development Studies*, 37(5): 104–40.

McGillivray, M. (1991) 'The Human Development Index: Yet Another Redundant Composite Development Indicator?', *World Development*, 19(10): 1461–8.

McGillivray, M. and H. White (1992) *Measuring Development? A Statistical Critique of the Human Development Index*, Institute of Social Studies Working Paper 135 (The Hague: Institute of Social Studies).

McGillivray, M. and H. White (1993) 'Measuring Development? The UNDP's Human Development Index', *Journal of International Development*, 5(2): 183–92.

McGillivray, M. and H. White (1994) 'Inter-country Quality of Life Comparison: Does Measurement Error Really Matter?', *Asian Journal of Economics and Social Studies*, 13(1): 1–13.

McGranahan, D. V., C. Richard-Proust, N. V. Sovani and M. Subramanian (1972) *Contents and Measurement of Socioeconomic Development*, A Staff Study of the United Nations Research Institute for Social Development (New York: Praeger).

Morris, M. D. (1979) *Measuring the Conditions of the World's Poor: The Physical Quality of Life Index* (New York: Pergamon).
Morse, S. (2003) 'For Better or for Worse, till the Human Development Index do us Part?', *Ecological Economics*, 45: 281–96.
Murray, C. J. L. (1991) *Development Data Constraints and the Human Development Index*, Discussion Paper 25 (Geneva: United Nations Research Institute for Social Development).
Neumayer, E. (2001) 'The Human Development Index and Sustainability – A Constructive Proposal', *Ecological Economics*, 39: 101–14.
Noorbakhsh, F. (1998a) 'A Modified Human Development Index', *World Development*, 26(3): 517–28.
Noorbakhsh, F. (1998b) 'A Human Development Index: Some Technical Issues and Alternative Indices', *Journal of International Development*, 10: 589–605.
Noorbakhsh, F. (2002) 'Human Development and Regional Disparities in Iran: A Policy Model', *Journal of International Development*, 14: 927–49.
Noorbakhsh, F. (2003) 'Human Development, Poverty and Disparities in the States of India', Paper presented in the UNU-WIDER conference on Inequality, Poverty and Human Well-being, 30–31 May, Helsinki.
Ogwang, T. (1994) 'The Choice of Principal Variables for Computing the Human Development Index', *World Development*, 22(12): 2011–114.
Osberg, L. and A. Sharpe (2002) 'An Index of Economic Well-being for Selected OECD Countries', *Review of Income and Wealth*, 48(3): 291–316.
Ram, R. (1982) 'Composite Indices of Physical Quality of Life, Basic Needs Fulfilment, and Income: A "Principal Component" Representation', *Journal of Development Economics*, 11: 227–47.
Ravallion, M. (1997) 'Good and Bad Growth: The Human Development Reports', *World Development*, 25(5): 631–8.
Sagar, A. and A. Najam (1998) 'The Human Development Index: A Critical Review', *Ecological Economics*, 25: 249–64.
Seers, D. (1972) 'What are we Trying to Measure?', *Journal of Development Studies*, 8(3): 21–36.
Sen, A. K. (1985) *Commodities and Capabilities* (Amsterdam: Elsevier).
Sen, A. K. (1990) 'Development as Capability Expansion', in K. Griffin and J. Knight (eds), *Human Development and the International Development Strategy for the 1990s* (London: Macmillan).
Sen, A. K. (1993) 'Capability and Well-being', in M. C. Nussbaum and A. Sen (eds), *The Quality of Life* (Oxford: Clarendon Press for UNU-WIDER).
Sen, A. (2000) 'A Decade of Human Development', *Journal of Human Development*, 1(1): 17–23.
Slottje, D. (1991) 'Measuring the Quality of Life Across Countries', *Review of Economics and Statistics*, LXXIII(4): 684–93.
Srinivasan, T. N. (1994) 'Human Development: A New Paradigm or Reinvention of the Wheel?', *American Economic Review*, Papers and Proceedings, 84: 238–43.
Streeten, P. (1995) 'Human Development: The Debate about the Index', *International Social Science Journal*, 47(143): 25–37.
Streeten, P. (2000) 'Looking Ahead: Areas of Future Research in Human Development', *Journal of Human Development*, 1(1): 25–48.
Thanawala, K. (1990) 'Economic Development and All That', *International Journal of Social Economics*, 17(2): 14–21.
Tilak, J. B. G. (1992) 'From Economic Growth to Human Development: A Commentary on Recent Indexes of Development', *International Journal of Social Economics*, 19(2): 31–42.

United Nations Development Programme (UNDP) (1990–2004) *Human Development Report* (New York: Oxford University Press).

United Nations Research Institute for Social Development (UNRISD) (1970) *Contents and Measurements of Socioeconomic Development* (Geneva: UNRISD).

Veenhoven, R. (1996) 'Happy Life Expectancy: A Comprehensive Measure of the Quality-of-Life in Nations', *Social Indicators Research*, 39: 1–58.

Zaim, O., R. Fare and S. Grosskopf (2001) 'An Economic Approach to Achievement and Improvement Indexes', *Social Indicators Research*, 51(1): 91–118.

6
Indicators of Inequality and Poverty

S. Subramanian

Introduction

In this chapter we shall take a rapid overview of certain salient issues in the measurement of inequality and poverty – two major sources of social 'illfare'. While the intention is to assign each of the two topics the same importance, this may not be reflected in the final outcome (which seems somewhat to favour 'poverty' over 'inequality') when judged according to the amount of space allocated to the two topics: the space-allocation pattern, it must be clarified, is largely a function of the expository demands – as they have seemed to present themselves – confronting the author. Both subjects are immensely vast, and built on foundations of considerable philosophical and conceptual import which, however, we shall have little space to review here. The best one can do is to point the interested reader toward Sen's (1981a, 1992) assessments of the conceptual underpinnings of the notions of poverty and inequality respectively. Our own concerns here will be restricted to issues in *measurement*, and that, principally though certainly not exclusively, in the space of *incomes*. This is not so much because of any underlying view to the effect that income is the most relevant dimension in which to measure inequality and poverty, as because this chapter is primarily a survey of the literature; and the literature on inequality and poverty has, as it happens, concerned itself very largely with measurement in the income dimension.

In discussing inequality and poverty measures as well-being (or rather 'ill-being') indicators, a twofold approach will be adopted. First, holding constant the dimension (say income) in which measurement is undertaken, the indicator will be varied, so as to furnish an idea of the greater or lesser adequacy with which alternative indicators capture features of aggregate well-being. This would call for a description of the more significantly desirable properties of inequality and poverty indexes, and an assessment of which indexes satisfy which properties. Second, holding the indicator fixed, the dimension in which measurement is undertaken will be varied, so as to furnish an idea of the greater or lesser appropriateness of alternative 'spaces' in which to assess aggregate well-being. This would call for a consideration of measurement in non-income dimensions – such as in the space of capabilities and functionings – in addition to the income dimension. Simply as a guide to unambiguous usage, the terms 'inequality' and 'poverty' will, in this chapter, be generally reserved for the space of incomes, while the terms 'disparity' and 'deprivation' will be employed for more inclusive spaces.

A select list of very fine surveys of issues in inequality measurement is constituted by Sen (1973, 1992), Kakwani (1980a), Anand (1983), Foster (1985), Shorrocks (1988), Jenkins (1991), and Foster and Sen (1997). A similar list for issues in poverty measurement would include Sen (1979, 1981a), Anand (1983), Kakwani (1980b, 1984), Foster (1984), Donaldson and Weymark (1986), Atkinson (1987), Seidl (1988), Ravallion (1994), and Zheng (1997). When it comes to assessing deprivation and disparity in more general spaces than solely income, the reader should consult, amongst others, Morris (1979), Sen (1980, 1981b, 1984, 1985a), Sen *et al.* (1987), Dasgupta (1993), McGillivray and White (1993), Anand and Sen (1995), Qizilbash (1996), Majumdar and Subramanian (2001), and Subramanian and Majumdar (2002).

Inequality measurement

Preliminary concepts

For specificity, we shall throughout work with the domain of *incomes* as the one in which inequality will be assessed. A fundamental unit of consideration will be an *income vector*. An income vector $\mathbf{x}$ is a list of n non-negative incomes $(x_1,...,x_i,...x_n)$, where $x_i (i = 1,...,n)$ stands for the income of person i in a community of n individuals. The set of individuals whose incomes are represented in the vector x will be designated by $N(\mathbf{x})$; $n(\mathbf{x})$ will stand for the number of individuals; and $\mu(\mathbf{x}) \equiv (1/n(\mathbf{x}))\Sigma_{i=1}^{n(x)} x_i$ will stand for the mean of the incomes in $\mathbf{x}$. What we have just discussed is a *discrete* income distribution. On occasion, it is helpful to work with a *continuous* distribution: here, x will stand for a random variable signifying income; $f(x)$ is the *density function* of x (that is, the proportion of the population with income x); $F(x)$ is the *cumulative density function* of x (that is, the proportion of the population with incomes not exceeding x); and $F_1(x)$ is the *first-moment distribution function* of x (that is, the share in total income of units with incomes not exceeding x). For a clear statement of concepts and definitions, the reader should consult Kakwani (1980a).

A visual representation of inequality: the Lorenz curve

One of the clearest ways of obtaining a visual picture of inequality in the distribution of incomes is to plot the *Lorenz curve* (due to Lorenz 1905) in the unit square. The Lorenz curve is just the plot of the first moment distribution function $F_1(x)$ against the cumulative density function $F(x)$. Or, more directly, it is the graph of the income share of the poorest pth fraction of the population, for every p between 0 and 1. If income is perfectly equally divided, then it is clear that the Lorenz curve will coincide with the diagonal of the unit square. But a typical, unequal distribution will be represented by a Lorenz curve that lies below the diagonal, and is convex in shape. The more unequal a distribution, the further away from the diagonal the Lorenz curve will lie. For the case of complete concentration, the Lorenz curve will be described by the two equal sides of the right-angled triangle of which the diagonal of the unit square is the hypotenuse.

Given a discrete, non-decreasingly ordered n-vector of incomes $\mathbf{x} = (x_1, \ldots x_i, \ldots, x_n)$, the Lorenz curve – noting that $\mu(\mathbf{x})$ is the mean of $\mathbf{x}$ – can be derived as a plot of the following points: (0,0); $(1/n, x_1/n\mu)$; $(2/n, (x_1 + x_2)/n\mu)$; $\ldots$; $((n-1)/n, (x_1 + x_2 + \ldots + x_{n-1})/n\mu)$; (1,1): these points, connected by straight lines, will then yield a 'piece-wise linear' Lorenz curve. In Figure 6.1, I have drawn the Lorenz curves for three hypothetical, unequal distributions **x**, **y**, and **z**. I shall now define the binary relation of *Lorenz dominance*, designated by L. Given any two distributions **x** and **y**, we shall say **x** Lorenz-dominates **y**, written $\mathbf{x}L\mathbf{y}$, if and only if the Lorenz curve for **x** lies somewhere inside, and nowhere outside, the Lorenz

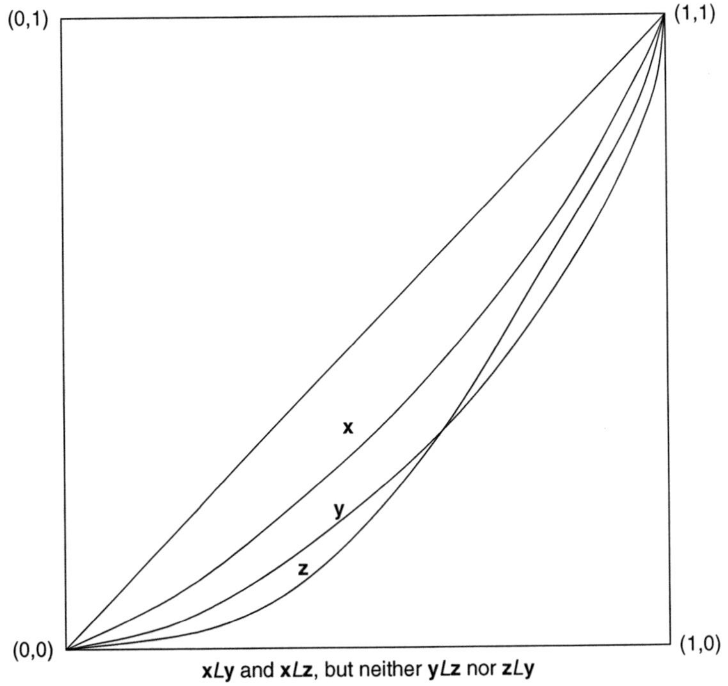

Figure 6.1 The Lorenz curve

curve for **y**. In the discrete case, for two equi-dimensional non-decreasingly ordered n-vectors of income **x** and **y**, we shall say **x***L***y** holds whenever $\Sigma_{j=1}^{i} x_j \geq \Sigma_{j=1}^{i} y_j$ for every $i = 1, \ldots, n$ and there exists at least one i for which $\Sigma_{j=1}^{i} x_j > \Sigma_{j=1}^{i} y_j$. If **x** Lorenz-dominates **y**, then it seems reasonable to conclude that **x** has unambiguously less inequality than *y*. Can any two distributions always be ranked according to the Lorenz-dominance relation? No. Note from Figure 6.1 that while it is certainly true that **x***L***y** and **x***L***z**, we can neither say **y***L***z** nor **z***L***y**: the relation *L* cannot rank intersecting Lorenz curves.

A simple numerical example may help to fix ideas. Consider a 5-person society and three ordered income vectors **x**, **y** and **z**, such that $\mathbf{x} = (10, 20, 30, 40, 50)$, $\mathbf{y} = (10, 15, 35, 40, 50)$, and $\mathbf{z} = (5, 25, 30, 40, 50)$. All three distributions have the same mean: $\mu(\mathbf{x}) = \mu(\mathbf{y}) = \mu(\mathbf{z}) = 30$. If the Lorenz curves for the three distributions are plotted, it can be verified that **x** Lorenz-dominates each of **y** and **z**, but that the Lorenz curves for **y** and **z** intersect. It is not difficult to see why this should happen. Note that **x** can be seen to be derived from **y** through a progressive transfer from person 3 to person 2, and that **x** can be seen to be derived from **z** through a progressive transfer from person 2 to person 1. These equalizing transfers are reflected in the Lorenz-dominance of **x** over each of **y** and **z**. However, when it comes to comparing distributions **y** and **z**, note that **y** can be seen to be derived from **z** through two opposing types of transfers: a progressive (or equalizing) transfer from person 2 to person 1, and a regressive (or disequalizing) transfer from person 2 to person 3. The resulting ambiguity is reflected in the intersection of the Lorenz curves of **x** and **y**.

What are the properties of the relation *L*? *L* is *irreflexive* – that is, there is no **x** such that **x***L***x** holds; it is *asymmetric* – that is, for all **x**, **y**, **x***L***y** implies (*not* **y***L***x**); it is *transitive* – that is, for all **x**, **y**, and **z**, if **x***L***y** and **y***L***z**, then **x***L***z**; but *L*, as we have seen, is *not complete*, in the sense that given any distinct **x** and **y**, it is not necessarily true that either **x***L***y** or **y***L***x** should hold. A binary relation such as *L*, which is irreflexive, asymmetric, transitive and incomplete, is called a *strict partial ordering*. The point to note is that the ordering is partial: this may well be how it should be, but nevertheless, if we were to provisionally view the completeness of a binary relation to be a desired virtue, then the question arises: how do we secure the possibility of obtaining an inequality ordering over all distributions of income that we may be interested in? This question is addressed in the following sub-section.

Real-valued indexes of inequality

An inequality index is a function *I* which assigns a real number to every non-negative income vector **x**. This real number is intended to measure the extent of inequality associated with the distribution **x**. The (arguable) advantage with a real-valued index of inequality is that it precipitates a complete ordering over income distributions, which follows from the fact that any two real numbers are always comparable in terms of the '>', '=', or

'<' relationship. (One says 'arguable', because the property of 'completeness' in a binary relation could be an over-praised attraction: as Sen has repeatedly pointed out, in a variety of contexts, it is not necessarily a virtue to force comparability on a pair of alternatives that are not inherently comparable. Further, there is always the possibility of loss of relevant information in the process of aggregation.)

How do we choose among alternative inequality indexes? A means to this end resides in recognizing the usefulness of first specifying what we may think are desirable properties for such measures. The properties of inequality indexes we shall review in the following sub-section have a fair measure of support from scholars working in the area. The ensuing exposition draws considerably on Shorrocks (1988) and Anand (1983).

Properties of inequality measures

If the sorts of populations we are dealing with are *homogeneous* populations, then the *symmetry* axiom (*Axiom S*), which requires an inequality index to be invariant with respect to an interpersonal permutation of incomes, has a certain natural appeal. Second, we may wish to specify a lower bound of 0 for an inequality index, and reserve this number for a distribution in which income is perfectly equally divided: this is the *normalization property* (*Axiom N*). Third, it is of the essence for an inequality measure to satisfy the *transfer property* (*Axiom T*), which is the requirement that the inequality index should register a decline in value following – other things equal – on a progressive rank-preserving transfer of income between two individuals. The transfer axiom – also called the Pigou–Dalton principle of transfers – is of crucial significance: any inequality index that violates this property can scarcely qualify for being called an inequality index. It may be as well to briefly explicate, here, the welfare basis of the transfer axiom. Suppose aggregate welfare W associated with any income vector $\mathbf{x}$ to be a sum of the utilities of all persons in a society, where utility is defined on income, and every person is assumed to have the same utility function U: $W(\mathbf{x}) = \Sigma_{i=1}^{n} U(x_i)$. If $U(.)$ increases with income but at a diminishing rate, then $U(.)$ will be said to be *increasing and strictly concave*. When the U-function is increasing and strictly concave, it is easy to see that a unit of income will be valued more highly when it accrues to a poor person than to one who is richer. That is to say, a progressive rank-preserving transfer of income will increase aggregate welfare W. This enables one to see that an inequality index that satisfies the principle of transfers will certify $\mathbf{x}$ to be inequality-superior to $\mathbf{y}$ when $\mathbf{x}$ is derived from $\mathbf{y}$ through an equalizing transfer, just as a social welfare function W of the type just described will certify $\mathbf{x}$ to be welfare-superior to $\mathbf{y}$. The next property of an inequality index is that of *continuity* (*Axiom C*), which demands, effectively, that 'like distributions should reflect like inequality values', so that the inequality index does not display abrupt changes for minor variations in the income distribution. The preceding four properties are what Shorrocks (1988) refers to as the 'basic' properties of an inequality index. These do not, of course, exhaust the set of desirable features one may look for in an index. One such additional desirable feature is the so-called *replication invariance* property (*Axiom RI*), which is the requirement that the inequality index should be invariant with respect to any k-fold population replication of an income distribution. Another such feature is captured in the *scale-invariance* property (*Axiom SI*), which stipulates that the inequality index be *mean-independent*; that is, invariant with respect to any uniform scaling up or down of an income distribution. The next property is a strengthening of the transfer axiom: *transfer-sensitivity* (*Axiom TS*) is Kolm's (1976) 'principle of diminishing transfers', and it requires that an inequality index be more responsive to income transfers at the lower than at the upper end of an income distribution (see also Shorrocks and Foster 1987). There are alternative ways of expressing this requirement, and a fuller treatment – adapted to the context of poverty measurement – is available on pp. 147–8. The next two properties are concerned with the relationship between sub-group inequality and overall inequality. *Sub-group consistency* (*Axiom SC*) – see Shorrocks 1988 – requires that, other things equal, an increase in any one sub-group's inequality level should not cause overall measured inequality to decline. *Decomposability* (*Axiom D*) is the requirement that an inequality index be amenable to decomposition into two components: a *within-group* inequality component and a *between-group* inequality component. The final property we shall consider is one that can scarcely be stated in any precise or formal way. It is the requirement that the inequality index be amenable to ready interpretation in terms of its intuitive appeal. I shall call this property *Axiom E*, for 'ease of interpretation'.

We have thus far discussed certain properties of inequality indexes in very general terms. It is time now to consider *specific* inequality measures.

Some specific inequality indexes

The literature on inequality measures differentiates between two types of measures – the so-called *ethical* measures, and the so-called *descriptive* measures. Ethical measures are those that seek to relate inequality in a distribution to *the loss in social welfare* arising from the presence of inequality: examples of this approach are to be found in the work of, among others, Dalton (1920), Aigner and Heins (1967), Kolm (1969), Atkinson (1970), and Blackorby and Donaldson (1978). For specificity, we shall briefly describe here the approach adopted by Atkinson (1970). Imagine that the social welfare function (SWF) is of the utilitarian type, and that each person has an (identical) increasing, strictly concave utility function, so that, given any income vector $\mathbf{x}$, the SWF is given by: $W(\mathbf{x}) = \Sigma_{i=1}^{n(x)} U(x_i)$, where $U(x_i)$ defines the ith person's utility level. Of crucial significance for an ethical inequality index is the notion of an *equally distributed equivalent income*, or 'ede income', for short. Given an income vector $\mathbf{x}$, the ede income x^{ede} is defined as that level of income such that, if it is equally distributed, then the resulting social welfare is exactly the same as that which obtains for the distribution **x**. That is, x^{ede} can be obtained as the solution to the equation:

$$\sum_{i=1}^{n(x)} U(x^{ede}) = \sum_{i=1}^{n(x)} U(x_i) \tag{6.1}$$

Since the $U(.)$ function is strictly concave, x^{ede} will be less than the mean $\mu(\mathbf{x})$ of the distribution **x**. The proportionate difference between μ and x^{ede} then furnishes us with a measure of inequality, interpreted as the welfare loss, in equivalent income units, occasioned by the presence of inequality.

Atkinson specialized the individual utility function to the so-called 'constant elasticity of marginal utility' type, given by:

$$\begin{aligned} U(x_i) &= [1/(1-\varepsilon)]x_i^{1-\varepsilon} \text{ for } \varepsilon > 0 \text{ and } \neq 1 \\ &= \log x_i \text{ for } \varepsilon = 1 \end{aligned} \tag{6.2}$$

To ensure strict concavity of $U(.)$, ε is confined to strictly positive values, and this parameter is interpreted as measuring a degree of 'aversion' to inequality: as ε becomes larger and larger, the U function becomes more and more concave, so that the social welfare function W becomes more and more 'equity conscious'. Given equations (6.1) and (6.2), it is easy to see that, in the Atkinson context, the equally distributed equivalent income is given by:

$$\begin{aligned} x^{ede} &= \left[(1/n)\sum_{i=1}^{n} x_i^{(1-\varepsilon)}\right]^{1/(1-\varepsilon)} \quad \text{for } \varepsilon > 0 \text{ and } \neq 1 \\ &= \exp\left[(1/n)\sum_{i=1}^{n} \log x_i\right] \quad \text{for } \varepsilon = 1 \end{aligned} \tag{6.3}$$

Atkinson's 'ethical' measure of inequality can then be written, for any given income vector **x**, as:

$$A(\mathbf{x}) = [\mu(\mathbf{x}) - x^{ede}(\mathbf{x})]/\mu(\mathbf{x}) \tag{6.4}$$

where x^{ede} is as given in equation (6.3).

While this approach to inequality measurement is strikingly interesting, the reader interested in a critical review should consult Sen (1978). Inequality may or may not be explicitly linked to any underlying welfare consideration. When an inequality index measures the loss in social welfare occasioned by inequality, a specific, welfare theoretic normative connotation is conferred on the index. It is, however, also possible to divorce an inequality index from any explicit engagement with the loss in welfare associated with the presence of inequality, and to assign a purely 'positive' role to the index. The rest of this sub-section will be devoted to a discussion of certain widely used *descriptive* measures of inequality, which are essentially statistical measures of dispersion, not explicitly motivated by a desire to link inequality to the welfare losses arising from the former.

In what follows, we present the expressions for five, fairly commonly used, descriptive indexes. Given any income vector **x**, the *Variance of Incomes* (V), the *Variance of Log Incomes* (V_L), the *Squared Coefficient of Variation* (S), *Theil's* (1967) *'Entropy' Index* (T), and the *Gini Coefficient of Inequality* (G) are given, respectively, by:

$$V(\mathbf{x}) = [1/n(\mathbf{x})]\sum_i (x_i - \mu(\mathbf{x}))^2 \tag{6.5}$$

$$V_L(\mathbf{x}) = [1/n(\mathbf{x})]\sum_i (\log x_i - \log \mu(\mathbf{x}))^2 \tag{6.6}$$

[*Note*: The version of V_L here is the one employed by Sen (1973): the mean income that figures on the right hand side of (6.6) is the *arithmetic* mean rather than the *geometric* mean, which latter – strictly – is the quantity customarily employed in the 'varlog' measure.]

$$S(\mathbf{x}) = [1/n(\mathbf{x})]\sum_i [(x_i - \mu(\mathbf{x}))/\mu(\mathbf{x})]^2 = V(\mathbf{x})/\mu^2(\mathbf{x}) \tag{6.7}$$

$$T(\mathbf{x}) = [1/n(\mathbf{x})]\sum_i (x_i/\mu)\log(x_i/\mu) \tag{6.8}$$

and

$$G(\mathbf{x}) = [n(\mathbf{x})+1]/[n(\mathbf{x})] - [2/\{n^2(\mathbf{x})\mu(\mathbf{x})\}]\sum_i [n(\mathbf{x})+1-i]x_i \tag{6.9}$$

where the individuals have been indexed in non-decreasing order of their incomes; namely, $x_i \leq x_{i+1}, i = 1, \ldots, n-1$ Two major problems with the indexes V and V_L respectively, which tend to disqualify them from further serious consideration, are that the one violates *Axiom SI* and the other violates *Axiom T* (on the latter problem, see Sen 1973; the problem also arises with the 'canonical' version of the 'varlog' measure, where the mean income employed is the geometric mean, on which see Foster and Ok 1999). This effectively narrows down the field to the set of indixes S, T, and G. A quick way of reviewing these three descriptive measures of inequality would be to consider them all together, and in relation to each other, in terms of the properties they satisfy. In the summary chart labelled Table 6.1, a '+' stands for fulfilment of a property, and a '–' stands for its violation. Where property E (ease of interpretation) is concerned, 'H' stands for 'high', 'M' for 'medium', and 'L' for low: it must be emphasized that the evaluation according to this particular criterion is, inevitably, infected by the author's subjectivism.

The three inequality indexes considered above have their respective merits and demerits. The squared coefficient of variation fails transfer sensitivity,

Table 6.1 Some descriptive inequality measures and their properties

Axioms	Squared coefficient of variation (*S*)	Theil's index (*T*)	Gini index (*G*)
Symmetry	+	+	+
Normalization	+	+	+
Transfer	+	+	+
Continuity	+	+	+
Replication invariance	+	+	+
Scale invariance	+	+	+
Transfer sensitivity	−	+	−
Subgroup consistency	+	+	−
Decomposability	+	+	−
Ease of interpretation	M	L	H

Notes: + = fulfilment of a given property; − = violation of the property; and 'H', 'M' and 'L' stand, respectively, for a score of 'high', 'medium' and 'low'.

unlike Theil's *T*, but it scores a little better with respect to ease of interpretation. Theil's index satisfies virtually all the desirable properties of an inequality index, except that getting an immediate intuitive handle on it – in terms of perceiving a transparent connection between the notions of inequality and entropy – is not the easiest of things (Sen 1973). Gini is not transfer sensitive; and it also disappointingly violates sub-group consistency (and therefore decomposability – see, among others, Cowell 1984). Where it does score high is in terms of its intuitive appeal: it lends itself to alternative, attractively neat interpretations – in terms of the pithy formula (conveyed forcefully to the author in personal communication by James Foster) of 'the expected distance between two randomly drawn incomes over twice the mean', in terms of a straightforward measure of dispersion (via the relative mean difference), in terms of welfare interpretations (via Rawls and Borda), and in terms of its link with the Lorenz curve (Gini is just twice the area enclosed by the Lorenz curve and the diagonal of the unit square) – which are reviewed in Sen (1973). Ultimately, our choice of an inequality measure must be guided by our larger intent and purpose. If, for instance, we are simply interested in ranking distributions, Gini, by virtue of the ease with which its meaning can be intuited, is a useful measure to employ. On the other hand, if we are interested in qualitative or quantitative assessments of the contributions of different sub-groups to overall inequality, then passing the test of sub-group consistency becomes important: indeed, as Shorrocks (1988) has shown, the choice then gets whittled down to the class of inequality indexes called Generalized Entropy Measures, of which the squared coefficient of variation and Theil's coefficient are special cases.

Connections amongst different orderings

It is useful, at this stage, to take stock of the ground we have covered, and to register any links there might be between different approaches to the problem of inequality measurement that we have examined. The reader will note that a good deal of what we have reviewed is concerned with three distinct sorts of orderings of income distributions: the Lorenz partial order, welfare orderings, and orderings by real-valued inequality indexes. It is interesting to ask what connections, if any, exist between these types of orderings.

It may be recalled first that at the basis of the 'ethical approach' to inequality measurement espoused by Atkinson is the postulation of an SWF given by $W = \Sigma_i U(x_i)$, where the $U(.)$ function is required to be increasing and strictly concave. There are any number of $U(.)$ functions that satisfy the stated requirements. The question therefore arises: under what conditions can two distributions **x** and **y** sharing the same mean income and the same population size be ranked without particularizing any further the form of the $U(.)$ function? Atkinson (1970) has presented a remarkable equivalence theorem which accords a central place to the Lorenz partial ordering L. What his theorem states is that given any two distributions **x** and **y** with the same mean income and population size, if $\mathbf{x}L\mathbf{y}$, then any social welfare function $W = \Sigma_i U(x_i)$ for which the $U(.)$ function is increasing and strictly concave will rank **x** above **y**; and conversely, if welfare from **x** is judged to be greater than welfare from **y** according to any social welfare function $W = \Sigma_i U(x_i)$ for which the $U(.)$ function is increasing and strictly concave, then it will be the case that $\mathbf{x}L\mathbf{y}$ holds (see Fields and Fei 1978, and Foster 1985). An additional interesting result is the following one. Let $\mathbf{I}^*$ be the set of all real valued inequality indexes that satisfy the properties of symmetry, normalization, continuity and transfer. Then the following can be asserted. Given any two distributions **x** and **y** with the same population sizes and mean incomes, if $\mathbf{x}L\mathbf{y}$, then we can be sure that $I(\mathbf{x}) < I(\mathbf{y})$ for every inequality index I that belongs to the set of indexes $\mathbf{I}^*$. Given the earlier result, it also then follows that if $W(\mathbf{x}) > W(\mathbf{y})$ for any social welfare function W that is a sum of identical increasing and strictly concave individual utility functions, then $I(\mathbf{x}) < I(\mathbf{y})$ as long as the inequality index I belongs to the set of indexes $\mathbf{I}^*$. (The intuitive basis of these results can be easily grasped by revisiting the brief discussion relating to the transfer axiom on p. 139.) More general results, involving a larger class of welfare functions through a dilution of the restrictions on their form, and extensions to comparisons of distributions with variable means and populations, are available in the literature. (The interested reader is referred to, among others, Dasgupta *et al.* 1973, Rothschild and Stiglitz 1973, Sen 1973, Anand 1983, and Foster and Shorrocks 1988c.)

Poverty measurement

A twofold exercise

Measuring poverty in the space of incomes entails a twofold exercise, the first of which is *identification*, and the second, *aggregation*. Identification calls for the specification of a distinguished positive level of income z, called the *poverty line*, such that those with incomes less than z are certified to be *poor*. The word 'those' in the preceding line avoids an explicit engagement with the important issue of the appropriate unit of consideration when it comes to specifying the income recipient: for example, should one be concerned with individuals or households? The household is a more 'natural' unit to consider, but it also raises difficult questions of how to make adjustments to the poverty line or to household incomes in order to allow for variations in household size and composition (see Blackwood and Lynch 1994). This is the problem of *heterogeneity*. The needs of a household consisting of two members (a 'couple') will typically be different from those of two single-member households, because of the existence of 'economies of scale'. The needs of a three-member household consisting of a parent and two children will also, typically, be different from the needs of a three-member household consisting of two parents and a child. Variations in the size and age-sex composition of households call for the construction of appropriate 'equivalence scales', as a means of establishing a common standard of comparability across heterogeneous income recipients. Heterogeneity poses deep conceptual and practical problems for both inequality and poverty analysis, as also for welfare analysis. The issue is only flagged here, but not dealt with, so that the reader is at least alive to the problem. For the purposes of this chapter, we shall steer clear of the important issue of heterogeneity, and simply assume that the income recipient units are homogeneous individuals. Turning next to the aggregation exercise, this calls for combining information on the distribution of incomes and the poverty line in order to arrive at a real-valued index of poverty. A poverty index is a function $P(\mathbf{x}; z)$ which assigns a real number to every combination of non-negative income vector $\mathbf{x}$ and positive poverty line z, where the number is intended to be a quantification of the extent of poverty associated with the regime $(\mathbf{x}; z)$.

Identification: absolute versus relative approaches

Should the poverty line be pitched in an *absolute* or a *relative* sense? The answer would seem to depend on what one means by the term 'relative', as becomes clear from a perusal of the Sen (1983)–Townsend (1985)–Sen (1985b) exchange. If the poverty line is 'relative' in the sense of being linked to some measure of central tendency of the income distribution, then Sen (1983) would appear to be right in the view that the notions of poverty and relative inequality would no longer lend themselves to easy distinction. For example, if the poverty line is pegged at, say, half the mean income, then, as Sen points out, halving everybody's income would leave the set of poor persons unchanged, even though some individuals just above the poverty line in the initial situation could be precipitated into conditions of hunger in the latter situation. If, on the other hand, the poverty line is 'relative' in the sense of being inter-personally or inter-regionally or inter-temporally variable, to reflect varying resource requirements according to variable patterns of resource needs, then there might be a case for admitting 'relativity': only, it may be more meaningful to characterize such an approach to conceptualizing poverty as 'flexibly absolute', rather than as 'relative'. Indeed, as Sen has clarified, it might be most productive to view poverty as 'absolute' in the space of 'functionings', but 'relative' in the space of resources, commodities and incomes. (On the notions of 'absolute' and 'relative' poverty in more general terms, a useful reference is Foster 1998.)

One distinguished strand of the 'absolute' approach is the so-called 'biological' (see Sen 1981a) conceptualization: here, the poverty line is identified in terms of the income needed to achieve a nutritionally adequate diet. There has been very considerable controversy on *what* constitutes – in terms of calories, say – a nutritionally adequate diet: both inter- and intra-individual variations in requirements have been postulated, with accompanying theories of 'adjustment' and 'adaptation' (see, in particular, Sukhatme 1978, 1981, Sukhatme and Margen 1982, and Seckler 1982). For a sorting out of the difficult issues involved, the reader is referred to Osmani (1992), and Dasgupta and Ray (1990).

Even when 'relativity' is interpreted in its 'flexibly absolute' sense, the identification exercise could present potential problems, of both a conceptual and a practical nature, in undertaking inter-temporal and cross-section poverty comparisons. Specifically: are poverty comparisons meaningful only when the *same* poverty line is employed across the board? If so, how is this view compatible with the notion that poverty in different regions (or at different points in time for the same region) should be assessed in terms of standards that are appropriate for these different regions (or different points in time)? These questions acquire a particular salience in the context of cross-country poverty comparisons (see, for example, Blackwood and Lynch 1994). The difficulty may well reside in, precisely, taking an 'either/or' view of the problem, and it is useful, in this context, to quote Sen (1981a: 21) at some length:

> There is . . . nothing contradictory in asserting both of the following pair of statements:
>
> (1) There is *less* deprivation in community A than in community B in terms of some common standard, e.g. the notions of minimum needs prevailing in community A.

(2) There is *more* deprivation in community A than in community B in terms of their *respective* standards of minimum needs, which are a good deal higher in A than in B.

It is rather pointless to dispute which of these two senses is the 'correct' one, since it is quite clear that both types of questions are of interest. The important thing to note is that the two questions are quite distinct from each other.

Briefly, then, there is no uncomplicated or non-controversial route to the problem of specifying a poverty line; but assuming that it has, somehow, been solved (usually by appeal to some consensual agreement around a 'reasonable' norm), the next step in poverty measurement would be constituted by the *aggregation* exercise, to which we now turn.

Aggregation: properties of poverty indexes

As in the case of inequality measurement, we consider in what follows a set of properties of poverty indexes on which the literature has produced a fair measure of agreement as to their appeal. First, the *focus* axiom (*Axiom F*), stipulates that the extent of measured poverty should, other things equal, be invariant with respect to increases in *non*-poor incomes. A focused income–poverty measure, therefore, reckons well-being in terms of the condition of the *poor*, and not – unlike other income-based indicators of aggregate well-being – in terms of the population *as a whole*. Second, *symmetry* (*Axiom S*) demands that interpersonal permutations of incomes among the population should leave the value of the poverty index unchanged. Third, *normalization* (*Axiom N*) requires that, if nobody is poor, the extent of poverty is taken to be 0. Fourth, *continuity* (*Axiom C*) is the property that the poverty index P should be continuous on the set of sub-vectors of poor incomes. *Monotonicity* (*Axiom M*) demands that, ceteris paribus, poverty should increase with a decline in any poor person's income. *Transfer* (*Axiom T*) is the property that, other things remaining the same, a progressive rank-preserving income transfer between two poor individuals should cause poverty to decline. *Transfer sensitivity* requires the poverty index to be more responsive to income transfers at the lower than at the upper end of the distribution of poor incomes. There are at least two ways of capturing this requirement (see Kakwani 1984, and Foster 1984). The first – call this property *transfer sensitivity-1* (*Axiom TS-1*) – says that a given progressive rank-preserving transfer between two poor individuals separated by a given *number of individuals* should cause poverty to decline by more the poorer the pair of individuals involved in the transfer. The second – call this property *transfer sensitivity-2* (*Axiom TS-2*) – says that a given progressive rank-preserving transfer between two poor individuals separated by a given *income* should cause poverty to decline by more the poorer the pair of individuals involved in the transfer. Next, a couple of invariance properties. *Replication invariance* (*Axiom RI*) demands that, for any given poverty line, and any positive integer k, a k-fold population replication of the income distribution should leave the value of the poverty index unchanged. *Scale invariance* (*Axiom SI*) demands that any uniform scaling up or down of the income vector and the poverty line should leave measured poverty unchanged. *Sub-group consistency* (*Axiom SC* – see Foster and Shorrocks 1991) is the property that poverty should increase with an increase in any sub-group's poverty, other things remaining the same. *Decomposability* (*Axiom D*) is a strengthened version of sub-group consistency: it requires the poverty index to be expressible as a weighted sum of sub-group poverty levels, the weights being the relevant sub-group population shares (see Foster *et al.* 1984). Finally, as in the case of inequality measurement, one could have an axiom of ready comprehensibility, or *ease of interpretation* (*Axiom E*).

The stock of desirable properties can certainly be expanded, but the more important of them have been covered in the preceding inventory. Clearly, not all poverty indexes satisfy all of the axioms listed; and, on occasion, the quest for poverty indexes satisfying specified sets of properties could end in the discovery of non-existence (for some impossibility theorems on poverty measures, see, among others, the articles by Kundu and Smith 1983, Donaldson and Weymark 1986, and Subramanian 2002). As in the case of inequality indexes, so in the case of poverty measures, the choice of index must be guided by the appeal of the underlying axiom structure in relation to intent, motivation, purpose, and the availability of data. (For instance, when detailed data on income distributions are unavailable, and all we have are binary classifications of the population into the 'poor' and the 'non-poor', then poverty comparisons in terms of even a 'partial' index – to use the terminology of Foster and Sen 1997 – such as the headcount ratio are better than no comparisons: there is a case for not making the infeasibly comprehensive the enemy of the feasibly partial.) We turn now to a consideration of some of the more widely known real-valued indexes of poverty that have been advanced in the literature.

Aggregation: some specific poverty indexes

All of the poverty indexes reviewed in this section are defined for every permissible combination of income distribution $\mathbf{x}$ and poverty line z: the arguments $\mathbf{x}$ and z of the poverty index will simply be taken as read in much of what follows. For every combination of $\mathbf{x}$ and z, $Q(\mathbf{x}; z)$ will stand for the set of all poor individuals whose incomes are represented in the vector $\mathbf{x}$, and $q(\mathbf{x}; z)$ will stand for the number of poor individuals.

The most commonly used index of poverty is the so-called *headcount ratio*, H, which simply measures the proportion of the poor population in total population. The *income-gap ratio*, Y, measures the proportionate shortfall of the average income of the poor, $\mu^P \equiv (1/q)\Sigma_{i \in Q} x_i$, from the poverty line z.

The product of H and Y, denoted by R, expresses the income-gap ratio in *per person* terms: R is the *per capita income-gap ratio*. The principal virtue of indexes like H and Y is that they satisfy *Axiom E*: the underlying meaning of both is very easy to grasp. A well-known problem with H is that it violates monotonicity; and while Y and R respect monotonicity, neither satisfies the transfer property. Sen (1976) sought to remedy this deficiency by pursuing an axiomatic approach to the construction of a 'distribution-sensitive' poverty index, P_S, expressed as a normalized weighted sum of the income gap ratios of the poor, the weights being the respective rank-orders in the sub-vector of poor incomes:

$$P_S = [2/(q+1)nz]\sum_{i\in Q}(z - x_i)(q+1-i) \tag{6.10}$$

where the poor individuals have been ranked in non-decreasing order of their incomes; namely, $x_i \leq x_{i+1}$ for all $i \in Q \setminus \{q\}$

Given the rank-order weighting system employed in the expression for P_S, it should not be surprising if the Gini index of inequality had a role to play in the poverty index. Indeed, it turns out that, for 'large' values of q, the Sen index can be asymptotically approximated to the following expression:

$$P_S = H[Y + (1-Y)G^P] \tag{6.10'}$$

where G^P is the Gini coefficient of inequality in the distribution of poor incomes. By combining information on the incidence, the depth, *and* the 'severity' of poverty, the Sen index furnishes a more comprehensive account of poverty than any of H, Y, or R: in particular, P_S satisfies both the monotonicity and transfer axioms. Among early critiques and modifications of the Sen index are those by Takayama (1979) and Thon (1979). Takayama proposed a variant of the Sen index, involving the use of a 'censored' income distribution, which, unfortunately, fails the monotonicity test. While the Sen index penalizes any regressive transfer among the poor that leaves the beneficiary of the transfer poor, it does not invariably punish a regressive transfer that enables the beneficiary to escape poverty. If this is seen as a shortcoming, then a way of rectifying it is to employ a weighting system on the right hand side of equation (6.10′) wherein the relevant weight is the rank-order in the entire income vector rather than in the sub-vector of poor incomes; and this leads to Thon's variant of the Sen index (see also Shorrocks 1995). Kakwani (1980b) sought a parametric generalization of Sen's index, in a bid to meet the requirement of *Axiom TS-1*, which the Sen index fails.

A distinguished class of poverty indexes – in which the Sen index and its variants are not included – is that constituted by the *additively separable* indexes (see Atkinson 1987, Foster and Shorrocks 1991, and Keen 1992). Here, resort is had to a set of *individual deprivation functions* $\phi(x_i; z)$, with the property that $\phi(x_i; z) > 0$ for $x_i < z$, and $\phi(x_i; z) = 0$ for $x_i \geq z$; and a poverty index P is additively separable if it can be written as a simple average of these deprivation functions, viz. for all $(\mathbf{x}; z)$:

$$P(\mathbf{x}; z) = (1/n) \sum_{i \in Q} \phi(x_i; z) \tag{6.11}$$

Many of the properties of poverty indexes discussed earlier are implied, in the context of additively separable measures, by restrictions on the individual deprivation functions. Given a deprivation function $\phi(x; z)$, if ϕ is a continuous function of $x \in [0, z)$, then P is continuous; if ϕ is a declining function of x in the range $[0, z)$, then P satisfies monotonicity; and if, additionally, ϕ is a strictly declining and convex function of x for all $x \in [0, z)$, then P satisfies the transfer axiom. A number of poverty indexes advanced in the literature are different specializations of the function $\phi(x; z)$. The more salient of these indexes are quickly reviewed in what follows.

For $x_i < z$, if we set $\phi(x_i; z) = \log_e(z/x_i)$ in equation (6.11), we obtain *Watts'* (1968) poverty index P_W; if $\phi(x_i; z) = (1/\beta)[1 - (x_i/z)^\beta]$, $\beta < 1$, we obtain the *Clark, Hemming, and Ulph* (1981) class of indexes $P_{CHU}(\beta)$; if $\phi(x_i; z) = 1 - (x_i/z)^\sigma$, $\sigma \in (0, 1)$, we obtain the *Chakravarty* (1983) set of indexes $P_C(\sigma)$; if $\phi(x_i; z) = (1 - x_i/z)^\alpha$, $\alpha \geq 0$, we obtain the *Foster, Greer, and Thorbecke* (1984) P_α family of indexes; and corresponding to $\phi(x_i; z) = e^{\gamma(1-x_i/z)} - 1$, $\gamma > 0$, we obtain *Zheng's* (2000) group of 'constant distribution-sensitivity' indexes $P_Z(\gamma)$.

All of the above indexes (or families of indexes) satisfy *Axioms F, SI, RI,* and *D* (and therefore, *SC*). Watts' index satisfies *Axioms M, T,* and *TS-2* as well. For the other families of indexes, *Axioms M, T,* and *TS-2* are satisfied for parameter values of β, δ, α, and γ which are lesser or greater than specified cut-off values for the fulfilment of the respective axioms. (For example, the P_α indexes all satisfy focus, and scale- and replication-invariance, for $\alpha \geq 0$; monotonicity for $\alpha > 0$; transfer for $\alpha > 1$; and *TS-2* for $\alpha > 2$.) A major feature of all these indexes is that they are decomposable – unlike the Sen index, which fails even the weaker condition of sub-group consistency.

Finally, mention may be made of the so-called 'ethical' indexes of poverty – see, among others, Blackorby and Donaldson (1980) and Hagenaars (1987) – which are similar in motivation to the Atkinson-type 'ethical' indexes of inequality we have encountered earlier. Here, the idea is to express the poverty index as a distinguished per capita income-gap ratio $R^* = HY^*$, where Y^* is the proportionate shortfall from the poverty line of Atkinson's 'equally distributed equivalent income' x_P^{ede} – computed for the distribution of poor incomes. Depending on which particular underlying 'social evaluation function' is favoured, one can obtain different expressions for x_P^{ede}, and therefore – *via* Y^* – for the ethical poverty index R^*.

Plurality and ranking

Plurality can interfere with the possibility of unambiguous poverty rankings in at least two ways. First, there may be a *range* of plausible poverty lines, rather than a unique line, to consider, and it could happen that a given poverty index measures more poverty in distribution **x** than in distribution **y** for one poverty line z_1, but measures more poverty in **y** than in **x** for some other poverty line z_2, where both z_1 and z_2 belong to the plausible range of poverty lines. Second, with more than one poverty index figuring in the analyst's menu, it is possible, given a poverty line z, that one index pronounces that **x** has more poverty than **y**, while another index pronounces that **y** has more poverty than **x**. Foster and Shorrocks (1988c) and Zheng (2000), among others, have investigated the first problem, while treatments of the second problem can be found in Foster (1984), Atkinson (1987), Foster and Shorrocks (1988a, 1988b), Spencer and Fisher (1992), Shorrocks (1995), Foster and Sen (1997), and Zheng (2000). Here we will simply note, very quickly, that the prospect of obtaining unambiguous poverty rankings, in respect of both categories of problems outlined, is linked to the fulfilment of various stochastic dominance, 'generalized Lorenz' dominance, 'poverty profile' dominance, and 'generalized poverty profile' dominance, conditions. A generic problem for poverty measurement, using the difficulty presented for unambiguous ranking by a multiplicity of poverty indexes as an example, is the following. It is true that the probability that the sorts of 'dominance conditions' we have mentioned will be satisfied increases as we restrict the set of poverty indexes in contention through restrictions on their properties (such as on 'distribution sensitivity', as in Zheng 2000); but even as the uncertainty of obtaining consensus on rankings declines, the uncertainty regarding the 'rightness' of the poverty indexes retained presumably increases, as one constricts the set of admissible indexes. The problem has a certain analogy with the conduct of an election. If a movement toward unanimity is preferred, then a means to that end would be to confine voting rights to a smaller and smaller set of 'like-minded' voters – until, in the limit, all ambiguity is eliminated, assuming no ambiguity is attached to the desirability of just one vote counting, through straightforward dictatorship! Briefly, the poverty analyst must always contend with the problem that while plurality can promote ambiguity in one sense, singularity can promote ambiguity in another sense. There is no simple golden rule for the 'right' choice of the range of poverty indexes and poverty lines that could be employed in poverty analysis.

Poverty indexes and anti-poverty policy

Direct income transfers to the poor, and wage employment schemes, are two instruments for combating poverty. Given a budget of fixed size, what is an optimal pattern of income allocation to the poor, or an optimal wage, depending on which instrument is wielded? The answers would typically depend on how poverty (which is the quantity being sought to be minimized) is measured. Bourguignon and Fields (1990) and Gangopadhyay and Subramanian (1992) address the income transfer problem. For specificity, one could measure poverty by the P_α class of indexes. It turns out that for $\alpha < 1$, the prescribed optimal allocation is one in which only the richest of the poor, close to the poverty line, are the beneficiaries; for $\alpha = 1$, the odd outcome is that any feasible transfer schedule that exhausts the budget is also optimal; and for $\alpha > 1$, one has a 'lexicographic maximin solution', whereby, through a sequence of progressive and income equalizing transfers, the poorest of the poor are raised to that level of income that is compatible with exhausting the budget. In the matter of wage employment programmes (see, among others, Basu 1981, Drèze and Sen 1989, Ravallion 1991, and Gangopadhyay and Subramanian 1992), for $\alpha = 0$, the optimal wage is the poverty line income z; and as α increases, the optimal wage declines and coverage increases until, in the limit, for α tending to infinity, the wage is pitched as low as is compatible with creating the maximum number of jobs for which there are takers, given the size of the budget. The nature of the solution, in each case – with specific reference to the question of 'distribution sensitivity' – is a comment on, and serves to clarify our intuitive grasp of, the poverty index employed.

It should also be clear from the above that in all but the last case (poverty minimization through wage employment in the 'α tending to infinity' setting, which is compatible with the phenomenon of 'self-selection'), the intended beneficiaries of the poverty redress scheme would have to be identified and targeted, through (presumably costly) 'means testing'. This raises questions pertaining to the relative merits of 'universal provisioning' and means testing (Besley 1990); the principles of targeting (Besley and Kanbur 1993); and the possibilities of 'imperfect targeting' in a variety of contexts (Kanbur 1987, Besley and Kanbur 1988, Ravallion and Chao 1989), all of which issues lend themselves to being addressed as part of the analytics of poverty measurement.

Some other issues in poverty measurement

Research in poverty measurement has made many advances, and clarified many sources of conceptual confusion, since the early systematic efforts initiated by Watts (1968) and Sen (1976). There are still many issues that require more sustained investigation. Simply by way of allusion, some of these issues are mentioned here. *Fuzzy* approaches to the measurement of poverty have been considered by, among others, Shorrocks and Subramanian (1994). In conventional poverty analysis, poverty status is taken to be a binary variable that takes on one of only two values, 0 and 1, to signify, respectively, that one is not, or is, poor. A fuzzy approach relaxes this tightness by allowing poverty status to be defined by any value between 0 and 1: in this framework, people are more or less poor, rather than only either poor or non-poor. Fuzziness addresses the problem of imprecision inherent in the requirement of specifying a poverty line designed to strictly separate the poor component of a population from its non-poor component. (Indeed, inequality measurement is also open to a fuzzy approach; for two examples of which, see Basu 1987, and Ok 1995.) The measurement of deprivation assessed *multi-dimensionally* presents difficulties for both identification and aggregation; for treatments of which, the reader is referred to Mukherjee (2001), Tsui (2002), Atkinson (2003), Bourguignon and Chakravarty (2003), and Dutta *et al.* (2003). A completely different variety of problem, revolving around the 'adjustment' of poverty indexes for premature excess mortality among the poor, is considered by Kanbur and Mukherjee (2002): the larger issue revolves around the ethical and logical sustainability of divorcing the *outcome* of poverty changes from the *processes* leading to these changes. Yet another problem arises from the competing claims of the *aggregate headcount A* and the *headcount ratio H* as the appropriate means of factoring the incidence of poverty into a poverty index: two accounts of the nature and implications of the conflict are available in Chakravarty *et al.* (2002) and Subramanian (2002). These, and other problems, may not be amenable to completely satisfactory 'solutions', but an identification and elaboration of these problems is arguably itself of some instructional value.

Inequality and poverty: links and disjunctions

The interconnections between poverty and inequality are apparent in a number of ways. For one thing, and as we have seen, for the entire set of 'distribution sensitive' poverty indexes (namely, those that satisfy the transfer axiom), an increase in inequality in the distribution of poor incomes will, ceteris paribus, cause measured poverty to rise. For another, letting $\mathbf{x}_z^P$ stand for the vector of *poor* incomes given any income vector $\mathbf{x}$ and poverty line z, it would be the case that, for any poverty line z and any pair of vectors $\mathbf{x}$ and $\mathbf{y}$ with the same mean and the same number of poor persons, if $\mathbf{x}_z^P$ Lorenz-dominates $\mathbf{y}_z^P$, and $\mathbf{x}$ Lorenz-dominates $\mathbf{y}$, then $P(\mathbf{x}; z)$ is less than $P(\mathbf{y}; z)$ for any poverty index P that belongs to the class $\mathbf{P}^*$ of indexes that are focused, monotonic, transfer-preferring and scale-invariant; while if the Lorenz curves of $\mathbf{x}$ and $\mathbf{y}$ coincide, the two vectors share the same number of poor persons, and the mean of $\mathbf{x}$ exceeds the mean of $\mathbf{y}$, then again $P(\mathbf{x}; z)$ is less than $P(\mathbf{y}; z)$ for any poverty index P belonging to the class of indexes $\mathbf{P}^*$. These considerations have led some analysts (Kakwani and Subbarao 1990, and Datt and Ravallion 1992) to seek to 'decompose' a poverty change into a 'growth' component (attributable to a change in mean income, holding the Lorenz curve fixed) and an 'inequality' component (attributable to a change in the distributional parameters of the Lorenz curve, holding the mean income fixed). These are instances of 'congruence' between poverty and inequality.

But there are clearly also cases of conflict. We have noted earlier that certain poverty indexes (such as Sen's) do not invariably register an increase following on a regressive income transfer between two poor individuals when the beneficiary is thereby enabled to cross the poverty line. This has led some commentators like Pyatt (1987) to characterize Sen-type indexes as being 'badly behaved'. The underlying presumption seems to be that the S(ocial) W(elfare) F(unction) should be of the standard 'two objective' type, increasing in mean income and declining in inequality, so that a 'three objective' SWF, with poverty also explicitly factored into it, is effectively reduced to what Brent (1986: 93) calls 'the two objective version in disguise'. (For a number of other treatments of the subject of poverty, inequality and social welfare, the reader is referred to Hagenaars 1987, Vaughan 1987, and Lewis and Ulph 1988.) However, Brent (op. cit.) has demonstrated plausible conditions under which a well-defined, 'equity-conscious' SWF can actually register an *increase* with an increase in the headcount ratio of poverty: an SWF that favours equality could be inimical to poverty reduction. The 'bad behaviour' of poverty indexes, then, is attributable to a notion that cannot simply be dismissed out of hand; namely, that the poverty line is a *distinguished* dividing line, such that the ability to cross it is invested with a special welfare significance. Furthermore, in situations wherein the mean income is less than the poverty line, poverty minimization may call for a 'man overboard' solution to the 'lifeboat dilemma': equalizing incomes across the board could leave the *entire* population in very straitened circumstances, whereas allocating no income to a sub-set of the population while permitting the rest to be raised to the poverty line level of income might prove to be a harsh but pragmatic necessity (see Subramanian 1989 and Dasgupta and Ray 1990).

Briefly, then, while there are clearly many congruent linkages between poverty and inequality, the conflicts between the two must also be recognized: there may be no particular virtue to insisting on a view of social welfare in which welfare increases through inequality reduction must necessarily always be accompanied by reductions in poverty. Poverty and inequality are related, but distinct, concepts.

Deprivation and disparity: towards a more inclusive approach

Income alone?

Are poverty and inequality assessed solely in the space of incomes sufficient to convey a picture of how well or badly a society is doing? Is an 'adequate' level of personal disposable income a sufficient guarantor of achievement in the dimensions of, say, literacy, nutrition, longevity and health? Inter- and intra-country comparisons do not invariably furnish an affirmative answer to these questions. Thus, for example, relatively income poor countries such as China or Ecuador or Costa Rica have relatively impressive records in dimensions of well-being such as literacy, life expectancy and health; while relatively income rich countries such as some of the Arab States display relatively poor performances in extra income aspects of well-being. Similarly, the Indian state of Kerala is way ahead of a relatively (income-wise) richer state such as Haryana when it comes to assessing well-being in dimensions such as fertility, expectation of life at birth, infant mortality, and literacy. These empirical findings strongly suggest the importance of going beyond the metric of income in assessing deprivation, disparity, and well-being.

Well-being beyond income

Much of our preceding review of the measurement of inequality and poverty has been related to a somewhat special and narrow conception of well-being. 'Well-being', in this view, has been largely conflated with 'welfare', which itself has generally been seen to be some aggregation of individual 'utilities', with a person's utility being taken to depend just on their *income*. In Sen (1980), and a host of related writings, we see the beginnings of a substantive engagement with the question 'equality of *what*?' Depending on what particular view of well-being we may be disposed to favour, we may choose to assess deprivation and disparity in the dimensions of income, or resources generally, or utilities, or, as in Rawls (1971), 'primary goods'. Sen himself (1985a) advances the view that the most relevant engagement with the notion of well-being obtains when one's concern is with *human capability*. Deprivation, in this reckoning, is fruitfully seen as a failure of capability; and the containment of disparity is reflected in moving towards equality in the space of capabilities. The capability in question is not an abstract capability, but the capability to function – a *functioning* being what Sen calls 'a state of being or doing'. In this expanded view of well-being, a concern with income (and therefore with measures of income poverty and inequality as indicators of 'ill-being') is not invalidated; what is, however, called into question is an *exclusive* preoccupation with income related indicators – which can result in a picture of development that is both partial and misleading. A more inclusive view of well-being such as is afforded by the capability approach underlines the need for data on, and measurement of, indicators that go beyond the income metric (Qizilbash 1996, 1997).

Generalized well-being/deprivation indicators

As part of the more expansive view of well-being dictated by the sorts of considerations just reviewed, there has been an increasing concentration of effort among scholars to derive and justify measures of human well-being and capability deprivations that transcend an exclusive concern with the space of incomes. Among salient contributions to this effort – with, naturally, differences in content and emphasis – are the 'basic needs' approach to reckoning achievement (Hicks and Streeten 1979); the concern with assessing the 'quality of life' (Morris 1979, Sen 1981b); the importance attached to individuals' 'capability to function' (Sen 1985a, Sen *et al.* 1987); and the primacy accorded to the evaluation of 'human development' (UNDP 1990–2002, McGillivray 1991, McGillivray and White 1993).

The Human Development Index (HDI) has, through successive annual compilations of its country-wise values by the United Nations Development Programme's *Human Development Report* (UNDP *HDR*, hereafter), become a widely known shorthand measure of aggregate well-being. This is the subject of an entirely separate chapter and will therefore not be dealt with here. Additionally, the emphasis in this chapter is on *deprivation*, as such: the HDI reckons the well-being of any given population by reference to the population *as a whole*, whereas, from a *poverty* perspective, there would be a case for measuring well-being with specific reference to the condition only of the *deprived* section of the population. (This would correspond to the distinction between (a) a *focused* income poverty measure, and (b) other income based measures of aggregate well-being of the population considered in its entirety.) Driven by this motivation, a number of measures of deprivation, seen in the light of capability failure, have been developed: these would include the 'Capability Poverty Measure' in UNDP's *HDR 1996*; the 'Human Poverty Index' in UNDP's *HDR 1997*; Mahbub ul Haq's (1997) 'Human Deprivation Measure'; and Majumdar and Subramanian's (2001) 'Capability Failure Ratio'. In the interests of specificity, and also because it is the most comprehensive deprivation measure among the indexes just mentioned, it is the Human Poverty Index (HPI) that will be the focus of attention here.

The Human Poverty Index

The HPI is a *multi-dimensional* index. It measures deprivation in three dimensions – those of longevity, knowledge, and standard of living – and thus achieves a certain correspondence with the components of the HDI, with the difference that there is no specifically *income* component in the HPI. The HPI can be written as a combination of distinguished headcount ratios of failure in selected dimensions of the capability to function. Specifically, let Π_1 be the proportion of the population that is expected not to survive to the age of 40; let Π_2 be the adult illiteracy rate; and let Π_3 be a composite of the proportion of the population without access to health services and to safe water, and the proportion of the under-5 population that is undernourished. Then, Π_1, Π_2 and Π_3 are measures of capability failure in the dimensions, respectively, of longevity, knowledge and standard of living. The HPI can be written – for a detailed treatment the reader is referred to 'Technical Note 1: Properties of the human poverty index' in UNDP's *HDR 1997* – in its most general form, as a weighted average of order η, HPI(η), which is given by:

$$\text{HPI}(\eta) = [(w_1\Pi_1^\eta + w_2\Pi_2^\eta + w_3\Pi_3^\eta)/(w_1 + w_2 + w_3)]^{1/\eta} \tag{6.12}$$

where $w_k > 0 (k = 1, 2, 3)$ is a weight attached to the headcount ratio of human poverty in the kth dimension, and $\eta \geq 1$ is an indicator of the extent of 'substitutability' between the components of the HPI (with a higher value of η reflecting a lower degree of substitutability: for $\eta = 1$, we have perfect substitutability, and as η becomes indefinitely large we move toward zero substitutability, so that $\lim_{\eta \to \infty} \text{HPI}(\eta) = \max\{\Pi_1, \Pi_2, \Pi_3\}$).

Certain distinguished members of the HPI(η) class of indexes, obtained for specified values of η and specified patterns of the weighting structure $\{w_k\}$, are presented below:

$$\text{HPI}^*(\eta) = [(\Pi_1^\eta + \Pi_2^\eta + \Pi_3^\eta)/3)]^{1/\eta}, \eta \geq 1 \tag{6.13}$$

$\text{HPI}^*(\eta)$ is the *ordinary mean of order* η, obtained by setting $w_1 = w_2 = w_3$:

$$\text{HPI}(1) = [(w_1\Pi_1 + w_2\Pi_2 + w_3\Pi_3)/(w_1 + w_2 + w_3)] \tag{6.14}$$

HPI(1) is the *weighted mean of order 1*, or *weighted arithmetic mean*, obtained by setting $\eta = 1$:

$$\text{HPI}^*(1) = (\Pi_1 + \Pi_2 + \Pi_3)/3 \tag{6.15}$$

$\text{HPI}^*(1)$ is the *simple arithmetic mean* of Π_1, Π_2, and Π_3, obtained by setting $\eta = 1$ and $w_1 = w_2 = w_3 = 1$. It may be noted that the measure $\text{HPI}^*(1)$ is *decomposable.* That is to say, if the population is partitioned into M mutually exclusive and exhaustive sub-groups; if Π_{mk} is the headcount ratio of deprivation for the mth group ($m = 1, \ldots, M$) in the kth dimension ($k = 1, 2, 3$); if $\text{HPI}_m^*(1) = (\Pi_{m1} + \Pi_{m2} + \Pi_{m3})/3$ is the simple arithmetic mean version of the HPI for group $m(m = 1, \ldots, M)$; and if t_m is the population share of group $m(m = 1, \ldots, M)$: then, it is true that:

$$\text{HPI}^*(1) = \sum_{m=1}^{M} t_m \text{HPI}_m^*(1) \tag{6.16}$$

Finally, the HPI, as it is computed in *HDR 1997*, is obtained by setting $\eta = 3$ and $w_1 = w_2 = w_3$: the resulting measure, $\text{HPI}^*(3)$, is written as:

$$\text{HPI}^*(3) = [(\Pi_1^3 + \Pi_2^3 + \Pi_3^3)/3)]^{1/3} \tag{6.17}$$

Does a multi-dimensional human poverty index convey the same information as a unidimensional income based poverty index? This, of course, in an empirical question, and the answer would depend on the precise indexes one uses, the particular poverty norms one adopts, and the units of observation one considers in performing the comparison exercise. In this connection, some of the cross-country findings reported in UNDP's *HDR 1997* are instructive. Employing 1993 data for a set of 36 countries on the index $\text{HPI}^*(3)$ of equation (6.17) and on the income based headcount ratio of poverty (call it H) obtained by employing a poverty line of a dollar a day (in 1985 purchasing power parity dollars), the *HDR* (1997: 22) states that 'regression analysis indicates a weak relationship between the headcount index of income poverty and [HPI*(3)]'. For a sub-set of 41 countries for which data on both HPI (as measured by HPI*(3)) and H are available in *HDR* 1997, it turns out that the coefficient of rank correlation between an ordering of countries by HPI and an ordering by H is fairly strong (Spearman's rank correlation coefficient is of the order of 0.82), but not perfect. These results suggest, at the least, that income based measures of poverty are not necessarily completely adequate surrogates for a more expansive, capability oriented reckoning of disparity. Additionally, the experiences of countries such as China, Costa Rica, Kenya, Peru, the Philippines, and Zimbabwe – see *HDR* 1997 – which have displayed greater success in reducing human poverty than income-poverty, point to the possibilities of enhancing achievements in the space of human functionings by routes different from those centred exclusively on income growth and the percolation of that growth to the poor. In particular, these experiences would stress the importance of state intervention in securing relief from human poverty – an emphasis that is at some variance with a view, increasingly gaining currency in some quarters, that somewhat sidelines the state in favour of the market and civil society as agents for the promotion of aggregate well-being.

It remains now to consider how, given a deprivation index that may or may not be multidimensional but is, like HPI*(1) in equation (6.15), decomposable, one may assess the extent of group related disparity in the distribution of that deprivation.

Reckoning inter-group disparities in the distribution of deprivation

A decomposable real-valued index of generalized deprivation – call it D – is really a measure of central tendency: it presents the aggregate deprivation in a society, averaged over the deprivations of specific groups constituting the society. That is, suppose the population is partitioned into M mutually exclusive and completely exhaustive groups, identified by the running index $m = 1, \ldots, M$; then, if D_m is the deprivation level of the mth group (and it will be assumed that the groups are arranged in non-increasing order of deprivation, so that $D_m \geq D_{m+1}, m = 1, \ldots, M-1$), and if t_m is the population share of the mth group, D can be written as: $D = \Sigma_{m=1}^{M} t_m D_m$. For future use, let us also define T_m to be the cumulate proportion of the population with deprivation levels not exceeding that of the mth group, for every group $m = 1, \ldots, M$. D, being a simple average of group-specific deprivation levels, conceals any inequality there may be in the inter-group distribution of deprivations. Such group related disparity is clearly an important datum in assessing aggregate well-being, and there is therefore a strong case for reckoning such disparity in the measurement of deprivation (see Stewart 2001). To this end, one can construct 'adjusted' measures of deprivation, where the adjustment takes the form of buttressing information on the average level of deprivation with information on the inter-group disparity of its distribution. Two such adjusted measures, D^* and D^{**}, are presented below:

$$D^*(\lambda) = \left[\sum_{m=1}^{M} t_m D_m^{\lambda} \right]^{1/\lambda}, 1 \leq \lambda < \infty \tag{6.18}$$

and

$$D^{**}(\delta) = [1/(M-1)] \sum_{m=1}^{M} [(M-1-\delta m)t_m + \delta T_m] D_m, 0 \leq \delta \leq 1 \tag{6.19}$$

λ and δ in equations (6.18) and (6.19) respectively are parameters of 'inter-group disparity aversion', with the extent of aversion being an increasing function of the values of the parameters. Consider the special case in which $M = 2$ (where, for example, the population has been partitioned into 'males' and 'females'). For $\lambda = 1$ (respectively, $\delta = 0$), D^* (respectively, D^{**}) just collapses to D: this the '(average) Benthamite' rule of reckoning aggregate deprivation simply in terms of the average level of deprivation; for $\lambda \to \infty$ (respectively, $\delta = 1$), D^* (respectively, D^{**}) just collapses to D_1: this is the 'Rawlsian' rule of reckoning aggregate deprivation in terms of the deprivation of the worst off group. In general, each of D^* and D^{**} is amenable to being expressed as the average level of deprivation D enhanced by a factor incorporating a measure of between-group inequality: as it happens, this inequality measure, in the case of D^*, is an Atkinson-type 'ethical' index of inter-group disparity and, in the case of D^{**}, a Gini-type 'descriptive' measure. D^* is essentially an adaptation of a procedure advanced by Anand and Sen (1995), and subsequently adopted by the UNDP's *HDR*, for constructing a 'gender-adjusted HDI'; and D^{**} – see Subramanian and Majumdar 2002 – is a generalization of what Majumdar and Subramanian (2001) call an 'adjusted capability failure ratio', which the authors have computed, in an application to Indian data, for a partitioning of the population according to gender, caste and sector of residence. For a version of the 'adjusted capability ratio', as applied to an assessment of disparity in the cross-country distribution of deprivation, the reader is referred to Subramanian (2003).

Expanding the interpretation of well-being: orientation, policy and data

By taking a more expansive view of well-being than is afforded by a wholly income centred approach, we have seen that the measurement emphasis also shifts from an exclusive concern with indicators of poverty and inequality to more general indicators of deprivation and disparity. From many perspectives, this is a welcome shift. For one thing, data on income or consumption expenditure, which are required for constructing indexes of poverty and inequality, are not always wholly reliable. Inter-temporal comparisons of poverty and inequality, based on sample surveys, are often vitiated by changes in concepts, definitions, and reference periods of recall. Additionally, the identification problem is notoriously difficult to solve, and eliciting consensus on a poverty line is frequently a vexed business, which is customarily disposed of through a stance of philosophical resignation to the inevitability of some measure of arbitrariness and subjectivism in the measurement exercise. Further, there is always room for (endless) controversies on the 'correct' choice of price deflators with which to update base-year poverty lines so that these may be expressed in current prices. All of these problems are amply reflected in, for example, the Indian literature on poverty. Few would agree that there is little difference between a decline, over a forty year period, in the headcount ratio from 50 per cent to 30 per cent according to one set of poverty norms and a decline, over the same period, from 70 per cent to 65 per cent according to another set of norms. For all of these reasons, there is a strong case for being guided by generalized indicators of deprivation and disparity rather than solely by indicators of poverty and inequality. By focusing directly on the capability to function, in addition to reckoning income based indicators, one can get a fuller picture of time-series and cross-section variations in well-being deprivations and disparities. This would call for the compilation, by official data generating agencies, and the use, by policy makers and researchers, of data that are richer and more extensive than a narrow preoccupation with income will allow. Indeed, both national and international agencies are increasingly turning to the compilation and use of data sets on achievements with respect to literacy, health, nutrition, longevity, fertility, and the like. From the points of view of both social explanation and collective redress, it is fruitful to address problems of, for example, child labour, women's well-being, demographic transition, and social exclusion, by paying attention not only to achievements in the income dimension but to achievements in, say, the provision of potable water, sanitation, energy for cooking, electricity, public health care, and roads. Hence, the catholic approach to measurement, in this chapter and in this book.

Concluding observations

In this chapter, an attempt has been made to cover, however quickly, certain crucial issues in the measurement of economic poverty and inequality, as well as more generalized deprivation and disparity. We have discussed Lorenz orderings, welfare orderings, and inequality orderings; we have examined the welfare bases of inequality comparisons; we have presented axioms for both inequality and poverty measurement; we have reviewed a number of both the so-called 'ethical' and descriptive measures of inequality and poverty; we have attempted to evaluate these indexes, and to take stock of the importance of being guided by motive and purpose in their choice for concrete applications; we have pointed to sources of ambiguity in the measurement of the phenomena under investigation; we have attempted to locate anti-poverty policy in the context of measurement issues; we have sought to elucidate the relationship between inequality and poverty within an overall framework of welfare; and we have presented a rationale for, and discussed measurement issues relating to, the assessment of deprivation and disparity in an expanded framework of human well-being which moves beyond the income dimension to a consideration of human capabilities and functionings. This, without a doubt, amounts to not much more than scratching the surface; but given the vastness of that surface, it is to be hoped that the exercise will have had something to offer to the reader who is looking for a helpful preliminary overview of the subject.

Note

This chapter, by its nature, is not an original piece of work: it is constructed around the writings of a number of scholars in the fields of inequality and poverty measurement, of whom specific mention may be made of S. Anand, A. B. Atkinson, J. E. Foster, N. C. Kakwani, R. Kanbur, A. Sen, and A. F. Shorrocks. It also draws heavily on the author's 'Introduction' in Subramanian (1997). The chapter has benefited from discussions with, and comments by, Mark McGillivray, and from detailed suggestions for improvement made by an anonymous referee. Thanks are due to A. Arivazhagan for help with the graphics. Adam Swallow has edited the typescript with an almost frightening eye to minute detail. Taina Iduozee has performed a truly heroic job of chasing up, and filling in, the gaps in the bibliographical list. The author's most considerable debt is to James Foster for his detailed comments on the chapter – comments that he himself inadequately describes as '[a] series of smallish critiques [and] general peevish questions': as it happens, the critiques were seldom smallish and the questions were uniformly peevish, both of which facts have helped greatly in improving the quality of the product. All errors and deficiencies are solely the author's.

References

Aigner, D. J. and A. J. Heins (1967) 'A Social Welfare View of the Measurement of Income Inequality', *Review of Income and Wealth*, 13(1): 12–25.

Anand, S. (1983) *Inequality and Poverty in Malaysia: Measurement and Decomposition* (New York: Oxford University Press).

Anand, S. and A. Sen (1995) 'Gender Inequality in Human Development: Theories and Measurement', Human Development Report Office Occasional Paper 19 (New York: UNDP).

Atkinson, A. (1970) 'On the Measurement of Inequality', *Journal of Economic Theory*, 2(3): 244–63.

Atkinson, A. (1987) 'On the Measurement of Poverty', *Econometrica*, 55(4): 749–64.

Atkinson, A. (2003) 'Multidimensional Deprivation: Contrasting Social Welfare and Counting Approaches', *Journal of Economic Inequality*, 1(1): 51–65.

Basu, K. (1981) 'Food for Work Programmes: Beyond Roads That Get Washed Away', *Economic and Political Weekly*, 16(1): 37–40.

Basu, K. (1987) 'Axioms for a Fuzzy Measure of Inequality', *Mathematical Social Sciences*, 14(3): 275–88.

Besley, T. (1990) 'Means Testing versus Universal Provision in Poverty Alleviation Programmes', *Economica*, 57(225): 119–29.

Besley, T. and R. Kanbur (1988) 'Food Subsidies and Poverty Alleviation', *Economic Journal*, 98(392): 701–19.

Besley, T. and R. Kanbur (1993) 'The Principles of Targeting', in M. Lipton and J. van der Gaag (eds) *Including the Poor* (Washington, DC: World Bank).

Blackorby, C. and D. Donaldson (1978) 'Measures of Relative Equality and Their Meaning in Terms of Social Welfare', *Journal of Economic Theory*, 18(1): 59–80.

Blackorby, C. and D. Donaldson (1980) 'Ethical Indices for the Measurement of Poverty', *Econometrica*, 48(4): 1053–60.

Blackwood, D. L. and R. G. Lynch (1994) 'The Measurement of Inequality and Poverty: A Policy Maker's Guide to the Literature', *World Development*, 22(4): 567–78.

Bourguignon, F. and S. R. Chakravarty (2003) 'The Measurement of Multidimensional Poverty', *Journal of Economic Inequality*, 1(1): 25–49.

Bourguignon, F. and G. S. Fields (1990) 'Poverty Measures and Anti-Poverty Policy', *Recherches Economiques de Louvain*, 56(3–4): 409–27.

Brent, R. J. (1986) 'An Axiomatic Basis for the Three Objective Social Welfare Function within a Poverty Context', *Economics Letters*, 20(1): 89–94.

Chakravarty, S. R. (1983) 'A New Index of Poverty', *Mathematical Social Sciences*, 6(3): 307–13.

Chakravarty, S. R., R. Kanbur and D. Mukherjee (2002) 'Population Growth and Poverty Measurement', at: www.people.cornell.edu/pages/sk145/papers.htm

Chiappero, M. E. (2000) 'A Multidimensional Assessment of Well-being Based on Sen's Functioning Approach', *Rivista Internazionale di Scienza Sociali*, 108(2): 207–39, (also at: www.unipv.it/iuss/esascs/didactics/mat_research/Chia_Wellbeing.pdf).

Clark, S., R. Hemming and D. Ulph (1981) 'On Indices for the Measurement of Poverty', *Economic Journal*, 91(362): 515–26.

Cowell, F. A. (1984) 'The Structure of American Income Inequality', *Review of Income and Wealth*, 30(3): 351–75.

Dalton, H. (1920) 'The Measurement of Inequality of Incomes', *Economic Journal*, 30(119): 348–61.

Dasgupta, P. S. (1993) *An Inquiry in Well-being and Destitution* (Oxford: Clarendon Press).

Dasgupta, P. S. and D. Ray (1990) 'Adapting to Undernutrition: The Clinical Evidence and its Implications', in J. Drèze and A. Sen (eds) *The Political Economy of Hunger*, vol. 1 (Oxford: Clarendon Press for UNU-WIDER).

Dasgupta, P. S., A. K. Sen and D. Starrett (1973) 'Notes on the Measurement of Inequality', *Journal of Economic Theory*, 6(2): 180–7.

Datt, G. and M. Ravallion (1992) 'Growth and Redistribution Components of Changes in Poverty Measures: A Decomposition with Applications to Brazil and India in the 1980s', *Journal of Development Economics*, 38(2): 275–95.

Donaldson, D. and J. A. Weymark (1986) 'Properties of Fixed-Population Poverty Indices', *International Economic Review*, 27(3): 667–88.

Drèze, J. and A. Sen (1989) *Hunger and Public Action* (Oxford: Clarendon Press).

Dutta, I., P. K. Pattanaik and Y. Xu (2003) 'On Measuring Deprivation and the Standard of Living in a Multidimensional Framework on the Basis of Aggregate Data', *Economica*, 70(278): 197–221.

Fields, G. S. and J. C. S. Fei (1978) 'On Inequality Comparisons', *Econometrica*, 46(2): 303–16.

Foster, J. (1984) 'On Economic Poverty: A Survey of Aggregate Measures', in R. L. Basmann and G. F. Rhodes, Jr (eds), *Advances in Econometrics*, vol. 3 (Greenwich, CT and London: JAI Press).

Foster, J. (1985) 'Inequality Measurement', in H. P. Young (ed.) *Fair Allocation* (Providence, RI: American Mathematical Society).
Foster, J. (1998) 'Absolute versus Relative Poverty', *American Economic Review, Papers and Proceedings*, 88(2): 335–41.
Foster, J., J. Greer and E. Thorbecke (1984) 'A Class of Decomposable Poverty Measures', *Econometrica*, 52(3): 761–6.
Foster, J. and E. A. Ok (1999) 'Lorenz Dominance and the Variance of Logarithms', *Econometrica*, 67(4): 901–7.
Foster, J. and A. Sen (1997) 'On Economic Inequality after a Quarter Century', in A. Sen (ed.) *On Economic Inequality* (expanded edn) (Oxford: Clarendon Press).
Foster, J. and A. F. Shorrocks (1988a) 'Poverty Orderings', *Econometrica*, 56(1): 173–7.
Foster, J. and A. F. Shorrocks (1988b) 'Poverty Orderings and Welfare Dominance', *Social Choice and Welfare*, 5: 179–98.
Foster, J. and A. F. Shorrocks (1988c) 'Inequality and Poverty Orderings', *European Economic Review*, 32(2–3): 654–62.
Foster, J. and A. F. Shorrocks (1991) 'Subgroup Consistent Poverty Indices', *Econometrica*, 59(3): 687–709.
Gangopadhyay, S. and S. Subramanian (1992) 'Optimal Budgetary Intervention in Poverty Alleviation Schemes', in S. Subramanian (ed.), *Themes in Development Economics: Essays in Honour of Malcolm Adiseshiah* (Delhi: Oxford University Press).
Hagenaars, A. (1987) 'A Class of Poverty Indices', *International Economic Review*, 28(3): 583–607.
Haq, Mahbub ul (1997) *Human Development in South Asia* (Karachi: Oxford University Press).
Hicks, N. and P. Streeten (1979) 'Indicators of Development: The Search for a Basic Needs Yardstick', *World Development*, 7(6): 567–80.
Jenkins, S. (1991) 'The Measurement of Income Inequality', in L. Osberg (ed.), *Economic Inequality and Poverty: International Perspectives* (Armonk, NY: M. E. Sharpe).
Kakwani, N. C. (1980a) *Income Inequality and Poverty: Methods of Estimation and Policy Applications* (New York: Oxford University Press).
Kakwani, N. C. (1980b) 'On a Class of Poverty Measures', *Econometrica*, 48(2): 437–46.
Kakwani, N. C. (1984) 'Issues in Measuring Poverty', in R. L. Basmann and G. F. Rhodes Jr (eds), *Advances in Econometrics*, vol. 3 (Greenwich, CT and London: JAI Press).
Kakwani, N. C. (1993) 'Performance in Living Standards: An International Comparison', *Journal of Development Economics*, 41(2): 307–36.
Kakwani, N. C. and K. Subbarao (1990) 'Rural Poverty and its Alleviation in India', *Economic and Political Weekly*, 25(13): A2–A16.
Kanbur, R. (1987) 'Measurement and Alleviation of Poverty: With an Application to the Effects of Macroeconomic Adjustment', IMF Staff Papers (Washington, DC: IMF).
Kanbur, R. and D. Mukherjee (2002) 'Premature Mortality and Poverty Measurement', at: www1.york.ac.uk/depts./econ/dept_seminars/mukherjee_fullpaper.pdf
Keen, M. (1992) 'Needs and Targeting', *Economic Journal*, 102(410): 67–79.
Kolm, S. Ch. (1969) 'The Optimum Production of Social Justice', in J. Margolis and H. Guitton (eds) *Public Economics* (London: Macmillan).
Kolm, S. Ch. (1976) 'Unequal Inequalities I, II', *Journal of Economic Theory*, 12(3): 416–42 and 13(1): 82–111.
Kundu, A. and T. E. Smith (1983) 'An Impossibility Theorem on Poverty Indices', *International Economic Review*, 24(2): 423–34.
Lewis, G. W. and D. T. Ulph (1988) 'Poverty, Inequality, and Welfare', *Economic Journal*, 98(390): 117–31.

Lorenz, M. O. (1905) 'Methods for Measuring Concentration of Wealth', *Journal of the American Statistical Association*, 9: 209–19.

Majumdar, M. and S. Subramanian (2001) 'Capability Failure and Group Disparities: Some Evidence from India for the 1980s', *Journal of Development Studies*, 37(5): 104–40.

McGillivray, M. (1991) 'The Human Development Index: Yet Another Redundant Composite Development Indicator?', *World Development*, 19(10): 1461–8.

McGillivray, M. and H. White (1993) 'Measuring Human Development? The UNDP's Human Development Index', *Journal of International Development*, 5(2): 183–92.

Morris, M. D. (1979) *Measuring the Condition of the World's Poor: The Physical Quality of Life Index* (Oxford: Pergamon Press).

Mukherjee, D. (2001) 'Measuring Multidimensional Deprivation', *Mathematical Social Sciences*, 42(3): 233–51.

Ok, E. A. (1995) 'Fuzzy Measurement of Income Inequality: A Class of Fuzzy Inequality Measures', *Social Choice and Welfare*, 12(2): 111–36.

Osmani, S. R. (1992) 'On Some Controversies in the Measurement of Undernutrition', in S. R. Osmani (ed.) *Nutrition and Poverty* (Oxford: Clarendon Press for UNU-WIDER).

Pyatt, G. (1987) 'Measuring Welfare, Poverty and Inequality', *Economic Journal*, 97(386): 459–67.

Qizilbash, M. (1996) 'Capabilities, Well-being and Human Development: A Survey', *Journal of Development Studies*, 33(2): 143–62.

Qizilbash, M. (1997) 'Pluralism and Well-being Indices', *World Development*, 25(12): 2009–26.

Ravallion, M. (1991) 'On the Coverage of Public Employment Schemes for Poverty Alleviation', *Journal of Development Economics*, 34(1–2): 57–79.

Ravallion, M. (1994) *Poverty Comparisons: A Guide to Concepts and Methods* (Chur: Harwood Academic).

Ravallion, M. and K. Chao (1989) 'Targeted Policies for Poverty Alleviation under Imperfect Information: Algorithms and Applications', *Journal of Policy Modelling*, 11(2): 213–24.

Rawls, J. (1971) *A Theory of Justice* (Cambridge, MA: Harvard University Press).

Rothschild, M. and J. Stiglitz (1973) 'Some Further Results on the Measurement of Inequality', *Journal of Economic Theory*, 6(2): 188–204.

Seckler, D. (1982) ' "Small But Healthy": Basic Hypothesis in the Theory, Measurement and Policy of Malnutrition', in P. V. Sukhatme (ed.) *Newer Concepts in Nutrition and their Implications for Policy* (Pune: Maharashtra Association for the Cultivation of Science).

Seidl, C. (1988) 'Poverty Measurement: A Survey', in D. Bos, M. Rose and C. Seidl (eds) *Welfare and Efficiency in Public Economics* (Heidelberg: Springer Verlag).

Sen, A. K. (1973) *On Economic Inequality* (Oxford: Clarendon Press).

Sen, A. K. (1976) 'Poverty: An Ordinal Approach to Measurement', *Econometrica*, 44(2): 219–31.

Sen, A. K. (1978) 'Ethical Measurement of Inequality: Some Difficulties', in W. Krelle and A. F. Shorrocks (eds) *Personal Income Distribution* (Amsterdam: North-Holland).

Sen, A. K. (1979) 'Issues in the Measurement of Poverty', *Scandinavian Journal of Economics*, 81(2): 285–307.

Sen, A. K. (1980) 'Equality of What?' in S. M. McMurrin (ed.), *Tanner Lectures on Human Values, I* (Salt Lake City and Cambridge: University of Utah Press and Cambridge University Press) (Reprinted in Sen 1982).

Sen, A. K. (1981a) *Poverty and Famines: An Essay on Entitlement and Deprivation* (Oxford: Clarendon Press).

Sen, A. K. (1981b) 'Public Action and the Quality of Life in Developing Countries', *Oxford Bulletin of Economics and Statistics*, 43(4): 287–319.

Sen, A. K. (1982) *Choice, Welfare and Measurement* (Oxford: Blackwell, Cambridge, MA: MIT Press and Delhi: Oxford University Press).

Sen, A. K. (1983) 'Poor, Relatively Speaking', *Oxford Economic Papers*, 35(2): 153–69.

Sen, A. K. (1984) 'Rights and Capabilities', in T. Honderich (ed.) *Morality and Objectivity: A Tribute to J. L. Mackie* (London: Routledge).

Sen, A. K. (1985a) *Commodities and Capabilities* (Amsterdam: North-Holland).

Sen, A. K. (1985b) 'A Sociological Approach to the Measurement of Poverty: A Reply to Professor Townsend', *Oxford Economic Papers*, 37(4): 669–76.

Sen, A. K. (1992) *Inequality Reexamined* (New York: Russell Sage Foundation and Oxford: Clarendon Press).

Sen, A. K., J. Muellbauer, R. Kanbur, K. Hart and B. Williams (1987) *The Standard of Living* (Cambridge: Cambridge University Press).

Shorrocks, A. F. (1988) 'Aggregation Issues in Inequality Measurement', in W. Eichhorn (ed.), *Measurement in Economics: Theory and Applications in Economic Indices* (Heidelberg: Physica Verlag).

Shorrocks, A. F. (1995) 'Revisiting the Sen Poverty Index', *Econometrica*, 63(5): 485–97.

Shorrocks, A. F. and J. E. Foster (1987) 'Transfer Sensitive Inequality Measures', *Review of Economic Studies*, 54(1): 485–97.

Shorrocks, A. F. and S. Subramanian (1994) 'Fuzzy Poverty Indices', Mimeo. University of Essex.

Spencer, B. and S. Fisher (1992) 'On Comparing Distributions of Poverty Gaps', *Sankhya The Indian Journal of Statistics, Series B*, 54(1): 114–26.

Stewart, F. (2001) 'Horizontal Inequality: A Neglected Dimension of Development', WIDER Annual Lecture 5 (Helsinki: UNU-WIDER).

Subramanian, S. (1989) 'Poverty Minimization in the Light of "Life-Boat Ethics"', *Journal of Quantitative Economics*, 5(2): 239–49.

Subramanian, S. (ed.) (1997) *Measurement of Inequality and Poverty*, Readers in Economics Series (Delhi: Oxford University Press) (Re-issued in paperback 2001, 2002).

Subramanian, S. (2002) 'Counting the Poor: An Elementary Difficulty in the Measurement of Poverty', *Economics and Philosophy*, 18(2): 277–85.

Subramanian, S. (2003) 'Aspects of Global Deprivation and Disparity: A Child's Guide to some Simple-minded Arithmetic', in F. Carlucci and F. Marzano (eds) *Poverty, Growth and Welfare in the World Economy in the 21st Century* (Bern: Peter Lang AG).

Subramanian, S. and M. Majumdar (2002) 'On Measuring Deprivation Adjusted for Group Disparities', *Social Choice and Welfare*, 19(2): 265–80.

Sukhatme, P. V. (1978) 'Assessment of Adequacy of Diets at Different Income Levels', *Economic and Political Weekly*, 13(31–3): 1373–84.

Sukhatme, P. V. (1981) 'On Measurement of Poverty', *Economic and Political Weekly*, 16(32): 1311–24.

Sukhatme, P. V. and S. Margen (1982) 'Relationship between Undernutrition and Poverty', *Indian Economic Review*, 16(1–2): 13–39.

Takayama, N. (1979) 'Poverty, Income Inequality and their Measures: Professor Sen's Axiomatic Approach Reconsidered', *Econometrica*, 47(3): 747–59.

Theil, H. (1967) *Economics and Information Theory* (Amsterdam: North-Holland).

Thon, D. (1979) 'On Measuring Poverty', *Review of Income and Wealth*, 25(4): 429–39.

Townsend, P. (1985) 'A Sociological Approach to the Measurement of Poverty: A Rejoinder to Prof. Amartya Sen', *Oxford Economic Papers*, 37(4): 659–68.

Tsui, K.-Y. (2002) 'Multidimensional Poverty Indices', *Social Choice and Welfare*, 19(1): 69–93.

UNDP (United Nations Development Programme) (1990–2002) *Human Development Report* (New York: Oxford University Press).

Vaughan, R. N. (1987) 'Welfare Approaches to the Measurement of Poverty', *Economic Journal*, 97 (supplement): 160–70.

Watts, H. (1968) 'An Economic Definition of Poverty', in D. P. Moynihan (ed.), *On Understanding Poverty* (New York: Basic Books).

Zheng, B. (1997) 'Aggregate Poverty Measures', *Journal of Economic Surveys*, 11(2): 123–62.

Zheng, B. (2000) 'Minimum Distribution-Sensitivity, Poverty Aversion, and Poverty Orderings', *Journal of Economic Theory*, 95(1): 116–37.

7
Gender-related Indicators of Well-being

Stephan Klasen

Introduction

There are large and persistent gender gaps in many indicators of well-being across the world. They include gender gaps in control over economic resources, education, earnings, mortality, access to employment, pay, time use, safety, and power in the public and the private sphere (e.g. UNDP 1995, World Bank 2001). Perhaps the most egregious form of gender inequality is that of gender inequality in survival in parts of the developing world, most notably South Asia and China where millions of females are 'missing' as a result of these inequalities (e.g. Sen 1989, Klasen and Wink 2002, 2003).

Yet, when it comes to constructing appropriate measures of well-being that take into account these gender differentials, numerous problems emerge. Among the many difficult conceptual issues to be considered are the space in which gender inequality in well-being is to be measured, whether the indicators should track well-being of males and females separately, create composite measures of gender equity, or adjust overall measures of well-being by the gender inequality in well-being, whether gender equality in every indicator is necessarily the goal, how to assess gender inequality that is apparently desired by males and females, and what role indicators of empowerment should play in gender related indicators of well-being.

These issues will be dealt with in the first sections of the chapter, which aim to discuss each issue in turn and propose solutions where they seem feasible.

In addition, there are many measurement issues one needs to tackle when devising gender related indicators of well-being. Among the most serious issues to be addressed is that most information about economic resources is only available at the level of households, and it is conceptually and practically difficult to 'assign' household incomes or assets to individuals of different gender within households. For example, this makes assessments about the share of the world's income-poor that is female extremely difficult (for claims about this suspect, see Marcoux 1998). Second, when assessing gender related indicators of well-being, the question of the relevant population appears particularly important. Finally, the data base for assessing gender inequality across space and time is often lacking or particularly shaky due to differences in definitions, approaches to measurement and interpretation, so that comparisons of gender-related indicators of well-being require particular care. These issues will be tackled in the latter sections of the chapter, alongside a critical discussion of the two most widely known indicators of gender related development.

In short, I will argue that it is critically necessary to consider gender when devising measures of well-being, but that such approaches must take special care to address these very difficult conceptual and measurement issues.

The case for including gender in an assessment of well-being

In principle, one can make a case for including gender in an assessment of well-being on instrumental or intrinsic grounds. On instrumental grounds, there is a large literature that documents that large gender gaps in critical aspects of well-being (particularly in education, health, and employment) not only disfavour females, but also compromise progress on overall development, with negative effects on economic growth, human development, poverty reduction, fertility and mortality decline, and educational improvements (e.g. Sen 1999, Ranis and Stewart 2000, World Bank 2001, Klasen 2002, Ravallion and Datt 2002, Klasen and Lamanna 2003). While these are weighty considerations that have clearly served to elevate gender issues in development policy debates, such an instrumental view sidelines questions of equity and justice, and limits the debate on gender inequality to the areas of instrumental significance, which is insufficient from a well-being perspective. Thus, I will now concentrate on intrinsic justifications for considering gender inequality in well-being.[1]

The intrinsic case for including gender inequality in an assessment of well-being rests primarily on two factors. First, gender differences in important well-being indicators are so large that they cannot and should not be ignored in an overall assessment of well-being. The large inequality existing in two very important indicators of well-being, survival and education, nicely illustrate this point. Regarding survival, there is a sizeable literature that has demonstrated that girls and women in parts of the developing world suffer from considerable inequalities in survival (e.g. D'Souza and Chen 1980, Sen 1989, Klasen 1994, Klasen and Wink 2002). This is mainly due to inequalities in access to resources within households but is increasingly also due, particularly in China, South Korea, and also recently in India, to sex selective abortions of female foetuses.[2] As a result of these past and present inequalities in survival, some 100 million women are 'missing' in today's populations in

South Asia, the Middle East, and East Asia (Klasen and Wink 2002, 2003).[3] Table 7.1 gives the distribution of missing women in different parts of the developing world. The death toll of gender bias in survival thus ranks among the most important human catastrophes of our present time and must therefore be considered when we are measuring the well-being of people.

Similarly, there are pervasive gender differences in access to education in most regions of the world. Although the size of gender inequality differs greatly and has generally narrowed in most regions (see Table 7.2), these gaps remain sizeable and must be taken into consideration when we consider well-being more generally (Abu-Ghaida and Klasen 2004).

The second factor that supports the case for including gender inequality in an assessment of well-being is that gender inequality is a consequence of a biological category, one's sex – that is, in general, not changeable – and thus rewards and punishes people for an ascriptive characteristic they

Table 7.1 Missing women, latest estimates

	Year	Actual number of women	Actual sex ratio	Expected sex ratio	Expected number of women	Missing women	% Missing
China	2000	612.3	1.067	1.001	653.2	40.9	6.7
Taiwan	1999	10.8	1.049	1.002	11.3	0.5	4.7
South Korea	1995	22.2	1.008	1.000	22.4	0.2	0.7
India	2001	495.7	1.072	0.993	534.8	39.1	7.9
Pakistan	1998	62.7	1.081	1.003	67.6	4.9	7.8
Bangladesh	2001	63.4	1.038	0.996	66.1	2.7	4.2
Nepal	2001	11.6	0.997	0.992	11.7	0.1	0.5
Sri Lanka	1991	8.6	1.005	1.006	8.6	0.0	0.0
West Asia	2000	92.0	1.043	1.002	95.8	3.8	4.2
of which:							
Turkey	1990	27.9	1.027	1.003	28.5	0.7	2.4
Syria	1994	6.7	1.047	1.016	6.9	0.2	3.1
Afghanistan	2000	11.1	1.054	0.964	12.1	1.0	9.3
Iran	1996	29.5	1.033	0.996	30.6	1.1	3.7
Egypt	1996	29.0	1.048	1.003	30.3	1.3	4.5
Algeria	1998	14.5	1.018	1.005	14.7	0.2	1.2
Tunisia	1994	4.3	1.021	1.000	4.4	0.1	2.1
Sub-Saharan Africa	2000	307.0	0.987	0.970	312.5	5.5	1.8
Total (World)		1774.8				101.3	5.7

Note: Turkey and Syria are subsumed in West Asia and are therefore not added separately. The expected sex ratio at birth is based on regressions 2 and 4 in Table 7.2. Actual and expected sex ratios refer to the number of males per females in the entire population; the expected sex ratio at birth refers to the number of males per females at birth.
Source: Klasen and Wink (2003).

Table 7.2 Enrolment and achievement in education by gender

	Primary gross enrolment rate				Secondary gross enrolment rate				Average years of attainment[b]			
	1975		1999		1975		1999		1970		1995	
Region	F	M	F	M	F	M	F	M	F	M	F	M
East Asia and Pacific	108	121	106	105	35	49	60	65	3.06	4.54	5.85	6.84
Europe and Central Asia	..	..	93	95	..	..	80	81	8.09	8.93	9.67	9.20
Latin America and Caribbean	97	100	130	133	34	35	87	80	3.52	4.14	5.58	5.91
Middle East and North Africa	64	99	91	99	24	44	67	72	1.39	2.75	4.21	5.74
South Asia	58	91	91	110	15	33	41	57	1.08	2.95	2.94	5.31
Sub-Saharan Africa[a]	45	66	73	85	6	13	23	28	1.56	2.60	2.82	3.98

Notes: [a] Latest available data on primary GERs are from 1998 and on secondary GERs from 1996.
[b] Attainment data include schooling beyond secondary. Since data are from Barro and Lee (2000), the regional classification includes some countries with per capita incomes too high to be included in the World Bank's database (the one used for the GERs).
Sources: World Development Indicators central database and Barro and Lee (2000).

are born with.[4] In contrast to income inequality which may, in part, occur despite equality of opportunities for everyone, gender inequality is precisely a case where there are inequalities of opportunities based purely on one's sex which is particularly objectionable in most theories of justice.[5]

To be sure, this second point does not apply to gender alone. Inequalities based on race or ethnicity would also need to be considered in the same vein, and such inequalities typically are considered in countries where there are significant racial and ethnic divides.[6] While other 'ascriptive' inequalities are thus important to consider as well, there are arguments why a consideration of gender inequality is particularly important and requires special care and attention, compared to other types of 'ascriptive' inequalities. First, some gender gaps observed are rooted in (or justified with) biological differences between males and females, and thus require particularly careful analysis. The most important two biological differences are the ability of women to bear children and the differences in average body size and strength between the sexes. While a lot of gender inequality is socially constructed, even those social constructions often relate to these biological differences. Second, while for most other 'ascriptive' inequalities, the locus of these inequalities is largely in the public sphere and often relate to markets (particularly the labour market, the housing market, and so on), a considerable portion of gender inequality is generated in the home, and thus outside of formal markets. As a result, gender inequality in the home is often less measurable and visible, compared to inequalities in markets such as the labour market, where racial (or gender) inequality can be assessed using standard theoretical and empirical methods.

Lastly, some of these gender inequalities that take place in households are unrelated to economic resources but are still likely to have a large impact on the well-being of females. They include items such as enforced female seclusion (purdah), female genital mutilation, or domestic violence. Considering them in a gender sensitive assessment of well-being would be important (although it is often difficult to quantify these phenomena as well as to assess the well-being impact of these practices).[7]

Thus, if we think that our measures of well-being should be reliable in the sense of not glossing over important inequalities within society, and if we believe they should be grounded in a theory of justice that at least calls for equality of opportunities for all, then gender inequality must be considered when devising meaningful measures of well-being. At the same time, a consideration of gender inequality must take careful note of the specific issues relating to gender, which are the link to biological differences and the importance of the household in generating gender inequality.

The space of gender-related indicators of well-being

The dimension (or space) in which to measure well-being is a general problem to be addressed when considering indicators of human well-being (see also other contributions in this volume). When gender is considered, this discussion assumes further urgency and possibly points to different solutions. In particular, specific spaces are quite unsuitable for examining gender dimensions of well-being. For example, focusing on the income space generates the problem that income can usefully be measured only at the household level and not easily ascribed to individual male and female members (see below).[8] Similarly, focusing on the work aspects of well-being, it is not immediately clear that gender inequalities in labour force participation and pay are the only important aspects to consider, as they ignore important gender gaps in time use outside of the market economy, including gender differences in home production and care responsibilities (e.g. Folbre, 2005).

Basing one's well-being assessment on the space of liberties (in the sense of Nozick 1974) might also not do justice to the realities of gender inequality and its impact on well-being, as many gender inequalities in the home or in the labour market occur despite equal procedural liberties for both sexes. While removing any legal and procedural inequalities, where they exist, is certainly an important step towards reducing gender inequalities in the household or in the labour market (World Bank 2001), it is clearly not sufficient as other economic, social, and cultural factors might continue to maintain these inequalities.

Examining well-being in the space of capabilities, as advocated by Sen (e.g. 1990, 1992), might be particularly suitable for capturing the gender dimension of well-being. The capability approach calls for people to have the largest possible set of valuable functionings from which people can then choose a life they have reason to value. Among the basic capabilities are the ability to be lead a long life in good health, be well nourished, educated, housed and adequately clothed, and integrated into the community.[9]

The advantages of considering this space are that they focus on substantive 'positive' freedoms that males and females have reason to value.[10] Moreover, it focuses on aspects of life that are amenable to measurement at the individual level and do not face the disaggregation problem of household based measures (such as income or assets), and it considers outcomes rather than focusing purely on procedures or means that might lead to different outcomes for males and females. By placing priority on freedoms (rather than just outcomes that he calls functionings), due recognition is also made of the fact that males and females might, for reasons of nature or nurture, end up with different outcomes despite enjoying the same capabilities.

This last point is, however, only a theoretical advantage. In practice, most applications of Sen's capability approach to measuring individual well-being (and aggregate indicators based loosely on it, such as the Human Development Index (HDI)), have ended up measuring functionings, rather than capabilities as it is exceedingly difficulty to observe people's choice sets, while their choices (outcomes or functionings) are more readily observable (e.g. Klasen 2000). Thus, in practice we ascribe a lack of the capability 'to be able to be adequately nourished' to those who are fasting and starving alike, even though only the latter is suffering from that short-fall. Similarly, we may observe women's poor health or nutrition (functioning failure) and may not distinguish between their inability to be adequately nourished (capability failure) or, for example, their willingness to sacrifice resources for the sake of their children (no capability failure?).[11]

It thus appears that the capability approach is particularly suited to considering gender dimensions of well-being but, as we have seen, limiting oneself to observing functionings might reduce one of the key advantages of that approach (although, as discussed below, this might generate different advantages).[12]

Is equality of outcomes the goal?

While a capability approach might call for equal capabilities for everyone, it is, as mentioned above, exceedingly difficult to observe people's capability sets and, instead, actual outcomes are usually measured to assess inequalities of well-being. Gender inequalities in such outcomes (e.g. health, nutrition, education, employment, earnings) are then usually seen as a well-being problem to be redressed, as the implicit assumption is that the inequalities constitute a well-being loss for those it disfavours. While, in most cases, this appears plausible, special care is necessary in a well-being assessment of such gender gaps in outcomes.

First, in some cases, biological differences might lead to problematic conclusions about the presence of gender gaps in opportunities or treatment. The best example of this is longevity. There is a sizeable literature documenting that males suffer from a survival disadvantage vis-à-vis females (e.g. Waldron 1983, 1993, 1998, Klasen 1994). This is particularly well-documented among infancy and old age, where males suffer from significantly higher mortality rates for well-known biological reasons (Waldron 1983, 1993). Equal infant mortality rates would therefore actually be an indication of significant gender bias in treatment favouring males. Consequently, the female life expectancy advantage of 3–7 years in most countries of the world (with the exception of those in South and East Asia) does not signify gender inequality favouring females. While it seems uncontroversial to consider any deviation from this apparent biological disadvantage evidence of 'gender inequality' as has been done, explicitly or implicitly, in the calculations of missing females by the authors active in that research area (e.g. Sen, 1989; Coale, 1991; Klasen, 1994; Klasen and Wink, 2002; 2003, see Table 7.1), it is less clear that, in a gender-related well-being indicator, one should consider the biological male survival disadvantage 'normal'. This will be of particular importance for well-being measures that have an implicit definition of gender equality (see below).[13]

Similar problems might emerge in the assessment of gender gaps in undernutrition. Males and females have different body sizes and their growth to attain these body sizes follows different patterns. Here, the solution has been to examine undernutrition of males and females by comparing the anthropometric shortfall of males and females with reference to a sex specific reference standard. In the case of children, this reference standard refers to male and female children who grew up in the USA between the 1930s and the 1970s (WHO 1995).[14]

To some extent, a portion of gender gaps in earnings might also be due to differences in strength in particular manual occupations where strength is an important determinant of productivity. Here, is it not a priori obvious how to separate these effects from discriminatory treatment. It is clear, however, that this can possibly explain only a small portion of the large gender gaps in earnings that exist in not only manual occupations.

Second, some inequalities in outcomes might be the result of informed choices by males and females, and thus do not signify inequalities in opportunities or capabilities. For example, there are plausible economic arguments for a sexual division of labour in the household (between market and household work) and if, as argued by Becker (1981), females have a comparative advantage in their ability to combine child-bearing and child-rearing, it might be optimal for couples to specialize in different forms of production, and the resulting inequality in time use and (market) labour force participation might be the result of this optimal decision. If this is anticipated, it could then also be an argument for females to invest less and differently in human capital than males, and gender gaps in education might emerge.

It is unlikely that the existing sexual division of labour, and the resulting gender gaps in education and employment, are largely based on this optimizing calculus. They are more likely an outcome of constraints and barriers facing women and girls, as well as different socialization. Nevertheless, it is possible that these considerations do play a role and thus full equality in labour force participation, time use and even education might not necessarily maximize well-being for both concerned.[15] In these cases, there are no easy solutions other than recognizing that not all gender differences in these outcomes necessarily reflect lower well-being for those who have the lower outcome.

Agency versus well-being

A related issue arises when considering Sen's distinction between agency and well-being. Sen (1990, 1999) argues that strengthening female agency, which he defines as the 'role of the individual as a member of the public and as a participant in economic, social, and political actions' (Sen 1999: 19), should be considered as a separate worthwhile goal alongside improving female well-being. While Sen (1999) makes this case largely on instrumental grounds by arguing that strengthening female agency tends to promote female well-being (as well as the well-being of children, male and female), the question arises as to whether strengthening female agency – that is, promoting female empowerment – is an integral part of female well-being.

There is overwhelming evidence for the important instrumental significance of female empowerment for female well-being. In particular, the bargaining approaches to intrahousehold resource allocation, which empirically are able to explain household behaviour much better than unitary household models (e.g. Haddad *et al.* 1997, World Bank 2001, Sen 1999), allocate a central role to the threat point of males and females. Improving the threat point of women outside of marriage (and also inside, see Lundberg *et al.* 1997) improves their well-being inside of marriage. Measures to improve the threat point include better education and income earning opportunities, better economic and legal support in the case of divorce, and resource transfers by the state directed at them. In short, economic and legal empowerment will improve their well-being.

There is also evidence that greater female political representation, particularly at local level, improves public policy favouring female well-being

(Bardhan and Klasen 1999, Chattophadhyay and Duflo 2003, UNRISD, 2005).

But is female empowerment a well-being end in itself? One may argue that the ability to achieve positions of economic and political power might be an important capability, and should thus be included in a measurement of well-being.[16] But, as above, one might have to exercise caution when claiming, for example, that less than 50 per cent female representation necessarily represents a well-being relevant inequality.

Related to this there arises a second question about the distinction between agency and well-being. This arises in situations where gender gaps in own well-being (measured in the space of functionings or capabilities) are accepted, and even wanted, by all concerned, including those it apparently disfavours. There is a sizeable literature that shows that women are more willing to sacrifice resources for their children (e.g. Thomas 1997, Klasen 1998, World Bank 2001), even if that means lower well-being outcomes for themselves. Similarly, Sen (1990) claims that women in some contexts, including in South Asia, might equate their well-being with the well-being of their family and thus accept lower allocations for themselves. The origins of this greater female altruism are somewhat controversial, but quite clearly socialization of girls and women into accepting such a role has played an important role. To the extent that women are the agents of their own lower achievements, how can one assess gender inequality in these outcomes? If one took a capability perspective, one would have to say that despite the functioning shortfall, there is no capability problem as these women could have secured more resources for themselves.[17] If one considered agency as an important aspect of well-being, the ability of women to pursue their goal of sacrificing themselves for the good of the family should positively influence their well-being, even though their own worse nutritional and health status would have to be assessed against that.

Sen (1990) argues that it is still possible to claim that females in South Asia are worse off than males as they suffer from lower objectively measurable functionings, despite being agents of their inferior outcomes (by agreeing to deprive themselves of nutrition and health care to favour their husbands or children). This is akin to arguing that these females suffer from 'false consciousness' in the sense of not putting their own interests first, and it repudiates a central starting point of much economic analysis which is not to question the preferences of individuals (e.g. Becker and Stigler 1977). While we may often have little grounds to question people's preferences, it appears perfectly possible to claim that such preferences will reduce well-being, as measured by objective indicators.[18] To the extent that this phenomenon is empirically relevant, it is actually an argument favouring the functioning over the capability space (or a broader agency perspective), for well-being assessments as functionings focusing on measuring own well-being outcomes while examining capability sets of goals beyond one's own might overlook these problems of 'false consciousness'.

In addition, one should also see the clear limitations of the claim that women are consenting agents of their own discrimination. While this may be due in some circumstances, most discrimination in survival in South Asia occurs in childhood (Klasen and Wink 2002), and it is not plausible that all women and girls (including very young girls where most discrimination occurs) freely consent to reduced allocations for themselves. Evidence of significant public discussion and activism by grass-roots organizations to improve women's well-being suggests that other factors, including lack of political, economic, and legal power to change matters, are often more important in explaining gender inequality in health, education, nutrition, and mortality than the willing consent of females to it.

A related problem emerges in the assessment of differences in self-destructive behaviour not motivated by self-sacrifice. For example, how is one to treat the fact that men in Russia, largely due to higher rates of alcoholism and related accidents, violence, and diseases, have life expectancies that are fully ten years below those of women? Is this gender inequality to be treated in the same manner as the reverse gaps in South Asia where women suffer from inequalities in health care that lead to similar gender gaps in mortality?[19] Interestingly, UNDP's Gender Related Development Index (GDI), which defined equality in survival as females having a five year higher life expectancy than males, thus treats the 10-year gap in Russia equivalently to the 0 year gap in Nepal (UNDP 1995, Bardhan and Klasen 1999). I would argue that the two situations are substantively different although, once again, one may simply state that from a well-being perspective measured in the functioning space, the outcome is equivalent.

Gender disaggregated measures, gender gap indices, and gender sensitive aggregate measures

In principle, one can tackle the issue of gender related measures of well-being using three different approaches. One simply disaggregates well-being measures by gender to see whether males and females fare differently in different well-being outcomes. The advantages of this approach are that it yields direct information about the well-being of both genders and that it side-steps the tricky issue of having to define what is meant by gender equality (see discussion above). Also, such disaggregations might be particularly useful for policy purposes, where such gaps can then focus the attention of policy makers as, for example, has been achieved through the Millennium Development Goal of achieving equality in educational enrolments between the sexes (UNDP 2003, Abu-Ghaida and Klasen 2004). The major disadvantage is that it is not always obvious how to interpret such indicators. In fact, when interpreting the gender disaggregated indicators, the question of what constitutes equality will again become relevant. Moreover, such an approach says nothing about the consequences of gender inequality for overall well-being in a society or the respective importance of the various gender gaps.

A second approach is, then, to create simple composite indexes of such gender gaps, by averaging the ratio of female to male achievements. There has been a proliferation of such measures in the academic and policy literature recently, including a Gender Equity Index (GEI) by Social Watch (Social Watch 2005), a Gender Gap Index (GGI) by the World Economic Forum (WEF, 2005), the African Gender Status Index by the Economic Commission of Africa (ECA 2004), the Relative Status of Women Index by Dijkstra and Hanmer (2001), and the Standardized Index of Gender Equality (SIGE) by Dijkstra (2002). All of these measures are averages of gaps in different dimensions of gender related well-being, ranging from 3 to 42 different dimensions. Usually, these indicators are unweighted averages, in the case of SIGE the weighting is adjusted by the standard deviation in each component (to avoid variation in one component dominating the final index), and in the case of the GEI, the average is based on rankings according to gaps in each component rather than the gap itself. The advantage of such measures is that they provide a rather comprehensive, yet simple, assessment of many dimensions of gender inequality in one figure. At the same time, they have the disadvantages of composite measures, including essentially arbitrary weighting schemes, and great sensitivity to the number and choice of dimensions included. The application of such indexes to the gender dimension poses additional problems, among them the inclusion of indicators where it is unclear whether a deviation from a ratio of 1 is necessarily a sign of gender inequality, and the implicit possibility of balancing out gender gaps in different dimensions. This last point might be particularly problematic where – for example, in the Gender Status Index – a country with a large gender gap favouring males in life expectancy, but an equal and opposite gender gap favouring females in parliamentary represention, would score as well as a country with gender equality in both dimensions. While such a problem used to be empirically rare, there are now many more countries, particularly among industrialized and transition countries, where females are advantaged in some dimension of well-being (particularly life expectancy, but sometimes also education) but continue to remain disadvantaged in others: this 'balancing out' of gender gaps in opposite directions is posing some real questions (see Klasen 2006).

The third approach is to construct (individual or composite) gender sensitive measures of well-being that try to assess the impact of gender inequality on aggregate well-being. UNDP's GDI is a prominent example of a composite version of such an approach. The approach is based on the notion that societies exhibit inequality aversion (which can be derived from concave utility functions or from axioms such as rank-order weighting (Grün and Klasen 2003)). One formulation of such an approach is to use Atkinson's concept of equally distributed equivalent achievement, which adjusts the average achievement of a certain well-being outcome downward by applying a penalty for gender inequality based on a presumed inequality aversion.[20] The advantage of this approach is that it assesses the aggregate well-being costs of gender inequality and thus rightly emphasizes that gender inequality is not only hurting females, but also imposes an aggregate well-being loss on societies. In contrast to the composite indicators of gender gaps, it also does not 'balance out' gender gaps in opposite directions but cumulates them, which might be seen as more desirable in some contexts.[21] The disadvantage is that it must include an implicit notion of equality upon which it can levy penalties for deviations from that equality standard. As argued above, such a definition of equality might in some cases be controversial. Moreover, it includes an assumption about the magnitude of inequality aversion which is equally controversial.

There is no reason to choose between the three approaches. Each yields important information, so it is useful to consult measures based on all three approaches (and the individual components that make up the indicators) for a comprehensive assessment of gender related well-being, bearing in mind the respective advantages and disadvantages.

Dealing with the household in gender-related measures of well-being

As argued above, a critical distinguishing characteristic of gender, compared to other social divisions, is that much of inequality is generated within households. As argued above, some of these inequalities (e.g. in labour force participation or time use) might partly be based on joint (or at least coordinated) household decisions with the aim of maximizing well-being for the household as a whole. Understanding such considerations necessitates models and theories that can explain household behaviour, particularly as they relate to division of labour and time use (e.g. Ermish 2003).

Moreover, it is also important to recognize that the household plays a very important and not always well-understood role in generating and allocating most well-being relevant resources. Households earn incomes and get other well-being resources and allocate them among primarily two types of goods. The first type refers to household specific private goods which are used by only one person. Spending on food, clothing, health care, education, and so on are all such private goods where it is, at least in theory, possible to identify the ultimate beneficiary of a certain expenditure of money (or time). While in theory the ultimate beneficiary is discernible, in practice it is exceedingly difficult to determine actually how much of certain private goods was used by particular members. Surveys of food intake (involving weighing of food after it has been allocated), for example, require intrusive survey methodologies that might have an impact on usual household behaviour. Thus, for important portions of private goods (especially food), it is not easy, in practise, to determine the ultimate beneficiary of a particular expenditure.

Facing this constraint, the literature has moved in two different directions. One direction has been to study how the structure of expenditures (and their associated well-being outcomes) of households varies with the contribution of different household members. This has been used to distinguish between unitary and collective household models and it was generally shown that the structure of expenditures and outcomes in households depends on the contributions of different household members (e.g. Lundberg *et al.* 1997, Thomas 1997). While this has generated useful information about the nature of intra-household decision making, the interpretation of these findings for well-being by gender is unclear, as this literature has not generated results on the total intrahousehold resource allocation by gender (merely the factors affecting it).[22]

The second approach has been to focus on expenditure on goods where the beneficiary is more readily discernible. For example, tobacco tends to be consumed primarily by adult men, women's clothing by adult women, and so on. Examination of these expenditure categories has been used to understand better marginal effects of certain policies or changed circumstances (e.g. Deaton 1997, Lundberg *et al.* 1997, World Bank 2001). These studies have examined whether changes in unearned income of males and females affect expenditures on these assignable goods (and found that they do, e.g. Lundberg *et al.* 1997), or whether males are more willing to give up resources for an additional son or an additional daughter (the evidence is rather mixed on this one, see Deaton 1997). While these are useful tests of models of intra-household resource allocation and of the presence of a preference for sons, they only are able to study these marginal effects and say very little about the *total* distribution of private goods within households.

The other types of goods are household specific public goods that have, within the household, the classical public goods qualities; that is, they are non-rival and non-excludable. Spending on housing, utilities, and many durable goods falls into this category. It is not possible to ascertain with any certainty how much these public goods are used by one person as opposed another.

There are also goods that are in between, in the sense that they are a private good consumed by one member which nevertheless provides positive externalities on other household members. There is some literature that argues that education is such a good, as it has been found to bring clear benefit to the person who receives it but also provides positive externalities on other household members (Basu and Foster 1998, Basu *et al.* 2002). Assigning the precise magnitude of this externality to all household members is, however, very difficult and requires significant further research.[23]

Faced with the serious practical problems associated with household specific private goods (and their externalities) and the insurmountable conceptual problems associated with assigning use of household specific public goods, it is impossible to say with any certainty how total consumption is distributed by gender within households. As a result, studies of income or consumption poverty have usually assumed an equal distribution of resources within the households and then determined whether a household as a whole is poor (i.e. everyone in that household is poor) or not (i.e. no one in the household is poor). While this is clearly unsatisfactory, it is not clear that one can do much better than that.

This has serious implications for attempting a gender disaggregation of income or consumption poverty. As we cannot say anything about intra-household distribution of consumption, gender differentials in income or consumption poverty can only come about by differences in poverty rates of different types of households depending on their sex composition.

It is all the more surprising that UNDP (1995) and many others thereafter have claimed that of the world's (income) poor, 70 per cent are female. To my knowledge, no clear methodology or evidence for this claim was ever provided (see also Ravallion 1997), and it is impossible to derive this figure by differences in poverty rates of different household types.

This has been shown convincingly by Marcoux (1998) and will be briefly discussed here. About one third of the world's population (and probably considerably more of its poor population) are children below the age of 15. It is not likely that households with more male than female children of those age groups are systematically richer.[24] A large share of adults live in families where there are as many adult males as there are adult females – one each in a nuclear or several couples in extended families – so that these households cannot contribute to differential poverty rates by gender. The most important household categories that are gender imbalanced are single households, and lone parent households. Single households consist primarily of widows/widowers or single men or women living alone. In developing countries, both types of household are quite rare (although increasing, see United Nations 2000). While it is likely the case that widow households are poorer than widower households, at least in some countries (Drèze and Srinivasan 1997), the share of these households is simply too small to generate such a huge imbalance in poverty by gender. The last group of households comprises lone parents. They do constitute a significant share of households in some regions (especially in Africa, see United Nations 2000), but as shown by many studies they are not invariably poorer than two-parent households (Marcoux 1998), nor is the gender imbalance in these households large enough to approach the aggregate gender imbalance of poverty that was claimed.

Not only is this particular claim not verifiable, but due to the problems described above, it appears conceptually impossible to arrive at a serious alternative estimate of total consumption disparities by gender.

While some might see this as a serious problem, it may simply be seen as another argument for not focusing on the income or consumption space when evaluating well-being by gender. When moving to a functioning or capability space, these problems are much less severe, as one can more easily observe individual well-being outcomes (and their gender differentials) even within households and thus can come to reliable estimates of gender inequality in these spaces.[25]

The relevant population for welfare assessments

Most well-being measures focus on the currently alive and often base their assessment on their situation in a particular year, ignoring longer-term horizons. Per capita GDP or the income based poverty rate are classic examples, where the income situation of households in a given year is used as the welfare measure. Such assessments can lead to absurd outcomes such as that per capita income goes up and poverty falls when the poor suffer from higher mortality rates (Kanbur and Mukherjee 2002).

The focus on the current situation of the currently alive is particularly problematic when it comes to gender related indicators of well-being. It appears to be the case that gender inequality in mortality in some countries, most notably China, has moved from post-birth to pre-birth discrimination. As parents use sex selective abortions to influence the sex of their off-spring, the survival conditions of girls that are allowed to be born have improved. Focusing purely on period measures such as period life expectancy would therefore indicate reduced gender bias, although this has come at the expense of killing female foetuses (Bardhan and Klasen 1999, Klasen 2003). Clearly, this is a problem of the relevant population for the assessment of well-being where the aborted foetuses are not part of the relevant population while the living girls are. In principle, one could address this problem by expanding the relevant population in the well-being assessment. In particular, if one took a 'normal sex ratio' at birth (about 1.06 males per hundred females rather than the actual sex ratio after sex selective abortions, which was 1.16 in China in 2000, see Klasen and Wink 2003) and assumed that average potential life expectancy for males is, say, 80, and for females it is 85, one could then compare the actual number of males and females with those who would be potentially alive based on the sex ratio and life expectancy assumption. Gender bias in mortality would be equally visible as a shortage of females relative to those potentially alive, regardless of whether it occurred pre-birth or post-birth.[26]

Data and measurement issues

While the availability and quality of data for some aspects of gender related well-being (e.g. life expectancy, education) has improved in many countries, there are large data and measurement gaps that need to be overcome when developing sensible gender related well-being measures.

The first important and well-recognized issue is that work in the home is not measured well and included in standard national income accounting (UNDP 1995). Related to this, we know very little about time use outside of time spent in formal labour market activities. As time use is a critical ingredient to well-being, this is a huge data gap that is only slowly being filled (UNDP 1995, 2005).

Third, much relevant well-being information at the household level is not available at all, or only in extremely patchy format. That includes information about issues such as domestic violence, about division of labour in household and caring activities, and about power over decision making. All of these aspects are likely to affect well-being in important ways, yet we do not know much about the nature of these issues or their well-being impact. More research and data gathering efforts in those aspects are critically needed (UN Division for the Advancement of Women 2005).

Fourth, a lot of gender related data suffer from inconsistencies over time and across countries. For example, data on female labour force participation, employment, and earnings suffer from particularly severe inconsistencies (e.g. Bardhan and Klasen 1999).

Last, despite improvements, there remain serious concerns about data quality for those data that do exist in many countries. In many countries, data on education, longevity, mortality, and incomes are estimated, not measured. As there are no reliable national income accounting data, recent censuses or household surveys, many of the existing micro data sets are not strictly comparable to one another, and there is a great shortage of reliable panel data.[27] The quality of these estimates is open to question. Much work remains to be done before consistent data are available reliably to assess and compare gender related indicators of well-being.

UNDP's gender-sensitive development indicators

As part of the 1995 *Human Development Report* focusing on gender, UNDP proposed two measures of tracking gender related well-being across space and time, which are probably the most visible attempts to date to devise gender related measures of well-being. The measures are discussed in detail in Bardhan and Klasen (1999, 2000) and, partly in response to the first paper the GDI was revised in 1999 to rectify a particular problem in the income component of the GDI. Here, we will briefly review them in light of the discussions above. For illustrative purposes, Table 7.3 provides these measures for a sample of countries in 1999 and 2003.

The first, the GDI, is an overall well-being indicator that simply adjusts the HDI downward by existing gender inequalities in longevity, education, and incomes. It thus tries to incorporate the aggregate well-being costs associated with existing gender inequality in critical well-being outcomes, rather than

Table 7.3 HDI, GDI, and GEM for selected countries in 2003

Country	HDI	GDI	Implied penalty*	GEM
Norway	0.944	0.941	0.003	0.837
United States of America	0.937	0.935	0.002	0.760
Italy	0.916	0.910	0.006	0.561
Korea, Rep. of	0.879	0.873	0.006	0.363
Poland	0.841	0.839	0.002	0.594
Mexico	0.800	0.790	0.010	0.516
Malaysia	0.790	0.784	0.006	0.503
Russian Federation	0.779	0.774	0.005	0.440
Saudi Arabia	0.769	0.743	0.026	...
Sri Lanka	0.730	0.726	0.004	0.272
South Africa	0.684	0.678	0.006	...
Honduras	0.667	0.656	0.011	0.408
Egypt	0.648	0.634	0.014	0.253
Botswana	0.614	0.611	0.003	0.564
Bangladesh	0.502	0.495	0.007	0.218
Pakistan	0.499	0.469	0.030	0.414
Yemen	0.470	0.424	0.046	0.127
Ethiopia	0.359	0.347	0.012	...
Mozambique	0.356	0.341	0.015	...

* The implied penalty is arrived at by subtracting the HDI from the GDI.
Source: UNDP (2003).

generate a separate index of well-being for males and females. The difference between the two measures (see fourth column of Table 7.3) is thus an indication of the well-being loss associated with gender inequality in the three components of the HDI. As shown in Table 7.3, the implied penalties are very small, particularly in countries with higher human development, so that neither value nor rank of the GDI differs greatly from the corresponding HDI. As shown in Bardhan and Klasen (1999, 2000) and Klasen (2006), the differences, where they do exist, are predominantly driven by large gender gaps in earned income, while gender gaps in education and longevity have a much smaller influence on the implied penalty.

The longevity component of the GDI assumes a survival advantage of five years of females and treats countries that have larger or smaller female advantages symmetrically. In light of the discussion above, it is unclear whether one should accept the five-year female survival advantage as 'normal' from a well-being perspective. Also, whether an advantage of five years is a good assumption for all countries of the world is debatable. The longevity component purely considers the mortality conditions of the currently living. As discussed above, this might be a problem if there is some substitution between pre-birth and post-birth discrimination; that is, if parents abort unwanted females and consequently give more equal allocations to the females that are allowed to be born (Klasen 2003).

One potential problem with the otherwise uncontroversial education component of the GDI relates to the question of whether some of the differences in educational achievement are based on optimal assessments of comparative advantage and sexual division of labour. But one should not overemphasize this point, as the empirical relevance of this issue is likely to be minor.[28]

The earned income component of the GDI, however, is deeply problematic in light of the discussions above. The earned income component calculates the earned income of males and females based on sex specific labour force participation rates and earnings differentials (in the non-agricultural sector). It then uses the gender inequality in these earned incomes to adjust the income component of the HDI downwardly.[29] The income component of the HDI is meant to be a proxy for important functionings such as nutrition, housing, clothing and other basic functionings relating to consumption that tend to be provided in markets, and thus the amount of functionings at one's disposal depends largely on incomes. The gender gap in this achievement should therefore measure gender gaps in consumption or access to these basic functionings. But gender gaps in earned income are unlikely to be a good proxy for gender gaps in consumption because of the role households play in the distribution of these resources. While earned incomes affect bargaining power, and thus access to resources at the margins, it is clear that women even without any earned incomes still have access to resources within the household. They consume the household specific public goods (especially housing), and they receive a share of household resources (e.g. food, clothing, and so on). To claim that women in, say, Saudi Arabia (where the share of female earned incomes is among the lowest in the world) have also a commensurately low access to consumption goods in households, is a vastly exaggerated claim and seriously distorts the well-being assessments in the GDI.[30]

Second, the earned income component implicitly assumes that equality in (market) labour force participation and earnings should be the goal of all societies. As discussed above, there might be economic and other reasons why such a goal is not necessarily shared by everyone.

Third, the measure ignores household production and thereby argues specifically for gender equality in market earnings. This ignores household production, including care work, as a significant source of well-being; conversely, it also ignores the well-being consequences of the double burden that many women, who work in the market but continue to work in the household, carry (Folbre 2005).

These problems are aggravated by severe data gaps in calculating the earned income component which were overcome using highly problematic assumptions discussed in detail by Bardhan and Klasen (1999).[31] As it turns out that the overall penalty for gender inequality implicit in the GDI is largely due to the gender gaps in earned incomes, these shortcomings in this component largely drive the rank changes between the HDI and the GDI. Due to the overwhelming influence of this component and the many problems associated with it, the GDI does not appear to be a reliable indicator of gender sensitive development. Due to these serious limitations of the earned income component, Bardhan and Klasen (1999) suggested that the GDI (and a corresponding reduced HDI) should concentrate on average achievements and gender gaps in longevity and education.[32]

Lastly, as shown in Table 7.3, the implied penalties for gender gaps are really so small that they might give the misleading impression that gender gaps are really irrelevant, particularly in richer countries. But this conclusion would be mistaken, as the components of the GDI are simply too crude to pick up the more subtle gender gaps (e.g. in type of education, in earnings in the labour market, in time use, in control over resources, and so on) that exist everywhere, including in industrialized countries (see Bardhan and Klasen 2000).[33]

The Gender Empowerment Measure (GEM) does not aim to measure well-being, but instead focuses on the relative empowerment of males and females in the political, economic and household sphere. Clearly, women's empowerment plays an important intrinsic and instrumental role in an assessment of well-being, although the discussion above showed that it is not entirely clear how empowerment should be treated in an assessment of well-being. But as a separate measure of empowerment, it serves a useful purpose. Using the classification above, the GEM is also a gender sensitive indicator (rather than a gender gap measure) as it also calculates a 'penalty' for deviations from equal representation of males and females, rather than simply combining the gaps in each dimension. As shown in Table 7.3, the GEM provides a drastically different picture from the HDI and GDI, so new insights are gained. For example, some successful developing countries in terms of GDP and human development perform terribly in the GEM (e.g. South Korea) and, to the extent that empowerment is not only means but also an end, this is useful information.[34]

While the GEM has thus usefully provided some cross-country comparisons on aspects of female empowerment, the GDI is at present still a highly problematic and unreliable indicator of gender sensitive development. There is scope for improvement, as suggested above, but also it is advisable to move beyond the three very crude indicators that are used to measure human development and gender gaps in these achievements, and consider more indicators of gender inequality that receive less attention. The section on data and measurement suggested a few such areas of investigation.

Conclusion

This survey of issues relating to gender related indicators of well-being has demonstrated that there is much value to be gained in considering the gender dimensions of well-being. At the same time, much more work is needed to arrive at reliable measures that track the gendered nature of well-being across space and time, and current measures and claims appear not to have always usefully advanced the measurement of gender related well-being.

But a few more constructive conclusions also emerge. First, it appears that a functioning or capability space might be preferable for considering gender related well-being issues. Second, it is useful to generate gender disaggregated indicators, composite gender gap measures, and gender sensitive aggregate well-being measures as all three yield useful information and complement each other well. Third, one should carefully examine the relevant population when considering gender related well-being. Fourth, there is much work to be done in improving available data to generate reliable gender disaggregated, composite and gender related measures of well-being. Fifth, there are many dimensions of gender inequality that have important well-being consequences about which we know very little. Here, it is critical to gather more data and work on analyzing the well-being consequence of these issues.

Notes

I thank participants at a WIDER meeting, a research seminar at the University of Munich, the IARIW conference in Cork, three anonymous referees, as well as Andrew Sumner, James Foster, Mark McGillivray and Kanchana Ruwanpura for helpful comments and suggestions. I also thank Katarina Smutna for excellent research assistance.

1 Clearly the instrumental view of gender inequality should be of concern when thinking about development policies and strategies, and thus it is right that many institutions and policy debates focus on this aspect. At the same time, gender issues should still attract attention as a well-being issue, even if these positive links to overall development did not exist. In this sense, gender issues should receive the same attention as other ascriptive inequalities (e.g. race or ethnicity) whose importance as well-being issues also does not depend on their potential instrumental role in furthering overall development.
2 For a discussion of the issue of sex selective abortions as a form of gender inequality, see Klasen and Wink (2003) and Klasen (2003).
3 While this problem is particularly severe in the regions mentioned above, it was historically prevalent in many other parts of the world, including Europe, the USA, Japan. For a discussion of these historical episodes, see Klasen (1999a).
4 Those very few people who do change their sex during their life-time are often subject to other forms of inequalities and discrimination.
5 For a discussion, see Sen (1992) and the World Bank's World Development Report on 'Development and Equity' which would also consider inequalities due to ascriptive characteristics objectionable (World Bank, 2005).
6 For an example, see Klasen (2000), which examines well-being in South Africa, where race plays an important role.
7 Also, here, some of the issues discussed on pp. 174–6 are particularly relevant. See UN Division for the Advancement of Women (2005) for a discussion of some of the empirical issues involved when measuring violence against women.

8 Using the space of primary goods, advocated by Rawls, would lead to similar problems. Other problems with choosing the income space for measuring well-being are that they focus on a well-being means rather than an end, and that the transformation of income into well-being might differ across people. For a discussion, see Sen (1999) and Klasen (2000).

9 For details on the approach, refer to Sen (1999) and the literature cited therein. For an application of the approach to measuring well-being, see Klasen (2000).

10 Also, by focusing on substantive freedoms, it is possible to highlight issues of violations of basic rights (such as freedom from domestic violence) and inequalities in de jure or de facto rights such as unequal marriage and divorce arrangements.

11 There is a large literature documenting that women are more willing to give up resources to their children than their husbands are (e.g. Haddad *et al.* 1997, World Bank 2001). See also discussion by Gasper (Chapter 2 in this volume) and below.

12 Unfortunately, it seems exceedingly difficult to measure capabilities in a comprehensive manner, so there appears to be no easy way out.

13 There is also some uncertainty about the magnitude of the 'biological' survival advantage of females as the empirically observed survival advantage is, to a considerable extent, due to differences in behavioural patterns between males and females, mainly relating to smoking, alcohol abuse, traffic behaviour, and violence. For a discussion of these issues, see Waldron (1993), Klasen and Wink (2002, 2003).

14 It is not clear whether this is the appropriate way to assess gender gaps elsewhere, as both genetic and environmental factors might affect the growth of males and females in ways they did not in the reference population of the USA (Klasen 1999b).

15 Empirically, it is difficult to assess whether such decisions are indeed based on informed consent based on these types of efficiency arguments. One possible way to examine this would be to study satisfaction of women and men in households that have chosen a sexual division of labour. It is important to point out, however, that the claim of higher efficiency of some inequalities needs to be carefully inspected. While there might be some efficiency gains to a sexual division of labour in households, it is not clear how large they are. Similarly, claims that favouring males over females to maximize household resources – which would thus help women themselves – usually do not stand up to closer scrutiny. In fact, many studies have documented that even if, for example, female education leads to lower labour market returns, there are significant externalities associated with female education that might more than outweigh these lower returns (e.g. World Bank 2001, Klasen 2002). Also, if individuals exhibit inequality aversion, this should significantly lower any well-being benefit of such inequalities.

16 See also the discussion by Gasper (Chapter 2, this volume). Gasper poses the question whether well-being should be confined to own achievements and capabilities, or also include agency achievements or even agency freedoms. He criticises Sen for confining the term 'well-being' to achievements and freedoms related to oneself and thus having a rather narrow concept of 'well-being' that ignores these important agency aspects as part and parcel of well-being.

17 This is, of course, only true to the extent that women would actually be able to secure equal resources for themselves if they chose to. Whether this is empirically correct, is somewhat doubtful. See also later discussion.

18 It might also be the case that mothers invest more in children as they see such investments as private investments towards a public good within the family and, since they value that public good more than their husbands, they are reluctantly

willing to invest more in it than their partners (who in turn get to free-ride more on their wife's investments). In this situation, there would be large gender inequality in private goods between husband and wife and no gender gap in public goods, but clearly women would have preferred a more equitable contribution of both towards the public good children. I thank a referee for raising this point.

19 Or should we treat it as 'rational addiction', as proposed by Becker and Murphy (1988).

20 See UNDP (1995), Atkinson (1970), or Bardhan and Klasen (1999) for a detailed description and discussion of this procedure.

21 Since the equally distributed equivalent achievement is lower than the average achievement regardless of the direction of the gender gap, the welfare loss of gender inequality in different dimensions is added even if they are in opposite directions. This is surely an advantage, insofar as it recognizes that a country with gender equality in all dimensions fares better as far as the welfare assessment of gender gaps is concerned than a country with large gender gaps in opposite directions. On the other hand, one might also convincingly argue that a country with gender gaps in opposite directions should fare better in a welfare assessment of these gaps than a country with all gender gaps only hurting one sex, which would support 'balancing out' of gaps in different directions. For a discussion, see Klasen (2006).

22 Using rather restrictive assumptions, Chiappori (1997a, 1997b) show that the total sharing rule (up to an additive constant) on private goods could be recovered if the collective model of household decision making was correct and the resource allocation was Pareto efficient. The conditions under which this result holds are highly restrictive and I know of no study that has empirically derived such a sharing rule. Also, the public good problem within the household would remain.

23 Basu *et al.* (2002) only demonstrate the labour market externality in one particular setting, Bangladesh. From a well-being perspective, other types of externalities are also important and the results would have to be generalized to other settings. This is a huge and daunting (but very interesting) research agenda.

24 This could only come about if male children were able to bring in considerably more resources than female children. As child labour rates are quite low in these age groups, the gender differentials in earnings are not large, and the absolute earnings constitute a small share of household resources (Cigno *et al.* 2002), this is not likely.

25 To a more limited degree, similar problems might emerge when the functioning space is considered. For example, one will have to assume that everyone in a household is equally well housed (or equally badly housed) as it is impossible to ascribe different functionings 'being housed' to different members of a household sharing the same housing unit. But here the assumption of equal access by all to this functioning might not be such a bad approximation. With many other functionings (e.g. health, nutrition, and so on), these problems do not arise.

26 Other complexities would arise when using such an approach. For a discussion and proposals see Bardhan and Klasen (1999) and Kanbur and Mukherjee (2002).

27 For a discussion, see Srinivasan (1994) and Sumner (2003).

28 While such considerations might justify some gender differentials in education subjects and degrees (especially at higher levels), the relevance for justifying gender gaps in literacy or the amount of primary, secondary, and tertiary education is likely to be small. Moreover, there are many more well-being benefits to education beyond the human capital considerations that are the focus in this criticism.

29 There was a mathematical error in the calculating this component in the GDI from the 1995 to the 1998 reports which we pointed out in Bardhan and Klasen (1999) and which led to a particularly high penalty for gender inequality in earned incomes in relatively rich countries. This was corrected in the 1999 *HDR* (without any comment) and commented briefly upon in the 2000 *HDR*. Bardhan and Klasen (2000) discussed the implications of the revised version of this measure.

30 This point was readily acknowledged in the *HDR* (UNDP 1995). It was justified by arguing that gender gaps in earnings reflect gender gaps in agency which have an important impact on well-being. But in the logic of the HDI and GDI, it is unclear how one can adjust the income component of the HDI with gender gaps in agency (rather than gender gaps in the consumption which that income is meant to track). See also Bardhan and Klasen (1999). As it is clear that gender gaps in earnings do have an impact on gender gaps in consumption but do not accurately reflect gender gaps in consumption, one way to address this would be to transform the gender gaps in earned income by some concave function that would be guided by the literature on the impact of bargaining power on relative consumption within households and use this transformed gender gap for the GDI calculation. It is not clear, however, that we have robust data on what such a concave transformation should look like.

31 The gender gaps in other components are also somewhat suspect, particularly since the data are often based on extrapolations from much older information.

32 For details on this and further recommendations, see Bardhan and Klasen (1999) and Klasen (2006).

33 The policy implications of the GDI are also somewhat unclear. Given the very close correlation with the HDI, it might even give the misleading impression that all one needs to do is boost the HDI and the GDI will rise accordingly, so that one need not worry too much about gender.

34 The GEM also suffers from a number of conceptual and empirical weaknesses. First, it is unclear whether it is appropriate to transfer the inequality aversion procedure to adjust for gender gaps from a well-being to an empowerment measure. Second, the earned income component not only considers gender gaps, but also income levels and gives the problematic impression that women can only be empowered in rich countries. Thus, a perfect score of 1 can only be attained for countries who have no gender gaps and the highest possible income for both males and females. Third, the GEM is only available for some 80 countries, thereby limiting its usefulness. See Klasen (2006) for further details and suggesions.

References

Abu-Ghaida, D. and S. Klasen (2004) 'The Economic Costs to Missing the Millennium Development Goal on Gender Equity', *World Development*, 32: 1075–107.

Atkinson, A. (1970) 'On the Measurement of Inequality', *Journal of Economic Theory*, 2: 244–63.

Bardhan, K. and S. Klasen (1999) 'UNDP's Gender-Related Indices: A Critical Review', *World Development*, 27: 98–110.

Bardhan, K. and S. Klasen (2000) 'On UNDP's Revisions to the Gender-Related Development Index', *Journal of Human Development*, 1: 191–5.

Barro, R. and J. Lee (2000) 'International Data on Educational Attainment: Updates and Implications', CID Working Paper 42, Center for International Development, Harvard University.

Basu, K. and J. Foster (1998) 'On Measuring Literacy', *Economic Journal*, 108: 1733–49.

Basu, K. A. Narayan and M. Ravallion (2002) 'Is Literacy Shared within the Household?', *Labour Economics*, 8: 649–65.

Becker, G. (1981) *Economics of the Family* (Chicago: University of Chicago Press).

Becker, G. and M. Murphy (1988) 'A Theory of Rational Addiction', *Journal of Political Economy*, 96: 675–700.

Becker, G. and G. Stigler (1977) 'De Gustibus non est Disputandum', *American Economic Review*, 67: 76–90.

Chattophadhyay, R. and E. Duflo (2003) 'Women as Policy-Makers', Mimeo, Cambridge, MA: MIT.

Chiappori, P.-A. (1997a) 'Introducing household production in collective models of labor supply, *Journal of Political Economy*, 105(1): 191–209.

Chiappori, P.-A. (1997b) ' "Collective" Models of Household Behaviour: The Sharing Rule Approach', in L. Haddad, J. Hoddinott and H. Alderman (eds), *Intrahousehold Resource Allocation in Developing Countries* (Baltimore, MD: Johns Hopkins University Press).

Cigno, A., F. Rosati and Z. Tzannatos (2002) 'Child Labour Handbook', Social Protection Discussion Paper 206 (Washington, DC: World Bank).

Coale, A. (1991) 'Excess Female Mortality and the Balance of the Sexes', *Population and Development Review*, 17: 517–23.

Deaton, A. (1997) *The Analysis of Household Surveys* (Baltimore, MD: Johns Hopkins University Press).

Dijkstra, A. G. (2002) 'Revisiting UNDP's GDI and GEM: Towards an Alternative', *Social Indicator Research*, 57: 301–38.

Dijkstra, A. G. and L. C. Hanmer (2001) 'Measuring Socio-economic Gender Inequality: Towards an Alternative to the UNDP Gender-Related Development Index', *Feminist Economics*, 6(2): 41–75.

Drèze, J. and P. Srinivasan (1997) 'Widowhood and Poverty in India', *Journal of Development Economics*, 54: 217–35.

D'Souza, S. and L. Chen (1980) 'Sex Differentials in Mortality in Rural Bangladesh', *Population and Development Review*, 6: 257–70.

Economic Commission for Africa (ECA) (2004) *The African Gender and Development Index* (Addis Ababa: ECA).

Ermish, J. (2003) *An Economic Analysis of the Family* (Princeton: Princeton University Press).

Folbre, N. (2005) 'Measuring Care: Gender, Empowerment, and the Care Economy', Mimeo, University of Massachusetts.

Grün, C. and S. Klasen (2003) 'Growth, Inequality, and Well-Being: Comparisons across Space and Time', *CESifo Economic Studies*, 49: 617–59.

Haddad, L., J. Hoddinott and H. Alderman (eds) (1997) *Intrahousehold Resource Allocation in Developing Countries* (Baltimore, MD: Johns Hopkins University Press).

Kanbur, R. and D. Mukherjee (2002) 'Premature Mortality and Poverty Measurement', Mimeo, Cornell University.

Klasen, S. (1994) 'Missing Women Reconsidered', *World Development*, 22: 1061–71.

Klasen, S. (1998) 'Marriage, Bargaining, and Intrahousehold Resource Allocation: Excess Female Mortality among Adults in Rural Germany (1740–1860)', *Journal of Economic History*, 40: 432–67.

Klasen, S. (1999a) 'Gender Inequality in Mortality in Comparative Perspective', Mimeo, University of Munich.

Klasen, S. (1999b) 'Malnourished and Surviving in South Asia, Better Nourished and Dying Young in Africa?', SFB Discussion Paper 214 (Bonn: SFB).

Klasen, S. (2000) 'Measuring Poverty and Deprivation in South Africa', *Review of Income and Wealth*, 46: 33–58.
Klasen, S. (2002) 'Low Schooling for Girls, Slower Growth for All?', *World Bank Economic Review*, 16: 345–73.
Klasen, S. (2003) 'Sex Selection', in P. Demeny and G. McNicoll (eds), *Encyclopedia of Population*: 878–81.
Klasen, S. (2006) 'UNDP's Gender-Related Measures: Some Conceptual Problems and Possible Solutions', Mimeo, University of Göttingen.
Klasen, S. and F. Lamanna (2003) 'The Impact Gender Inequality in Education and Employment on Economic Growth in the Middle East and North Africa', Mimeo, University of Göttingen.
Klasen, S. and C. Wink (2002) 'Is there a Turning Point in Gender Bias in Mortality?', *Population and Development Review*, 28: 285–312.
Klasen, S. and C. Wink (2003) 'Missing Women: Revisiting the Debate', *Feminist Economics*, 9: 263–99.
Lundberg, S., R. Pollack and L. Wales (1997) 'Do Husbands and Wives Pool their Resources?', *Journal of Human Resources*, 32: 224–35.
Marcoux, A. (1998) 'Feminisation of Poverty?', *Population and Development Review*, 24: 131–9.
Nozick, R. (1974) *Anarchy, State, and Utopia* (New York: Basic Books).
Ranis, G. and F. Stewart (2000) 'Strategies for Success in Human Development', *Journal of Human Development*, 1(1): 49–70.
Ravallion, M. (1997) 'Good and Bad Growth: The Human Development Reports', *World Development*, 25(5): 631–8.
Ravallion, M. and G. Datt (2002) 'Why Has Economic Growth Been More Pro-Poor in Some States of India than Others?', *Journal of Development Economics*, 68: 381–400.
Ray, D. (1998) *Development Economics* (Princeton: Princeton University Press).
Sen, A. (1989) 'Women's Survival as a Development Problem', *Bulletin of the American Academy of Sciences*, 43: 14–29.
Sen, A. (1990) 'Gender and Cooperative Conflicts', in I. Tinker (ed.), *Persistent Inequalities* (New York: Oxford University Press).
Sen, A. (1992) *Inequality Re-examined* (New York: Oxford University Press).
Sen, A. (1999) *Development as Freedom* (New York: Knopf).
Social Watch (2005) *Roars and Whispers Gender and Poverty: Promises versus Action* (Montevideo: Social Watch).
Srinivasan. T. N. (1994) 'Data Base for Development Analysis: An Overview', *Journal of Development Economics*, 44, 3–28.
Sumner, A. (2003) 'Economic and Non-Economic Well-Being', Paper presented at UNU-WIDER Conference on Inequality, Poverty, and Human Well-Being, Helsinki 30–31 May.
Thomas, D. (1997) 'Incomes, Expenditures and Health Outcomes: Evidence on Intra-household Resource Allocation', in L. Haddad, J. Hoddinott and H. Alderman (eds), *Intrahousehold Resource Allocation in Developing Countries* (Baltimore, MD: Johns Hopkins University Press).
UN Division for the Advancement of Women (2005) 'Violence against women: a statistical overview, challenges and gaps in data collection and methodology and approaches for overcoming them', Mimeo, New York: United Nations.
United Nations (2000) *The World's Women* (New York: United Nations).
United Nations Development Programme (UNDP) (1995, 1999, 2000, 2003, 2005) *Human Development Report* (New York: Oxford University Press).

UNRISD (2005) *Gender Equality: Striving for Justice in an Unequal World* (Geneva: UNRISD).

Waldron, I. (1983) 'The Role of Genetic and Biological Factors in Sex Differences in Mortality', in A. Lopez and L. Ruzicka (eds), *Sex Differentials in Mortality* (Canberra: Australian National University Press).

Waldron, I. (1993) 'Recent Trends in Sex Mortality Ratios for Adults in Developed Countries', *Social Science Medicine*, 36: 451–62.

Waldron, I. (1998) 'Sex Differences in Infant and Early Childhood Mortality', in United Nations (ed.), *Too Young to Die* (New York: United Nations).

WHO (1995) 'Physical Status: The Use and Interpretation of Anthropometry', WHO Technical Report Series 854 (Geneva: WHO).

World Bank (2001) *Engendering Development* (Washington, DC: World Bank).

World Economic Forum (WEF) (2005) *Women's Empowerment: Measuring the Global Gender Gap* (Davos: WEF).

8
Sustainability and Well-being Indicators

Eric Neumayer

Introduction

Most indicators of well-being ignore sustainability and most indicators of sustainability ignore (current) well-being. A prominent example for the former is the United Nations Development Programme's Human Development Index (hereafter UNDP and HDI), whereas the World Bank's Genuine Savings (GS) is characteristic of the latter. This chapter provides a critical assessment of those efforts, which have tried to integrate both concepts into one single indicator or have combined the measurement of both without full integration. Well-being often comes under the name welfare or utility, and we will use all three terms interchangeably here. In spite of its common use in economics and other social sciences, it is not easily defined in a concrete sense. Other chapters of this book discuss the meaning of well-being and how best to measure it in detail.

Sustainability is sometimes narrowly defined in physical terms as environmental sustainability, where it refers to the maintenance of certain environmental functions. Economists, however, prefer a broader definition that is not confined to environmental sustainability. Definitions differ slightly, but the most common one sees sustainability as the requirement to maintain the capacity to provide non-declining well-being over time. Contrary to well-being itself, which has an orientation towards the presence, sustainability is therefore a future oriented concept. To make the notion of maintaining the capacity to provide non-declining well-being over time operational, economists have resorted to the idea of maintaining the value of total capital intact, which usually comprises manufactured capital, human capital, natural capital and sometimes social capital. Manufactured capital consists of factories, machineries, infrastructure and the like. Human capital refers to human skills and knowledge. Natural capital encompasses everything in nature that provides human beings with well-being, from natural resources to the provision of amenity value to the pollution absorptive capacity of the environment. Social capital is difficult to define. It refers to things like the amount of trust, the extent of social networks, the willingness of individuals to cooperate with each other and their 'civic engagement' in social groups such as churches and unions (Putnam 1993). Even with this definition of sustainability, there are different conceptual paradigms of the conditions for achieving sustainability; specifically, *weak* sustainability holds that natural capital is substitutable with other forms of capital, whereas *strong* sustainability rejects such substitutability and therefore focuses on environmental sustainability (Neumayer 2003).

The pursuit of well-being of the current generation is easily justifiable, notwithstanding the fact that in reality many policy makers pursue other and often contrary objectives. The pursuit of sustainability can be justified by a universalist ethic in the Kantian (1785) and Rawlsian (1972) tradition, which treats all human beings equally independent of their position in time (Anand and Sen 2000, Neumayer 2003). In addition, it can also be justified under the notion of 'usufruct rights', where each generation has the right to enjoy the fruits of accumulated capital without depleting it (Anand and Sen 2000: 2035).

The next section provides a critical discussion of the Index of Sustainable Economic Welfare (ISEW) or Genuine Progress Indicator (GPI), which is the most prominent current example of an attempt to integrate fully the measurement of well-being and sustainability into one single indicator. Another indicator falling in this category is Osberg and Sharpe's (2002a, 2002b) Index of Economic Well-Being. Such attempts encounter formidable conceptual problems, which render it questionable whether well-being and sustainability should, or even could, be measured with one single, fully integrated indicator. I then assess various proposals to combine sustainability with the measurement of well-being without full integration. For no clear reason, all these proposals have focused on adding sustainability considerations to the HDI. None of these proposals is entirely convincing, either because they do not really tackle the sustainability issue, or because they conflate the conceptually different measurement of human development with that of sustainability similar to the fully integrated indicators. As an alternative, we therefore propose to use so-called GS as a sustainability check for well-being indicators. We discuss the proposal in the context of the HDI, but stress that our proposal can be applied to any well-being indicator.

Fully integrated indicators of well-being and sustainability

Gross national product (GNP) or gross domestic product (GDP) were originally created as indicators of total economic output for macroeconomic stabilization policy and were therefore not meant to be indicators of well-being.[1] On the other hand, it is certainly true that policy makers, the media and the public alike seem to equate GNP/GDP with well-being. In international comparison as well, we tend to think of the countries with a high GNP/GDP as not only the rich, but also the well-off countries. However, because income is just one of the components of well-being, GNP/GDP have long since been criticized as misleading and deficient indicators of well-being. Consequently, there have been many attempts at constructing better indicators. Since our objective is to review and critically assess indicators that have combined the measurement of well-being with that of sustainability, we cannot discuss these efforts here. For an overview and references, see Hagerty *et al.* (2001), as well as the other chapters contained in this volume.

Let us start with indicators that have tried to integrate fully the measurement of sustainability into that of well-being. The Index of Sustainable Economic Welfare (ISEW), also known under the name Genuine Progress Indicator (GPI), is the most prominent example. It stands in the tradition of earlier attempts to incorporate sustainability aspects into a well-being indicator – see, for example, Nordhaus and Tobin's (1972) Measure of Economic Welfare (MEW), Zolotas' (1981) Economic Aspects of Welfare (EAW) and Eisner's (1990) Total Incomes System of Accounts (TISA).[2] The MEW and the EAW take environmental aspects into account, but only rudimentarily so. The MEW adjusts the welfare measure for 'disamenities of urban life' such as 'pollution, litter, congestion, noise' based on hedonic valuation studies.[3] The EAW subtracts air pollution damage costs together with half of the estimated control costs for air and water pollution and the full control costs for solid wastes from the welfare measure. The TISA on the other hand does not include any environmental aspects in its measurement, but as with the MEW and the EAW, seeks to broaden the concept of capital and investment accounted for.

Because of space limitations, we will concentrate on the ISEW/GPI, which take a more comprehensive set of environmental factors into account than either the MEW or the EAW does. Also, these older indicators are somewhat outdated now. An ISEW/GPI has been constructed for Australia (Hamilton 1999), Austria (Stockhammer *et al.* 1997), Chile (Castañeda 1999), Germany (Diefenbacher 1994), Italy (Guenno and Tiezzi 1998), the Netherlands (Rosenberg *et al.* 1995), Scotland (Moffatt and Wilson 1994), Sweden (Jackson and Stymne 1996), Thailand (Clarke and Islam 2003), the UK (Jackson *et al.* 1997), and the USA (Redefining Progress 2001). The methodology differs slightly from study to study, but all follow the same basic concept, which is well captured by the example of the GPI for the USA. It starts by adjusting personal consumption expenditures for unequal income distribution and subtracts net foreign lending or borrowing as well as the cost of consumer durables. It then subtracts a whole range of so-called social costs, such as the costs of crime, traffic accidents, commuting, divorce, underemployment and loss of leisure time. The next group of deductions refers to the costs of environmental pollution such as air, water and noise pollution; environmental degradation such as loss of wetlands, farmlands and old-growth forests; and resource depletion. Two of these are by far the most important ones in this group: first, the costs of replacing non-renewable resource use with renewable resources under the assumption that the per unit costs of replacement rise by 3 per cent per annum; and second, the future or long-term damage costs due to carbon dioxide (CO_2) emissions, which are accumulated from year to year. Finally, a number of welfare enhancing items are added such as the value of housework and volunteer work, the service value of consumer durables, public infrastructure and net capital investment.

All studies that have computed an ISEW/GPI come to the same basic conclusion: starting from around the 1970s or early 1980s, depending on the country, the ISEW/GPI no longer rises very much or even falls, whereas GNP/GDP continues to rise. As an explanation for this widening gap between ISEW/GPI and GNP/GDP, Max-Neef (1995: 117) has put forward the so-called 'threshold hypothesis': 'for every society there seems to be a period in which economic growth (as conventionally measured) brings about an improvement in the quality of life, but only up to a point – the threshold point – beyond which, if there is more economic growth, quality of life may begin to deteriorate'. This 'threshold hypothesis' is referred to in almost every recent ISEW/GPI study and Max-Neef (1995: 117) himself regarded the evidence from these studies 'a fine illustration of the Threshold Hypothesis'.

The ISEW/GPI has been criticized on many accounts – see, for example, Nordhaus (1992), several authors in Cobb and Cobb (1994), Atkinson (1995), Crafts (2002), Neumayer (1999, 2000a, 2003, 2004). The two components that have encountered the greatest critique are resource depletion and long-term environmental damage. On resources, critics have argued that the replacement method overestimates the true loss of resource value with a bias that grows bigger over time due to the erroneous assumption of increasing per unit costs of replacing non-renewable resources. If anything, the costs of renewable resources such as wind and solar energy are falling rather than rising over time. In addition, the implicit assumption that the full amount of current non-renewable resource use needs to be replaced by renewable resources is also questionable, given that there is no imminent danger of a running out of most non-renewable resources. On long-term environmental damage costs, its accumulation over time has been contested as flawed due to multiple counting. The damage costs for carbon dioxide emissions already cover the full future damage cost discounted to present value terms such that accumulation would count the same damage over and over again – see Neumayer (2000a, 2003, 2004) for details.

Some of the problems of the ISEW/GPI are avoided in Osberg and Sharpe's (2002a, 2002b) Index of Economic Well-Being. For example, they include a value for increases in life expectancy over time, which is ignored in ISEW/GPI (Crafts 2002). They also value leisure time and do not count human capital investment as regrettable or defensive expenditures as the ISEW/GPI does for 50 per cent of education expenditures. They do not commit the fallacy of multiple counting of long-term environmental damage in the form of carbon dioxide emissions. On the other hand, their environmental component is rather weak, with resource consumption not included at all and carbon dioxide is the only pollutant accounted for.

As fully integrated indicators of well-being and sustainability both the ISEW/GPI and Osberg and Sharpe's Index of Economic Well-Being encounter another fundamental problem, on which we will concentrate here. The problem is that, for measurement purposes, one should not attempt fully to integrate well-being and sustainability into one single indicator. This is because what affects current well-being need not affect sustainability and vice versa – either, not at all or, at least, not in the same way. This seems counter-intuitive given the conceptual links between well-being and sustainability. However, current well-being is affected by the way in which current total capital is used. Sustainability is only affected if the total capital stock itself is affected.

Take the depletion of non-renewable resources and long-term environmental damage from carbon dioxide emissions as examples. They affect sustainability as, all other things equal, they diminish the value of the total capital stock available to future generations. They rightly form a component of a sustainability indicator. But neither resource depletion nor long-term environmental damage negatively affect current welfare. They affect future, but not current welfare. One could therefore argue that they should be excluded from an indicator of current welfare. Against this reasoning, one might argue with Osberg and Sharpe (2002a: 300) that 'if individuals alive today care about the well-being of future generations, measurement of trends in current well-being should include considerations of changes in the well-being of generations yet unborn'. This is a good argument, but it depends on the assumption that changes to future well-being really do affect the current generation's welfare. More importantly, the argument cannot hold in the other direction, as future generations cannot care for the welfare of the current generation. Hence, what affects the current generation's welfare should not be included in an indicator of sustainability. There are items in the ISEW/GPI and in Osberg and Sharpe's Index of Economic Well-Being that affect current welfare, but are only loosely connected to sustainability, if at all. A good example for this is income inequality. The indicators fall if income inequality increases. Many would agree that the current welfare of society is negatively affected by a more unequal distribution of incomes. A society with a more unequal distribution of income generates less current welfare out of the available stock of capital than another one with the same capital stock but a more equal distribution of income. Not necessarily so with sustainability, however. A more unequal distribution of present incomes does not in itself diminish the value of the total capital stock available to future generations. There could be indirect effects as the distribution of income can affect savings, and therefore investment decisions, which then affects sustainability. The available evidence is not unambiguous (Schmidt-Hebbel and Servén 2000), but if anything evidence seems to suggest that a more unequal distribution of income can be in the interest of the future because rich people have a higher marginal propensity to save than poor people (Smith 2001).[4] Hence, more income inequality could lower current welfare, but enhance sustainability.

The co-existence of factors within one integrated indicator of welfare and sustainability, which affect one but not the other (or only weakly and ambiguously so), means that as the indicator rises or falls we do not know what rises or falls. A rising indicator could mean rising welfare and sustainability, rising welfare, and a decline in sustainability (that is, less in value terms than the rise in welfare), or falling welfare and a rise in sustainability (that is, more in value terms than the fall in welfare); however, which is not clear. The lesson is that one needs two separate indicators to trace two distinct concepts.

Indicators combining well-being and sustainability without full integration

Let us, therefore, turn to efforts at combining the measurement of well-being with that of sustainability without trying to integrate both into one single indicator. These efforts have concentrated on the UNDP's HDI, first published in 1990, which is also perhaps the most prominent and best known indicator of well-being. The exact methodology of the HDI has changed somewhat throughout time. Other chapters of this book explain the HDI in detail. Suffice it to say here that it is made up of three equally weighted components, the income, the education and the health/longevity components. For each variable a maximum and a minimum is defined. An index is then calculated as follows:

$$\text{X\_index} = \frac{(\text{actual value} - \text{minimum value})}{(\text{maximum value} - \text{minimum value})}$$

$$\text{HDI} = \frac{1}{3} \times (\text{Income\_index} + \text{Longevity\_index} + \text{Education\_index})$$

The validity of the HDI as an indicator of well-being has been disputed in many respects – see, for example, McGillivray and White (1993), Hicks (1997), Noorbaksh (1998a, 1998b), Sagar and Najam (1998). We will not discuss the criticism it has encountered, as other chapters in this volume pursue this task. Instead, I will concentrate on my major objective, which is to examine how indicators of well-being and sustainability have been combined with each other.

Sustainability extensions to the HDI

There have been many proposals on how the HDI could be amended to take environmental aspects or sustainability into account. First, Desai (1995) has developed an 'index of intensity of environmental exploitation', which ranks countries similarly to the HDI methodology according to a composite index comprising greenhouse gas emissions per capita, water withdrawal as per cent of annual internal renewable water resources and energy consumption per unit of GNP. Desai does not, however, attempt to integrate this index into the HDI itself.

Second, Dahme *et al.* (1998) have proposed to rank countries according to their total material requirements and to use this data to construct an extension to the UNDP's HDI, called 'Sustainable Human Development Index' (SHDI). Total material requirement refers to the sum of all material inputs required to produce a country's national economic output. All material inputs are grouped into abiotic raw materials (mineral and energy resources), biotic raw materials, moved soil (agriculture and forestry), water and air, and are aggregated in weight terms.

Third, Sagar and Najam (1996: 14) suggest that an increase in income per capita 'above a selected threshold – selected to represent a point that allows a reasonably high standard of living but beyond which consumption pressures on the environment start becoming excessive – the standard-of-living index should reflect this unsustainable lifestyle through a penalization on the index'. The resulting 'index of sustainable living' would go some way towards a SHDI according to its proponents.

Fourth, De la Vega and Urrutia (2001) have proposed to adjust the HDI's income component to reflect the environmental damage caused in generating the income. Their proposal focuses on carbon dioxide since it is the only pollutant for which comprehensive cross-country and over time data exist. Setting 60 tonnes of carbon dioxide emitted per capita as the maximum and 0 as the minimum, they compute an 'environmental behaviour indicator' (EBI) according to the formula $EBI = 1 - CO_2/60$. The harmonic mean of the EBI and the HDI's income component forms the so-called pollution sensitive income component. This pollution sensitive income component is then used in the usual way as one of the three unweighted components together with the longevity and education component to create a so-called pollution sensitive HDI.

The fifth proposal by Ramanathan (1999) is close to the HDI methodology in setting maximum and minimum values for an index of deforestation; an index of the number of rare, endangered or threatened species; a greenhouse gas emissions; and a chlorofluorocarbon emissions index, which are combined to an overall environment endangerment index (EEI). This aggregate EEI is then used to calculate a so-called Environment Sensitive HDI as the product of the HDI and the EEI. He does not, however, attempt to compute such an Environment Sensitive HDI.

A critical assessment of the proposed extensions

All these proposals encounter substantial problems and criticism. Desai's (1995) proposal refers to rather incomplete and partly irrelevant aspects of environmental pollution. For example, how much water a country withdraws as a per cent of annual internal renewable water resources is substantially determined by geological and climatic conditions, and a higher percentage of use is not necessarily worse than a low percentage. Similarly, energy consumption per unit of GNP is just an efficiency measure. Carbon dioxide emissions are certainly relevant, but they capture just one aspect of environmental pollution. Also, to rank countries according to their carbon dioxide emissions does not tell us anything about the actual environmental damage caused or its unsustainability. Furthermore, Qizilbash (2001) demonstrates that the ranking of countries is very sensitive to the choice of environmental factors looked at. If other environmental factors are included, such as commercial and traditional fuel consumption per capita (instead of per unit of GNP), water resource consumption per capita (instead of as a percentage of annual internal reserves), and forest and woodland change, then the ranking is quite different from the one arrived at by Desai (1995).

De la Vega and Urrutia's (2001) pollution sensitive HDI is similar to Desai's proposal in focusing on carbon dioxide emissions, but it attempts to integrate the pollution index into the income component. Again, no attempt at valuation is undertaken. Their proposal suffers from a major setback, however. Countries with very high per capita emissions, such as some of the Middle East oil producing countries, Luxembourg, Australia, Norway and the USA, move down in the pollution sensitive HDI ranking, and vice versa for countries with very low emissions. This would erroneously suggest that the achieved human development of these countries is lower than the original HDI indicated. However, this is not the case. Instead, very high per capita carbon dioxide emissions merely signal that the high human development of these countries is bought at the expense of carbon dioxide emissions that would be unsustainable on a global scale as they would cause drastic climate change. Never mind that this is no new information, but rather something we knew all the time. More importantly, given that this is the true information content, the HDI itself should be unaffected since human development is unaffected. Again, as with the case of the ISEW/GPI and Osberg and Sharpe's (2002a, 2002b) Index of Economic Well-Being, the conflation of factors relevant for current well-being with those of sustainability leads to a flawed overall indicator that can no longer measure correctly either current well-being or sustainability. Ramanathan's (1999) proposal encounters the very same critique.

Dahme *et al.*'s (1998) proposal is very removed from actual environmental damage. From an environmental point of view, two forms of material flows with differing environmental damage impacts cannot be added together just because one can express both in weight terms. Without further analysis of what the material flows consist of and what are their environmental implications, it is pointless simply to rank countries according to the size of their material flows (for a more detailed critique of material flows as a measure of sustainability, see Neumayer 2003, 2004).

More fundamentally, neither of these proposals directly addresses the sustainability problem. A ranking of countries according to environmental factors or material flows does not tell us anything about their sustainability, not even if we focus on environmental sustainability only. Sagar and Najam's (1996) proposal is, also, too simplistic. There does not exist a threshold of income, after which further income increases are unsustainable due to 'excessive consumption'. Without further knowledge about the environmental impact of the consumption level, one cannot infer whether it is sustainable or not. Also, none of the proposals discussed so far deals seriously with resource depletion, even though resource depletion forms an important component of the depreciation of the natural capital stock.

An alternative proposal: assessing the sustainability of well-being with Genuine Savings

As an alternative to fully integrated indicators of sustainability and well-being, and as an alternative to the suggested extensions to the HDI discussed in the last section, Neumayer (2000a) has proposed to combine the HDI with a measurement of sustainability that can signal whether the achieved level of human development can be maintained into the future. The measurement of sustainability is that of so-called Genuine Savings (GS), which measures the total investment in all forms of capital minus the total depreciation of all forms of capital. In simple terms, if GS is persistently negative, then the total capital stock available to future generations is eroded – a clear indication of unsustainability (Pezzey and Toman 2002). Hence, Neumayer (2000a) proposes to qualify a country's HDI as unsustainable if the country's GS rate is below 0. Note, however, that the proposal can, in principle, be applied to any indicator of well-being, not just the HDI.

Genuine Savings has been pioneered by Hamilton (1994, 1996) with the World Bank's Environment Department. The World Bank publishes GS data in its annual statistical compendium World Development Indicators under the name 'adjusted savings'.[5] Within its GS computations, the World Bank takes depletion of the following natural resources into account in computing natural capital stock depreciation: oil, natural gas, hard coal, brown coal, bauxite, copper, iron, lead, nickel, zinc, phosphate, tin, gold, silver, and forests. As can be seen, the measure is strong on non-renewable resources since, for these marketed resources, the necessary data for valuation are not too difficult to access. The harvesting of forests is the only renewable resource taken into account so far, others such as water depletion, fish catch, biodiversity loss, soil erosion and the like encounter formidable data problems.

The same is true for environmental pollution, for which carbon dioxide is currently the only pollutant included.

The World Bank counts current education expenditures as a proxy for investment in human capital. This is certainly rather crude, but it is difficult to see how investment in human capital could be estimated otherwise for so many countries over such a long time horizon.[6] Dasgupta (2001b: C9f.) argues that it is an overestimate since human capital is lost when people die. Against this, one might object that part of the human capital might have been passed on so that the human capital is not really lost once individuals die or, to be precise, leave the workforce. In any case, such correction would be difficult to undertake.

Table 8.1 lists the HDI of countries in five-year steps from 1975 to 2000 and qualifies the achieved level of human development as potentially unsustainable if the country's GS was negative in or around that year. Note that, for a number of technical reasons, the qualification is one of *potential* unsustainability rather than outright unsustainability. First, given the sometimes shaky quality of the data, one must be cautious about making strong assertions. Second, the World Bank counts the full value of resource depletion as natural capital depreciation ([price – average cost] ∗ quantity of resource extracted or harvested). As argued in detail in Neumayer (2000a, 2003) the World Bank's computation of the full value of natural resource extraction might overestimate natural capital depreciation. What has become known as the El Serafy method (El Serafy 1981, 1989) corrects this upward bias, but it requires information about reserve stocks, which is not available for many countries for many resources for many years. Our computations therefore, by necessity, apply the World Bank method. Third, a negative value of GS in one time period is not enough to signal unsustainability. What matters is whether GS is persistently below zero.

Table 8.1 shows that most countries with high human development are not detected as weakly unsustainable. This is because investments in human and man-made capital far outweigh depreciation of capital. It is only such countries as Kuwait, and Trinidad and Tobago, with a strong dependence on natural resource extraction, that have negative GS rates. Although not shown, the world as whole also has positive GS rates. Most countries whose human development achievement needs to be qualified due to negative GS rates are those with low human development, or in the lower part of medium human development. Another observation following from Table 8.1 is that unsustainability is persistent in the sense that often countries with negative GS in one year have similarly negative rates in other years as well. Unsustainability is not inescapable, however, as such examples as Chile and Jamaica show, which started off with negative GS, but turned these into positive rates in the 1990s. In the case of sub-Saharan Africa (SSA), from which many countries with signs of unsustainability come, a more detailed analysis shows that even their net savings – that is, before natural capital

Table 8.1 HDI with Genuine Savings qualification

Rank	Country	1975	1980	1985	1990	1995	2000
High human development							
1	Norway	0.859	0.877	0.888	0.901	0.925	0.942
2	Sweden	0.863	0.872	0.883	0.894	0.925	0.941
3	Canada	0.868	0.883	0.906	0.926	0.932	0.940
4	Belgium	0.844	0.861	0.875	0.896	0.927	0.939
5	Australia	0.844	0.861	0.873	0.888	0.927	0.939
6	United States of America	0.863	0.884	0.898	0.914	0.925	0.939
7	Iceland	0.863	0.885	0.894	0.913	0.918	0.936
8	Netherlands	0.861	0.873	0.888	0.902	0.922	0.935
9	Japan	0.854	0.878	0.893	0.909	0.923	0.933
10	Finland	0.836	0.856	0.873	0.896	0.908	0.930
11	Switzerland	0.874	0.886	0.892	0.905	0.914	0.928
12	France	0.848	0.863	0.875	0.897	0.914	0.928
13	United Kingdom	0.841	0.848	0.858	0.878	0.916	0.928
14	Denmark	0.868	0.876	0.883	0.891	0.907	0.926
15	Austria	0.840	0.854	0.867	0.890	0.909	0.926
16	Luxembourg	0.831	0.846	0.860	0.884	0.912	0.925
17	Germany	n.a.	0.859	0.868	0.885	0.907	0.925
18	Ireland	0.818	0.831	0.846	0.870	0.894	0.925
19	New Zealand	0.849	0.855	0.866	0.875	0.902	0.917
20	Italy	0.828	0.846	0.856	0.879	0.897	0.913
21	Spain	0.819	0.838	0.855	0.876	0.895	0.913
22	Israel	**0.790**	0.814	0.836	0.855	0.877	0.896
23	Hong Kong, China (SAR)	0.756	0.795	0.823	0.859	0.877	0.888
24	Greece	0.808	0.829	0.845	0.859	0.868	0.885
25	Singapore	0.722	0.755	0.782	0.818	0.857	0.885
26	Cyprus	n.a.	0.801	0.821	0.845	0.866	0.883
27	Korea, Rep. of	0.691	0.732	0.774	0.815	0.852	0.882
28	Portugal	0.737	0.760	0.787	0.819	0.855	0.880
29	Slovenia	n.a.	n.a.	n.a.	0.845	0.852	0.879
30	Malta	0.731	0.766	0.793	0.826	0.850	0.875
31	Barbados	n.a.	n.a.	n.a.	n.a.	n.a.	0.871
32	Brunei Darussalam	n.a.	n.a.	n.a.	n.a.	n.a.	n.a.
33	Czech Republic	n.a.	n.a.	n.a.	n.a.	0.843	0.849
34	Argentina	0.785	0.799	0.805	0.808	0.830	0.844
35	Hungary	0.777	0.793	0.805	0.804	0.809	0.835
36	Slovakia	n.a.	n.a.	0.813	0.820	0.817	0.835
37	Poland	n.a.	n.a.	n.a.	0.792	0.808	0.833
38	Chile	**0.702**	**0.737**	**0.754**	0.782	0.811	0.831
39	Bahrain	n.a.	n.a.	n.a.	n.a.	n.a.	0.831
40	Uruguay	0.757	0.777	0.781	0.801	0.815	0.831
41	Bahamas	n.a.	0.805	0.817	n.a.	n.a.	n.a.
42	Estonia	n.a.	n.a.	n.a.	n.a.	n.a.	0.826
43	Costa Rica	0.745	0.769	0.770	0.787	0.805	0.820
44	Saint Kitts and Nevis	n.a.	n.a.	n.a.	n.a.	n.a.	0.814
45	Kuwait	**0.753**	**0.773**	**0.777**	n.a.	**0.812**	**0.813**

Table 8.1 (Continued)

Rank	Country	1975	1980	1985	1990	1995	2000
46	United Arab Emirates	n.a.	n.a.	n.a.	n.a.	n.a.	n.a.
47	Seychelles	n.a.	n.a.	n.a.	n.a.	n.a.	n.a.
48	Croatia	n.a.	n.a.	n.a.	n.a.	n.a.	n.a.
49	Lithuania	n.a.	n.a.	n.a.	0.816	0.781	0.808
50	Trinidad and Tobago	0.722	**0.755**	**0.774**	**0.781**	**0.787**	**0.805**
51	Qatar	n.a.	n.a.	n.a.	n.a.	n.a.	0.803
52	Antigua and Barbuda	n.a.	n.a.	n.a.	n.a.	n.a.	0.800
53	Latvia	n.a.	n.a.	n.a.	0.804	0.763	0.800
Medium human development							
54	Mexico	n.a.	0.734	**0.752**	0.761	0.774	0.796
55	Cuba	n.a.	n.a.	n.a.	n.a.	n.a.	n.a.
56	Belarus	n.a.	n.a.	n.a.	0.809	0.776	0.788
57	Panama	n.a.	0.731	0.745	0.747	0.770	0.787
58	Belize	n.a.	0.710	0.718	0.750	0.772	0.784
59	Malaysia	0.616	0.659	0.693	0.722	0.760	0.782
60	Russian Federation	n.a.	n.a.	n.a.	n.a.	0.779	**0.781**
61	Dominica	n.a.	n.a.	n.a.	n.a.	n.a.	n.a.
62	Bulgaria	n.a.	0.763	0.784	0.786	0.778	0.779
63	Romania	n.a.	n.a.	n.a.	0.777	0.772	0.775
64	Libyan Arab Jamahiriya	n.a.	n.a.	n.a.	n.a.	n.a.	0.773
65	Macedonia, TFYR	n.a.	n.a.	n.a.	n.a.	n.a.	n.a.
66	Saint Lucia	n.a.	n.a.	n.a.	n.a.	n.a.	0.772
67	Mauritius	0.630	0.656	0.686	0.723	0.746	0.772
68	Colombia	0.660	0.690	0.704	0.724	0.750	0.772
69	Venezuela	0.716	**0.731**	**0.738**	**0.757**	**0.766**	**0.770**
70	Thailand	0.604	0.645	0.676	0.713	0.749	0.762
71	Saudi Arabia	**0.587**	**0.646**	**0.670**	**0.706**	**0.737**	**0.759**
72	Fiji	0.660	0.683	0.697	0.723	0.743	0.758
73	Brazil	0.644	0.679	0.692	0.713	0.737	0.757
74	Suriname	n.a.	n.a.	n.a.	n.a.	n.a.	**0.756**
75	Lebanon	n.a.	n.a.	n.a.	0.680	**0.730**	0.755
76	Armenia	n.a.	n.a.	n.a.	n.a.	n.a.	**0.754**
77	Philippines	n.a.	0.684	0.688	0.716	0.733	0.754
78	Oman	n.a.	n.a.	n.a.	n.a.	n.a.	n.a.
79	Kazakhstan	n.a.	n.a.	n.a.	n.a.	n.a.	**0.750**
80	Ukraine	n.a.	n.a.	n.a.	n.a.	n.a.	**0.748**
81	Georgia	n.a.	n.a.	n.a.	n.a.	n.a.	**0.748**
82	Peru	n.a.	0.669	0.692	0.704	0.730	0.747
83	Grenada	n.a.	n.a.	n.a.	n.a.	n.a.	0.747
84	Maldives	n.a.	n.a.	n.a.	n.a.	0.707	0.743
85	Turkey	0.593	0.617	0.654	0.686	0.717	0.742
86	Jamaica	**0.687**	**0.690**	**0.692**	0.720	0.736	0.742
87	Turkmenistan	n.a.	n.a.	n.a.	n.a.	n.a.	n.a.

88	Azerbaijan	n.a.	n.a.	n.a.	n.a.	n.a.	0.741
89	Sri Lanka	0.616	0.650	0.676	0.697	0.719	0.741
90	Paraguay	0.665	0.699	0.705	0.717	0.735	0.740
91	Saint Vincent and the Grenadines	n.a.	n.a.	n.a.	n.a.	n.a.	0.733
92	Albania	n.a.	n.a.	n.a.	n.a.	0.702	0.733
93	Ecuador	n.a.	**0.673**	**0.694**	**0.705**	**0.719**	**0.732**
94	Dominican Republic	0.617	0.646	0.667	0.677	0.698	0.727
95	Uzbekistan	n.a.	n.a.	n.a.	n.a.	**0.714**	**0.727**
96	China	n.a.	n.a.	0.591	0.625	0.681	0.726
97	Tunisia	0.514	0.566	0.613	0.646	0.682	0.722
98	Iran, Islamic Rep. of	**0.556**	0.563	**0.607**	**0.645**	**0.688**	**0.721**
99	Jordan	n.a.	0.636	0.658	0.677	0.703	0.717
100	Cape Verde	n.a.	n.a.	0.587	0.626	0.678	0.715
101	Samoa (Western)	n.a.	n.a.	n.a.	n.a.	n.a.	n.a.
102	Kyrgyzstan	n.a.	n.a.	n.a.	n.a.	n.a.	0.712
103	Guyana	n.a.	**0.679**	**0.671**	n.a.	0.703	n.a.
104	El Salvador	0.586	0.586	0.606	0.644	0.682	0.706
105	Moldova, Rep. of	n.a.	0.720	0.741	0.759	0.704	0.701
106	Algeria	n.a.	**0.550**	0.600	0.639	n.a.	n.a.
107	South Africa	n.a.	0.663	**0.683**	**0.714**	0.724	0.695
108	Syrian Arab Republic	0.538	0.580	0.614	**0.634**	**0.665**	**0.691**
109	Viet Nam	n.a.	n.a.	n.a.	0.605	0.649	0.688
110	Indonesia	n.a.	n.a.	0.582	0.623	0.664	0.684
111	Equatorial Guinea	n.a.	n.a.	n.a.	n.a.	n.a.	n.a.
112	Tajikistan	n.a.	n.a.	n.a.	n.a.	0.669	0.667
113	Mongolia	n.a.	n.a.	0.650	0.657	0.636	0.655
114	Bolivia	n.a.	**0.548**	**0.573**	**0.597**	0.630	0.653
115	Egypt	0.435	0.482	0.532	0.574	0.605	0.642
116	Honduras	0.518	0.566	0.597	0.615	0.628	0.638
117	Gabon	n.a.	n.a.	n.a.	n.a.	n.a.	**0.637**
118	Nicaragua	n.a.	**0.576**	0.584	0.592	**0.615**	0.635
119	São Tomé and Príncipe	n.a.	n.a.	n.a.	n.a.	n.a.	n.a.
120	Guatemala	0.506	0.543	0.555	0.579	0.609	0.631
121	Solomon Islands	n.a.	n.a.	n.a.	n.a.	n.a.	n.a.
122	Namibia	n.a.	n.a.	n.a.	n.a.	n.a.	0.610
123	Morocco	0.429	0.474	0.508	0.540	0.569	0.602
124	India	0.407	0.434	0.473	0.511	0.545	0.577
125	Swaziland	0.512	0.543	0.569	0.615	0.620	0.577
126	Botswana	0.494	0.556	0.613	0.653	0.620	0.572
127	Myanmar	n.a.	n.a.	n.a.	n.a.	n.a.	n.a.
128	Zimbabwe	n.a.	0.572	0.621	0.597	0.563	n.a.
129	Ghana	0.438	**0.468**	0.481	0.506	0.525	0.548
130	Cambodia	n.a.	n.a.	n.a.	n.a.	0.531	0.543
131	Vanuatu	n.a.	n.a.	n.a.	n.a.	n.a.	n.a.
132	Lesotho	n.a.	n.a.	n.a.	n.a.	n.a.	n.a.
133	Papua New Guinea	n.a.	n.a.	n.a.	n.a.	n.a.	n.a.
134	Kenya	0.443	0.489	0.512	0.533	0.523	0.513
135	Cameroon	0.410	**0.455**	0.505	0.513	0.499	**0.512**

Table 8.1 (Continued)

Rank	Country	1975	1980	1985	1990	1995	2000
Low human development							
136	Congo	0.417	**0.467**	**0.517**	**0.510**	**0.511**	n.a.
137	Comoros	n.a.	0.480	0.498	0.502	0.506	n.a.
138	Pakistan	**0.345**	0.372	0.404	0.442	0.473	0.499
139	Sudan	**0.346**	**0.374**	n.a.	n.a.	**0.462**	**0.499**
140	Bhutan	n.a.	n.a.	n.a.	n.a.	n.a.	0.494
141	Togo	0.394	0.443	0.440	0.465	0.476	0.493
142	Nepal	0.289	0.328	0.370	0.416	0.453	0.490
143	Lao People's Dem. Rep.	n.a.	n.a.	n.a.	n.a.	n.a.	0.485
144	Yemen	n.a.	n.a.	n.a.	**0.399**	**0.439**	**0.479**
145	Bangladesh	**0.335**	**0.353**	0.386	0.416	0.445	0.478
146	Haiti	n.a.	0.430	0.445	0.447	0.457	**0.471**
147	Madagascar	**0.399**	**0.433**	**0.427**	0.434	**0.441**	0.469
148	Nigeria	0.328	**0.388**	**0.403**	**0.425**	**0.448**	**0.462**
149	Djibouti	n.a.	n.a.	n.a.	n.a.	n.a.	n.a.
150	Uganda	n.a.	n.a.	0.386	**0.388**	0.404	0.444
151	Tanzania, U. Rep. of	n.a.	n.a.	n.a.	0.422	0.427	0.440
152	Mauritania	**0.337**	**0.360**	**0.379**	**0.390**	**0.418**	0.438
153	Zambia	n.a.	**0.463**	**0.480**	**0.468**	n.a.	n.a.
154	Senegal	0.313	**0.330**	**0.356**	0.380	0.400	0.431
155	Congo, Dem. Rep. of the	n.a.	n.a.	n.a.	n.a.	n.a.	**0.431**
156	Côte d'Ivoire	0.369	0.403	0.412	**0.415**	0.416	0.428
157	Eritrea	n.a.	n.a.	n.a.	n.a.	n.a.	n.a.
158	Benin	0.288	0.324	**0.350**	**0.358**	0.388	0.420
159	Guinea	n.a.	n.a.	n.a.	n.a.	n.a.	0.414
160	Gambia	**0.272**	n.a.	n.a.	n.a.	0.375	0.405
161	Angola	n.a.	n.a.	n.a.	n.a.	n.a.	**0.403**
162	Rwanda	0.336	0.380	0.396	0.346	0.335	0.403
163	Malawi	0.316	0.341	0.354	0.362	0.403	0.400
164	Mali	0.252	0.279	**0.292**	0.312	0.346	0.386
165	Central African Republic	n.a.	**0.351**	0.371	0.372	**0.369**	0.375
166	Chad	n.a.	n.a.	**0.298**	0.322	0.335	**0.365**
167	Guinea-Bissau	n.a.	n.a.	0.283	0.304	0.331	0.349
168	Ethiopia	n.a.	n.a.	0.275	0.297	0.308	**0.327**
169	Burkina Faso	0.232	0.259	0.282	0.290	0.300	0.325
170	Mozambique	n.a.	**0.302**	**0.290**	**0.310**	0.313	0.322
171	Burundi	n.a.	n.a.	0.338	0.344	0.316	**0.313**
172	Niger	0.234	0.254	0.246	**0.256**	**0.262**	0.277
173	Sierra Leone	n.a.	n.a.	n.a.	n.a.	n.a.	n.a.

Notes: Numbers in bold represent negative GS rates; n.a. means that either the HDI or GS is not available.
Sources: UNDP (2002) and World Bank (2004).

depreciation – are often already negative,such that their economies are on a weakly unsustainable path quite independently of depreciation due to natural resource exploitation (Neumayer 2004).

One of the problems of the existing published GS data is that it does not take into account population growth. The correct accounting for population growth depends on whether population growth is assumed to be exponential and whether social welfare only depends on per capita utility or also on population size (see Hamilton 2000, Asheim 2002, Arrow *et al.* 2003) If one were to take the change in the total per capita capital stock as a first approximation, then many more developing countries with fast growing populations would run into problems with weak sustainability. Dasgupta (2001a: 158) computes that Bangladesh, India, Nepal, Pakistan and the SSA region as a whole have all had net depreciation of their total per capita capital stock over the period 1970 to 1993. China, the only other country looked at by Dasgupta, has just so escaped this fate. World Bank (2006: ch. 5) estimates suggest that almost all African countries exhibit negative total per capita capital stock changes. Note, however, that technological progress is a force in the opposite direction. If it is at least partly exogenous in the sense that it is not fully captured by total capital (Weitzman 1997), then even negative GS rates at any moment of time need not imply weak unsustainability. The same is true for what Dasgupta (2001a: 149) calls 'costless accumulation of public knowledge'. We cannot resolve these difficult issues and simply take existing published GS data as a first approximation.

What are the policy implications of our analysis? Countries with negative GS rates need to invest more and consume less to achieve sustainability. There is a fundamental problem with this policy implication, however. We saw already that developing countries with low and lower medium human development form the majority of countries with unsustainable human development. To demand from these poor countries to save more and consume less is likely to impose the burden of sustainability achievement on the shoulders of poor, powerless and vulnerable people. This, however, would contradict the universalist foundation of sustainability, as Anand and Sen (2000: 2030) make clear:

> universalism also requires that in our anxiety to protect the future generations, we must not overlook the pressing claims of the less privileged today. A universalist approach cannot ignore the deprived people today in trying to prevent deprivation in the future.

Without help from the intra-generationally rich (i.e. the developed countries), these countries will not only be unable to improve their welfare, but they also risk losing the little welfare they have, since even this low level is unsustainable. Such help in the form of aid, trade or investment can be justified with recourse to the fact that development in rich countries has partly been achieved via imposing a negative externality in the form of greenhouse gas emissions, the costs of which are mainly borne by future developing countries (Neumayer 2000b). Given that the poor and unsustainable countries are often major resource extractors, could render such assistance to be in the interest of developed countries. Without such help, resource extracting countries might be inclined to over-exploit their natural resources, which could have negative knock-on effects on resource importing developed countries in the future.

Conclusion

We have argued that besides methodological flaws that are specific to the ISEW/GPI, fully integrated indicators of well-being and sustainability encounter a fundamental conceptual problem: what affects current well-being need not affect sustainability at all or not in the same way, and vice versa. Fully integrated indicators therefore tend to conflate the measurement of two items that should be kept conceptually different. Whereas well-being refers to the current use of the available capital stock in terms of preference satisfaction, sustainability refers to sustaining the value of the total capital stock for the future. The inclusion of sustainability in a measure of current well-being can be justified if one assumes that the current generation's welfare fully takes the welfare of future generations into account. However, no similar justification exists for a measure of sustainability, which should be free of items that affect only current well-being as future generations cannot care for current welfare.

As we have seen, even some proposals combining the measurement of well-being with that of sustainability without full integration at times fall into this trap. We have therefore developed a proposal that combines the measurement of well-being with that of sustainability and which avoids the trap. Well-being is measured in the conventional way, but the sustainability of the achieved level of well-being is checked with a GS test. Where GS is below 0, there is a danger that the achieved level of well-being is bought at the expense of liquidating the total capital available to a country, which cannot be sustainable. We have illustrated our proposal with reference to the HDI, but hasten to add that it is a general proposal in that the GS test can be added to any indicator of well-being.

Of course, our proposal to combine the HDI with a sustainability check according to the GS rule is not without its problems and limitations, either. Currently, GS is not computed for all countries for which UNDP calculates a HDI, but using GS as a sustainability qualification only makes sense if it is available for all relevant countries. Coverage is also a problem with respect to the extent to which natural capital is fully taken into account. Ideally more renewable resource depletion such as water, soil and fish should be included. The same goes for pollutants such as sulphur and nitrogen dioxides, particulate matter, volatile organic compounds and many more. That developed countries are not regarded as unsustainable according to GS is partly due to their high investment in manufactured and human capital. However, if more pollutants could be taken into account, their sustainability position would no longer be as favourable as it is currently. This is because as UNDP (1998: 66) correctly points out: 'It is the rich who pollute more ... who generate more waste and put more stress on nature's sink'. Of course, it is doubtful whether we will ever have such data available for all countries. However, for the developed countries better and more comprehensive data exist and there is no reason why a more comprehensive GS measure could not be estimated for this group of countries. As a first step, the World Bank now includes estimates of the damage caused by particulate matter emissions for developed countries.

The main reason why the world as a whole, and developed countries are not detected as unsustainable by GS has to do with the concept of sustainability underlying the measure, however. This concept is one of weak sustainability, which, as pointed out in the introduction, assumes substitutability of natural capital through other forms of capital. The competing concept of strong sustainability rejects such substitutability. It requires to keep pollution within the absorptive capacity of nature and to replace depleted non-renewable resources with a functionally equivalent stock of renewable resources or non-depletable resources (such as solar and wind energy) (Neumayer 2003). Why not combine the HDI with a measure of strong sustainability then? The reason is that there are likely to be very few, if any, countries that achieve strong sustainability. Most developed countries emit more greenhouse gases than the atmosphere can cope with. Those developing countries that do not exceed the natural absorptive capacity of the global atmosphere with their greenhouse gas emissions still often deplete their non-renewable resource stock without adequate replacement investments in renewable or non-depletable resources, or degrade their local environment. The information content of such a measure would therefore be minimal. The lesson is to take GS as a first step in the right direction. A country, which is not weakly sustainable cannot be strongly sustainable either, and since there are so many poor, weakly unsustainable countries in the developing world, making them weakly sustainable is what we should concentrate on for now, with a view toward achieving stronger forms of sustainability in the future.

Notes

I would like to thank Mark McGillivray and G. Srinivasan, as well as various participants at the project meeting, for their constructive comments.

1 The revised United Nations system of national accounts makes this very clear: 'Neither gross nor net domestic product is a measure of welfare. Domestic product

is an indicator of overall production activity' (Commission of the European Communities – Eurostat *et al.* 1993: 41).

2 See Eisner (1990) for an overview.

3 Such studies derive the value from environmental disamenities in comparing, for example, house prices from real estate, which is similar in all respects but the environmental disamenity.

4 Anand and Sen (2000: 2038) also point out that redistribution to the poor in the form of better nutrition, health and education rather than income is likely to contribute to sustainability unambiguously. I agree, but the mere redistribution of income need not be sustainability promoting.

5 As Dasgupta (2001a, 2001b), I prefer the term 'genuine investment', as investment is really what GS refers to. However, GS has now become the established nomenclature.

6 Note that, in the traditional national accounts, capital expenditures on education are already counted towards investment in man-made capital.

References

Anand, S. and A. Sen (2000) 'Human Development and Economic Sustainability', *World Development*, 28: 2029–49.

Arrow, K. J., P. Dasgupta and K.-G. Mäler (2003) 'The Genuine Savings Criterion and the Value of Population', *Economic Theory*, 21: 217–25.

Asheim, G. B. (2002) 'Green National Accounting with a Changing Population', Working Paper (Oslo: University of Oslo).

Atkinson, G. (1995) *Measuring Sustainable Economic Welfare: A Critique of the UK ISEW*, Working Paper GEC 95-08 (Norwich and London: Centre for Social and Economic Research on the Global Environment).

Castañeda, B. E. (1999) 'An Index of Sustainable Economic Welfare (ISEW) for Chile', *Ecological Economics*, 28: 231–44.

Clarke, M. and S. M. N. Islam (2003) *Diminishing and Negative Returns of Economic Growth: An Index of Sustainable Economic Welfare (ISEW) for Thailand*, Mimeo (Melbourne: Victoria University).

Cobb, C. W. and J. B. Cobb (eds) (1994) *The Green National Product: A Proposed Index of Sustainable Economic Welfare* (Lanham: University Press of America).

Commission of the European Communities–Eurostat, International Monetary Fund, Organisation of Economic Co-operation and Development, United Nations and World Bank (1993) *System of National Accounts 1993* (Brussels; Luxembourg; New York; Paris; Washington, DC).

Crafts, N. (2002) 'UK Real National Income, 1950–1998: Some Grounds for Optimism', *National Institute Economic Review*, 181(1): 87–95.

Dahme, K., F. Hinterberger, H. Schütz, and E. K. Seifert (1998) *Sustainable Human Development Index: A Suggestion for 'Greening' the UN's Indicator*, Mimeo (Wuppertal: Wuppertal Institute for Climate, Environment and Energy).

Daly, H., H. E. Cobb and J. B. Cobb (1989) *For the Common Good* (Boston: Beacon Press).

Dasgupta, P. (2001a) *Human Well-being and the Natural Environment* (Oxford: Oxford University Press).

Dasgupta, P. (2001b) 'Valuing Objects and Evaluating Policies in Imperfect Economies', *Economic Journal*, 111: C1–C29.

De la Vega, M. C. L. and Urrutia, A. M. (2001) 'HDPI: A Framework for Pollution-Sensitive Human Development Indicators', *Environment, Development and Sustainability*, 3: 199–215.
Desai, M. (1995) 'Greening of the HDI?', in A. MacGillivray (ed.), *Accounting for Change* (London: New Economics Foundation) 21–36.
Diefenbacher, H. (1994) 'The Index of Sustainable Economic Welfare: A Case Study of the Federal Republic of Germany', in C. W. Cobb and J. B. Cobb (eds), *The Green National Product: A Proposed Index of Sustainable Economic Welfare* (Lanham: University Press of America) 215–45.
Eisner, R. (1988) 'Extended Accounts for National Income and Product', *Journal of Economic Literature*, 26: 1611–84.
Eisner, R. (1990) *The Total Incomes System of Accounts* (Chicago: Chicago University Press).
El Serafy, S. (1981) 'Absorptive Capacity, the Demand for Revenue, and the Supply of Petroleum', *Journal of Energy and Development*, 7: 73–88.
El Serafy, S. (1989) 'The Proper Calculation of Income from Depletable Natural Resources', in Y. J. Ahmad, S. El Serafy, and E. Lutz (eds), *Environmental Accounting for Sustainable Development: a UNDP–World Bank Symposium* (Washington, DC: World Bank) 10–18.
Guenno, G. and S. Tiezzi (1998) 'An Index of Sustainable Economic Welfare for Italy', Working Paper 5/98 (Milano: Fondazione Eni Enrico Mattei).
Hagerty, M. R., R. A. Cummins, A. L. Ferriss, K. Land, A. C. Michalos, M. Peterson, A. Sharpe, J. Sirgy and J. Vogel (2001) 'Quality of Life Indexes for National Policy: Review and Agenda for Research', *Social Indicators Research*, 55: 1–96.
Hamilton, C. (1999) 'The Genuine Progress Indicator: Methodological Developments and Results from Australia', *Ecological Economics*, 30: 13–28.
Hamilton, K. (1994) 'Green Adjustments to GDP', *Resources Policy*, 20: 155–68.
Hamilton, K. (1996) 'Pollution and Pollution Abatement in the National Accounts', *Review of Income and Wealth*, 42 (1), 13–33.
Hamilton, K. (2000) 'Sustaining Economic Welfare – Estimating Changes in Per Capita Wealth', Policy Research Working Paper 2498 (Washington DC: World Bank).
Hicks, D. A. (1997) 'The Inequality-Adjusted Human Development Index: A Constructive Proposal', *World Development*, 25: 1283–98.
Jackson, T., F. Laing, A. MacGillivray, N. Marks, J. Ralls and S. Stymne (1997) *An Index of Sustainable Economic Welfare for the UK 1950–1996* (Guildford: University of Surrey Centre for Environmental Strategy).
Jackson, T. and S. Stymne (1996) *Sustainable Economic Welfare in Sweden: A Pilot Index 1950–1992* (Stockholm: Stockholm Environment Institute).
Kant, I. (1785) [1968] *Grundlegung zur Metaphysik der Sitten*, Werke Band XI. (Frankfurt: Suhrkamp).
Max-Neef, M. (1995) 'Economic Growth and Quality of Life: A Threshold Hypothesis', *Ecological Economics*, 15: 115–118.
McGillivray, M. and H. White (1993) 'Measuring Development? The UNDP's Human Development Index', *Journal of International Development*, 5: 183–92.
Moffatt, I. and M. C. Wilson (1994) 'An Index of Sustainable Economic Welfare for Scotland, 1980–1991', *International Journal of Sustainable Development and World Ecology*, 1: 264–91.
Neumayer, E. (1999) 'The ISEW: Not an Index of Sustainable Economic Welfare', *Social Indicators Research*, 48: 77–101.
Neumayer, E. (2000a) 'On the Methodology of ISEW, GPI and Related Measures: Some Constructive Suggestions and Some Doubt on the "Threshold" Hypothesis', *Ecological Economics*, 34: 347–61.

Neumayer, E. (2000b) 'In Defence of Historical Accountability for Greenhouse Gas Emissions', *Ecological Economics*, 33: 185–92.

Neumayer, E. (2001) 'The Human Development Index and Sustainability – A Constructive Proposal', *Ecological Economics*, 39: 101–14.

Neumayer, E. (2003) *Weak versus Strong Sustainability: Exploring the Limits of Two Opposing Paradigms*, 2nd rev. edn (Cheltenham: Edward Elgar).

Neumayer, E. (2004) 'Indicators of Sustainability', in T. Tietenberg and H. Folmer (eds), *International Yearbook of Environmental and Resource Economics 2004/05* (Cheltenham: Edward Elgar).

Noorbakhsh, F. (1998a) 'A Modified Human Development Index', *World Development*, 26: 517–28.

Noorbakhsh, F. (1998b) 'The Human Development Index: Some Technical Issues and Alternative Indices', *Journal of International Development*, 10: 589–605.

Nordhaus, W. D. (1992) *Is Growth Sustainable? Reflections on the Concept of Sustainable Economic Growth*, Paper prepared for the International Economic Association Conference, Varenna, October.

Nordhaus, W. D. and J. Tobin (1972) 'Is Growth Obsolete?', in National Bureau of Economic Research, *Economic Growth*, Research General Series 96F (New York: Columbia University Press).

Osberg, L. and A. Sharpe (2002a) 'An Index of Economic Well-Being for Selected OECD Countries', *Review of Income and Wealth*, 48: 291–316.

Osberg, L. and A. Sharpe (2002b), 'International Comparisons of Trends in Economic Well-Being', *Social Indicators Research*, 58: 349–82.

Pezzey, J. C. V. and M. A. Toman (2002) 'Progress and Problems in the Economics of Sustainability', in T. Tietenberg and H. Folmer (eds), *International Yearbook of Environmental and Resource Economics 2002/2003* (Cheltenham and Northampton: Edward Elgar) 165–232.

Putnam, R. D. (1993) *Making Democracy Work – Civic Traditions in Modern Italy* (Princeton: Princeton University Press).

Qizilbash, M. (2001) 'Sustainable Development: Concepts and Rankings', *Journal of Development Studies*, 37: 134–61.

Ramanathan, B. (1999) 'Environment Sensitive Human Development Index: Issues and Alternatives', *Indian Social Science Review*, 1: 193–201.

Rawls, J. (1972) *A Theory of Justice* (Oxford: Oxford University Press).

Redefining Progress (2001) *The 2000 Genuine Progress Indicator* (San Francisco: Redefining Progress).

Rosenberg, D., P. Oegema and M. Bovy (1995) *ISEW for the Netherlands: Preliminary Results and some Proposals for Further Research* (Amsterdam: IMSA).

Sagar, A. and A. Najam (1996) *Sustainable Human Development: A Zero-Sum Game?*, Mimeo (Cambridge, MA: Boston University).

Sagar, A. D. and A. Najam (1998) 'The Human Development Index: A Critical Review', *Ecological Economics*, 25: 249–64.

Schmidt-Hebbel, K. and L. Servén (2000) 'Does Income Inequality Raise Aggregate Saving?', *Journal of Development Economics*, 61: 417–46.

Smith, D. (2001) 'International Evidence on How Income Inequality and Credit Market Imperfections Affect Private Saving Rates', *Journal of Development Economics*, 64: 103–27.

Stockhammer, E., H. Hochreiter, B. Obermayr and K. Steiner (1997) 'The Index of Sustainable Economic Welfare (ISEW) as an Alternative to GDP in Measuring GDP in Measuring Economic Welfare. The Results of the Austrian (revised) ISEW Calculation 1955–1992', *Ecological Economics*, 21: 19–34.

United Nations Development Programme (UNDP) (various years) *Human Development Report* (New York: Oxford University Press).
Weitzman, M. L. (1997) 'Sustainability and Technical Progress', *Scandinavian Journal of Economics*, 99: 1–13.
World Bank (2004) 'Green Accounting and Adjusted Net Savings', website: http://lnweb18.worldbank.org/ESSD/envext.nsf/44ByDocName/ GreenAccounting Adjusted Net Savings.
World Bank (2006) *Where is the Wealth of Nations?* (Washington, DC: World Bank).
Zolotas, X. (1981) *Economic Growth and Declining Social Welfare* (New York: New York University Press).

9
Subjective Measures of Well-being

Ruut Veenhoven

There are two approaches in social indicators research: the 'objective' and the 'subjective' approach. In the objective approach the focus is on measuring 'hard' facts, such as income in dollars or living accommodation in square metres. The subjective approach, in contrast, considers 'soft' matters, such as satisfaction with income and perceived adequacy of dwellings. The objective approach has its roots in the tradition of social statistics, which dates back to the nineteenth century. The subjective approach stems from survey research, which took off in the 1960s. The objective approach is similar to mainstream economic indicators research; though the topics differ, the method is the same. The subjective approach is akin to the psychological stream found in economic indicators research, which is used to monitor things such as consumer trust (Katona 1975) and subjective poverty (VanPraag *et al.* 1980).

The subjective approach originates from the USA. Landmark studies have been published by Campbell *et al.* (1975) and by Andrews and Withey (1976). This approach is further refined in the German 'welfare studies' (Glatzer and Zapf 1984). Specializations have been developed on subjects such as perceived poverty (VanPraag *et al.* 1980), values (Inglehart 1990), and happiness (Veenhoven 1997).

What are 'subjective' measures?

At first sight, the distinction between 'objective' and 'subjective' indicators is fairly clear. Yet, when a closer look is taken there are two dimensions of difference.

First, there is a difference in the *substance* of the matter measured. Objective indicators are concerned with things that exist independent of subjective awareness. For instance: someone can be ill in an objective sense, because a tumour is spreading in the body, without that person knowing. Likewise, Marxists maintain that workers are objectively underclass people, even if they see themselves rather as middle class. Both the doctor and the Marxist give more weight to the objective condition and will press for treatment even if the 'patient' protests.

Second, there is a difference in *assessment*. Objective measurement is based on explicit criteria and performed by external observers. Illness can be measured objectively by the determining presence of antigens in the blood, and class membership by noting the possession of means of production. Given these operational definitions, any impartial observer will come to the same conclusion. Yet, subjective measurement involves self-reports based on implicit criteria. When we say we feel sick, we mostly cannot explain in much detail why we feel so and someone else, with the same symptoms, may be less apt to define himself as unwell.

These examples show that the differences in substance and measurement do not necessarily concur. The possible combinations are presented in Figure 9.1.

The two top quadrants concern objective substance matters. The quadrant top left denotes the combination of objective substance and objective measurement. An example is the actual 'wealth' of a person when measured by her bank account. The top right quadrant also concerns objective substance, but now measured using self-estimate. An example is measuring wealth using self-perceived wealthiness.

The two bottom quadrants in Figure 9.1 concern subjective matters, such as identity, happiness and trust. The bottom left quadrant combines subjective substance with objective measurement. An example would be measuring happiness by relating it to the use of anti-depressants. The bottom right quadrant measures subjective substance using subjective appraisal; for instance, measuring happiness using self-report. The shading indicates the degree of subjectivity in Figure 9.1, the darker the field, the more subjective the indicators.

The reality of social indicators research is more complex than these two dichotomies suggest. The substance of indicators cannot always be classified as either 'objective' or 'subjective', and the methods of measurement that are used do not always fit this dichotomy. Insertion of a *mixed* category on

Substance	**Assessment**	
	Objective	*Subjective*
Objective		
Subjective		

Figure 9.1 Objective–subjective difference: basic configurations
Source: Veenhoven (2002)

Substance	**Assessment**		
	Objective	*Mixed*	*Subjective*
Objective	**1**	**2**	**3**
Mixed	**4**	**5**	**6**
Subjective	**7**	**8**	**9**

Figure 9.2 Objective–subjective differences; elaborate configurations

both axes results in the 3 by 3 classification of Figure 9.2. The numbers in the cells reflect the position on the joined objective–subjective range, the higher the number, the more subjective the indicator.

The following indicators of health can be used to exemplify this classification.

Type 1 Illness revealed by symptoms such as weight loss or biochemical tests;
Type 2 Illness diagnosed by a doctor on the basis of a patient's complaints;
Type 3 Perception of being ill by one-self (possibly without feeling sick);
Type 4 Being and feeling ill as apparent in sickness behaviours such as absenteeism and visiting the doctor;
Type 5 Being and feeling ill measured by a health questionnaire that involves both perceptions of functional health and health complaints;
Type 6 Being and feeling ill as reported directly by a person;
Type 7 Feeling ill as apparent by consumption of relief drugs, such as painkillers or tranquilizers;
Type 8 Feeling ill measured using a sickness complaint inventory;
Type 9 Feeling ill measured using a response to a single question on how fit or sick one feels.

What is 'well-being'?

The term 'well-being' is used to denote that something is in a good or a bad state. The term does not specify what that something is or what is considered to be 'good' or 'bad'. So, it is a typical catch-all term without a precise meaning, incorporating words such as 'progress' and 'welfare'. This notion can be specified in two ways: (i) by specifying the 'what', and (ii) by spelling out the criteria of 'well'ness.

Well-being of *what*?

The term is used for social systems and for individual beings. This difference is often left implicit and used to suggest that what is good for society is also good for citizens. The focus of this volume is on 'human well-being', hence on the well-being of individuals. In this sense the term 'well-being' is synonymous with 'quality-of-life'.

What is being *well*?

Sometimes, the term 'well-being' is used as a generic for all that is good for someone or society. Yet mostly, the word is used for specific varieties of goodness. The main meanings are presented in Figure 9.3.

The classification of meanings in Figure 9.3 depends on two distinctions. Vertically there is a difference between *chances* for a good life and actual *outcomes* of life. Chances and outcomes are related, but are certainly not the same. This distinction is quite common in the field of public health research. Pre-conditions for good health, such as adequate nutrition and professional care are seldom confused with health itself. Yet, means and ends are less well distinguished in the discussion on well-being.

Horizontally there is a distinction between *external* and *internal* states of being. In the first case, the wellness is in the environment, in the latter it is in the individual. This distinction is also quite commonly made in public health. External pathogens are distinguished from inner afflictions, and researchers try to identify the mechanisms by which the former produce the latter. Yet again, this basic insight is lacking in many discussions about well-being. Together, these two dichotomies mark four different concepts of well-being, which are explained below.

Quality of the environment

The left top quadrant of Figure 9.3 denotes the meaning 'good living conditions'. Sociologists use the word 'well-being' mostly in this sense. Economists sometimes use the term 'welfare' for this meaning. Ecologists and biologists also use the term 'livability' in this context, and then refer to the suitability of an environment for a particular species.

Politicians and social reformers typically stress this concept of well-being. In their use of the word, they typically refer to pre-conceptions of what constitutes a good living environment, such as a good standard of living and social equality.

	Outer qualities	*Inner qualities*
Life-chances	Living in a good environment	Being able to cope with life
Life-results	Being of worth for the world	Enjoying life

Figure 9.3 Four kinds of being 'well'
Source: Veenhoven (2000)

Life-ability of the person

The right top quadrant of Figure 9.3 denotes inner life-chances. That is: how well we are equipped to cope with the problems of life. Psychologists typically use the word 'well-being' in this sense. This variant is also known by different names. In the medical profession, this matter is called 'health' in the medium variant of the word.[1] Biologists call it 'fitness'. Sen (1993) calls this variant of well-being 'capability'. This concept is central in the thinking of therapists and educators; the former associate the term with public health, the latter with schooling.

Worth for the world

The left bottom quadrant of Figure 9.3 represents the notion that a good life must be good for something more than itself. This presumes some higher value, such as ecological preservation or cultural development. In fact, there is a myriad of values on which the worth of a life can be judged. Gerson (1976: 795) referred to this matter as 'transcendental' conceptions of well-being. Another appellation is 'meaning of life', which is then used to denote 'true' significance instead of mere subjective sense of meaning. Moral advisors emphasize this kind of well-being.

Enjoyment of life

Finally, the bottom right quadrant of Figure 9.3 represents the inner outcomes of life; that is, well-being in the eye of the beholder. As we are dealing with conscious humans, this quality boils down to subjective appreciation of life. This is commonly referred to by terms such as 'satisfaction' and 'happiness'. There is no professional interest group that stresses this meaning. Yet, this concept is central in utilitarian moral philosophy, which is enjoying a revival (Veenhoven 2004).

Measures of well-being

Using the distinctions made in Figures 9.2 and 9.3, I can now provide a systematic overview of measures of well-being. Below I will take the quadrants shown in Figure 9.3 and consider for each of these concepts which of the measurement methods given in Figure 9.2 apply. Though the focus of this chapter is on subjective indicators, I will also mention objective indicators, since this will help me to place the subjective ones in context.

Indicators of quality of the environment

Starting with the left top quadrant of Figure 9.3, I begin with well-being in the sense of living in good conditions. How can this kind of well-being be measured? Substantially, this is an objective matter, since an environment is something that exists independent of personal perceptions. Following

Figure 9.2, we can distinguish three measurement methods: types 1, 2 and 3. Below, I give examples of each of these. When considering the indicators used for measuring the quality of an environment I will distinguish between indicators that refer to specific qualities and indicators of overall quality.

Specific qualities

A living environment has many aspects, physical aspects, economic aspects, and social aspects. Each of these aspects can be judged by several standards; for example, a social environment can be evaluated for the safety it provides, for the freedom it allows, and for the fairness it achieves. As I cannot review all these matters, I will use the example of 'social equality'. This aspect of objective well-being can be measured in the following ways:

Type 1 indicators Objective measurement of social inequality requires that impartial outsiders assess differences in access to scarce resources among members of a society. Typically, this boils down to differences in income, which are assessed using national income statistics that draw on registrations of taxes and salaries. Other indicators of this kind involve differences in access to education or medical care within a country.

Type 2 indicators Since income statistics have many limitations, the distribution of incomes in a country can also be assessed using questionnaires. This brings a subjective element into this otherwise objective assessment, especially when income is assessed using global questions. The Luxembourg Income Study is an example of this approach.

Another example of mixed measurement of social inequality is considering inequality in subjective outcomes of life. In this context, I have proposed measuring social inequality in nations using the dispersion of life-satisfaction in representative samples of the general population (Veenhoven 2005a). An advantage of this method is that it covers all relevant resources, and not just the few that are easily measurable and deemed relevant. Other advantages are that this indicator of social inequality is readily comparable across time and nations. A disadvantage is the causes of inequality remain unknown.

Type 3 indicators A purely subjective assessment of social inequality can be gained by asking people how much inequality they think there is in their country. An advantage of this approach is that such perceptions also reflect less palpable differences regarding access to scarce resources than just income. The disadvantages are that the perceptions may be incorrect and public discussion about social inequality may influence people's perceptions of this reality.

Overall quality

We can discern three ways to assess the overall quality of living conditions.

Type 1 indicators The objective approach is to add together registration based indexes of quality of living conditions. This is practised in several indexes of well-being, such as Estes's (1984) 'Index of Social Progress' and Slottje's (1991) index of 'quality of life' in nations. Such indexes combine indicators of material affluence, safety in the streets, political stability, rule of law, unemployment, and so on. Though commonly used, this type of indicator is very questionable. There are a number of problems: such indexes cannot cover all the relevant issues and the weighing of items in these indexes is quite arbitrary. The relevant qualities of an environment depend to some extent on the capabilities of its inhabitants; living in a free society may be beneficial for well educated autonomous people, but possibly not so for dumb conformists. I have discussed the limitations of these indexes in more detail elsewhere (Veenhoven 1996b, 2000).

Type 2 indicators Several indicators combine such registration-based indexes of quality of living conditions with subjective satisfaction with these conditions. An example is Rogerson's (1997) measure of quality-of-life in British counties. That measure considers ten environmental attributes, such as 'cost of living', 'pollution', and 'shopping facilities', and then weights these qualities using public opinion with respect to their importance. The overall quality of an environment can also be measured indirectly, by considering how well people thrive in it. When people flourish in an institution or in a country the quality of that environment is apparently sufficient, though not necessarily ideal. In that vein, I have proposed to measure the livability of a society by using the average happiness of its citizens (Veenhoven 2000). This is a mixed measure, since subjective information is used in an objective way; it is an interpretation of self-reported happiness that goes beyond the individuals' awareness, just as a doctor's diagnosis adds to the patients' complaints.

Type 3 indicators An example of a purely subjective assessment of the overall quality of a person's environment is to ask them to rate the quality of their town or country. This indicator is commonly is used in surveys on the 'best place to live' and in questionnaire studies on the quality of life provided by institutions, such as the army or homes for the aged. This approach also avoids the preconceptions of type 1 measures. Yet, the major disadvantage is again that the perceptions may be false. People may be unaware of shortcomings in their environment, due to misinformation or defensive denial.

Indicators of ability to cope with life

This kind of well-being is depicted by the top-right quadrant in Figure 9.2. Life-ability can be thought of as an entirely objective substance, someone being capable or not, independent of how capable that person thinks they are. As such, it can be measured using indicators type 1, 2 and 3.[2] As for in the case of an environment, we can again distinguish between indicators of specific capabilities and estimates of overall life-ability. In this context, I will also make a distinction between indicators of the well-being of separate individuals and social indicators for the well-being of collectivities, such as citizens of a country.

Specific capabilities

Being 'well' in this sense involves many capabilities, both physical and mental. Good physical ability entails absence of obvious dysfunction in the first place, often referred to as 'health', but may also call for positive functioning,[3] as exemplified in endurance or motor skill. Mental abilities concern intellectual capability, emotional control and various social skills, such as empathy and assertiveness. I will not try to review all the indicators of all capabilities, since this would cover the entire field of psychological assessment. Let me suffice with the example of 'intelligence'.

Type 1 indicators Intelligence can be measured objectively using 'tests' of performance in standardized tasks, mostly in a paper and pencil format. Intelligence tests entail sampling intellectual capabilities such as counting, memorization and verbal logic. Intelligence is also assessed using real life performance, such as educational achievement and success at work.

These individual level indicators can be aggregated to the nation level. Average scores on intelligence tests are commonly compared across nations and over time. In a similar way, the level of literacy in a country can be used to assess this kind of well-being in nations.

Type 2 indicators Emotional intelligence is typically measured in another way. Since performance during emotional tasks is not immediately visible to an outsider, common EQ-tests draw on self-ratings. Typical items are: 'How well do you get along with your family?' and 'Do you feel you understand what is going on in other people?' The objective element in these 'tests' is to be found in the selection and weighing of items, which sometimes depends on their predictive power. Average scores on such indicators can also be used to compare across social categories and nations, and for trend analysis. To my knowledge this is not common practice.

Type 3 indicators A purely subjective indicator of intelligence is a simple self-rating; for instance, the answer to the question: 'Do you feel you are smarter than most people of your age? Much smarter, a bit smarter, about equal, a bit less, much less'. A common result with such measures is that most people think that they are better than average (Headey and Wearing 1988). This sense of relative superiority is commonly attributed to self-serving bias, but it may also be due to under-estimation of others, due to selective publicity. Whatever the reason, this pattern of response makes this kind of indicator less suitable for comparison across nations and over time.

Overall life-ability

Comprehensive capability cannot really be 'measured' but can, to some extent, be 'estimated'. This is done in the following ways:

Type 1 indicators The objective way would seem to be to aggregate scores on tests of various capabilities. This approach can yield informative capabilities 'profiles' but not a meaningful sum score. The same objections brought against indexes of environmental quality also apply in this case. Performances of different skills cannot meaningfully be summed and the mix of capabilities that a person's life calls for depends on environmental demands. In restricted settings, such as psychiatric hospitals, one can also assess capability using behavioural observation. Trained observers or attendants rate the patient's ability to deal with the problems of daily life. Various rating systems are used for this purpose. This method can work if the required capabilities can be fairly unequivocal defined, which is mostly the case in such settings.

Type 2 indicators Such neutral estimates of life-ability are often completed with self-reports. This is common practice in psychological measurement, especially for estimates of overall ability. Such measurement mostly involves interviews and it is therefore difficult to ignore a subject's self-appraisal.

Type 3 indicators A purely subjective measure is someone's self-estimate of capability. This is commonly measured using responses to questionnaire items on self-reliance and self-confidence. When such items figure in nationwide surveys, the mean can serve as an indication of the competence of the average citizen.

As noted, some conceptions of life-ability involve both objective and subjective elements. A good example is the concept of 'positive mental health' as described by Jahoda (1958). Objective elements in this capability syndrome are 'adequate perception of reality' and 'integration' of personality. Subjective features are 'self-confidence' and 'liking' of other people. This mixed concept can be measured using indicator types 4, 5 and 6.

Indicators of worth for the world

Let me now consider the well-being concept denoted by the bottom-left quadrant in Figure 9.3. This view on well-being stresses the consequence of a life. This notion is not very prominent in the social policy discourse and therefore remains marginal in social indicators research. It is a greater issue in the discussion about the meaning of life in philosophy and in existential psychology: for the sake of completeness, I will review the possible indicators of this matter.

Substantively, this kind of well-being is 'objective'. The concept deals with actual effects on an environment, not about illusions. So, the possible indicators are again of the types 1, 2 and 3. Measurement is quite difficult in this case, since it is difficult to ascertain the effects of a life – in particular, its effects on a wider environment.

Aspects of worth

The worth of a life for its environment can be judged in many ways. One can consider long-term effects on an ecosystem and on society, or limit the scope to short-term worth for one's business or family. I will illustrate this point with indicators of environmental damage, which have emerged from current discussions about sustainable development.

Type 1 indicators An objective measure of this objective substance is the 'ecological footstep'; that is, the amount of non-renewable resources consumed during a life. At the national level, this is typically estimated using statistical data about sales of materials. An example can be found in the *Living Planet Report* (WWF 2002).

Type 2 indicators The ecological footprint can also be measured at the individual level, using questionnaires and consumption diaries. This objective matter is then measured using subjective data. These individual level scores can be aggregated to the national level in principle, provided that these data can be raised in representative samples of the general population.

Type 3 indicators Using up non-renewable resources is also estimated by simple self-ratings. Since this is difficult to judge, I see little value in such ratings.

Overall worth of life

It is easier to think of the overall worth of life than to strike a balance of effects. This notion is almost unmeasurable, although some attempts have been made.

Type 1 indicators To my knowledge there have been no attempts to measure overall worth at the individual level by objectively summing a measurable value to the world, such as good citizenship and cultural innovations. Yet, such indicators are being used at the national level. An example is Naroll's (1984) estimates of national contribution to the progress of science and international peace.

Type 2 indicators The worth of life has also been assessed using questions about perceived contributions of one's life to several causes. Chamberlain and Zika (1988) have reviewed some of the questionnaires. Again, the objective element in this method of measurement is that the investigator selects the aspects of worth and determines the weights. It is difficult to ascertain whether such scales reflect perceived worth of life or satisfaction with that perception.

Type 3 indicators The most subjective measure is to ask people how useful, all in all, they think their life is: the problem with such questions is that people rarely know, and therefore the responses are likely to be guided by other cues, such as their enjoyment of life.

Indicators of satisfaction with life

The bottom-right quadrant in Figure 9.3 denotes personal appreciation of life. This kind of well-being is substantially subjective. As such, the assessment methods 7, 8 and 9 from Figure 9.2 apply. Below, I will give examples of each of these indicator types; again, first, for satisfaction with aspects of life and then for satisfaction with life-as-a-whole.

Aspects of life

Subjective appreciation can be about different domains of life, such as work, family, or leisure. Satisfaction can also deal with specific qualities of life, such as comfort of one's life or challenges that one faces. People appraise life in numerous ways and often combine aspect appraisals to arrive at multifarious notions, such as 'loneliness'. A good overview of domains and criteria can be found in Andrews and Withey (1976). I have chosen to use the domain 'job satisfaction' for my example.

Type 7 indicators Since job satisfaction is a mental state, it is not easily observed by an outsider. Job satisfaction can be inferred, to some extent, by objectively observing behaviours, such as strikes, job-hopping, absenteeism, and productivity. These indicators can be used at the individual level and for aggregates. An obvious weakness of this method is that behaviour depends on more things than mere satisfaction.

Type 8 indicators An example of mixed objective and subjective measurement is found in common job satisfaction 'scales'. These are based on questionnaires dealing with multiple aspects, such as perceived job-security, the quality of contacts with colleagues, difficulty of work tasks, days sick, interest in other jobs, and so on. A commonly used scale of this type is the Job Descriptive Index of Smith *et al.* (1969). This kind of indicator draws on subjective information, but the information is processed in an objective way, by computing a sum score.

Type 9 indicators The most subjective measures of job satisfaction are simple self-reports, such as an answer to the question: 'Taking everything into consideration, how do you feel about your job as a whole?' (Warr *et al.* 1979).

Life-as-a-whole

Subjective appreciation of one's life-as-a-whole is called 'life satisfaction' or 'happiness', and is measured using indicator type 7, 8 and 9.

Type 7 indicators Suicide is sometimes used as an objective indicator of life satisfaction, both at the individual level and at the national level. Life satisfaction is also inferred from other behavioural indications of despair, such as alcoholism and political extremism.

Many such indicators are combined in Lynn's index of distress in nations. This index sums the following incidence rates: (i) consumption of stress related stimulants, such as tobacco, coffee, and alcohol; (ii) risky behaviours leading to accidents and criminality, including murder; (iii) psychiatric disorders as measured by hospitalization for psychosis; (iv) deviant behaviour, such as divorce rates and illegitimate birth rates; and (v) despair, as apparent in suicide (Lynn 1971, 1982). For more on this subject, see Veenhoven (1993: ch. 5), where I looked at the correlations of such behaviour with self-reported life satisfaction, and found that these are mostly weak.

Type 8 indicators There are several kinds of mixed measures of life satisfaction. One method is to infer satisfaction from behavioural intentions, such as plans to leave a country or having a suicidal ideation. Such questions often form a part of wider happiness 'tests', which also involve items about things deemed to be related to happiness, such as having plans for the future, seeing meaning in life and thinking one self to be happier than average. A much-used questionnaire of this kind is the Neugarten *et al.* (1961) *Life Satisfaction Index.*

This approach has several flaws. One is that such sum scores lack clear conceptual meaning; it is often unclear whether such questionnaires tap happiness or broader notions such as 'adjustment' or 'optimism'. A related weakness is that the things deemed related to life satisfaction do not always go together with it; for instance, not all happy people make plans. Further, such measures introduce contamination into the correlational analysis; if goal orientation is part of the happiness indicator, one cannot investigate the relation between happiness and goal orientation using this measure.

Another kind of mixed indicator departs from the type 9 subjective self-reports of life satisfaction, and combines these with objective data. One example is Veenhoven's (1996b) 'Happiness Adjusted Life-Years'. Analogous to 'Disability Adjusted Life Years' (DALY's), this measure combines subjective happiness with objective longevity (Veenhovens 1996b). This measure can be used at the individual level and at the national level. Another composite of this kind is 'Equality Adjusted Happiness', which is computed by dividing average life satisfaction in a nation by the standard deviation (Veenhoven and Kalmijn 2005). This measure applies only at the societal level.

Type 9 indicators The most subjective way of measuring subjective satisfaction with life is simply to ask people how much they enjoy their life as a whole. A common item used in the *World Values Surveys* (n.d.) is:

'All things considered, how satisfied are you with your life-as-a-whole now?'

1 2 3 4 5 6 7 8 9 10

Dissatisfied Satisfied

Such questions can be framed in several ways, using different keywords, time frames and response formats. The *World Database of Happiness* (n.d.)

contains an 'Item Bank', which provides a good overview of the questions used for this purpose.

Indicators of overall well-being

So much for the indicators of the separate well-being concepts delineated in Figure 9.3. Let us now consider attempts to measure wider well-being. Following the fourfold classification in Figure 9.3, we can see that there are seven possible kinds of composites: one combination of the two top quadrants, one combination of the two bottom quadrants, four three-quadrant combinations and a combination of all four quadrants. It would be too much to try to deal with all these combinations and their measurement variants. I will give a few examples and explain why we should avoid using any of these indexes.

UNDP Human Development Index

The most commonly used indicator in this field is the 'Human Development Index' (HDI). This index was developed for the United Nations Development Programme, and is used to describe the progress in all the countries of the world in UNDP's annual *Human Development Report* (e.g. UNDP 1999). The HDI is the major yardstick used in these reports. The basic variant of this measure involves three items: (i) public wealth, measured by buying power per head; (ii) education, as measured by literacy and schooling; and (iii) life-expectancy at birth. Later variants of the HDI involve further items: (a) gender equality, measured by the so-called 'Gender empowerment index' which involves male–female ratios in literacy, school enrolment and income; and (b) poverty, measured by prevalence of premature death, functional illiteracy, and income deficiencies. Note that we deal with scores drawn from national statistical aggregates instead of individual responses to questionnaires.

When placed in our fourfold matrix, this index can be seen to indicate three things (see Figure 9.4). First, it is about living conditions, in the basic variant of material affluence in society, with the addition of social equality. These items belong in the top left quadrant. In the case of wealth, it is acknowledged that this environmental merit is subject to diminishing utility,

	Outer quality	*Inner quality*
Life-chances	Material wealth Gender equality Income equality	Education
Life-results		Life expectancy

Figure 9.4 Meanings measured by the Human Development Index

however, this is not so with the equalities. Second, the HDI includes abilities. The education item belongs in the top right quadrant. Though a high level of education does not guarantee high social competence, it means that many citizens at least have basic knowledge. Last, the item 'life expectancy' is an outcome variable and belongs in the bottom right quadrant. The bottom left quadrant remains empty.

The HDI is certainly a useful measure of 'catch-up': it indicates how well developing nations meet some attainments that are characteristic of the leading nations of the world. Yet, the HDI is of little value as a measure of overall well-being. Figure 9.4 helps us to see why. The HDI adds apples and oranges: *chances* for a good life, wealth and education, are added to *outcomes*, life expectancy; and *outer* qualities, wealth and equality, are added to an *inner* one, education. This simply makes no sense. The HDI is also not suited for monitoring progress in well-being in advanced nations, since its items are subject to the law of diminishing utility. More is not always better. This is acknowledged in the case of wealth, but not in the cases of equality and education. We can have too much social equality and schooling. Further, life expectancy is of value only if life remains satisfying in old age. The HDI does not take enjoyment of life into account.

Allardt's welfare index

In his seminal study on comparative welfare, Allardt (1976) measured well-being in Scandinavian nations using self-reports on nine items: (i) income, (ii) quality of housing, (iii) political support, (iv) social relations, (v) health, (vi) education, (vii) being irreplaceable, (viii) doing interesting things, and (ix) life satisfaction. These indicators cover all the variants of well-being in Figure 9.3 (see Figure 9.5). Most of the items belong in the left-top quadrant because they concern pre-conditions for a good life rather than good living, as such, and because these chances are in the environment rather than in the individual. This is the case for income, housing, political support, and social relations. Two further items also denote chances but these are internal capabilities, the health factor and level of education. These items are placed in the top-right quadrant of personal life ability.

	Outer quality	*Inner quality*
Life-chances	Income (h) Housing (h) Political support (h) Social relations (l)	Health (h) Education (h)
Life-results	Irreplaceable (b)	Doing interesting things (b) Life-satisfaction (b)

Figure 9.5 Meanings measured by Allardt's *Dimensions of Welfare* (1976): having (h), loving (l) and being (b)

The item 'irreplaceable' belongs in the utility bottom left quadrant. It denotes value of a life to others. The last two items belong in the enjoyment bottom right quadrant. 'Doing interesting things' denotes appreciation of aspects of life,[4] while life satisfaction concerns appreciation of life as a whole.

WHO Quality of Life scale

Recently, a similar indicator has been developed in the field of health related quality-of-life research. The World Health Organization Quality of Life (WHOQOL) scale is a questionnaire about self-perceived well-being over a two-week period. The domains addressed are: (i) physical health, (ii) psychological health, (iii) social relationships, and (iv) environmental conditions; the questionnaire also includes an item on perceived overall quality of life. The full questionnaire involves 100 items, the short version 26 (WHOQOL Group 1998).

The main themes are summarized in Figure 9.6. Although this scale is meant for individual level analysis in the first instance, it is also used for comparing well-being across nations and for this reason considerable effort has been invested in making accurate translations of the questionnaire.

Why all these indexes fall short

looseness-1All these attempts to summate across quadrants fall short. The main reason is that, as stated above, it involves adding apples to oranges. There is no sense to be had from adding 'chances' and 'outcomes'. This is akin to measuring public health in a country by adding the quantity of sewage to the number of days of illness per capita. No serious epidemiologist would do this, since the question is rather how these phenomena are related. Policy makers must know what quantity of sewage is required to reduce the number of days of illness per capita

	Outer quality	*Inner quality*
Life-chances	Physical environment Home environment Financial resources Social support Safety Information Transportation	Physical health Mental health Work capacity Learning capacity Energy
Life-results		Pain Depression Satisfaction with health Satisfaction with self Satisfaction with life

Figure 9.6 Meanings measured by the WHO's QOL scale

and a summation of these matters' measures will not give a meaningful answer.

Likewise, it makes no sense to summate 'outer' environmental conditions and 'inner' capabilities. Such simple summations do not acknowledge the contingencies involved. The livability of outer conditions depends to a great extent on the inner capabilities of people. If outer conditions are poor, inner capabilities must be strong for a good life, but in good external conditions lower capabilities may suffice. It is the 'fit' that matters, not the sum. The fit is also situation specific; modern urban environment calls for different capabilities than traditional agrarian society. Schooling is more fitting in the former condition than in the latter.

All these indexes are also incomplete, because they are limited to a few aspects, typically issues that are on the political agenda and happen to be measurable. Most of the indexes give equal weight to all items, while it should be evident that the importance of aspects will vary. None of the indexes acknowledges that weights vary with satiation and that they are contingent on situations and personal capabilities. I have analyzed these shortcomings in more detail elsewhere (Veenhoven 1996b, 2000).

Best indicator is happy life years

The most comprehensive measure of well-being is how long and happily people live. Though this latter measure covers only the bottom right quadrant in Figure 9.3, it is likely also to reflect the top quadrants. When a person lives long and happily, the preconditions are apparently sufficient; both the environmental conditions and the person's coping abilities must surpass the minimum level. Moreover, the person's capabilities (top right quadrant) apparently fit environmental demands (top left quadrant). Note: I do not proclaim that long and happy living is the essence of well-being; what I claim is that it is the most comprehensive indicator of this multi-facetted concept.

The degree to which people live long and happily in a country can be measured by combining data on length of life, using civil registration data with data on satisfaction with life as assessed in surveys, using type 9 questions mentioned above. A simple measure is to multiply life expectancy with life satisfaction. For example: in the United States in 1995, life expectancy at birth was 76.4 years and average life satisfaction on a 1 to 10 scale, 7.4. Hence, the average American citizen could be expected to enjoy 56.9 happy life years in that era ($76.4 \times 7.4/10$). This method is described in more detail elsewhere (Veenhoven 1996b).

This measure of how long and happily people live is called 'Happy Life Expectancy'[5] and abbreviated as HLE. Analogous to 'Disability Adjusted Life Years' (DALYs), 'Happiness Adjusted Life Years' can be abbreviated as HALYs. This measure was ranked top in a recent review of indicators of quality-of-life in nations (Hagerty *et al.* 2001).

Data on happy life years are now available for 90 nations in the early 2000s, and the number of countries covered continues to expand. Trend data are available for ten nations, some of which cover around fifty years. These data are published on the World Database of Happiness and are regularly updated (http://worlddatabaseofhappiness.eur.nl, select 'Distribution in Nations' and next click 'Finding Reports').

A look at the data shows great variation across nations. HLE is currently highest in Switzerland (63 years) and lowest in Moldova (20.5 years). About 75 per cent of the cross-national differences can be explained by 'hard' societal characteristics such as economic development, political freedom and rule of law (Veenhoven 1996b). Comparison over time shows a steady increase in first world nations in the last decade.

There is, of course, much doubt about the value of subjective life satisfaction and these misgivings also apply to this measure of happy life years, another paper would be required to discuss these qualms. Suffice to note that I have done this elsewhere (Veenhoven 1996a, 1996b), and showed that these philosophical fantasies have little ground in reality. One thing is that happiness cannot be disposed of as false consciousness; happy people appear to be typically realistic and well informed (Veenhoven 2004). Another point is that happiness is not the same as carefree living. Happiness can go with considerable hardship and even seems to require some challenge (Veenhoven 2005b). Nor does happiness require dictatorial control, such as depicted in a 'Brave New World', since happiness appears to require autonomy (Veenhoven 2004). I will touch on some further qualms about happiness in the next section.

Use of measures of subjective well-being

Defenders of the objective approach hold that social indicators serve to guide social policy, and that social policy makers need information about (i) the actual state of social problems, and (ii) the effects of attempts to solve these problems. This information should be of an indisputable nature – in other words 'objectively true' – and this scientific truth should enable rational social engineering. In this view, subjective indicators will distort the technocratic policy process and will give a voice to the irrationalities that have always hampered scientific management.

This position is quite common in the field of social indicators. Several international agencies rule out subjective indicators (OECD 1999) or ignore them (UNDP 1999). The Swedish level of living tradition is also quite critical of subjective indicators (Vogel 2002). Below, I will take a closer look at the misgivings about subjective indicators and argue why social policy still needs subjective indicators and why objective indicators taken alone are inadequate.

Qualms about subjective measures

Recalling Figure 9.1 will help us to chart the doubts about subjective indicators. Misgivings about attitudinal matters must be distinguished from misgivings about measurement by self-reports.

Misgivings about attitudinal matters

It is commonly objected that matters to do with the mind are unstable, incomparable, and unintelligible. It is argued that attitudinal phenomena vary over time and that this variation has little link with reality conditions. For instance, attitudes about safety on the streets may depend more on media sensationalism than on actual incidence of robbery. In this view, subjective indicators cannot provide a steady policy compass and fail to protect policy makers against the whims of the day.

It is also argued that subjective appraisals cannot be compared between persons. One assertion is that different people use different criteria, so two persons stating they are 'very happy' could say so for different reasons. Another claim is that people have different scales in mind, and that people who report they are 'very happy' may, in fact, be equally as happy as someone who characterizes their life as 'fairly happy'. In economics, this reasoning is known as the theorem of 'incomparable utilities'. If true, this would mean that subjective appraisals cannot show whether one person (or social group) is better off than another and, hence, that this kind of indicator is of little help when selecting those most in need of policy support.

Likewise, it is argued that subjective appraisals cannot be compared across cultures. The example of poverty is often given in this context. Notions of poverty and, hence, definitions of oneself as poor, will differ greatly between rich and poor nations, and within nations between upper and lower classes. This would mean that, for social policy, these kinds of indicators tell policy makers little about relative performance.

A related objection is that the criteria used for these subjective appraisals are largely implicit. Though people know fairly well *how* satisfied, anxious, or trustful they are, they typically know less well *why* they think this is so. The appraisal process is quite complex and partly unconscious; this creates at least an interpretation problem for social policy. The declining trust in government (Vile 1999) is an illustrative case. Though the trend is fairly clear, at least in the USA, the causes are not and, hence, neither is the remedy.

This all merges into the position that subjective valuation is, in fact, irrelevant. Satisfaction judgments, in particular, can depend too little on real quality of life and too much on fashionable beliefs and arbitrary comparison. In this view, policy makers would do better to ignore appraisals of citizens, just as some doctors disregard their patients' complaints. Instead, policy makers should look to objective statistical information and behave like doctors, who believe only in the results of laboratory tests.

These objections do, indeed, apply to some subjective indicators. There is good evidence that most of them apply to satisfaction with domains of life and, in particular, to satisfaction with income. Income satisfaction is highly dependent on social comparison and, hence, largely unrelated to objective welfare (VanPraag 1993).

Yet, these objections do not apply to any subjective indicator, and especially not to overall satisfaction with life. Unlike most domain satisfaction, life satisfaction is not relative, because life satisfaction judgements draw on affective information in the first place – 'how well one feels' – and not on cognitive comparison with standards of a good life. Research findings have also shown that subjective life satisfaction is strongly related to several indicators of objective welfare, especially at the national level. Illusive happiness exists only in fiction.

Misgivings about measuring by self-reports

Several objections concern matters of validity. It is doubted that self-reports tap the things we want to access, even if the aim is inner matters. Next, there are qualms about reliability. Self-reports are said to be imprecise and too vulnerable to distortions. Though much of this criticism is overdone, there is some truth in it.

Doubts as to validity When objective matters are measured by self-report there is always the problem that survey questions may evoke responses to different matters than the investigator had in mind. Even with a seemingly clear-cut matter such as 'income', there are problems as to whether it is personal income or family income, gross or net, whether capital revenues and non-monetary income should be included, and so on. This problem is particularly noticeable for ill defined concepts such as 'health' and 'social prestige'.

When subjective substance is measured, a further problem arises: people may not have thought much out in their mind. For instance, not everybody has a crystallized 'self-concept' or a clear 'class conscience'. Even when the person has some idea, this is not always fully consciously understood. For example, racists often fail to acknowledge their own opinions and unhappy people may seek comfort in defensive reversal and thus believe that they enjoy life.

Again, these problems vary with subject matter. Elsewhere, I have reviewed the various qualms about the validity of self-reported happiness and inspected the empirical evidence for these claims. I found no evidence for specific distortions and good evidence for general predictive validity. At the individual level, happiness appears to be a strong predictor of longevity, stronger than smoking or not and, at the national level, research shows quite strong correlations with societal characteristics such as economic affluence and political democracy, which together explain about 75 per cent of the variance in average happiness (Veenhoven 1997).

Doubts as to reliability Even when self-reports fit the subject matter, there is still the problem of precision. Self-reports are typically made based on fixed response options, the number of which is mostly no greater than 10. Not only are these scales rather crude, but the responses to them are also fickle. The same amount of satisfaction may be rated by one person using the number 6 and by another person using the number 7. Such random error is no great problem for average scores, but it greatly deflates correlations. Next, there is the problem that responses may be distorted in a systematic way, such as by a tendency for respondents to conform to social desirability. There is some evidence that desirability bias inflates ratings of income and social prestige. Alongside such cultural biases, there may also be systematic distortions due to interviewing techniques, item sequences and response formats.

In this case, the distortions are also not the same for any subjective indicator. Research on happiness has demonstrated that self-reports are affected by the mood of the moment and characteristics of the interviewer (Schwarz 1999). Yet, in national averages such random errors appear to balance out, given the high percentage of explained variance mentioned above.

Uses of subjective indicators in policy process

In spite of these weaknesses, subjective indicators are indispensable in social policy, both for assessing policy success and for selecting policy goals. Objective indicators alone do not provide sufficient information, especially not on the subject of well-being.

Assessing policy success

Success in some goals can be measured objectively. Improvement of housing conditions can be measured using the gain in square metres per person or improvement in education using the student/teacher ratio. Yet, such measures have their limitations and, in some cases, additional subjective indicators are required.

This is, for instance, the case with public 'health'. Considerable problems exist regarding assessment of average health based on medical consumption and registered incidence of disease. Longevity does not fully capture the phenomenon either, and the effect appears only in the long term. Therefore, all developed nations run health surveys to gather data on subjective health complaints and reports of general feelings of health. Likewise, a reduction in xenophobia will only partly manifest in objective indicators such as racist attacks and interethnic marriage. Attitudinal data are needed to complete the picture.

Success in social policy depends typically on public support. Without public backing most programmes perish in the long run, even if planned goals are reached. Public opinion is not always fully expressed in the political process; hence, polls are needed to obtain additional information. Survey data are particularly needed for issues that are not on the political agenda and for groups that are poorly represented.

Selecting policy goals

Social policy makers also need information to enable them to decide on future directions. Political entrepreneurs must have an idea of what people want in order to mobilize the necessary support. They must also have a good overview of what people really need in order to select the most meaningful objectives. Such an overview would be incomplete without the use of subjective indicators to determine peoples' needs.

When deciding on new directions, time and again, policy makers come up against the problem that the political process does not always adequately reflect public preferences. Representatives sometimes fail to pick up latent concerns, and vested interests often keep appealing issues from the political agenda. Good political marketing, therefore, requires additional public opinion research – in particular, polls on worries, aspirations, and satisfactions. These indicators are subjective in both substance and measurement. This kind of research is common practice in all developed democracies.

Policy makers also operate in a more technocratic way and try to grasp what people really need. Here, the problem is that expressed wants do not always reflect true needs. A good example is the case of materialist aspirations in affluent society. The Western public wants ever more money and consumption, and this demand is served well by politicians. Yet, in spite of the stunning rise in the material level of living, people keep asking for more, while average happiness has remained about at the same level. According to Frank (1999), this is because our material needs are already satiated. In his view, the constant craving for more luxury draws on an underlying need for supremacy, which could be equally well met in less wasteful ways. Lane (2000), likewise, has observed a decline in happiness in modern market economies, which he attributes to the institutional neglect of social needs.

In this example, the gratification of needs in a population is measured by happiness, which is, at the very most, a subjective indicator. Elsewhere, I have argued that overall happiness is, indeed, the best available indicator of the degree to which true needs are met, especially if combined with the number of years lived (Veenhoven 2000).

Why objective indicators fall short

The need for subjective indicators must also be judged against the limitations of objective indicators. Objective indicators provide only a part of the required information and give generally a better view of details than on the whole. Hence, a categorical rejection of subjective indicators leaves the policy maker with an information deficit, which is inevitably filled by private observations and hearsay.

Limits to observation

We have already noted above that social policy is not only concerned with objective matters such as 'income', but also with subjective well-being. Hence, in a policy mix there is always a combination of objective and subjective substance. We have also seen that objective measurement falls short on a lot of issues, in attitudinal matters and in the assessment of objective substance. Remember that even the objective measurement of income is problematic. Objective measures also have limited validity and reliability. Joint use of objective and subjective measures is mostly helpful if one wants to get a complete picture, while rigid restriction to objective indicators considerably narrows the perspective.

Limits to aggregation

Though objective counts are often quite useful for assessing detail, they are typically less helpful for charting the whole. For example, when assessing the quality of housing, objective indicators can help a great deal when quantifying aspects such as space, light, and sanitation, but these aspects' scores cannot simply be added to get a meaningful overall estimate of dwelling quality. There have been many attempts to combine piecemeal objective observations into a comprehensive index, but all these attempts labour under the same problems of incomplete information and arbitrary weights (Veenhoven 1996a; 2000).

Aggregation is less problematic with subjective indicators, because we can simply ask people to give their overall judgement. Research has shown that people are quite able to strike a balance, both in life domains such as housing and for their life-as-whole. Subjective appraisals have sometimes been used to assign weights to items in objective sum scores, mostly avowed value priorities and correlations sometimes observed with regard to satisfaction. This gives poor results: rather than use subjective appraisals to construct a comprehensive index, it is better to start with a request for an overall judgement.

Use in developing countries

The use of subjective measures of well-being is limited largely to developed nations, where periodical social surveys are common practice. In developing nations, social indicators research is largely lodged in the objectivist tradition. A notable exception is the Social Weather Station in the Philippines (Mangahas 1998). Periodical survey programmes have recently started in Latin America (Latino barometro n.d.) and in Asia (Asia barometer n.d.).[6]

In addition to the above-mentioned arguments for using subjective indicators, there are four further reasons why this approach is particularly advisable for developing nations:

1 Information about subjective well-being is simply lacking in most developing nations. For all nations, we know the average income and the

number of physicians per thousand of population, but for most we do not know how happy the population is. This marks not only an information deficit for these nations, but also limits the comparative study of subjective well-being.

2 Representation of political interest falls short in many developing countries; survey data on aspirations, needs and satisfactions of citizens are all the more required.
3 Since the quality of data registration in developing countries is often poor, so too are the derived objective indicators. Hence, survey data are needed all the more to obtain an adequate picture of reality.
4 Surveys are relatively cheap in developing nations and the quality of survey data could be better controlled.

Taken together, this means it would be a valuable exercise to carry out periodical social surveys in developing countries. Such surveys could be linked up with the newly established European Social Survey to provide comparable data.

Conclusion

Social indicators cannot be classified as either 'objective' or 'subjective', since there are many gradations. Neither can one measure 'well-being' in the main, because this term is used to denote different matters that cannot be meaningfully summated. The most subjective measures of subjective well-being are self-reports of satisfaction, and the most comprehensive measure of this kind is satisfaction with life-as-a-whole, abbreviated to 'life satisfaction' or 'happiness'. Subjective enjoyment of life can be meaningfully combined with objective length of life and expressed as a number of 'happy life years'. Since this outcome depends on the fit between environmental conditions and personal capabilities, it is also the best indicator of overall well-being.

Information about perceptions and satisfactions of citizens is useful for making policy choices, while the degree to which citizens live long and happily is an important criterion for final policy effectiveness. Data on this matter should also be made available for developing nations by introducing periodical welfare surveys in such countries.

Notes

1 There are three main meanings for health: the maxi variant is all the good (WHO definition); the medium variant is life-ability; and the mini-variant is absence of physical defect.
2 One can also think of life-ability as involving some self-confidence. In that case, we deal with a substantially mixed concept which can be measured using indicators type 4, 5 and 6.

3 Sometimes called '*eu*functioning', in contrast to '*dis*functioning'.
4 'Doing interesting things' can also be seen as a quality in itself, especially when the person does not like it; in this interpretation this item should be placed in the meaning quadrant, because it represents some kind of perfection.
5 Also referred to as 'Happy Life Years' (HLY).
6 Bhutan is often mentioned as a developing country that does take subjective indicators seriously because of its claim to pursue 'Gross National Happiness'. Yet the indicators used to monitor progress to that end are largely of the objective kind.

References

Allardt, E. (1976) 'Dimensions of Welfare in a Comparative Scandinavian Study', *Acta Sociologica*, 19: 227–39.
Andrews, F. and S. Withey (1976) *Social Indicators of Well-being: American Perceptions of Quality of Life* (New York: Plenum Press).
Asia barometer (n.d.): http://avatoli.ioc.u-tpkyo.ac.jp/~asiabarometer/
Campbell, A., P. E. Converse and W. L. Rodgers (1975) *The Quality of American Life* (Ann Arbor: Institute for Social Research).
Chamberlain, K. and S. Zika (1988) 'Measuring Meaning of Life, Examination of Three Scales', *Journal of Personality and Individual Differences*, 9: 589–96.
Estes, R. (1984) *The Social Progress of Nations* (New York: Preager).
European Social Survey (ESS) (n.d.): http://ess.nsd.uib.no
Flax, M. J. (1972) *A Study in Comparative Urban Indicators* (Washington, DC: The Urban Institute).
Frank, R. H. (1999) *Luxury Fever. Why Money Fails to Satisfy in an Era of Excess* (New York: Free Press).
Gerson, E. M. (1976) 'On Quality of Life', *American Sociological Review*, 41: 793–806.
Glatzer, W. and W. Zapf (1984) *Lebensqualität in der Bundesrepublik* [Quality of Life in West Germany] (Frankfurt am Main: Campus) [English summary in *Social Indicators Research* (1987) 19: 1–171].
Hagerty, M. R., R. A. Cummins, A. L. Ferriss, K. Land, A. Michalos, M. Peterson, A. Sharpe, J. Sirgy and J. Vogel (2001) 'Quality of Life Indexes for National Policy: Review and Agenda for Research', *Social Indicators Research*, 55: 1–96.
Headey, B. and A. Wearing (1988) 'The Sense of Relative Superiority: Central to Well-being', *Social Indicators Research*, 20: 497–516.
Inglehart, R. (1990) *Culture Shift in Advanced Industrial Society* (Princeton: Princeton University Press).
Jahoda, M. (1958) *Current Concepts of Positive Mental Health* (New York: Basic Books).
Kanahan, D., E. Diener and N. Schwartz (eds) (1999) *Well-being, the Foundations of Hedonic Psychology* (New York: Russell Sage Foundation).
Katona, G. (1975) *Psychological Economics* (Amsterdam: Elsevier Scientific Publishers).
Lane, R. E. (2000) *The Loss of Happiness in Market Democracies* (New Haven: Yale University Press).
Latino barometro (n.d.): http://www.latinobarometro.org
Lynn, R. (1971) *Personality and National Character* (London: Pergamon Press).
Lynn, R. (1982) National Differences in Anxiety and Extraversion', *Progress in Experimental Personality Research*, 11: 213–58.
Mangahas, M. (1998) *Self-Sustained Quality of Life Monitoring: The Philippine Social Weather Reports*, Occasional Report (Social Weather Station: Philippines).
Naroll, R. (1984) *The Moral Order* (London: Sage).

Neugarten, B. L., R. J. Havighurst and S. S. Tobin (1961) 'The Measurement of Life Satisfaction', *Journal of Gerontology*, 16: 134–43.

OECD (1999) *Social Indicators: A Proposed Framework and Structure* (Paris: Organization for Economic Cooperation and Development).

Rogerson, R. (1997) *Quality of Life in Britain*, Quality of Life Research Group, Department of Geography, University of Strathclyde.

Schwarz, N. (1999) 'Reports of Subjective Well-Being: Judgmental Processes and Their Methodological Implications', in D. Kahneman, E. Diener and N. Schwarz (eds) *Well-Being: The Foundations of Hedonic Psychology* (New York: Russell Sage Foundation) 61–84.

Sen, A. (1993) 'Capability and Well-being', in M. Nussbaum and A. Sen (eds) *The Quality of Life* (Oxford: Clarendon Press for UNU-WIDER).

Slottje, D. J. (1991) 'Measuring the Quality of Life across Countries', *Review of Economics and Statistics*, 73: 684–93.

Smith, P. C., L. H. Kendall and C. L. Hulin (1969) *The Measurement of Satisfaction in Work and Retirement* (Chicago: Rand-McNally).

UNDP (1999) *Human Development Report 1999* (Oxford and New York: Oxford University Press for the United Nations Development Programme).

VanPraag, B. M. (1993) 'The Relativity of the Well-being Concept', in M. Nussbaum and A. Sen (eds) *The Quality of Life* (Oxford: Clarendon Press for UNU-WIDER) 362–85.

VanPraag, B. M., Th. Goedhart and A. Kapteyn (1980) 'The Poverty Line: A Pilot Survey in Europe', *Review of Economics and Statistics*, 63: 461–5.

Veenhoven, R. (1993) 'Happiness in Nations: Subjective Appreciation of Life in 56 Nations 1946–1992', RISBO, Erasmus University Rotterdam, Studies in Social and Cultural Transformation.

Veenhoven, R. (1996a) 'Developments in Satisfaction Research', *Social Indicators Research*, 36: 1–46.

Veenhoven, R. (1996b) 'Happy Life-expectancy. A Comprehensive Measure of Quality-of-Life in Nations', *Social Indicators Research*, 39: 1–58.

Veenhoven, R. (1997) 'Progrès dans la compréhension du bonheur', *Revue Québécoise de psychologie*, 18: 29–74. [English version available at: www2.eur.nl/fsw/research/veenhoven/Pub1990s/1997c-txte.pdf]

Veenhoven, R. (2000) 'The Four Qualities of Life', *Journal of Happiness Studies*, 1: 1–39.

Veenhoven, R. (2002) 'Why Social Policy needs Subjective Indicators', *Social Indicators Research*, 58: 33–45.

Veenhoven, R. (2004) 'Happiness as a Public Policy Aim: The Greatest Happiness Principle', in A. Linley and S. Joseph (eds), *Positive Psychology in Practice* (Chichester: Wiley) 658–78

Veenhoven, R. (2005a) 'Return of Inequality in Modern Society? Test by Dispersion of Life-satisfaction across Time and Nations', *Journal of Happiness Studies*, 6: 457–87.

Veenhoven, R. (2005b) 'Happiness in Hardship', in L. Bruni and P. Porta (eds) *Economics and Happiness* (Oxford: Oxford University Press) 243–66.

Veenhoven, R. and W. M. Kalmijn (2005) 'Inequality-Adjusted Happiness in Nations: Egalitarianism and Utilitarianism Married in a New Index of Societal Performance', *Journal of Happiness Studies*, 6: 421–55.

Vile, M. J. C. (1999) *Politics in the USA* (New York: Routledge).

Vogel, J. (2002) 'Strategies and Traditions in Swedish Social Reporting: A 30-year Experience', *Social Indicators Research*, 58: 1–3.

Warr, P., J. Cook and T. Wall (1979) 'Scales for the Measurement of Social Work Attitudes and Aspects of Psychological', *Journal of Occupational Psychology*, 52: 129–48.

WHOQOL Group (1998) 'Development of the World Health Organization WHOQOL–BREF Quality of Life Assessment', *Psychological Medicine*, 28: 551–8.

World Database of Happiness (n.d.) Continuous register of research on subjective appreciation of life, Version 2005, Erasmus University Rotterdam, http://worlddatabaseofhappiness.eur.nl

World Values Survey (n.d.) ICPRS file 6160, Ann Arbor, MI: World Values Survey.

WWF (2002) *Living Planet Report* (WWF: Gland, Switzerland).

10

Participatory Approaches and the Measurement of Human Well-being

Sarah White and Jethro Pettit

Introduction

'We are all democrats now,' wrote John Dunn ironically in his 1979 review of *Western Political Theory* (Dunn 1979). Twenty-five years on, the democratic ethic of people centred governance has acquired the status of a sacred totem that commands obeisance far beyond the arena of formal politics. Rites and symbolic acts of participation have accordingly been 'mainstreamed' across a remarkable range of institutions, from neighbourhood school boards to multilateral agencies. Though very different in their form and practice, the promise is similar. Incorporating participation will mean that processes of policy making, administration and research become more inclusive, more responsive, more equitable, and so represent more fully the interests of 'the people' they claim to serve.

This chapter considers one aspect of these dynamics, the use of participatory methods in international development research, and asks what contribution these can make to the measurement of well-being. We begin by charting the terrain, setting out very briefly some main dimensions of well-being and participation, and noting some connections between them. We then identify the two main issues that the chapter will consider: the contribution of participatory methods to the *definition* of well-being on the one hand, and its *measurement* on the other. Discussion of each of these issues concerns not only *technical*, but also *political* questions, regarding how participatory methods are placed within the broader context of institutions and policy processes. In the next section, we introduce some of the main techniques and principles of participatory research in international development. The main body of the chapter then considers how these have been used in practice to define and assess poverty and well-being. This draws on general lessons arising from the practice of participatory research at project level, and on the experience of two larger-scale policy research processes sponsored by the World Bank. These are the participatory poverty assessments (PPAs), undertaken to counter criticisms of the narrowly economic focus of the poverty assessments; and the *Voices of the Poor* study (Narayan *et al.* 2000), commissioned as a background for the *World Development Report* of 2000/01.[1] Since measurement of well-being has been most rigorously pursued through quality of life research,[2] we also consider the role that participatory approaches have played in this. We then reflect on Kanbur's (2002) discussion of the potential for complementarity between qualitative and quantitative methods in poverty appraisal, and the emerging experiments with 'participatory numbers', using participatory methods to generate quantitative data. Bringing this review of experience to a close, we consider some more general issues concerning the validity and limitations of participatory methods. In the final section, we assess the future trajectory of participatory approaches in well-being research, and reflect on some of the dilemmas regarding the use of participatory data in the policy making process.

Well-being and participatory research: some interconnections

The concepts of well-being and participation share an obvious similarity: they are both highly contested, internally diverse umbrella terms. This makes the issue of measurement a somewhat fraught one! They also share the quality of being 'hurrah' words: they are good things, engendering a warm glow and drawing people to them.[3] For participation, the reason for this lies in its association with the sacred value of the democratic ethic. In the case of well-being, it is clearly founded in the positive 'well' qualifier it contains. This can be something of a problem in the context of international development research where many people are experiencing serious deprivation. Early responses in Ethiopia to research on well-being thus included the query: if the study was limited to 'well-being', then who was going to be looking at everyone else? The *Voices of the Poor* study addressed this issue by exploring together concepts of both well-being and ill-being (Narayan *et al.* 2000).

Complicating the issue still further, the relationship between well-being and participation is not simply an external one of two entirely separate, independently defined entities. Rather, there exists already an internal relation between the two concepts. Inherent in the concept and practice of participatory research is the assumption that participation will enhance well-being, both as a good in itself, and as the means for the better representation of other interests. Similarly, people's capacity to participate has long been a critical variable in discussions of poverty (Townsend 1979), human need (Doyal and Gough 1991), human development (Sen 1999), and well-being (Nussbaum 2000). Indeed, the extent of participation and responsiveness to 'other' voices has featured as one of the criteria for judging the legitimacy of a paradigm of well-being. In terms of the philosophy of well-being, this is particularly evident in discussion of Martha Nussbaum's work. In empirical studies, it is perhaps most striking in the work of health policy and social indicators researchers on quality of life (for example, Cummins 1996; Michalos 1997; Veenhoven 2000; Hagerty *et al.* 2001). The formation of the World Health Organization's quality-of-life instrument, the WHOQOL, for example, involved the extensive use of focus groups reflecting different national contexts and sees its cross-cultural legitimacy as significantly founded in its participatory approach (Camfield and Skevington 2003).

Well-being is a complex notion with many different dimensions whose definition is disputed. The 'well' qualifier makes the concept irreducibly normative, concerned with values and assessment. Its focus on 'being' suggests attention to states; not only of body and material endowments, but also of mind and subjective perceptions. In order to understand these, however, it is necessary to explore the processes through which both 'subjective' states of mind and 'objective' endowments have arisen, and to which they in turn give rise. This introduces a third, social or process dimension that shows how subjective perceptions and objective welfare outcomes are constituted through social interaction and cultural meanings (McGregor and Kebede 2003). This chapter therefore considers the potential of participatory methods for exploring each of three levels of observation. The first is what (different) people have or do not have (material and human resources, social relationships); the second is what people do, or do not or cannot do with these resources, and why (social or cultural action); the third is how people judge, assess, and feel about these things: how they make or cannot make sense of what happens (meaning).[4]

As with well-being, participation also has many aspects and generates many controversies, both in terms of the range of practices that go under that name, and in the objectives they are hoped to achieve. In this chapter, we aim to focus primarily on the use of participatory *research* methods for assessing poverty and well-being, rather than the action related dimensions of appraisal, planning and social mobilization.[5] As will become clear, however, this is a somewhat difficult line to hold, since a practical orientation towards making a difference through action has been a primary and abiding characteristic of participatory research.

The diversity and multiple objectives that participation may serve are well illustrated within one of the most influential traditions of participatory poverty research, the participatory rural appraisal (PRA) approaches, which emerged in the late 1980s and 1990s.[6] On the one hand, PRA traces its ancestry to innovative methods developed and used by community organizers in rural areas across the world, as they sought to engage communities in reflecting on their situations in order to design strategies for change. On the other hand, it also derives from the techniques of 'rapid rural appraisal'

(RRA), developed in the late 1970s and 1980s by researchers working as consultants in international development, who had become frustrated with expensive and unwieldy household surveys, and sought quicker and more cost effective techniques. A further dimension, mixing democratic and efficiency motivations, concerned suspicions of the bias and ignorance of highly paid outside 'experts'. This coincided with recognition in the development industry more generally that the failure to consult local people or generate a sense of ownership amongst them had resulted in a plethora of high cost inappropriate technologies and ineffective programmes (Burkey 1993). Since the people living within a situation could plausibly be expected to have a better understanding of the many issues facing them than outside experts 'bussed in' for a few days or weeks, it made sense to elicit and employ this 'local knowledge'. Seeking such knowledge, in turn, required a different range of research techniques from those conventionally used in 'scientific' approaches. Last, but not least, was a political dimension. For community organizers working within a Freirean paradigm of conscientization,[7] participatory research was seen as a means to empower disadvantaged people through giving them tools of analysis and awareness. Advocates of PRA, similarly, saw these methods as a means to give more voice to the intended 'beneficiaries' of development programmes, and so greater opportunity to shape what is done in their name. This 'democratic' promise of participatory approaches is clearly of prime significance to their present incorporation within larger-scale processes of policy making such as participatory poverty assessments (PPAs) and poverty reduction strategy papers (PRSPs). Inevitably, of course, the political aspect also has a shadow side. As many critiques have pointed out, participatory methodologies can also be used to obscure differences within target communities, legitimize extractive and exploitative processes of information gathering, impose external agendas, and contain or co-opt potential popular resistance.

From this brief review, it is clear that there are two distinct but related contributions that a participatory approach can make to the understanding and measurement of well-being. In the first place, the key promise of participatory methodologies is that they are 'experience-near' in terms of their participant/respondents: they are able to reflect more closely the knowledge and world view of people themselves than more formal, abstract, or 'scientific' approaches. Along with other hermeneutic social science approaches, participatory methods have thus contributed to the much wider recognition of contextual, subjective and non-material dimensions of human experience, and of the complex dynamics and causalities behind poverty and well-being. Current understandings of well-being thus already, in part, reflect the influence of participatory research. This is evident, for example, in livelihoods analyses, which built substantially on RRA-style innovations in the analysis of agro-ecosystems and households' resource portfolios. At their best, these stress not only the diversity of livelihoods but also the importance of appreciating the dynamic interaction within and between different aspects of ecological, social and political systems. This process continues as the focus of development research expands from aspects of poverty and livelihoods to broader dimensions of ill-being and well-being, as was the case in both the PPAs and the *Voices of the Poor* study. Projecting this trend forward, participatory approaches therefore have clear potential to contribute to 'scoping' the concept and meaning of well-being, and ensuring, in particular, that people's own perceptions of well-being and the dimensions they comprise are properly understood. This is not as straightforward a process as it might at first appear. As we consider below, participatory approaches, just as other more conventional research, carry with them baggage of assumptions and methods that can act as a filter on genuinely alternative perspectives. They are also critically affected by the broader political and institutional contexts in which they are undertaken.

The second potential contribution of participatory methods concerns the measurement of well-being. The issue of measurement has been an area of controversy since the early days of RRA. As Andrea Cornwall describes it, two principles were adopted. These were ' "optimum ignorance" (find out as much as you need to know now) and "appropriate imprecision" (there is no need to know everything exactly)' (Cornwall 2000: para. 4.1). While perhaps raising fearsome spectres for convention bound quantitative economists, these could, of course, simply be seen as sensible guidelines for any data collection process that does not want to be burdened with such a weight of information that it is unmanageable to analyze. For well-being as for more conventional investigations of poverty, measurement issues concern both the *distribution* of well-being across a population and the *extent* of well-being enjoyed by a particular individual, household, or community. The much more inclusive character of well-being than poverty, and especially its less tangible dimensions, however, make such measurement a complicated issue. Assuming the threefold distinction into subjective, objective, and interactive or process dimensions of well-being suggested above, there are clearly questions to be asked as to *which aspects* of these are best explored by participatory methods as well as *how* these may be pursued. Reflecting on practice to date, as well as possible future directions, may yield rather surprising findings. Prima facie, for example, research into subjective perceptions might be thought to lend itself most easily to qualitative analysis. In fact, however, this is the area in which, to date, participatory methods have been used to produce the most rigorously quantitative data through the generation of numerical profiles reflecting people's self-assessed quality of life.

Finally, there may be a further aspect that should be present in poverty analyses but is often overlooked. This concerns the question of *how* people experience well-being – the analysis not of subjective components of well-being, but the subjective, socially and culturally constructed experience of well-being as a whole. Such questions may not easily lend themselves to incorporation within policy perspectives, but are nonetheless critical to the promise of participatory approaches genuinely to reflect people's own values and orientations. One may be able, for example, to get people to participate in generating numerical values to represent their assessments of the relative importance of different aspects of their quality of life. This does not, however, necessarily mean that this rather abstract exercise reflects the ways that people live their lives, or captures the underlying rhythms within which they take action and understand the meaning of their experience overall.

Participatory methods: what are they?

Participatory research methods involve a wide range of tools, techniques and processes, which are often applied in a customized mix and sequence that is iterative and complementary in order to 'triangulate' perspectives and to build progressively from one stage of inquiry to the next (cf. Pretty *et al.* 1995). Some of these techniques are common to other social science methods, such as small group discussions and in-depth, semi-structured interviews. Others are more visual and interactive, involving the creation of tangible maps, matrices and lists which can in turn be analyzed using visual methods of scoring, and ranking using tokens of some kind as counters. These visual and interactive techniques often involve the analysis of trends or seasonal cycles using timelines and calendars, or diagrams that can be used to explore the flow of causes, symptoms and impacts. The methods may be repeated with different individuals or sub-groups in order to draw out and then discuss differences in perspective within communities; for example, by age, gender, ethnicity, occupation, or social status. Table 10.1 gives a list of the principal tools and methods used in the World Bank sponsored participatory research projects drawn on in this chapter.

Table 10.1 Principal methods used in PPAs and the *Voices of the Poor* study

Participatory poverty assessments	***Voices of the Poor***
Focus groups	Focus groups
Preference ranking or scoring	Small group discussions
Wealth or well-being ranking	Well-being ranking
Charts indicating cyclical change	Listing
Trend analysis	Scoring
Causal flow diagrams	Cause-impact analysis
Participatory mapping	Trend analysis
Institutional diagramming	In-depth interviews with individuals or households
Drawings – pictorial representations	

Sources: Norton *et al.* (2001: 33); Narayan *et al.* (2000: 307–13).

The genesis of these methods lies mostly in small-scale programmes of non-governmental and community-based development organizations, and the action of researchers and social scientists working alongside them. 'Well-being ranking', for example, evolved from the earlier practice of 'wealth ranking,' which drew on work in social anthropology and was developed in PRA. 'Wealth ranking' involves sorting households – usually depicted on cards – into different categories and, in the process, generating a range of locally defined criteria for wealth. The concern here is with capturing significant differences in levels of economic prosperity, not to produce exact calculations of income. While criteria typically include income, therefore, they also go beyond this but, in most cases, are limited to ownership of or access to tangible assets or resources.[8]

The kinds of measures generated in this process are well illustrated in Table 10.2. This shows the classification of five levels of wealth produced in a village in South Africa. The levels of poverty in Table 10.2 were defined by local people for the purposes of identifying the poorest families to join a micro-credit programme. The criteria were generated during a ranking process by small 'reference groups' of villagers, while sorting the households into levels. Up to four reference groups sorted the same households to ensure consistency of results and to identify outliers. Although the criteria used to define the levels and to rank the households varied from one exercise, section or village to another, the levels of poverty and wealth turned out to be remarkably consistent and comparable from one area to the next, even in very large villages. The numerical data generated by this process proved to be highly accurate and commensurable in identifying the poorest families over populations numbering in the thousands (Simanowitz 2000). The results from participatory wealth ranking exercises in eight villages were used to produce a quantitative household economic status index in which participants' criteria were used to define the poverty lines (Hargreaves *et al.* 2004).

While it is tempting to focus on its distinctive methods and techniques, the essence of participatory research – and, as we review later, the focus of the most profound criticisms of it – lies not in these, but rather the commitment to certain principles that guide the conduct of the research. These include the primary principle that researchers should act as facilitators, guarding against their own biases and seeking to minimize any power differentials between themselves and the respondents, so as to enable local knowledge and perspectives to emerge. Reflecting this, second, the research design should be flexible, able to respond to changing contexts and emergent findings as these arise. This does not mean that a larger research design and guidelines cannot be in place, particularly if there is a need for comparability. But flexibility is encouraged in the way that methods are applied and sequenced in order to give maximum scope for local perceptions and analysis to emerge. A third principle is to use methods that are visual and interactive,

Table 10.2 Characteristics of different wealth groups identified in Sofaya, South Africa

Poorest	
• Single parent, unemployed, or two parents both unemployed • Many children • Being unmarried and having no family to assist • Dependent on temporary jobs • No means of provision except by begging • Widows with many children	• Insufficient and poor quality food; sometimes have to beg food • No proper place to sleep; poor quality housing • Orphans with no parents • Inability to educate children • No clothes; almost never buy • No assets
Poor	
• Temporary jobs (e.g., farm labourers) • Have some food, but struggle • Working widows and pensioners with many children • Parents dependent on working children who also have their own families in the same house hold sharing resources • Working on agriculture scheme	• Many children • No pension/pensioners with many children • Unmarried • Have some house (though not good); some made of mud bricks and show cracks • Can provide something from their temporary job
Quite poor	
• Earns enough to cope daily – mostly temporary work/self-employed • Those with smaller number of children to look after • Pensioners with fewer children • Widows with pensions from late husbands	• Have sleeping place • Unmarried • Payouts from old jobs • Children attend school irregularly • Able to buy enough food
OK	
• Pensioners with only themselves to look after* • Few children • Good supply of food • Families where at least one parent has a permanent job	• Children attend school regularly • Good house • More than enough food
Wealthy	
• Professionals and business owners • Good money to supply their family adequately • Children attend school properly • Migrant labourers	• Eating bread with margarine • Children nicely clothed • Children attending tertiary education • Company pensions

Table 10.2 (Continued)

• Electricity in the house • Owning a television • Smaller families • Owning a car/gun	• Food in abundance • Excellent housing

Note: * That a pensioner who supports few or no people is considered moderately well off should give information about absolute levels of poverty and allow comparison with national figures.
Source: Simanowitz (2000)

to allow participants of all backgrounds and levels of education to engage in both generating and analyzing data. Many PRA methods were developed specifically for use with people with mixed or low levels of literacy. This relates to a fourth principle, which is that participants should be involved in the process of analysis, not just in the collection of data. This does not necessarily preclude further analysis by external researchers or, indeed, the use of participatory methods at some stages and more conventional methods at others.

These inclusive methods of analysis, often using forms of group dialogue and deliberation, are an important aspect of the power of these approaches in identifying people's own perspectives, knowledge, values, categories, definitions and priorities. In principle, at least, the process is as important as the outcome. The perspectives that emerge should not simply reflect aggregations of individual or household responses, but rather the shared understandings or differences among the people and groups involved that have been identified through dialogue and debate. The researchers' skill in facilitating the interaction involved in this process is critical. Such an approach clearly makes it difficult to sustain the conventional separation between 'data' such as measures and indicators, and the 'methods' used to generate them. While this relationship is particularly evident in the case of participatory research, critical reflection in the sociology of science suggests that this is a feature of research more widely. The separation of theory, methods and data is, in fact, far harder to sustain than has typically been assumed, even within the most conventional of natural science contexts (for example, Knorr-Cetina and Mulkay 1993).

Participatory methods and defining well-being

As noted above, perhaps the most obvious contribution of participatory research to the understanding of well-being is in its capacity to draw out culture, location and social group specific understandings of the dimensions of well-being. A review of experiences with PRA methodologies in eight countries thus notes the value of these methods in identifying 'improved quality of life according to local standards' (Cornwall and Pratt 2002, 2003) and in 'capturing local perspectives' (Cornwall *et al.* 2001: 6). In Mexico, for example, locally defined indicators for 'improved quality of life' ranged from jobs, income, health and housing to gender relations, self-esteem and reaffirmation of cultural identities (Garcia and Way 2003: 30). Karen Brock's (1999) review of the micro-level participatory research being done by NGOs and research institutes during the 1990s documents in more detail the diverse and context specific views of poor people, finding that these could indeed be identified and measured, even if not easily aggregated.[9] Drawing on qualitative data from 58 sources in 12 countries, she notes the frequency with which different indicators were mentioned. Concerning the objective endowments of material resources and social relationships, certain broad indicators emerged time and again, with marked differences for men and women, and for people living in rural and urban areas:

> Respondents in rural areas placed a strong emphasis on food security in their definitions of poverty, ill-being and vulnerability, as well as lack of work, money and assets. They also emphasized the vulnerability of particular groups within the community: the old, the disabled, female-headed households and those living alone, isolated from social networks. The definitions of those in an urban setting place far more emphasis on the immediate living environment: crowded and unsanitary housing, lack of access to water, dirty and dangerous streets and violence both within and outside the household (Brock 1999: 9).

Similar patterns are evident in the World Bank sponsored PPAs (Brock and McGee 2002: 3). Echoing earlier livelihoods analyses, these show the importance of time and seasonality, differences by gender, the value of safety nets to tide over bad times and the value to the poor of multiple sources of food and income (IDS 1996: 3, summarized in McGee and Norton 2000: 28).

The importance of social processes and interaction to people's experience of well-being also emerges from these studies. These include the ways in which social factors 'shape people's experiences of poverty and determine their priorities', poor people's own explanations of causes, and the 'dynamics of deprivation at levels other than the household' (Robb 1999: 22–4, cited in McGee and Norton 2000: 28–32). Brock's study also sheds light on connections between social processes and interactions, and people's subjective experiences, particularly as these concern issues of power and powerlessness.

> The disaggregated findings clearly demonstrate that different kinds of poor people experience their lives in very different ways, and that relationships of power are often a crucial component in understanding the dynamics of poverty and ill-being (Brock 1999: 1).

The mix of the three dimensions of 'objective' endowments, social interaction and subjective experience is also reflected in the *Voices of the Poor* project, with the participants themselves drawing attention to the linkages and dynamics of causality between them. The study thus reports that powerlessness has many inter-related dimensions. Some of these relate to livelihoods, food, income and assets, but others are grounded in experiences of social isolation and exclusion, unequal gender relations, physical isolation and vulnerability, and abusive behaviour by the more powerful. They also include the political dimensions of being excluded from or disempowered by institutions, or of being only weakly organized as poor people (Narayan *et al.* 2000: 248–50).

Many of these findings were obtained through the aggregation of focus group discussions, a key methodology used in both the PPAs and the *Voices of the Poor* research. In general, however, there seems to be a trade-off between the scale of research methods and their explanatory power to reveal these more subtle connections. Larger-scale PPAs may miss the 'intangible' dynamics and causes of poverty that ought to be addressed by policy, particularly relations of power, gender and social exclusion. Even when these do surface, evidence of a more complex, dynamic social picture appears to be more problematic for policy makers to respond to (McGee and Norton 2000: 33). Thus, while the *Voices of the Poor* project identified, as one of its more important conclusions, an 'inter-connected web' of the 'dimensions of powerlessness and ill-being' (Narayan *et al.* 2000: 249), this finding hardly appeared in the resulting *World Development Report 2000–01* (Chambers 2002: 302). As will be considered further in the concluding section, there are important 'technical' issues here about the relationship between the local and the universal, and the need for recognition of proper distinctions between these, which confound any default assumption that universal models are simply a reflection of the local, 'writ large'. There are also political issues that concern sensitivity not only to the micro-politics of particular 'community' contexts, but also to the institutional structures, cultures and interests of the development agencies that make use of any data gathered in participatory ways.

Reflecting on such observations has led some to advocate a return to the activist inheritance of PRA, albeit in a new form. This involves a shift away from seeing participatory methods primarily as a source of data and inputs for policy, and towards seeing them as vehicles of more direct policy influencing, engagement and advocacy. Norton *et al.* (2001: 11) thus suggest there may be 'second generation' PPAs, the chief contribution of which is to act as catalysts for enhancing participation and voice in policy making. Such a shift does not deny the unique informative role of participatory methods, but reflects caution regarding the high expectations and misunderstandings about the use of PPAs for more 'objective' monitoring of poverty and well-being:

> PPAs will not produce a precise pseudo-scientific measure of a single indicator ... [and] thereby give a comforting sense that things are definitively getting better or worse ... PPAs can contribute to monitoring trends in poverty in the following ways: by eliciting people's perceptions of trends in well-being and factors that effect it ... by highlighting significant indicators of well-being which can then be followed by more orthodox survey methods ... [and] by investigating trends in areas which are difficult to monitor through orthodox quantitative methods (Norton *et al.* 2001: 14).

Participatory methods and measuring well-being

While participatory research is typically associated with qualitative methods, it can, and often does, produce quantitative data. There is no simple equivalence between a low tech approach – such as the use of visual methods, with local materials to map out a matrix, rather than a printed questionnaire – and qualitative data. In fact, as is discussed further below, the reverse may be the case, since many hermeneutic, qualitative approaches depend heavily on language and sensitivity not only to *what* is said but the *ways* in which it is said. In practice, both qualitative and quantitative data may be produced at once. A group process, for example, of identifying local problems through a matrix, and then assigning weightings to them, may produce a quantitative outcome in terms of numerical scores reflecting the significance of different problems to people's welfare. But it may at the same time produce a qualitative output through the discussion that it stimulates, which reveals the processes underlying such problems, and the meanings they have in people's lives.

Regarding the three dimensions of well-being identified above, participatory methods can and have been used to measure both 'objective' endowments and 'subjective' perceptions. It is more difficult to see what measurement and issues of numerical quantification have to offer in understanding the dimension of social processes and interaction. This is true not only of participatory methods, but also of more conventional survey based approaches.

The strength of a participatory approach is its capacity to reflect local categories of value and assessment. This concerns objective endowments, not only subjective perceptions. The distribution of housing of varying quality, for example, could be assessed by an external researcher. Alternatively, participatory methods could be used to identify what local people regard as the key factors in house quality, and the different social meanings these express. The advantage of the first, more 'objective' approach, is easy comparability across different sites. The advantage of the second is that it works with local categories, which may give a simpler method of classification, and more accurately reflect the particular factors that give housing its social significance as an indicator of well-being. Despite the attraction of 'hard' categories held constant across different contexts, if the research focus is on 'well-being effects', rather than the character of housing per se, it is arguable that, in fact, the proper factor for comparative analysis are these 'socialized categories', which a participatory approach is better equipped to deliver. Probably the best approach lies in a combination. Initial qualitative and participatory research can identify certain critical factors in local understandings of well-being. Building these into the structure of a household survey enables the questionnaire both to reflect the specific social realities of the communities being researched, and to generate internationally comparable data. This may, in turn, lay the basis for further, more detailed qualitative and quantitative studies, to explore specific aspects of the well-being matrix in greater depth.

Well-being ranking which, as mentioned above, offers an expanded version of the earlier wealth ranking methodology, uses a participatory process to generate and rank criteria that make up 'the good life', and assess how well-being is seen to be distributed within the group (Norton *et al.* 2001).[10] The key issue in terms of measurement then becomes whether the data produced are valid only within that particular context, or whether they can in some way be aggregated with data produced through similar exercises undertaken in different locations. As Laderchi (2001: 11) notes, since wealth and well-being rankings typically arrive at some form of ordinal information, their numerical nature is relatively undisputed. Wealth rankings have been found to result in similar patterns as economic surveys (Scoones *et al.* 1995, in ibid.) and even to produce greater accuracy than formal surveys, particularly in identifying very poor people for programme benefits (for example, Simanowitz 2000; Barahona and Levy 2003). The degrees of symmetry may also differ with the profile of respondents, with data from women differing most significantly from the survey data, suggesting the importance of gender as a key variable in both knowledge (for example, of differing income sources) and values (Norton *et al.* 2001). This is consistent with the findings of the *Voices of the Poor* research (Brock 1999) and with detailed micro studies of household budgeting and markets in other contexts (see, for example, Johnson 2004).

Some studies, however, have raised questions regarding the reliability of quantitative data gathered through PRA compared with that gained through surveys or key informant interviews (for example, Davies *et al.* 1999, in Laderchi 2001). While direct comparisons between different pieces of research are often difficult to draw, such asymmetries in findings between PRA and other forms of data collection may lead to better understanding of the conditions in which both are produced, and thus more precise understanding of what is being measured. Laderchi (2001) gives an example of this, as she reports McGee's (2000) discussion of discrepancies between the Ugandan PPA, in which poor people recorded a deterioration in well-being, and the household survey (UNHS), which showed rising consumption per capita over four subsequent years. In part, this reflected the broader focus of the PPA, differences in the time spans considered, and the distinction between the national span of the household survey versus the selection of particular 'representative' districts in the PPA. But it also pointed to the importance in poor people's perceptions of rising expectations and increased market dependence, and the significance of the PPA's disaggregation by region and gender. In general, the discrepancies emerging from the Uganda PPA suggest that a more nuanced and differentiated set of insights may be achieved with participatory approaches.

As mentioned above, the issue of measurement has been addressed most robustly in the area of quality-of-life research, which seeks to assign a numerical value to people's subjective perceptions, and so enable comparison across contexts. The origins of this research lie, on the one hand, with the social indicators movement and, on the other, in the area of medicine and health, where the information has been sought as a means of testing the comparative utility of different drugs or treatments. While all of the quality-of-life approaches involve some elements of participation, they differ considerably in the form and level at which this occurs. The WHOQOL project of the World Health Organization (WHO) represents one pole, with a highly structured, relatively bureaucratic approach, backed up by extensive psychometric testing. Focus groups made up of people with a range of professional experience, scientific knowledge and cultural background participated in defining 25 key 'facets' of the six 'domains' (physical, psychological, level of independence, social relationships, environment, and spirituality) identified by the WHO. The measures for overall quality of life and general health perceptions were developed simultaneously in 15 centres, and the core instrument was then translated into different cultural and linguistic contexts through a rigorous iterative process (Camfield and Skevington 2003). The result is a formidable instrument of 200 questions in the full version or 52 in the summary version (WHOQOL–BREF), which respondents are encouraged to answer using a five-point scale.[11] This is now being used in more than 50 countries. Some hold that scores from the different domains should be recorded independently, while others advocate amalgamating them all into a single indicator, implying either an equivalence of importance across the different domains or a weighting between them. Even if the domains are considered separately, however, the data are rendered comparable across context, and amenable to complex statistical analysis.

An alternative example, from near the opposite pole of maximum flexibility and participation at the level of the individual respondent, is the person generated index or PGI (Ruta *et al.* 1994).[12] In this case, the individual respondents themselves specify the areas (or domains) of life that are important to them, and then evaluate their performance with respect to these. Such individualized measures are becoming increasingly influential within medicine because they have high 'face' and 'content' validity and directly address the changes that are important to patients. From the perspective of well-being research, the attraction of this more individualized approach lies in the way it is designed both to identify the value system of individual respondents and to use this system in working with them to gauge their quality of life. While it clearly has much to offer in terms of sensitivity to local culture, conditions, and the social identities of participants, it also gives scope for comparative analysis. One aspect of this would concern the frequency with which different domains are identified, and the range of scores that they attract. The PGI can also be used to yield a single indicator of overall subjective quality of life, defined as 'the extent to which our hopes and ambitions are matched by experience' (Calman 1984). In order to be meaningful, however, it is likely that this figure showing the gap between what people have and what they desire would need to be matched by another, externally defined measure (Camfield, personal communication). In terms of the measurement of well-being, there is clearly scope to broaden out such an instrument from its particular focus on health, and this is already being developed (Ruta 1998). It could also potentially be used in pre-appraisal or evaluation of development programmes, by identifying the critical areas of people's lives where intervention is required, or showing the perceived impact of an intervention according to a range of locally or personally defined criteria. In an exploratory study considering the scope for developing from these approaches a broader profile for 'development related quality of life', the participants involved in piloting the PGI in Ethiopia 'visibly enjoyed' allocating coins to indicate their priorities and were 'amused and pleased' by the outcome (Bevan *et al.* 2003).

The logic of this discussion of participatory measurement is the need to move beyond a negatively cathected qualitative/quantitative or, indeed, 'participatory/objective' divide, and recognize the ways in which different approaches may complement or enable one another sequentially. This view is put forward strongly by Kanbur (2002)[13] reporting on a workshop concerned with methodologies for poverty research. By developing a more nuanced typology of 'qual-quant', and by avoiding the common tendencies to conflate 'methods' with 'data' and 'quantitative' with 'numerical' and so on, participants in this 'q-squared' workshop created a five dimensional spectrum for locating data and methods within the two traditions, shown in Table 10.3.

This typology, and the analyses and discussion that produced it, illuminate three key points about the contribution of participatory methods in measuring well-being. First, by separating data from methods (Booth *et al.* 1998, in Kanbur 2002: 6), we recognize that both traditions can and do produce both kinds of *data*, which Kanbur more helpfully describes as 'numerical' and 'non-numerical'. What differentiates qualitative *methods* is their 'attempt to capture a social phenomenon within its social, economic and cultural context' while quantitative methods seek data 'untainted by

Table 10.3 Characteristics of qualitative and quantitative poverty appraisal

1	Type of information on population	Non-numerical to numerical
2	Type of population coverage	Specific to general
3	Type of population involvement	Active to passive
4	Type of inference methodology	Inductive to deductive
5	Type of disciplinary framework	Broad social sciences to neoclassical economics

Source: Kanbur (2002: 1).

the context in which it is described' (ibid., in Kanbur 2002: 6). This distinction, with some modification, is represented by the spectrum of 'population coverage', ranging from 'specific' to 'general'. Second, there is the question of who is involved in research *design* and in the *collection* of data, captured in the spectrum of 'population involvement' ranging from 'active' (subject-driven) to 'passive' (researcher-driven). Third, there is the process of *analysis* or 'inference methodology', which may be characterized as ranging from 'inductive' to 'deductive'. The latter is positivist and logical, seeking an unbiased process that aims to capture a single objective reality. The former is 'interpretive and constructivist', accepting the possibility of multiple realities and seeking 'to involve many stakeholders and to obtain multiple perspectives on the subject of the research and the meaning of the concepts' (Christiansen 2002: 115).

The Q-squared dialogue recognizes the potential for going much further in using participatory methods to generate and process numerical data. Reflecting this, there is a wealth of methodological experimentation occurring in this realm of 'participation and numbers' (Chambers 2003).[14] In some cases, these approaches involve local 'ownership' and participatory analysis of the data, while in others the data are aggregated and processed by outsiders in the same way conventionally generated quantitative data are treated, including the use of standard statistical methods. Barahona and Levy (2003) give a good example of this from Malawi, and a thorough consideration of some of the methodological issues it raises. There are also new innovations emerging in larger-scale, participatory monitoring of aspects of poverty and ill-being. One is the use of visual diaries by people in more than 2000 villages in South India to monitor their experiences of discrimination and abuse.[15] Another is a 'participatory poverty index' created for use in poverty alleviation planning in rural China. This index has recently been adopted by the Chinese government for use in nearly 600 of the country's poorest counties as an alternative to the national poverty line (Weldon 2002).[16] Table 10.4 shows the eight 'village-friendly poverty indicators' that were found to have a certain universality.

Many of the trade-offs in terms of process and quality in such larger-scale and aggregated approaches have already been discussed. There remains,

Table 10.4 Indicators used in participatory poverty index, China

Livelihood poverty	Cash flow through the household Food insecurity Poverty of personal environment, especially shelter
Infrastructure poverty	Potable water Isolation/access/all-weather road Energy poverty (e.g. no reliable electricity)
Human resource poverty	Women's health (e.g. unable to work) Education (drop-outs as indicator)

Source: Weldon (2002).

however, further potential for mixing participatory and conventional approaches, and especially for the added value and insight that participatory methods can bring to more complex and context specific issues (Hargreaves *et al.* 2004). A synthesis of experiences with 'participatory numbers,' including a recommended 'code of good practice', is now being developed (Holland and Abeyesekera, forthcoming).

The validity and limitations of participatory methods

The quality and ethics of practice have been major themes of self-critical reflection among participatory researchers, especially as these methods have been promoted and scaled-up (cf. Cooke and Kothari 2001, Cornwall and Pratt 2002). As noted above, the key issue in participatory research is not so much the techniques used as the way in which the research is conducted and the relationships established between researchers and research participants. Questions of ethics and quality thus bear directly on the validity of the findings. The Pathways project, a major review of PRA experience in eight countries, thus identified the quality of practice as a key issue, due in part to the rapid mainstreaming of PRA methods and the sheer volume of people claiming 'expertise' in using the methods.[17] Unfortunately, as Laderchi (2001) points out, while the quality of the research practice is clearly critical to the validity of the output, it is very difficult to assess this quality post hoc. In some ways, the active involvement of research subjects makes ethical issues a particular concern in participatory, more than other forms of research. It would, however, be a mistake to overemphasize the specificity of participatory research in this regard. It may be, in fact, that participatory researchers have much to offer others in more conventional research traditions in the strength of their self-critical reflection on practice, as the increasing interest in ethics across the research community suggests. The 'social life' of any research project – its principles, conduct and relationships established with respondents – is, in fact, central not only to its morality, but also to the quality of information it can yield.

An important area of criticism – discussed extensively amongst PRA practitioners – is the danger that participatory research hides diversity, and can present a falsely homogenous view of 'the people' whose views it represents. Dissenters may feel too shy or fearful to speak up in an open meeting, and even allowing for private meetings with individuals can leave them too exposed. As with other research methods, PRA necessarily involves some labelling – into women, men, young, old, rich, poor, household or village – which can mask internal distinctions within groups. In practice, the scope of participation may be very narrow. Research participants are often assumed to 'represent' others from a similar social group, without any broader involvement of members of that group in their selection, or processes for canvassing their opinions or providing feedback amongst them. Specific individuals can therefore gain unwarranted voice, while other perspectives within the group they supposedly speak for are silenced or distorted. The key populist notion of 'community' – another 'hurrah' word conceptually linked to both well-being and participation – offers a particular temptation in this regard:

> This mythical notion of community cohesion continues to permeate much participatory work, hiding a bias that favours the opinions and priorities of those with more power and the ability to voice themselves publicly . . . the language and practice of 'participation' often obscures women's worlds, needs and contributions to development . . . (Gujit and Shah 1998: 1)

While some labelling and generalization are endemic both to social science and development policy (see Wood 1985), there is a particular issue here for participatory research. As noted above, an important line in the ancestry of PRA methods lies in their use for raising awareness, community mobilization and collective action. In this context, the dialogic approach noted above is critical to the *forging* of community, the creation of a common interest, a shared version of reality, which can be put to work in the service of a collective project. Differences between individuals within such a community do not thereby cease to exist, but they are set aside *for the present* in the pursuit of a common, shared goal. The facilitators – or 'facipulators', as some have perhaps more honestly termed themselves (White and Tiongco 1997) – are therefore not simply allowing an existing consensus to emerge, but are actively involved in *creating* that community, and the shared interpretation of reality that animates it. Community is indeed a myth, in a positive sense, a myth that motivates and energizes, a myth to live by. It is when this shared consensus is divorced from a shared project for action, or when important intra-community differences are so obscured by 'consensus' that some groups are in fact further marginalized by the project, that problems arise. Then the representation of community becomes something flat, a unity borne not of a shared vision of where people wish to go, but a false representation of identity in where people are coming from.[18] The abstraction of participatory research from people's own analysis and action, and its incorporation as data for external policymakers, may therefore not only carry the moral hazard that it becomes extractive and even exploitative (Laderchi 2001). It may also produce poor quality information, representing a false consensus and apparent identity of interest where none in fact exists.

The different ways in which participatory researchers use 'triangulation' – multiple methods or sources to explore the same issue from different angles – offers another instance of this tension between an emphasis on unity and diversity. For those concerned with the measurement potential of participatory research in particular, triangulation is used to validate, to check a variety of sources so as to establish the reliability of a particular item of data. Others, however, use it with 'the intention of highlighting different viewpoints' and to ensure that these 'are not buried under singular versions' (Cornwall *et al.* 2001: 32). This reflects a broader tension between those who use PRA methods with positivist aims, seeking unbiased outcomes, and those for whom 'producing knowledge is always an inter-subjective process' (ibid.).

The related issues of 'facipulation' and the inter-subjective production of knowledge raise questions about the critical claims of participatory approaches that they can represent reality simply as people themselves see it. As Laderchi (2001) comments, where a report must be written, and particularly where the research forms part of a policy process, there must always be issues regarding the extent to which analysis arises simply from the respondents themselves unsullied by any contact with researcher concerns. As noted above, the more participatory approaches are 'scaled up', and the more they are 'mainstreamed' and aligned with unreconstructed, dominant development institutions, the further they are likely to get from any straightforward representation of poor people's realities. But even when research remains small-scale and context specific, the choice and phrasing of questions inevitably reflect the values and orientation of the researchers, as does the selection, presentation, and interpretation of findings. This is the case, of course, for any research. It is perhaps ironic, however, that the myth of 'hands-free' research, which derives ultimately from a 'hard-science' positivist empiricism, should be so central to the legitimacy of participatory approaches, which see themselves in many ways as opposed to such a paradigm. In other contexts, it is now accepted as axiomatic that researchers are always actors, crafting a representation of others' reality. This is so, for example, in social anthropology where its own version of 'hands-free' research – the participant observer who simply recorded without influencing what he (sic) saw – was a constituent myth in the emergence of the discipline (see, for example, Geertz 1988). The persistent credibility of the promise of PRA to deliver 'the people's' views perhaps owes more to the politics of development than it does to its connections with the wider intellectual community.

This leads into a final concern with the potential of participatory methods, at least as narrowly defined, to generate genuinely new and surprising information about the frames through which people see the world. These are what mark the limits of 'what is possible', the values that lie so deep they are 'forgotten', the unconscious sense of where the limits lie (Bourdieu 1977; Mitchell 1990). What is at stake here is not only the words used and references made, but also the 'tacit understandings' (Giddens 1977: 169) that constitute the 'common-sense' that shapes people's life-worlds. These are made up of assumptions and ways of seeing that people have so profoundly internalized that they cannot be asked about directly, but are grasped intuitively, as they emerge 'crab-wise' through the stories that are told (White 1992: 8). The 'well-being ranking' noted above, for example, asks for local perceptions of 'the good life,' and may clearly generate unexpected information in terms of the dimensions people identify and the ways in which they prioritize them. However, it may be that the formulation of 'the good life' does not adequately capture the deepest values of what people consider well-being. It may be, for example, that there is a critically moral dimension to this, better captured by the notion of 'living a good life' which lies outside the frame that the 'well-being ranking' unconsciously imposes. An example of what we mean is offered by Veena Das (2000: 224) in a footnote to her discussion of a woman's responses over her lifetime to the disasters that the partition of India and Pakistan wrought in her family:

> I must emphasize that the moral stakes for Asha can only be understood if we can enter a lifeworld in which she felt that her eternity was in jeopardy.

There is a danger that all forms of research, especially when undertaken cross-culturally, will be tone deaf to such subtle harmonies. For researchers of well-being, however, this may mean missing the underlying melody, which makes sense of the themes and variations sung through the more tangible data. This is, of course, not primarily an issue about methods and techniques but, as mentioned earlier, the conduct and principles of research. However, the danger of misrepresentation is particularly acute in the case of participatory methodologies. When their findings reconfirm rather than challenge the dominant hegemonies, it seems a more grievous failure than when other research approaches do the same, simply because they often make such strong moral claims about being able genuinely to represent 'other' voices.

Conclusion: trajectories and challenges

As this chapter makes clear, there is considerable scope for participatory methods to extend understanding of how people experience well-being, addressing all of the three dimensions identified above: objective endowments, subjective perceptions, and interactive processes. They also have a significant potential, particularly in combination with other approaches, to contribute to its measurement. Larger-scale studies may aggregate findings to generate potential indicators of well-being that can be used with larger populations of a similar character. PRA is also increasingly being combined with conventional survey and statistical methods: micro-level and qualitative participatory research methods can be used to identify appropriate criteria and questions, and to design better surveys which are then implemented in a conventional manner. There is growing interest in the potential of participatory methods to generate numerical data. Recent innovations in combining methods that are qualitative and quantitative, numerical and non-numerical, participatory and conventional, are likely to lead to greater use of participatory methods in not only conceptualizing well-being, but also in monitoring and measuring it on a larger scale. While attention needs to be paid, as ever, to methodological concerns with quality and epistemological concerns with the hybridization of research paradigms, this train has already left the station!

Despite the high profile given to participatory research, however, there remain significant institutional barriers to putting the findings to good use. Brock (1999: 4) notes the huge amount of data being collected continually by NGOs and research institutes, but finds that 'such information is usually marginalized in planning top-down poverty alleviation strategies'. Despite the progress that has been made in integrating qualitative and quantitative poverty data, she found that 'this does not often include making the full use of the micro-level qualitative data which already exists', due in part perhaps to 'the absence of relationships between micro and macro institutions in the policy process' (ibid.). This information gap from micro-level participatory research findings persists in a context (or perhaps even as a result) of widespread efforts to scale up participatory poverty assessment in national policy processes. Implicit in the commitment to participatory methods is the need not only to link indicators and techniques, but also to bridge gaps between diverse actors at different levels, often with quite distinct knowledge and interests (Brock and McGee 2002). The generation and integration of appropriate data are not enough: there is also a need to strengthen the engagement and relationships among key actors within processes of research, policy and practice. This means that 'the people' should not be the only participants in the research process. Rather, participatory research ought to involve key officials as stakeholders within the design and process, and so help them own the findings, and influence knowledge and action at the levels of policy formulation and programme implementation, rather than simply relying on the research report to achieve results. One risk in 'extracting' participatory tools for well-being measurement is that this action-research dimension may easily be lost, as the goal shifts to finding useful indicators and away from including key stakeholders in the process of finding relevant indicators and measuring them. Officials and middle managers are often those who could best benefit from an enhanced understanding of poverty and well-being, and from more experiential immersion and knowledge of poor people's realities. There are many innovative examples of this approach to participatory poverty research (see, for example, Brock and McGee 2002, and Jupp 2002).

While there is, no doubt, scope for working with institutional actors in this way, it is important not to forget the politics and dangers of cooption that have beset participation from its earliest adoption within development agency discourse (Selznick 1949/53). As mentioned above, many of the scaled-up and mainstreamed practices of participatory research have not been particularly effective at (or even interested in) measuring or analyzing things such as exclusion or power (Gujit and Shah 1998: 3). Rather, there has been a tendency to overstress technical issues and under recognize political dimensions of poverty and well-being. Even where the more complex dynamics of power, exclusion and relationships have emerged within the PPAs and *Voices of the Poor* research sponsored by the World Bank itself, there has often been resistance to the recognition of these elements within the relevant policy arenas. Laderchi (2001:5) thus advises that the view that PRA is widely accepted 'as a "serious" source of hard evidence on poverty' should not be too easily adopted. Rather, she cautions:

> The alternative, i.e. the widespread adoption of PRA as an expensive window dressing exercise, cannot be entirely ruled out.

Even where this degree of pessimism does not seem justified, three major conditions need to be met if participatory methods are to be used effectively in enabling genuinely alternative understandings of well-being to emerge and assessing the extent to which people are able to live good lives. First, while the question of measurement lends itself to debates regarding technical validity, it is important to locate these within discussion of more substantive issues. These concern, on the one hand, the *meaning and interpretation* of numerical data when removed from the contexts in which they are generated and, on the other hand, broader questions regarding the *purposes* of measurement: what kinds of data are required for what and by whom.

Second, and following on from this, there needs to be far greater sophistication in appreciating the relations between local and universal models of reality, and what characteristics are proper to each. There may indeed be some generic differences between the worldviews of 'policy makers' and 'the poor', especially in the realm of the complexity, and multi- and interdimensionality of the problems that poor people face; and it is without doubt important that these be recognized. However, it is not simply the case that micro-studies can be 'scaled up' to provide macro-level data, that universal models of reality are simply local models 'writ large', or that data remain 'the same' when they are abstracted from context. These are not simple issues, but they are critical to address if there is a genuine commitment to render the lives of research subjects as more than 'cases' of poverty or deprivation (Wood 1985) and to pursue interventions that are appropriate to the real contexts in which people live their lives.

Finally, the close associations between 'participation' and 'well-being', noted above, mean that it is rather easy for 'well-being' simply to be adopted as a virtual antonym for poverty or synonym for development, albeit in wide-angle lens.[19] This danger is very evident in the slippage between 'wealth ranking' and 'well-being ranking', where the second can easily be simply a more inclusive – or invasive – version of the first. While 'well-being' as presented, for example, in the *Voices of the Poor* study, undoubtedly wears a more human face than economic growth models of development, there is nonetheless a worrying familiarity about the shape of many 'new' findings and their resonance with 'old' development rhetoric and priorities. This familiarity intensifies the closer in and higher up one gets in the development policy nexus, with the clear danger that 'well-being' may simply offer a new euphemism for old agendas. There is no doubt, of course, that 'development', as with 'well-being,' is a very broad, contested, normative concept, for which many competing definitions are offered. The days of a simple faith in economic growth as the means of bringing 'progress' and 'modernization' are, for most of us at least, long past. However, it seems difficult to empty 'development' entirely of its grounding in an enlightenment view of the world, and the conviction that improvement in the material conditions of people's lives is the primary focus of concern. This may indeed be the way that people always and everywhere identify their 'well-being', but whether this is, or is not, the case should be a matter for *empirical* exploration, not assumed by definition. The promise of both participatory research and the focus on well-being is that they will enable genuinely different voices to be heard, voices that speak from and about realities other than those configured by development discourse and institutions. While definitions and indicators of 'development' may be determined by outsiders on a 'universal' template, a participatory approach would suggest that notions of 'well-being' must include local social and cultural values and meanings, as well as the subjective perceptions of individuals and groups. If this is the case, it should be possible to ask the question, 'Does more development bring greater well-being?' Only when such a question can be asked, and answered, will the critical criteria for the participatory definition and measurement of well-being be met.

Notes

The authors would like to give special thanks to Robert Chambers (IDS Sussex) for his comments and examples related to participatory approaches to defining poverty and well-being, Laura Camfield (WeD Bath) for her guidance on quality of life research, and Ian Gough (WeD Bath) for his perceptive comments.

1 The research study itself was entitled 'Consultations with the Poor'. However, since the major publication of its findings appeared under the title *Voices of the Poor*, we use this term throughout for the sake of clarity.
2 This refers to the defining and measuring of subjective and objective well-being by two separate groups of researchers: economists, psychologists and sociologists from the social indicators movement; and collaborations between clinicians and psychologists.
3 This point was originally made in relation to participation by Judith Turbyne (1992).
4 This conceptual framework is taken from the approach to well-being developed by the ESRC Research Group on Well-being in Developing Countries (WeD) at the University of Bath. An interdisciplinary study with country teams in Peru, Ethiopia, Thailand and Bangladesh, this explores the social and cultural construction of well-being through a major programme of comparative empirical research. See www.welldev.org.uk
5 This means that we do not discuss some major current examples of the incorporation of participation within policy making processes in development. Most obviously, these include the World Bank sponsored Poverty Reduction Strategy Papers (PRSPs) which aim to generate national ownership across state and civil society of an overall strategy for poverty reduction within aid recipient states.
6 The evolution and spread of PRA, often associated with the work of Robert Chambers at IDS Sussex, can be more accurately traced to a global network of practitioners not only at IDS, but also at the International Institute of Environment and Development (IIED) and at a host of innovative institutions in the global south. An overview of the evolution and spread of PRA, including critical reflections by practitioners, can be found in the *Pathways to Participation* reports cited later in this chapter (Cornwall and Pratt 2002, and in Chambers 1997).
7 Paulo Freire (1970) was a Brazilian educator whose methods of adult literacy had a profound, worldwide influence on community development and social change strategies. Freire's 'pedagogy of the oppressed' uses participatory research methods to enable poor people to gain awareness, analyze their reality and take steps to address the causes of their poverty. Freire's methods shaped a continuing tradition of participatory action research (PAR), often seen as more empowering and less extractive than participatory research used to generate data for analysis and action by outsiders.
8 For more detail see Pretty *et al.* (1995) and Simanowitz (1999).
9 Brock's study was undertaken as part of the *Voices of the Poor* project. This was a study carried out by the World Bank in 23 countries using participatory and qualitative methods to identify poor people's own perspectives on their poverty, ill-being, and priorities and to inform the *World Development Report 2000–01* (World Bank 2000). For other outputs, see Narayan *et al.* (1999). For a critical reflection, see Chambers (2002).
10 Norton *et al.* note that well-being ranking 'can only be used within the limitations of the shared mutual knowledge of the group carrying out the analysis (detailed knowledge is needed to establish the ranking)' (2001:33).
11 The WHOQOL also makes available specific modules for different countries, people living with HIV/AIDS, older people and on spirituality and personal beliefs.
12 This was originally entitled the Patient Generated Index.

13 Kanbur's edited volume presents the contributions made toward a workshop at Cornell in 2001 on 'Qualitative and Quantitative Poverty Appraisal: Complementarities, Tensions and Ways Forward' and is relied upon in this section because, agreeably, it 'represents a remarkable statement on the state of the art and debate' (Kanbur 2002).

14 Many useful innovations and guidelines for practice have emerged from the 'Combining Qualitative and Quantitative Methods in Development Research' conference held at Swansea in July 2002, and from 'discussion of the informal "participatory numbers" group which has met in the UK at the Centre for Development Studies, Swansea, the Centre for Statistical Services, Reading, the Institute of Development Studies, Sussex, the International HIV/AIDS Alliance, Brighton and the Overseas Development Institute, London' (Chambers 2003: 11). See also Barahona and Levy (2003) and Holland and Abeyesekera (forthcoming).

15 The 'Internal Learning System' of the Bangalore based NGO New Entity for Social Action (NESA) is using participatory methods to monitor human rights abuses with Dalit, Adivasi and other vulnerable communities. In 2000 villages, literate and non-literate men and women make entries every six months to score degrees of abuse, on a range of 1 to 5. Aspects of life monitored include husbands drinking, domestic violence, Dalits having to drink out of separate glasses, Dalits being made to carry dead bodies or dead animals, whether a girl can select her life partner (personal communication: Vimalathan, S. Nagasundari and H. Noponen). The diaries are aggregated to give an indication of social change (Chambers personal communication 2004).

16 The 'County Poverty Alleviation Method' in China uses eight indicators representing livelihoods, infrastructure and human resources. These can be modified and weighted according to local context and to participatory input from residents; 'since the weightings given will be used in the econometric formula used to calculate the final "participatory poverty index" (PPI), this means that the villagers' own priorities will be reflected quite strongly' (Welden 2002: 3) The overall process, which draws on a range of PRA techniques, is backed by the Asian Development Bank, the World Bank and bilateral donors. Thanks to Robert Chambers for calling this example to our attention.

17 The 'Pathways to Participation' project, hosted by the Institute of Development Studies at Sussex, was a collaborative, critical review of practitioner experiences using PRA methods in Kenya, the Gambia, Mexico, Nepal, India, Vietnam, China and Pakistan. Findings can be found in Cornwall and Pratt (2002, 2003) and in a series of papers available at: www.ids.ac.uk/particip/research/pathways/

18 This is a development of Jordan's (1989) analysis, that significant dimensions of identity derive not from abstract structural characteristics such as gender and class, but rather where we want to go and what we can offer one another.

19 Our thanks to Jane French (WeD) for this image.

References

Barahona, C. and S. Levy (2003) 'How to Generate Statistics and Influence Policy Using Participatory Methods in Research: Reflections on Work in Malawi 1999–2002', IDS Working Paper 212 (Brighton: Institute of Development Studies).

Bevan, P., K. Kebede and A. Pankhurst (2003) 'A Report on a Very Informal Pilot of the Person Generated Index© of Quality of Life in Ethiopia', Mimeo (Bath: WeD, University of Bath).

Booth, D., J. Holland, J. Hentschel, P. Lanjouw and A. Herbert (1998) 'Participation and Combined Methods in African Poverty Assessment: Renewing the Agenda' (London: Social Development Division, DFID).
Bourdieu, P. (1977) *Outline of a Theory of Practice* (Cambridge: Cambridge University Press).
Brock, K. (1999) 'It's not only Wealth that Matters – It's Peace of Mind Too: A Review of Participatory Work on Poverty and Ill-being', Study prepared for the World Development Report 2000/01 (Washington, DC: PREM, World Bank).
Brock, K. and R. McGee (eds) (2002) *Knowing Poverty: Critical Reflections on Participatory Research and Policy* (London: Earthscan).
Burkey, S. (1993) *People First: A Guide to Self-Reliant, Participatory Rural Development* (London: Zed Books).
Calman, K. C. (1984) 'Quality of Life in Cancer Patients: A Hypothesis', *Journal of Medical Ethics*, 10: 124.
Camfield, L. and S. Skevington (2003) 'Quality of Life and Well-being', WeD Working Paper (Bath: WeD, University of Bath).
Chambers, R. (1997) *Whose Reality Counts? Putting the First Last* (London: Intermediate Technology Development Group Publishing).
Chambers, R. (2002) 'The World Development Report: Concepts, Content and a Chapter12, *Journal of International Development*, 13: 299–306.
Chambers, R. (2003) 'Participation and Numbers', PLA Notes 47 (London: International Institute for Environment and Development).
Christiansen, L. (2002) 'The Qual-Quant Debate within its Epistemological Context: Some Practical Implications', in R. Kanbur (ed.), *Q-Squared: Qualitative and Quantitative Methods of Poverty Appraisal* (Delhi: Permanent Black).
Cooke, B. and U. Kothari (eds) (2001) *Participation: the New Tyranny?* (London: Zed Books).
Cornwall, A. (2000) 'Beneficiary, Consumer, Citizen: Perspectives on Participation for Poverty Reduction', Mimeo (Sussex: Institute of Development Studies).
Cornwall, A. and G. Pratt (2002) 'Pathways to Participation: Critical Reflections on PRA', Summary Report (Brighton: Institute of Development Studies).
Cornwall, A. and G. Pratt (eds) (2003) *Pathways to Participation: Reflections on PRA* (London: Intermediate Technology Development Group Publications).
Cornwall, A., S. Musyoki and G. Pratt (2001) 'In Search of a New Impetus: Practitioners' Reflections on PRA and Participation in Kenya', IDS Working Paper 131 (Brighton: Institute of Development Studies).
Cummins, R. A. (1996) 'The Domains of Life Satisfaction: An Attempt to Order Chaos', *Social Indicators Research*, (38): 303–28.
Das, V. (2000) 'The Act of Witnessing: Violence, Poisonous Knowledge, and Subjectivity', in V. Das, A. Kleinman, M. Ramphele and P. Reynolds (eds), *Violence and Subjectivity* (Berkeley/Oxford: University of California Press) 205–41.
Davies, J., M. Richards and W. Cavendish (1999) 'Beyond the Limits of PRA? A Comparison of Participatory and Conventional Economic Research Methods in the Analysis of Ilala Palm Use in South-Eastern Zimbabwe', Working Paper (London: ODI).
Doyal, L. and I. Gough (1991) *A Theory of Human Need* (London: Macmillan).
Dunn, J. (1979) *Western Political Theory in the Face of the Future* (Cambridge: Cambridge University Press).
Freire, P. (1970) *Pedagogy of the Oppressed* (New York: Seabury Press).
Garcia, X. M. and S.-A. Way (2003) 'Winning Spaces: Participatory Methodologies in Rural Processes in Mexico', IDS Working Paper 180 (Brighton: Institute of Development Studies).

Geertz, C. (1988) *Works and Lives: The Anthropologist as Author* (Oxford: Polity Press).

Giddens, A. (1977) *Studies in Social and Political Theory* (London: Hutchinson).

Gujit, I. and M. K. Shah (eds) (1998) *The Myth of Community: Gender Issues in Participatory Development* (London: Intermediate Technology Publications).

Hagerty, M. R., R. A. Cummins, A. Ferriss, K. Land, A. C. Michalos, M. Peterson, A. Sharpe, J. Sirgy and J. Vogel (2001) 'Quality of Life Indexes for National Policy: Review and Agenda for Research', *Social Indicators Research*, 55: 1–96.

Hargreaves, J., L. A. Morison, J. S. S. Gear, J. D. H. Porter, M. B. Makhubele, J. C. Kim, J. Busza, C. Watts and P. M. Pronyk (2004) 'Hearing the Voices of the Poor: Assigning Poverty Lines on the basis of Local Perceptions of Poverty; A Quantitative Analysis of Qualitative Data from Participatory Wealth Ranking in Rural South Africa', Unpublished manuscript (London: London School of Health and Tropical Medicine; and Johannesburg: University of Witwatersrand, Rural Aids and Action Research Programme (RADAR).

Holland, J. and S. Abeyesekera (eds) (forthcoming) *Who Counts?* (unpublished manuscript).

IDS (1996) 'The Power of Participation: PRA and Policy', IDS Policy Briefing 7 (Brighton: Institute of Development Studies).

Johnson, S. (2004) 'Gender Norms in Financial Markets: Evidence from Kenya', *World Development*, 32(8).

Jordan, J. (1989) 'Report from the Bahamas', in J. Jordan (ed.), *Moving Towards Home: Political Essays* (London: Virago) 137–46.

Jupp, D. (2002) 'Views of the Poor: Some Thoughts on How to Involve Your Own Staff to Conduct Quick, Low Cost but Insightful Research into Poor People's Perspectives', Unpublished manuscript (UK: DIPM).

Kanbur, R. (ed.) (2002) *Q-Squared: Qualitative and Quantitative Methods of Poverty Appraisal* (Delhi: Permanent Black).

Knorr-Cetina K. and M. Mulkay (eds) (1993) *Science Observed* (Beverly Hills, CA: Sage).

Laderchi, C. R. (2001) 'Participatory Methods in the Analysis of Poverty: A Critical Review', QEH Working Paper Series 62 (Oxford: Queen Elizabeth House, University of Oxford).

McGee, R. (2000) 'Analysis of Participatory Poverty Assessment (PPA) and Households Survey Findings on Poverty Trends in Uganda', Mission Report 10–18 February, Mimeo (Sussex: Institute of Development Studies).

McGee, R. and A. Norton (2000) 'Participation in Poverty Reduction Strategies: A Synthesis of Experience with Participatory Approaches to Policy Design, Implementation and Monitoring', IDS Working Paper 109 (Brighton: Institute of Development Studies).

McGregor, J. A. and B. Kebede (2003) 'Resource Profiles and the Social and Cultural Construction of Well-being', WeD Working Paper (Bath: WeD, University of Bath).

Michalos, A. C. (1997) 'Combining Social, Economic and Environmental Indicators to Measure Sustainable Human Well-being', *Social Indicators Research*, 40: 221–58.

Mitchell, T. (1990) 'Everyday Metaphors of Power', *Theory and Society*, 19(5): 545–78.

Narayan, D., R. Chambers, M. K. Shah and P. Petesch (1999) *Global Synthesis: Consultations with the Poor* (Washington, DC: World Bank).

Narayan, D., R. Chambers, M. K. Shah and P. Petesch (2000) *Voices of the Poor: Crying out for Change* (New York: Oxford University Press for the World Bank).

Norton, A., with B. Bird, K. Brock, M. Kakande and C. Turk (2001) 'A Rough Guide to PPAs: Participatory Poverty Assessment: An Introduction to Theory and Practice' (London: ODI).

Nussbaum, M. (2000) *Women and Human Development: The Capabilities Approach* (Cambridge: Cambridge University Press).

Pretty, J., I. Gujit, J. Thompson and I. Scoones (1995) 'Participatory Learning and Action: A Trainer's Guide' (London: International Institute for Environment and Development).

Robb, C. (1999) 'Can the Poor Influence Policy? Participatory Poverty Assessments in the Developing World' (Washington, DC: World Bank).

Ruta, D. A. (1998) 'Patient Generated Assessment: The Next Generation', *MAPI Quality of Life Newsletter*, 20: 461–89.

Ruta, D. A., A. M. Garratt, M. Lengm, I. T. Russell and L. M. Macdonald (1994) 'A New Approach to the Measurement of Quality of Life: The Patient-generated Index', *Medical Care*, 11(1): 109–26.

Scoones, I., J. Pretty, I. Gujit and J. Thompson (1995) 'Participatory Learning and Action: A Trainers' Guide, Sustainable Agriculture Programme' (London: International Institute for Environment and Development).

Selznick, P. (1949/53) *TVA and the Grass Roots: A Study in the Sociology of Formal Organization* (Berkeley, CA: University of California Press).

Sen, A. (1999) *Development as Freedom* (Oxford: Oxford University Press).

Simanowitz, A. (1999) 'Pushing the Limits of Mapping and Wealth Ranking', Participatory Learning and Action Notes 34 (London: International Institute for Environment and Development).

Simanowitz, A. (2000) 'Targeting the Poor: A Comparison between Visual and Participatory Methods', *Small Enterprise Development: an International Journal*, 11(1): March.

Townsend, P. (1979) *Poverty in the United Kingdom* (Harmondsworth: Penguin).

Turbyne, J. (1992) 'Participation and Development', Mimeo (Bath: University of Bath).

Veenhoven R. (2000) 'Freedom and Happiness: A Comparative Study in Forty Four Nations in the early 1990s', in E. Diener and E. M. Suh (eds), *Culture and Subjective Well-being* (Cambridge, MA: MIT Press).

Weldon, J. (2002) 'Planning Participatory Fixes', *China Development Brief*, 5(3): Winter, available at: www.chinadevelopmentbrief.com

White, S. C. (1992) *Arguing with the Crocodile: Gender and Class in Bangladesh* (London: Zed Books).

White, S. C. and R. Tiongco (1997) *Doing Theology and Development: Meeting the Challenge of Poverty* (Edinburgh: Saint Andrew Press).

Wood, G. (ed.) (1985) *Labelling in Development Policy* (London: Sage).

World Bank (2000) *Poverty and Development: The World Development Report 2000–2001: Attacking Poverty* (New York: Oxford University Press for the World Bank).

Index

Notes: f = figure; n = note; t = table; **bold** = extended discussion or heading emphasized in main text.

Printed in the United States
94229LV00001B/46/A

9 780230 004986

DATE DUE
